THE NEW ICON

THE NEW ICON

SAVARKAR AND THE FACTS

ARUN SHOURIE

PENGUIN
VIKING
An imprint of Penguin Random House

PENGUIN VIKING

Penguin Viking is an imprint of the Penguin Random House group of companies
whose addresses can be found at global.penguinrandomhouse.com

Published by Penguin Random House India Pvt. Ltd
4th Floor, Capital Tower 1, MG Road,
Gurugram 122 002, Haryana, India

First published in Penguin Viking by Penguin Random House India 2025

ISBN 9780143474333

Typeset in Minion Pro by MAP Systems, Bengaluru, India
Printed at Thomson Press India Ltd, New Delhi

www.penguin.co.in

For
Adit and Anita,
always

Hum kuchh nahin kehtey, koi kuchh nahin kehtaa
Tum kyaa ho tumhee sab se kehalvaaye chalo ho . . .

—*Kalim Ajiz*

Contents

Gratitude

It was 1957. Public meetings were being held to mark a hundred years of the uprising of 1857. In our school in Delhi too, eminent speakers were invited to address the students. That is how we first learnt of events and the dramatis personae of those times. Even though decades have flown by, I still remember how stirred I was on reading *The Indian War of Independence* in the school library. The name of the writer made no impression on me. I certainly did not realize that he was among those who had been tried for the assassination of Gandhiji. Savarkar completely slipped my mind, to the point that today I can't even recall how I reacted to the controversies that must have surrounded his name in the years that followed. I do not remember, for instance, the accusations and answers that must have swirled when—in 1970, Mrs Indira Gandhi was the Prime Minister at the time—a stamp was issued in his honour. Inexcusably—and incredibly, even to me—I do not recall the accusations and counter-accusations that must have flown around when a portrait of Savarkar was unveiled in the Central Hall of Parliament and a plaque installed in his honour in the Cellular Jail in the Andamans. These happened in 2003 when Atal ji's government was in office—and I was a part of it. It sounds incredible, as I said, but it is true— that is how far Savarkar had receded. Today, I am surprised when I look up an account of the unveiling of that portrait in Parliament. The entire Opposition, I learn, except Chandra Shekhar, had boycotted the event. That means there must have been much *tu-tu main-main*, shouting and hurling blame at each other. I used to often skip functions; however, being a part of the government, it is entirely possible that I attended this one. But I cannot excavate the memory.

The occasion that I remember when I came across Savarkar's name was when I read Ambedkar's case for the creation of Pakistan: *Pakistan, Or the Partition of India*.[1] In it, Ambedkar had recounted how Savarkar had argued that India was not one nation, but two—Hindus and Muslims. In doing so, Ambedkar observed, Savarkar was saying exactly what Jinnah was saying. Ambedkar pointed to the contradiction at the heart of Savarkar's assertions: Hindus and Muslims were two nations, but they must remain yoked in one country, Savarkar is saying, Ambedkar wrote—the Muslims in a position of subordination. Ambedkar's own argument in the book, of course, was that given the way things were—the book was published in 1945—Hindus and Muslims just could not live together, and the only feasible solution was to partition India into two countries. I was writing about Ambedkar, and so it was his advocacy of partition that stayed in my mind. Savarkar was just a marginal figure who had appeared in support of that thesis. All that registered in my mind was what Savarkar had said. Ambedkar was saying what the British would have probably wanted said— that there was no alternative to partitioning the country. And that, the British would add, was not because the British wanted to divide and rule us, but because we could not get along with each other.

It is now, in the recent past, with all this talk of Hindutva that I started looking for Savarkar's writings. English editions of some of his books were readily available in bookshops—*The Indian War of Independence, My Transportation for Life, Six Glorious Epochs of Indian History, Hindu Pad-padshahi, Essentials of Hindutva, Inside the Enemy Camp,* and a collection of Presidential Addresses at the annual sessions of the Hindu Mahasabha, published as *Hindu Rashtra Darshan*. His own biography,

---

[1] B.R. Ambedkar, *Pakistan or the Partition of India*. The book was published in 1945, and now forms Volume VIII of *Dr Babasaheb Ambedkar, Writings and Speeches*, Government of India, New Delhi, 1979/2014.

rather a hagiography, *Life of Barrister Savarkar,* that, in all probability, he wrote himself under the pen name 'Chitragupta', was available from an old books' shop. A selection, *Rationalism of Veer Savarkar,* and another collection of speeches and statements he made during his 'Whirlwind Propagandistic Tours' were available online. But he had written much, much more. A ten-volume set in Hindi of his writings, *Savarkar Samagra,* had been published. The bookshops in Delhi did not seem to have the set, and Amazon.in listed some of the volumes as being out of stock.

But fortunately, the set had been published by Prabhat Prakashan in Delhi,[2] and I had known Prabhat Kumar for many years as they had published Hindi translations of some of my books. He sent a complete set from their godown. Therefore, the first pile of thanks I owe is to him.

I soon discovered—much to my dismay—that several scholars had already written about Savarkar: R.C. Majumdar, U.R. Ananthamurthy, A.G. Noorani, Vinayak Chaturvedi, Jyotirmaya Sharma and others. Two biographies of him had also been published recently: one by Vaibhav Purandare and another by Vikram Sampat. It is always very discouraging to read books that have already been written on a subject on which you are thinking of writing—they seem to have already said everything about the matter. Joan Robinson had written about how, after trudging all the way, it is somewhat painful to meet others at the Pole![3] But there was an easy solution: I focused on what Savarkar had written himself and tried not to read too carefully what others had written about him.

---

[2] *Savarkar Samagra,* Volume 1 to 10, Prabhat Prakashan, Delhi, 2014–2020. Henceforth, *Savarkar Samagra.*

[3] That is what I remembered from the days at college when we used to memorize some of her writings. The exact passage, I find now, is somewhat different: 'A moment has been reached in the development of economic theory when certain definite problems require to be solved, and many writers are at work upon them independently. There are many occasions, therefore, when several explorers are surprised, and somewhat pained, on meeting each other at the Pole.': Joan Robinson, *The Economics of Imperfect Competition,* Macmillan, London, 1933/1946, p. vi.

But it wasn't just disappointment that lay on the way. Danger lurked. In all probability, authors who have traversed a subject earlier would have examined the same material that a latecomer would now do. That is, of course, manifestly the case with 'primary texts'. Everyone writing a commentary on the Gita would be quoting the same verses. In Savarkar's case, his mercy petitions, for example, are by now so well-known, they have been so frequently invoked and reproduced in recent public controversies that they are bound to figure in every book written about him. Anyone can be picking their text from anyone else. But this difficulty is not limited to 'primary texts'. The questions that are whirling around when one is studying and writing on a subject are more than likely to attract an author's gaze. Today, to take an obvious instance, Hindutva is much in the news, and Savarkar is most often talked about in the context of what he said about Hindutva, and about a pan-Hindu consciousness having suffused people and rulers alike from time immemorial. I had read Sir Jadunath Sarkar's *Shivaji and His Times* when I was in school. I read his volumes on the *History of Bengal* when I was in college. But if you asked me at the time what in these books had a bearing on claims about Hindutva and pan-Hindu consciousness, I would have had a hard time answering. My friend, T.C.A. Raghavan's arresting book, *History Men*,[4] led me to read both *Shivaji and His Times* and the three volumes of *History of Bengal* again. *History Men* also had such riveting exchanges between Sarkar, G.S. Sardesai and Raghubir Sinh—the three historians Raghavan had written about—that I was immediately led to read the collection of essays and letters, *Sir Jadunath Sarkar, Life and Letters*,[5] and Raghubir Sinh's *Malwa*

---

[4] T.C.A. Raghavan, *History Men, Jadunath Sarkar, G.S. Sardesai, Raghubir Sinh, and Their Quest for India's Past,* HarperCollins, NOIDA, 2020.

[5] *Life and Letters of Sir Jadunath Sarkar,* Hari Ram Gupta [ed.], Punjab University, Hoshiarpur, 1957.

in Transition.[6] This time, one passage after another struck me as manifestly crucial to the assertions about Hindutva and pan-Hindu consciousness. I diligently noted these down. Only to discover to my dismay that they overlapped to an embarrassing degree with the passages that had struck Raghavan as being relevant to his argument. And this to such an extent that I rang up Raghavan to get his counsel: how may I avoid the charge of having merely picked them up from his book?

These books had another effect. Even glancing through them sent me looking for original documents. Allusions to Savarkar's vociferous support of the British at a time when the country was in the thrall of the Quit India Movement led me to look for his exchanges with the British. This pull of original documents was often sharpened by casual, passing references in books. While reading a book that had nothing to do with this subject— Arthur Herman's *Gandhi and Churchill*—I came across a passing reference to the statement that Madan Lal Dhingra made at his trial for murdering Sir Curzon Wyllie.[7] Dhingra was an understudy of Savarkar, and the statement was rumoured to have been written by Savarkar.[8] Herman wrote of Churchill's admiration for the statement: his friend, Wilfred Blunt, had recorded in his diary that Churchill called it 'the finest ever made in the name of patriotism', and so impressed had Churchill been that he could recite it from memory. This had happened in 1909. But from where was I to get Blunt's diary? It is for such out-of-reach books that Internet Archive proved immensely useful. I am, therefore, most grateful to the organization, and all who take the trouble of digitizing old publications.

---

[6] Raghubir Sinh, *Malwa in Transition, Or a Century of Anarchy,* D.B. Taraporevala, Bombay, 1993.

[7] Arthur Herman, *Gandhi and Churchill: The Epic Rivalry that Destroyed an Empire and Forged Our Age,* Bantam Books, New York, 2008.

[8] Cf., Chitragupta, *Life of Barrister Savarkar,* Veer Savarkar Prakashan, Bombay, 2nd edition, 1987, p. 68, a book to which we will return subsequently.

But, of course, nothing could substitute for British files of the period. Those of Savarkar's mercy petitions that are available have been published often and so, even though Savarkar, who had written in copious detail about all aspects of his incarceration, had not written about these, there was no difficulty in getting the text. But, to take one example, in her excellent study, *Under the Shadow of the Swastika*, Marzia Casolari had said in passing that Savarkar had carried on extensive correspondence with the Viceroy in 1941.[9] What exactly had he been writing to Linlithgow? Did it accord with what he was saying in public at the time? And what were the British aiming to get out of him?

On other occasions, it was variance that worked as a propeller. To continue with Casolari, she had alluded to 'purses' that Savarkar used to be presented at public functions. To mark his 61st birthday, at a Training Camp, he had been presented Rs 1,80,000, she reported. A few days earlier, at another function in Bombay, he had been presented Rs 61,000. Casolari mentioned that 'other large sums were donated by members of Hindu organizations at the towns he visited during one of his political campaigns in the same period. In early June, Savarkar was in Ahmedabad, invited by the Gujarat Provincial Hindu Mahasabha. He received a similar sum there (the exact figure is not specified).'[10] And she had cited reports that the government had received to this effect. The website Savarkar.org described one of the functions in Bombay and the amount of Rs 61,000 Savarkar had been gifted at this function—along with a silver replica of SS *Morea*, the ship from which he had jumped in Marseilles. The website did not mention the other occasions.[11] To compound matters, in his thorough

---

[9] Marzia Casolari, *In the Shadow of the Swastika, The Relationships Between Indian Radical Nationalism, Italian Fascism and Nazism*, Routledge, London, 2020.

[10] Ibid, pp. 86–87.

[11] Cf: 'Felicitation function of Savarkar on occasion of his 61st birthday, Mumbai,' https://savarkar.org/en/Encyc/2017/5/26/Felicitation-function-of-Savarkar-on-occasion-of-his-61st-birthday-Mumbai.html, accessed on 24 July 2024.

History of the Indian National Congress, Pattabhi Sitaramayya had put the figure at Rs 3,00,000, adding that it was for the party.[12]

In 1943, these were huge amounts. More than that, they seemed to have caused considerable disquiet—even in a person by whose visit once Savarkar had felt so honoured. As is well-known, the great historian, G.S. Sardesai was a self-effacing, reticent man. Having been nudged out of Baroda, he had settled in Kamshet, a village fifty kilometres from Poona. In 1938, he learnt that his colleagues in the profession were preparing a commemoration volume to honour him and his work. To make matters worse, he learnt that his close friend of decades, Sir Jadunath Sarkar, had given his consent to the project and was even associated with getting essays for the volume. Sardesai was driven to exasperation. He wrote an angry letter to Sarkar:

Kamshet 7 March 1938

Your letter to hand together with the draft of this poor wretch's early life. What is all this! I altogether dislike the idea of a Commemoration vol. I have done nothing to deserve it. I have worked, as so many others have done, on my own account & with no idea of doing any service. There is no service at all. I have served myself. If my little humble work is appreciated that is enough reward & ample purse for me. I am now publicly repudiating the affair. So many of my friends and others of high worth & reputation have been similarly trapped. This has pained me most & I feel awfully ashamed. The Satara affair itself three years ago was an uncalled for affair & happily it is relegated to the past. I do not want any more ceremonies.[13]

---

[12] Pattabhi Sitaramayya, *History of the Indian National Congress,* Volume 2, 1969, p. 466.

[13] For the letters, *Life and Letters of Sir Jadunath Sarkar, Sir Jadunath Sarkar, Commemoration Volume,* Hari Ram Gupta [ed.], Punjab University, Hoshiarpur, 1957, pp. 317–18.

A few days later, he learnt that it was not just the commemoration volume, amounts were being collected to gift him a 'purse'. He was incensed, and shot off another angry letter to Sarkar:

Kamshet 24 March 1938

I did not know you had tried so much to secure first-rate articles from most of our common friends for a volume to be issued on my birthday. What irritated me most, apart from my aversion to such memorials, was the public announcement in the papers for collecting contributions towards the presentation of a purse, a beggary for which Savarkar & all his kind have made themselves notorious.[14]

What a delicious morsel—'. . . *a beggary for which Savarkar & all his kind have made themselves notorious*'. And manifestly the 'beggary' had been going on for quite a while. The figures I reproduced from Casolari, Sitaramayya and Savarkar.org related to 1943 while these letters of Sardesai were written five years earlier, in 1938.

In listing the figures, Casolari had cited files from the Archives. Did they contain more? Were they intelligence reports? Had they in turn cited some sources? There was no way for me to get to Bombay and look for the documents in the Maharashtra State Archives, to say nothing of going to London and looking through the records at the India Office: other things apart, because of the dangerous illnesses that had seized Anita, my wife, I was confined to a hospital and our home. I could not have learnt what was in the original records but for a dear friend, Sanjay Suri. Sanjay had been the chief reporter at *Indian Express* when I was at the paper. He has been in England since then. With the barest suggestion about a document, its possible date and location, Sanjay would track it down. I, therefore, owe him more than I can repay.

---

[14] Ibid.

Much to Learn

Much to Learn

The cow is a useful animal, as are the buffalo, the horse, the dog, and even the donkey. It is a useful animal—it is not our mother, it is not one in which *devatas* reside, it certainly is not a devata itself.[1]

Because it is useful, we should look after it, not worship it—'*Gau paalan ho, gau pujan nahin*'—let us nurture cows, not worship them. And we should look after it as long as it is useful. When human interests are no longer served by it, cow-protection in the extreme should be avoided.

That is Savarkar writing.[2] '*Paagalpan*' (madness), '*vaahiyaatpan*' (vulgarity), '*pongaapan*' (stupidity), '*moorakhtaa*' (foolishness), '*shuddha moorakhtaa*' (unadulterated foolishness), making people believe in such things is to make a donkey of man, venerating the cow has become the cause of '*rashtra ki buddhi-hatyaa kaa paap*' (the sin of killing the intelligence of the rashtra)—such are the words Savarkar uses while shredding people's beliefs and practices regarding cows. At one stage, the orthodox denounced him for an article he had written setting out views

---

[1] Throughout this book, unless otherwise indicated, italics have been added. Words or expressions that occur within parentheses (and) are in the original. Words that occur between [and] are mine.

[2] Several of Savarkar's essays regarding cows, their care and worship are in Volumes VII and VIII of *Savarkar Samagra*: for instance, *Savarkar Samagra*, Volume VII: pp. 315–16, 433–46, 445–49; Volume VIII: pp. 356–68, 376–97, 421–34. V.S. Godbole's *Rationalism of Veer Savarkar*, Itihas Patrika Prakashan, Mumbai, 2004, and the website savarkar.org also has several passages that bear on the subject of this chapter. For the last sentence in the previous paragraph, *Samagra Savarkar Vangmaya*, Volume 2, p. 678; Volume 3, p. 341, extracts at savarkar.org.

of this kind about cows. They demanded that the article be banned, that he be boycotted. He announced that he would go on writing about the absurdities in Hindu beliefs and practices regarding cows, that he would continue doing so for an entire year.[3]

The Uber-Mother

The fact is that having regarded the cow to be our mother, Savarkar wrote, over time she came to be accorded a status even higher than that of a mother.[4] The milk of both is drinkable. But in the case of the cow, its *panchgavya*[5] is imbibed . . . At least, first ascertain which are the ailments for which *gaumootra aur gaumaya*[6] have been verified to be efficacious . . . We have heard that cow urine has medicinal qualities. But, *bhai*, he asked, what doesn't? One's own urine also has some medicinal qualities as gaumootra has . . . As one's own urine also has medicinal qualities, should we keep imbibing our panchgavya on every religious occasion and for pure *sanskaars* (inborn traits), faculties? Brandy also is a medicine for *kafkshayaadi vikaar*.[7] Should we, therefore, imbibe it during *shraavandi*[8] also? Poison too is a medicine for some ailments. Use it for persons who have those ailments. One does not take it in the form of *dharmic sanskaars*

---

[3] The article that the orthodox got worked up about had appeared in *Maharashtra Sharda*, April 1934; it is reproduced in Volume VIII of *Savarkar Samagra*, pp. 356–67. Savarkar's scathing reply to his critics appeared in *Maharashtra Sharda*, July 1935; it is reproduced in Volume VIII of *Savarkar Samagra*, pp. 376–86. See also Ibid, pp. 387–96. For his declaration that he would continue writing about this topic for a year: Ibid, pp 423–24.

[4] *Savarkar Samagra*, Volume VIII, pp. 356–67, 376–86.

[5] Five products of the cow: milk, curd, ghee, urine, dung. Used in some rituals and in Ayurveda.

[6] Urine and dung among five products obtained from the cow.

[7] A cure for imbalance in particular humours of the body.

[8] The twenty-third lunar asterism.

(religious values). Shoot down such *thoonth aur moorkhataapoorand sanskaars*[9]—this alone will bring lustre to our dharma and *sanskriti . . .*

When a person announced that it was because she partook of panchgavya that the mother of Lokmanya Tilak gave birth to a son as great as him, Savarkar mocked him and asked, why were not the other things she ate—flour, rice, vegetables, fruit, etc.—the cause?[10]

If cow's dung and urine are actually useful in curing some ailment, Savarkar pointed out, so is the urine of a horse, the milk of a she-donkey, the *vishthtaa*[11] of a hen. If they cure certain ailments, then let those suffering from those ailments consume them, just as medicines are taken by individuals afflicted with the specific conditions those medicines treat. But do the droppings of the hen cure snakebite? If not, then would you eat them if bitten by a snake? If cow dung is fertiliser, then spread it in the field. Why put it into your stomach? Dead rats are excellent manure for roses. Does that mean that we should take them up to our noses and smell their odour?

In any case, even if the panchgavya is useful as a medicine, how does drinking cow urine become a *punya?* Savarkar asked. By cleansing our soul? The truth, Savarkar said, is that the innocence which has led to making a goddess of an ordinary animal, the same innocent religiosity has led people to take its defecating outside their door as auspicious, to regard brushing its tail over our eyes as beneficial, to consider praying to it as religion, and, in the end, crossing the limits of madness, to consider its urine and dung as sacred and *pavitra* (pure), to believe that eating or drinking it cleanses our soul, destroys our sins, and constitutes punya in this as well as the next world—innocence has reached a peak.

After all, where does the notion that the cow and everything emanating from it is sacred and purifying come from, where does it lead? The cow

---

[9] Worthless and absolutely foolish practices.

[10] *Savarkar Samagra*, Volume VIII, pp. 433.

[11] Droppings.

which, standing in the cowshed, chews on grass and *chaaraa* (fodder),
the one which, even as she is eating, urinates and defecates, upon getting
tired while masticating sits down in the same mix of urine and excreta,
the one who with its tail tosses on itself the filth lying on the ground, the
one who, the moment the rope breaks, runs and puts its mouth in garbage,
Savarkar observes, touching the tail of that animal the Brahmin, decked in
clean and spotless clothes and shielding his own purity, mixes that animal's
excreta and urine in a silver vessel and drinks it and believes that his life
has become pure. Is it right to believe this? There is the further belief that
the purity, which is tarnished by even the shadow of such a learned person
as Dr Ambedkar, which is destroyed by sitting in the same line for food
with a saint such as Tukaram, becomes even purer by touching the tail
drenched in the urine and excreta of that cow which is eating all sorts of
things in the cowshed, and its excreta and urine purifies everything . . .
Can there be a better example of how the intelligence of a man is killed?[12]

In response to the accusation that he was denigrating our revered
sanskriti, Savarkar retorted that if anything is defaming our great Hindu
sanskriti, it is the naive tradition of eating cow dung and drinking cow
urine. If our *sanatani* brothers do not want our tradition to be a subject
of derision, then they should bring about an end to this book-based
foolishness or *pothinishtha moorkhataa*. They should not prohibit our
writings through which we have drawn the attention of our people towards
that foolishness.

There is one more thing I want to say before we part, he wrote. In the
past, a person would have been made to eat cow dung and drink cow urine
as a punishment for something he had done, Savarkar recounted. That is
how he expiated the wrong. Later, the eating of dung and drinking of urine
per se came to be regarded as expiating sins. It is worth finding out how
this came to be because, if we set aside the question of drinking cow urine

---

[12] *Savarkar Samagra,* Volume VII, p. 435.

and eating cow dung, the expression 'Eat dung, drink urine' is even today regarded as an abuse, not a *sanskaar*.[13]

After all, do we not regard our country as our 'Motherland'? Having taken her to be our mother, do we go around eating mud and drinking from the nearest gutter as purifying panchgavya while chanting, '*Hey gutterjal! Yatvag sthigatan paapan dehey tishthati maamakey, veh sab kuchch tumharey praashan se jalkar raakh hone do.*'[14]

Look, don't Turn Away

Persons who are not accustomed to Savarkar's prose will shrink back from such forthrightness. The ones who are appropriating him these days will turn away and paste some motive on the one who recalls such writings of their new icon. The least they will say is that one should not go by isolated lines like these. But Savarkar's writings of this kind and about this subject are not just a few lines, they are essays followed by essays. Moreover, remember what happened when Savarkar was denounced for his writings, he continued in this vein for an entire year.

Out of Context?

'But you are plucking the lines out of context,' will be the next defence. Actually, Savarkar explained the context himself. He said that he had written about cows in the way he had, not just to get people to look after cows better or to improve the working of institutions that had been set up for serving cows. It was to undermine the stamp of religion that was being put on such beliefs and practices and to encourage people to learn to test everything on the touchstone of evidence, of science, and to worship the new deity, the Goddess of Reason. By regarding every practice, every

---

[13] *Savarkar Samagra*, Volume VII, pp. 444–45.

[14] 'O, Gutter water, Sir, let all sins wherever they reside in my body burn to ashes upon my consuming you.' *Savarkar Samagra*, Volume VIII, pp. 387–88.

ritual, every belief, all matters of ordinary conduct—beard and tuft, the length and breadth of hair—to be part of our dharma, and by taking the assertion 'esheh dharma sanaatanah'[15] to be the reason for clutching on to them, our religious life too had become 'kulshit aur rogi'.[16] So long as this sticking to anything and everything that is ancient or in a book is not shed, he wrote repeatedly, our people will not progress, they will not learn and the very practices and beliefs that figured in those religious texts because of the circumstances prevailing long ago will become the cause of the destruction of that very 'sanatana dharma'.[17]

Not the Maanbindu

As is well-known, Pandit Madan Mohan Malviya was as orthodox in his beliefs as he was in his day-to-day conduct. He said that the cow is the maanbindu[18] of Hindu sanskriti. Even as he addressed Malviyaji as parampujya (most respected), Savarkar chastised him for proclaiming this. The cow gives milk—that is its only significance. All the rest is shudh moorakhtaa (unadulterated foolishness). The cow is the dugdhbindu (symbol of milk of the Hindu Rashtra). It certainly is not the maanbindu. The maanbindu of devotees should be so much loftier than them, in the same way the maanbindu of the rashtra should be so lofty that it lifts everyone to the pinnacle of valour, that it ignites daring, one that transforms man into superman. A cow which every passer-by can twist and turn, any lallu-panju (any and every stray fellow) can eat up, is the symbol befitting our current weakness. Such a ghatiya (inferior) thing should not be the maanbindu of the rashtra—at least not for the future . . .[19] The maanbindu of our rashtra should be Narasimha.

---

[15] 'This is the eternal Dharma'.

[16] Foul and baneful.

[17] Savarkar Samagra, Volume VIII, pp. 421–24.

[18] Symbol of distinction.

[19] Savarkar Samagra, Volume VIII, pp. 431–33.

Therefore, instead of trying to fabricate reasons for looking away, we should—especially those who are appropriating him should—look at what Savarkar said.

The Abode of Gods?

The advocates of cow-worship get so carried away, Savarkar noted, that they proclaim that thirty-three crore gods reside in it. As the Vaarkaaries on the pilgrimage to Pandharpur are pushed and packed into the third-class railway compartment, in that very way, in the cow's body, the devas *ki ragdaa-ragdee hoti hai,* [20] and it becomes difficult for them to even breathe. The *dhakkam-dhakkaa* [21] going on in this animal . . . Vishnu, Chandra, Surya, Yama—some in the throat, some between the teeth, some in the nose, each god stuffed wherever he can be fitted. The crowding on the rear part of the cow becomes so great that when some *sanatani* gets angry at the cow kicking the bucket as he milks her and for that strikes her with a staff, five–ten devas are dispatched for *swargvaas* (dispatched to heaven). The condition of the devas who are rolled into the malodourous secretions in the nose and mouth is pitiable. But even worse than their condition is that of Marut and Varun. Because of the difficulties and confusion about finding a place for them, in the end they have been consigned to live in silence in the remaining two places: 'aaapney tu maru devi yonee ch varun sthitha/aur mootrey ganga.' [22] In the *dhaandali* [23] of making an animal into a god, they have reduced god into a *badtar* [24] animal . . . If anyone degrades our sanskriti in this scientific age, it is not our writing but the Sanskrit *shlokas* that place gods in conditions

---

[20] Crushed and squeezed.

[21] Pushing and shoving.

[22] The aperture for defecation and the Ganges of urine.

[23] High-handedness.

[24] Lowly.

worse even than those of animals . . . It would be like calling Shivaji the . . .[25] of Raipur and calling the . . .[26] at home 'Shivaji'—that would not be chanting a shloka, it would be hurling abuse . . . And none of these thirty-three crore gods are able to save the head of the cow in which they are residing as it is severed by the butcher. And why does not even one of the *maai kaa laal*[27] step forth and punish the butcher?[28] . . .

The sacred texts say that the cow is the abode of thirty-three crore gods. Well, the sacred texts also say that the *Varaahaavtari devata*[29] became a pig. Then why protect only cows? Why not set up organizations to protect pigs also?[30]

Worthy of Worship?

Man becomes like the gods he worships, Savarkar explained. Believing the cow to be god, worshipping the cow, the entire Hindu nation has become a cow. And so, like the cow's legs, it just collapses to the ground with a *dhaddaam* at the first stroke of danger. Let the Hindu nation be founded not on the feet of a cow but at the feet of a lion . . . I am not an enemy of cows, he explained. But we should look after it, not worship it. Continue to work to enhance the cow-wealth of the country, and simultaneously organize a massive campaign against the abattoirs. These abattoirs are being run to humiliate us, to cut off our noses, Savarkar said . . . But if you continue to just worship the cow, you will become a cow. Become lions. . . I look upon the cow as one that deserves to be protected. You look upon it as one that has to be worshipped . . .[31] Yes, sometimes making an entity worthy of worship

---

[25] I have omitted the name of the animal that Savarkar used.

[26] I have omitted the name of the animal that Savarkar used.

[27] The true, loved son of a mother.

[28] *Savarkar Samagra*, Volume VII, p. 444, Volume VIII, pp. 361–62.

[29] The wild-boar incarnation of Vishnu.

[30] *Savarkar Samagra*, Volume VIII, p. 351.

[31] *Savarkar Samagra*, Volume VII, pp. 315–16.

does lead people to begin looking after it. But in the case of the cow, having come to worship it, Hindus have forgotten to look after it.

Eating Beef? Eating Pork?

Should one eat beef? Should one eat pork? This is a matter not of religion but of your stomach, Savarkar maintained. What the doctors advise, what you can digest, what will be best for your body as you recover from an illness, these should be the determinants, according to Savarkar, not what a book says or what has been the traditional practice. The life of all—cows, dogs, horses, parrots, donkeys—is equally precious.[32] If the cows of Bharat are so sacred, what is the harm in eating the cows of America, a country where they eat their cows in any case?[33] Savarkar reiterated such arguments on several occasions. The cow is a useful animal so we should look after it well. But—and here we see his 'utilitarianism', something to which we will have occasion to return as we proceed—when kindness to it entails cost to humans, we should not: when the enemy armies used to encircle themselves with cows, these should have been killed, got out of the way so that the enemy could be dealt with. The cows of the countries of enemies are not worthy of kindness just because they are cows, he wrote. By their milk, our enemies are strengthened and not us. The cow and bullock of our country, being useful to us, should ordinarily not be eaten, but there is no harm in eating their meat like the meat of any other animal in England or America . . .[34]

The Example of the Lokmanya

As the controversy continued, a critic invoked the example of Lokmanya Tilak. Tilak had not eaten meat even when he was in England, the critic

---

[32] See, for instance, *Savarkar Samagra*, Volume VII, pp. 554–55.

[33] *Savarkar Samagra*, Volume VIII, pp. 424–26.

[34] *Savarkar Samagra*, Volume VIII, pp. 446–47.

pointed out. Savarkar pounced back. True, Tilak had not—but that was his personal choice, what does it have to do with shastras? Savarkar asked. After all, if it was a matter of obeying the shastras, how did Tilak cross the seas, how did he dine with *malechhas* (the sinful and filthy ones)? These too are forbidden.[35]

And What Does the Manusmriti Prescribe?

Savarkar was not one to leave an argument midway. He pointed out that, in fact, Manusmriti does not merely permit the eating of meat, it makes it obligatory to do so in *yagyas* and during shraadha.[36] Savarkar reproduced passages from Manusmriti to show that Brahmins and Kshatriyas partook of animals and birds at many yagyas; that during shraadha, eating and serving meat is extremely shaastriya, it is an imperative duty of the Brahmin/*Brahman kaa aavashyak kartavya*. Not just this, Manusmriti declares that he who does not eat meat during shraadha, will be born of an animal *yoni* for twenty-one births—such is the severe penalty prescribed for such a defaulter. And the meat of which animals is to be eaten? Of the *bhainsaa,* the bullock, and the *varaah,* the wild pig. When the progeny does so, their forefathers are satiated not just for one day but for ten months.[37] And the same is prescribed for the newborn son, Savarkar reminded his critics: the first food that is given to the newborn should contain the meat of a lamb, partridge and fish in *shorbaa* (broth) form.[38]

As the controversy continued, as part of his dissection of Manusmriti—and he took this merely as an example of texts that had come to be regarded as the final word for how we should conduct ourselves—Savarkar

---

[35] *Savarkar Samagra,* Volume VIII, pp. 472–73.

[36] Prayers and ceremonies in honour of and for the benefit of ancestors.

[37] Savarkar reproduced *Manusmriti,* 3/270, 5/23 and 5/35.

[38] *Savarkar Samagra,* Volume VIII, pp. 473–75, originally in *Kirloskar,* February 1937.

reproduced chapter and verse on this business of eating meat, of killing animals, etc.

Adhyaya 3, verses 55, 56, 60, 61 clearly show that Brahmins and others used to eat meat and fish during shraadha days as well as on days when yagyas were being performed, Savarkar observed while reproducing them. For the Brahmin, eating the meat and fish served on such days was made compulsory. Several verses set out how these dishes were to be prepared and served.[39] The food must be served hot—as our ancestors eat food only when it is hot, the ogres eat food when it is cold. It must be served in silence. No untouchable, no pig, cock, dog, menstruating woman or impotent man should be allowed to look at the priests as they eat the food.

The verses also list the periods for which these different dishes would satiate the hunger of our ancestors: *til*, rice, *jau*, *phaliyaan*—beans, water, roots, fruit satiate their hunger for one month; fish for two months; meat of deer for three months; mutton for four months; bird flesh for five months; goat for six months; for seven months with meat of *chitra*—spotted deer; for eight months with meat of a black antelope; for nine months with the meat of a gazelle, the small barasingha. From the meat of wild boar and wild buffalo, the ancestors remain satiated for ten months, from that of rabbit and tortoise for eleven months. They remain content forever from the milk of a cow or its kheer, from the flesh of a *mahaashalk matsya*— the fish with large scales, a red goat, the meat of a rhino, honey and food eaten by *munnies*. . . The animals, fish, birds that have been killed for the shraadha meal ascend to a good life . . . The Brahmin who kills an animal during *madhurpak,* yagya, shraadha and *devapuja* ensures *uttam gati* (highest fortune) not just for himself, but also for the animal . . .

---

[39] Savarkar lists, *Manusmriti, Adhyaya* 3, verses 228, 267, 269, 270, 271, 273.

Brahmins as Letterboxes

As one puts a letter in the letterbox, Savarkar pointed out with some glee, the Brahmins who have been appointed to reach this food to the ancestors must eat the meat, etc. because there is no other way of reaching the food to the ancestors in the other world.[40] He who, having been invited to a shraadha, refuses to eat meat out of obstinacy shall be reborn as an animal twenty-one times. . . The shlokas declare that there is no difficulty in a Brahmin eating meat during shraadha, when his life is in danger or when he feels like doing so. Just as God has created the ones who will eat meat, He has created the animals, fish, birds for man to eat. On the other hand, the texts insist that a twice-born who knowingly eats kukurmutta (mushroom), *graam-varaah* (wild boar), garlic, *graam-kukkut* (wild chicken), onion and turnip becomes a fallen one at once . . .

God Himself has created animals, etc. for yagyas. The violence used in killing an animal for a yagya that is done for the welfare of all is in fact nonviolence. The animals killed for yagya attain *shreshthtaa* (the best of births upon births).[41] Savarkar noted that between such verses, others too have been inserted, which declare that one should not eat meat under any circumstances.[42] These are a reflection not on the validity of the preceding verses but on the character of texts that we revere, he pointed out—something to which we will revert in a moment.

In a word, Savarkar said, whether one should eat meat or not is not a question to be answered by looking up a book like Manusmriti. It is to be settled by what medical science says today and what suits the physical constitution of the person . . .[43]

---

[40] See 'Shraadha diwas aur maansaashan', *Savarkar Samagra*, Volume IV, pp, 437–441.

[41] As examples, Savarkar reproduces verses 35, 27, 30, 32, 39, 40 from *Manusmriti, Adhyaya* 5.

[42] Like shlokas 41, 42, 48, 49 of the same *Adhyaya* 5.

[43] On the foregoing, *Savarkar Samagra*, Volume Volume VIII, pp. 437–41.

The Example to Emulate

And look at the harm such beliefs inflict, Savarkar reminded readers. Confronted with a Hindu army, the Mussalmaan invaders would put a ring of cows in front. The Hindu soldiers and army would refuse to fight lest a cow be killed, he said. No one taught them that to stop the ingress of enemies of the nation and dharma was a great punya. They let the rashtra die so that the cow-mother may live . . . And once the Mussalmaan had conquered all, the cows too were butchered . . . If you resist, we will break the Surya temple in Multan, the Mussalmaans warned . . . and the Hindu forces withdrew . . . If you take a step towards taking Kashi back, we will reduce the temple there to rubble, the Mussalmaans proclaimed. The nawab had but to threaten them in this way that the Hindus sat down in dharna to keep the Peshwa from attacking Kashi. The entire kingdom of devtas was sunk to save one temple . . . As if in the reign of Aurangzeb and Allauddin Khilji cows were not being butchered, as if temples were not being destroyed. They took *gau-rakshand* (cow protection) to be dharma and made *gau-bhakshand* (devouring cows) widespread. Intelligence goes first, and then . . .

If only, instead of desisting from fighting the enemy because of the herd of cows between the adversary and themselves, the Hindu forces had swiftly slaughtered the cows, and then washed their hands in the blood of the *malechhas* hiding behind them—so many temples, and cows would have been saved, and the Hindu rashtra would have survived, Savarkar said . . . If only they had replied, 'Just bring down the sun-temple, then take it that this Hindu army will not return home, and instead, having liberated Multan, it will advance and will have every mosque till Kabul ploughed under by ploughs pulled by donkeys. Not just that, on the foundations of the Shahi mosque in Kabul the sun-temple will be reconstructed . . .'[44] The counter-example that Savarkar held up was that of the Commander-in-

---

[44] *Savarkar Samagra*, Volume VII, pp 437–38.

Chief of the Sikh empire, Hari Singh Nalwa.[45] Scoring victory after victory, Hari Singh reached the banks of the Kabul river, Savarkar recounted. The Pathans surrounded his troops and cut off food supplies. As the Sikhs were looting the stores of grain in the villages, the Pathans sprinkled cows' blood over the stored grain. Hari Singh Nalwa had wild pigs killed and had the grain 'purified' by sprinkling *their* blood and flesh on the grain. The Muslim Pathans were furious. Now they could not eat the grain. They began to go hungry. Hari Singh ate both lots to set an example for his troops . . . Hari Singh triumphed. The moral, Savarkar said, is, 'Real cow-protection is that which becomes a weapon for protecting the nation. It is immaterial whether the Hindu, who himself becomes a cow with straws in his mouth roams moaning all over the world, dies or lives to partake of cow urine and manure. He is not a cow protector, he is a *dharmabrhashth pandaa*.'[46] The two in fact are the same: 'Being a cow he waits for someone else to come and free him from the grasp of the lion . . .' [. . .] 'Let there be reason in worship,' Savarkar wrote. 'Let only that be considered dharmic which manifestly benefits the nation . . .'[47]

The Sacred Peepal Tree

Savarkar's views about other things that we hold sacred were the same. The majestic, bountiful peepal tree, its cool shade in summer, the rustle of its leaves as the breeze blows through it—people don't just admire it for all these things. They believe gods live in it. They tie *mauli*, the auspicious red thread around its trunk. They perambulate around it. They look after it dutifully. They will not cut it. To all this Savarkar says, it is sheer foolishness to think that if one cuts down a peepal tree, ill will befall us. Muslims and

---

[45] Under his command, Sikh forces extended the frontier of the Sikh empire up to the Khyber Pass.

[46] A fallen Brahmin.

[47] *Savarkar Samagra*, Volume VIII, pp. 384–85, 391.

Christians do not hesitate to cut it down, he points out, and no ill befalls them on that count. Eventually, the learned pandit says, '*Jaisaa bhaav vaisaa Bhagwaan*'[48]—because we believe that harm will come to us if we harm the *peepal*, harm does come to us. As they do not have this belief, no harm comes to them. The answer is simple, says Savarkar: stop believing that harm will come to us, then no harm will come to us. To think that sages or gods live on the tree is just innocent blind faith. How is it that the gods on it come down on Hindus when the tree is harmed or they do one *parikramaa* less, but run away with their tails between their legs when a Mussalmaan or Christian comes to them, axe in hand? The God of the Hindus should be Narasimha. The peepal tree is just another tree. Where and when it is useful, it should be nurtured and helped to grow. But when its roots are endangering a building, or the tree is obstructing a path, it should be cut down . . . The vat, peepal, tulsi are worthy of being protected because they are useful to man. They should be protected as plants and trees. That is all. The moment the stamp of religion is put on a belief or practice, know that it is no more than blind belief, whether the belief is of a Hindu, Mussalmaan, Christian or Jew. At that point, intelligence ceases, and *bhakti* begins.[49]

Rituals

What holds for objects—an animal, a tree—holds as much for observances: rituals, fasts, vows.

The movement and position of the *Navagraha*—the nine 'planets'—are said to influence the outcome of our efforts, the crops we will get, our health, our relationships, in a word our lives. Well, their positions, their orbits, the velocity at which they move through the heavens are all fixed, Savarkar reminded his readers. Those nine are going to go on moving

---

[48] 'As the belief so the God.'

[49] *Savarkar Samagra*, Volume III, pp. 673–74; Volume VIII, pp. 462–65.

in their accustomed orbits, at those velocities. Therefore, if they have any effect on your fortunes, on your crops that effect will come to pass whether or not you pray to them, prostrate before their images and go round them, offer flowers and milk. Nor can the timing or duration of eclipses be altered one bit by our prayers and *havans,* nor by whether we give something in charity. Moreover, these are inert bodies: they do not know, they *cannot* know that you are or are not doing any of these things; they do not, they *cannot* know the purposes you want fulfilled by what you are doing.[50] To pray to them as if they are living beings, to seek to please them with offerings, yagyas, by giving gifts to and feeding Brahmins will be to worship untruth.[51]

We may love the moon and the sun for many things but to consider them to be living beings who have to be propitiated, etc. is foolishness, Savarkar wrote. If you are in the scorching summer sun whether you recite the Gayatri mantra or not, it will rain its heat on you. The protection against that is not some mantra but an umbrella, a headcover, and shoes to shield your feet from the ground.[52] Instead of praying to the goddess of roads, repair the roads, keep your vehicles in good condition, drive carefully: that way there will be better chances that you will reach your destination safe.[53]

Today the myths that accompanied or triggered the rituals, fasts, offerings, etc. hinder our people from learning the way the world works, Savarkar emphasized repeatedly. Therefore, they should be discarded. We have been taught, 'Never look at a full eclipse, remain indoors.' But the best moment to study some aspects of the sun and its flares is precisely that moment of total eclipse. In Europe, scientists observe the

---

[50] *Savarkar Samagra,* Volume III, pp. 659–60.

[51] Ibid, pp. 667–68.

[52] Ibid, pp. 665–66.

[53] Ibid, pp. 669–70.

eclipse, and, far from being harmed, they are able to acquire greater understanding.[54]

That we should not milk a cow or a buffalo, not cut grass, not clean our teeth during Sankranti[55] . . . and that because of the beneficence of this Sankranti, people in the East will suffer and those in the West will prosper . . . Instead of such *vaahiyaat* and *moorkhataapoorand*[56] observances, from and with friends, '*Til-gud lo, Madhur vaani bolo.*' [57]

It is plain wrong to believe that by smearing some oil and *sindoor* on any stone lying around, by reading this or that book and giving two handfuls of rice to some *airey-gairey panchkalyaandi*,[58] Mangal or Shani will be calmed, that it will be pleased. They will go about their routes whether you sing their praises or curse them, just like a kerosene lamp or an electric bulb: these will continue to emit light whether you do some ritual around them, curse them or sing hymns to them.[59]

What is being preached and conveyed through *panchaangs*[60] is *paagalpan aur kuch had tak thug vidya.*[61]

When it was very difficult to relight a fire, it was prescribed that the flame should not be allowed to die out. Now that electricity is available, it is foolish to go on burning an oil lamp because our ancestors used to do so.[62]

The final defence of these rituals and observances is that they help strengthen our minds and thereby better equip us to deal with the

---

[54] Ibid, pp. 657–58.

[55] Days that mark the passage of the sun from one Zodiac to another. Taken in some parts of India to be as the first day of the new month, and in some parts as the last day of the month that is passing.

[56] Observances that are vulgar and full of foolishness.

[57] 'Receive sesame-jaggery, Speak sweetly.' *Savarkar Samagra*, Volume III, pp. 662–63.

[58] Any and every nondescript do-gooder.

[59] Ibid, pp. 663–64.

[60] Almanacs.

[61] Madness and to an extent proficiency in looting the innocent. Ibid, pp. 669–70.

[62] *Savarkar Samagra*, Volume III, p. 671.

difficulties that may arise. The answer to that is evident: true, therefore work directly on the mind.

Ridicule

Savarkar ridiculed those who preyed on the innocence of the people and prescribed rituals of this kind. Bharatiyas are surpassing all in their inventions, he wrote. They are setting new records.

The Shankaracharya of Kamkoti announced that the way to bring about world peace—and he would be personally exerting to ensure this—is to have everyone drink cow's milk and eat fresh fruit. By doing so, everyone would lose their innate aggressiveness, and so peace would reign. Savarkar poured ridicule. The bullock drinks cow's milk, and yet he rushes at you to strike you with his horns. Perhaps because he does not eat ripe fruit? Perhaps because he has developed a taste for tea? And what about the cow itself? She occasionally kicks the bucket over as she is being milked and rushes at you and butts you with her horns. Possibly because there is some residual evil in her which she has imbibed through her horns? But trees have no horns, so the other way of acquiring merit and wholesome traits—i.e. eating ripe fruit—should work. The monkeys eat fruit and yet ruin your trees, they nibble at and throw away half-eaten fruit, and fight among themselves. They even attack children and snatch things from shops. Perhaps because they don't drink cow's milk, and they don't wait for the fruit to ripen before plunging their teeth into them? What about Krishna who tended cows? He participated in war and made sure that Arjuna fought and killed. Perhaps because he ate meat and drank liquor, of which there is specific reference in the Mahabharat? But what about him as a child, Bal Krishna? Ferocious, he killed Kansa . . .

Another authority on such matters, Chaubey Baba, had another prescription for total, universal peace. He announced that if Bharatiyas would chant 'Shri Ram Jai Jai Ram' together a crore of times, world peace would be established . . .[63]

We perform yagyas, we chant mantras, we undertake fasts, we give *daan* (donation) because we have been taught that these will bring 'divine blessing'. They will not, Savarkar wrote. He gave scores of examples of people who were certain that their God was the only true God, that he was the most powerful God. They propitiated that God through these and similar means, driven by the belief that God was with them—not just individuals but as entire peoples. They had the great, revealed books with them. They had the greatest saints amidst them. Yet, they were wiped out by adversaries. No 'divine blessing' saved them. The way to acquire 'divine blessing' is to acquire the competence and strength—worldly competence, worldly strength—that the task at hand requires. If you have acquired the requisite competence and strength, you will gain the objective. If you have not, nothing you do to please God is going to deliver success.[64]

The Twin Tests, the Many Alternatives

The beliefs and rituals that were prescribed and which we hang on to, Savarkar pointed out, reflect what the state of knowledge and understanding of natural phenomena were in those times. Today, we know much more about how things work. Therefore, to begin with, discard every ritual, practice, belief that has been superseded by scientific advancements or proven wrong by historical experience. Chanting did not save the Somnath temple. Why will it bring universal peace? . . . When we were stricken by a plague, our Hindu-Mussalmaan sanskriti—old as the devas though it is—resorted to vows, yagyas,

---

[63] For examples of Savarkar's piercing comments on such cures and those propagating them see, *Savarkar Samagra*, Volume VIII, pp. 397–405, 415–20. See also his comments on the value or otherwise of *yagyas*: *Savarkar Samagra*, Volume VII, pp. 410–32.

[64] *Savarkar Samagra*, Volume VII, pp. 385–94. Also, *Rationalism of Veer Savarkar*, op. cit., e-Edition, pp. 340–44.

turning rosaries, imploring deities, sacrificing goats, killing chicken, wearing amulets, qurbaani-namaz, prayers, etc. None of these worked. In Europe, they invented and deployed a vaccination. They cleaned their cities and houses; they killed off the rats . . . We float boats by breaking a coconut and chanting mantras. But when the boat develops a hole, no mantra, no shloka from the Gita, no *ayat* of the Quran, no verse from the Bible, no *taweez* (amulet) is going to save the boatmen. On the other hand, what to say of mere holes, the devices that engineers develop keep ships afloat even through storms . . . In engineering and science, the wish of God, whether the deed is virtuous or sinful according to the *dharmashastras, jyotish,* etc. have no place. If you take two parts of hydrogen, one of oxygen, you will get water. Whether this is done at an auspicious moment or not, whether the right kind of goat is sacrificed or not, whether on Eid because of your sacrificing or not sacrificing a cow God is angry or not, whether a Christian or a Mussalmaan or a Hindu makes that compound, water will come to be, Savarkar pointed out. Are the palaces, secretariats, bungalows, made by the British without bothering either about the auspicious time and date or whether the elements had been pacified by rituals and configuration and layout of the buildings—are these not as strong as our buildings? he asked. And have the buildings that were constructed by choosing the right *mahurat* (auspicious moment), by diligent application of Vaastu Shastra not been levelled by time, while the Governors' Houses constructed by the British have remained standing? . . . The huge airplanes made by those unbelieving Britishers are flying in the sky while the buildings constructed on the ground by us in full accord with Dharmashastras have gone to dust . . . [65]

A newspaper carries a report of a man crawling on his stomach from Prayagraj to Haridwar to please God. Savarkar mocks the man, the practice, the belief. Why are you crawling on a stomach to please the God who has given you two legs to walk on? He contrasts such pledges with the pledges

---

[65] *Savarkar Samagra,* Volume VII, pp. 415–16, 499–500.

that the young in Europe are making—of plumbing the depths of the ocean, of flying into space. So much for the stupidity of crawling on one's stomach in the name of religion, he writes, here is yet another example—in Nasik, a sadhu named Lahirimaharaj is observing silence for some days at present. He has vowed to wrap fragrant flour in paper and write the name of Rama on it and make an offering of eleven lakh such tablets in the river. He says that doing so will benefit the human race and save it from catastrophes such as earthquakes. Would it not be better if that flour is used to make bread, which then is distributed to the destitute? Savarkar asks. If their hunger is satisfied, surely God would be pleased. Let us suppose that the sadhu wants to create tablets for the benefit of mankind, then there is another way. He could make eleven lakh quinine tablets and distribute them to those affected by malaria . . .[66]

Alternatives

The only tests that should prevail are two. Does the practice or belief accord with current knowledge, with our experience? Will it benefit the nation? For this reason, Savarkar proposed many alternatives to these age-old and much-revered practices. They punctuate his writings. You will find several of them listed in Godbole's compilation, *Rationalism of Veer Savarkar,* as well as on savarkar.org. Here are just a few examples.

Ladies, instead of going round and round temples and trees, why not start a small oil mill—tie one end of a rope around your waist and the other to a press so that as you go round, you produce cooking oil that can be given to the poor? Instead of taking the vow to perambulate around a tree, why not take the vow to promote *swadeshi* products? Why not go around the town in the name of God and convert five persons every day to support our industries? In one of his essays, Savarkar showed how one could help

---

[66] *Savarkar Samagra,* Volume VIII, pp. 347–51.

even in little ways. He published a list of shops in Ratnagiri which stocked items produced in India. Not a difficult task, and yet so helpful.

Ladies, you go to fields in search of special blades of grass called *Durva* and offer 1,00,000 of them to God. Instead of this, go to the fields, cut grass and provide fodder for cows. Or cut beautiful flowers and give them away to working-class girls. Or plant flower shrubs in your own garden or in the houses of your friends. You observe so many *vratas* (fasts) during the four lunar months—Shravan, Bhadrapat, Ashwin and Kartik. Why not be up to date? Grow vegetables in the back garden and give them away to orphanages or make clothes and give them to the children of former untouchables who are now trying to go to school. Instead of paying pandits, offer money to persons like Masurkar Maharaj, who has been trying to convert Christians and Muslims back to Hindu Dharma . . . go round the city, meet those who have been recently converted to other religions and persuade them to come back to Hindu Dharma. Instead of spending money in the memory of your forefathers, why not supply saris to helpless women? Instead of offering a cow, clothes, utensils and money to Brahmins at the twelfth day ritual of a deceased relative, why not give them to an orphanage? Or support a Hindu student, who wishes to become an airline pilot? Even Lord Krishna has said in the Gita, 'The gift which is given only with the thought of "giving", which is given to a worthy person who has done no previous favour, at the proper place and time, that gift is held pure.' 'Let us adopt the same test to our vratas and ensure that they benefit the poor, helpless and downtrodden in the Hindu nation. Your physical sufferings and financial contributions should ultimately lead to the betterment of the Hindu nation.'[67]

---

[67] For Savarkar's general view on why and to what alternatives fasts, vows, etc. should change with time, *Savarkar Samagra*, Volume VII, pp. 405–32, and 490–97. For examples given in the paragraph, and similar ones, *The Rationalism of Veer Savarkar*, V.S. Godbole, compiler, Itihas Patrika Prakashan, Bombay, e-edition, pp 584–87; and on the website of savarkar.org. They give particulars of *Samagra Savarkar Vangmaya* where these and other examples can be found.

Instead of women taking vows to do so many thousand perambulations around a tree or temple or the fire, let them take a vow: 'I will visit ten houses every day for a month, and persuade them to buy swadeshi goods.' Instead of rationalizing the *pheras* (circumambulation) on the ground that they will improve the women's health, teach them the importance of physical activity and encourage them to go for a walk early in the morning. Let them help women less fortunate than themselves, let them help in orphanages. Let them earn something and donate it to organizations doing *shuddhi* (purification) work . . .[68]

To encourage others to take up such tasks instead of expending their funds and time in rituals, Savarkar listed the sorts of things that had been actually done in villages in Ratnagiri:

- Going to Mahar colonies and singing bhajans
- *Parikrama* of a temple by all—persons of all castes as well as untouchables
- At the spring festival: Brahmin ladies going to the Mahar, chamar, etc. colonies, and applying the same *haldi, rori* (turmeric and tilak) on women and giving the same prasad as they have been doing in localities of upper caste households
- Opening schools so that children do not have to go to the school run by missionaries because it is the only school in the village

Do as many and as much of these three–four things as your circumstances allow, Savarkar counselled. Every night before going off to sleep reflect, 'Have I done what I could have done?' And make it your belief that *nar ki sewa hi Narayan ki puja hai, patit kaa paalan hi Patit Pavan ki puja hai*— that service of man is prayer of Divinity, that helping the fallen is prayer of the Patit Pavan, the succour of the fallen . . . [69]

---

[68] *Savarkar Samagra*, Volume III, p. 675.

[69] *Savarkar Samagra*, Volume II, pp. 578–81.

He listed tasks of other kinds too: instead of spending all your time and resources organizing religious festivals, help set up *akharas* (wrestling areas), find out where and by what arguments missionaries and *maulvis* are spreading their net to ensnare Hindus, and work to save the Hindus . . .[70]

A Ready Test, and a Comparison

And he gave a ready test. When all sorts of rituals and expensive donations are prescribed, he said, and a book is cited as authority, look at the end: if it prescribes a hefty daan to the Brahmins, know it to be a fraud, written by some Brahmins for Brahmins.[71]

How do these views and prescriptions compare with what those who appropriate him today are doing? M.S. Golwalkar is a revered figure within the RSS. He was the *sarsanghchalak* for almost three decades. You will find his pictures in the house of every RSS member. And one of the most common among these are a picture of him performing a havan, and the reproduction of a painting done from that picture. Savarkar spent decades decrying ghee being poured onto the fire in havans and other similar rituals. Hindu rashtra is not going to benefit from these, he would write in essay after essay and repeat in lecture after lecture. Nothing will come of the hoary yagyas that went on for twelve years, the *japas* (chanting) done lakhs of times to ward off the difficulties heaped by Navagraha, the one lakh recitations from the Atharva Veda, the crores of recitations of the Gayatri mantra, of burning tubs full of ghee in the sacrificial or havan pit etc.[72] And yet the current lot has no compunction appropriating him. We have just seen how insistently and how sternly Savarkar urged Hindus to give up ostentatious ceremonies and structures. He urged people to use the resources instead for the welfare of the destitute. And look at the

---

[70] Ibid, p. 577.

[71] *Savarkar Samagra*, Volume III, pp. 676–78.

[72] For instance, *Savarkar Samagra*, Volume VII, p. 518.

ostentatious religiosity today: inaugurations and consecrations for the cameras, the *aarti* (light offering) at Haridwar and Benares recreated for television. Lighting lakhs of *diyas* in Ayodhya so as to get into the Guinness Book of Records. Instead of penitential pilgrimages, 'Religious *Tourism*' ... and yet, no qualm in appropriating Savarkar.

And this is done with the fullest confidence—because the high-priests of 'Religious Tourism' know that no one would have read Savarkar!

But to get back to Savarkar's views and work.

Creative Response

Apart from the specific things that we should learn from this set of Savarkar's writings, there is the general lesson. As we shall see, to obtain release from his imprisonment in the Andamans, Savarkar had been filing 'mercy petitions'. He used to propose several conditions by which he would abide were he to be released. In the end, he did accept the conditions for his release. Among these were two: he will desist from political activity and he will remain within Ratnagiri district for a specified period. In one of the final interviews with officials of the Bombay Presidency, he was asked whether, although it was not a condition for his release, he would like to state that the trial that led to his life imprisonment in the Andamans[73] was fair? He had accepted that also and certified that the trial had been fair and just.

But we will come to these things later. For the moment, the conditions that concern us are these two: that he would desist from political activity and that he would not venture out of Ratnagiri district.

Instead of lamenting these conditions, Savarkar put them to creative use. He wrote extensively, mostly for small circulation magazines, and through these writings, he urged people to shed beliefs and practices that

---

[73] In which he had been convicted on the charge of abetment to murder and on account of which he had been imprisoned in the Andamans for all those years.

were mere excrescences of time. He sought to encourage them to think and conduct themselves rationally.

Second, he strove to eliminate untouchability in Ratnagiri.

Third, he waged well-documented and forceful campaigns in the district against caste.

The campaigns reflected his rationalism. It is to these that we turn now.

The Raakshasi and the Raakshas

Savarkar called untouchability, the age-old curse of our religion, *asprishyata raakshasi,* the demoness of untouchability. Similarly, he called the caste system *jaatibhed kaa raakshas*, the demon of caste differentiation, the *vishvriksha,* the poison tree.[1]

Even in the dungeon of Andamans, where it was enough if one survived, Savarkar found some fellow prisoners being scrupulous about keeping their distance from those whom they regarded as untouchables. Savarkar encouraged all to sit in the same row for meals, to treat each other as fellow human beings.

In Ratnagiri, he could work against this evil on a broader scale. Invited to inaugurate a Hanuman temple, he said he would do so provided untouchables were also called to sit together with others inside the temple to sing bhajans. The organizer agreed. Savarkar entered the temple along with untouchables. And thus, the temple was inaugurated. During his address, Savarkar strongly criticized the practice of denying entry into temples to untouchables. 'The untouchables have as much natural right to worship God as other Hindus. Having them exercise that right is true dharma,' he told the devotees. 'The temples and surroundings of Trayambakeshwar or Kashi temples are very large,' he pointed out. 'There on the path of perambulation, dogs, cats, donkeys roam and do all their business. But Mahars, Mangs, Bhangis who are humans like the others, who are our Hindu brethren, who worship the same God are forbidden

---

[1] See, for instance, *Savarkar Samagra,* Volume VII, pp. 86, 87, 95.

from doing the perambulation. For this reason, this small little temple seems to me to be greater than those large temples . . .'[2]

A report stated that at a meeting of Brahmins in Bombay, it was mentioned that a *milan* (gathering) of untouchables should be held in front of the idol of Sri Ganesh. Where others might have seen in this a welcome sign of progress, Savarkar was moved to near anger at the condition of the people. He wrote that the surprising thing was not that such a thing had been said, but that it should have been necessary to say it. What kind of a God is it who by the mere sight of an untouchable becomes fallen? he asked. The most loved name of God is Patit Pavan. But here, instead of His touch and sight lifting the fallen, He falls by their merely seeing Him or touching Him. Is He made of wax or *gobar* (dung)? Savarkar demanded. He is a Brahmin who has acquired knowledge of Brahma, of reality. For such a person to believe that if any untouchable even gets to have darshan of God, the God becomes impure is as laughable as if a person with beautiful eyes were to proclaim day to be night. You Brahmins are yourself the guardians and lords of the earth. You should be *patit pavan*, the succour of the downtrodden. Does fire freeze by coming in contact with cold? It is darkness which is rent asunder by the lamp—does the lamp become blind by coming in contact with darkness? That which purifies the rivulet is Bhagirathi. So also, He alone by merely touching whom the *patit* become *pavan,* is God. By the mere touch of Sri Hari animals like Gajendra were elevated. To exclude the Mahar, Mang and others who believe in this legend, who are our own, to prevent them from even having darshan of the Lord to say nothing of touching Him, is a matter of regret and ignorance.

If it is just a question of purity, Savarkar pointed out, then the sinners among Brahmins, etc. should also be kept away. For the same reason, those among the Mahars and Mang who are learned and of good conduct

---

[2] *Savarkar Samagra*, Volume VII, pp. 304–05.

should be allowed darshan . . . Rocks are not going to rain down from the sky, the earth is not going to quake if Mahars sing bhajans in the temple . . . He drew attention to a counterexample: in Ratnagiri, a young lad, the son of a sweeper woman has been singing in the temple. The heavens have not fallen, Ganapati does not seem to have got upset . . .

No one has come up with a counterargument when the terrible consequences of this practice of untouchability are narrated, Savarkar told his readers. This practice is just a bad habit, like smoking bidis. Even when we are told that smoking them is bad for our health, it is not easy to get rid of the habit. . . from those living as servants of malechhas, those who do not act even when their wives and daughters are taken away by the Muslims, those who keep wagging their tails even as their temples and thrones are being smothered underfoot, those living on crumbs thrown down from tables, those sitting mute in offices and swallowing the abuse of sahibs, to those *mahamahopadhyayas* (learned scholars) and teachers wrapped in shawls waxing eloquent on the glories of English literature—none among them has a right to invoke smritis. And if it is a question of smritis, if someone says that the practice is mandated in the smritis, ask yourself how many of the observances mandated by these scriptures you have adhered to since you woke up in the morning.

Brahmins, Kshatriyas, he warned, these seven crore people are your brothers who are pleading that you allow them to worship in the temples. For the sake of justice, permit them, welcome them with affection. Today, they are performing *satyagraha* peacefully. Tomorrow, at the instigation of some hypocrites, they will take up weapons. Persons of foreign religions are trying to turn their minds . . . Is it your duty to increase the number of devotees of the one you call 'God', or is it to diminish their number? . . . In Kenya, the Europeans and adherents of foreign religions look upon you as untouchables. You are enraged at this, and that is justified too. But then, by the same mouth and contrary to that very reason, you dub your own fellow-religionists as untouchables. Reflect on this. Which is the shruti? Which is the smriti? . . .

And there was the ultimate answer. The ancient shrutis and smritis are with us. In case they say the opposite, then they should be made to conform. Smritis are for the nation. Those that become the cause for its destruction, how can they be smritis? That is the misapprehension of smritis. . .[3]

Programmes to Root Out the Evil

Nor did Savarkar stop at writing. He organized programmes to root out the evil. At these, persons from all castes would sit together and eat together—food cooked and served by individuals of all castes, especially those previously considered as untouchables. Until then, the practice in Ratnagiri, as in other places, was that if an untouchable requested tea, they had to bring their own vessel and stand outside the shop. The tea would be poured outside into the vessel and the untouchable would drink it standing outside. Savarkar had a restaurant opened in which all would eat snacks and drink tea together. He persuaded those controlling temples to allow whoever wanted to do the perambulations to do so, irrespective of his or her caste. He went to and urged others to go to the houses of those whom they regarded as untouchables, to befriend them, eat with them in their houses. He urged audiences, invite them to your houses and serve food to them as you would to anyone else. He got women to visit localities of untouchables, especially on religious occasions, sing bhajans with them, apply *haldi* (turmeric) and *kumkum* (vermilion) to their foreheads . . .

The best of these ventures was the Patit Pavan Temple. A local Seth had not been allowed to pray and do *archana* (propitiation) in the old Bhageshwar Mandir because he was from the Bhandari caste. He had resolved that he would construct a temple where he could pray and do archana. Savarkar said that he told him that there were many who spent their lives in a worse condition—they could not even have darshan of the

---

[3] *Savarkar Samagra,* Volume IX, pp. 110–15.

deity, they could not even pray in the compound of the temples. He urged the Seth to set up a temple where all could enter and pray. And the priests would be those who had learnt the rituals, mantras, etc., not those who were, say, Brahmins by birth. A residence would be constructed alongside the temple. In this residence, one Brahmin, one Kshatriya, one Vaishya, one person from the untouchable classes and one representative of the Seth would reside. The temple was indeed built.

Functions would be regularly held at the temple. Persons from all castes would attend. There would be a meal after the function. All would eat together. And the names of all who had eaten together would be printed the next day. No one was cast out of his caste as a result.

Unsparing

Savarkar toured the district, exhorting all to break the evil. Are you going to be imprisoned for doing so? he asked. Will you be hanged? All you have to do is to proclaim, '*Sparsh karoongaa, Svikaar karoongaa,*' [4] and do so. He was unsparing. Reflect on how you deal with some Abdul Rashid,[5] an Aurangzeb and those who butchered Hindus in East Bengal, he told audiences. If these *dharmashatru,* these enemies of the religion, come to you, you invite them into your home, you sit with them. You fondle dogs, you feed milk to snakes, you let the cat which gobbles mice every day lick your thali. You caress cows and buffaloes. But you do not touch fellow Hindus. You do not let even their shadow fall on you. By this kind of inhuman boycott, you have robbed their lives of meaning. You have pushed them into becoming informers of your enemies about the secrets of your home. You have pushed them into becoming the enemies of our religion by converting to some non-Hindu religion. For these reasons, and

---

[4] 'I will touch, I will accept.'

[5] Abdul Rashid murdered Swami Shraddhanand, the well-known Arya Samaj leader.

from the point of view of sheer justice, once we give them their due as human beings, the maulvis will be weakened, no one will be seen in the majority of missionary establishments . . .[6]

To the Victims Too

'He was unsparing,' I just typed. He was unsparing of the victims, too. The 'untouchables' were not a monolith group; within them, there were grades upon grades—layers of grades: *Mang, Paandi-mahar, Bekey-mahar, Daamoki-chamar, Ghati-chamar, Mochi, Mehtar, Dhed.* Among these also the Bengali, Punjabi, Madrasi, Megh, Mochi, Mahar, etc. were not at par. They also had strict taboos about eating with each other. The Mahars—Dr Ambedkar had been born into this caste—had the same deplorable attitude towards the Mang, Dhor, Chamar, etc. as Brahmins and Kshatriyas had towards the Mahars.

April 1931, the Somvanshi Mahar Parishad was meeting. They had invited Savarkar to preside. He scolded them for how they looked down on others. He scolded them for not doing enough for their own upliftment. You blame the Brahmins, etc. for not touching you, he told the audience. But you yourself treat subcastes like Dom, chamar, mehtar as untouchables. You will have to reform yourself also. In any case, if Brahmins, etc. touch you, what will you gain? he asked. They touch dogs also. By their touch, the dog does not become a lion. A lion is a lion by his *gunas* (characteristics). Become lions by your own efforts—you have to beat the others in competition. We are trying to get your children to sit with others in the classrooms, he reminds them, adding, but you are not sending your children to school. You must wrest your rights. You must be strong enough to do so: *samay par maar-peet karney aur sehney ki taiyaari chaahiye* (you should be ready to give and receive blows also). If you want a child, then you have to go through labour pains. The population of Mahars

---

[6] *Savarkar Samagra*, Volume IX, pp. 170–71.

in Ratnagiri is the same as that of Mussalmaans. But just see how much is their *dhauns-patti* (swagger and bullying). Look at that and look at your condition. This is because they take their rights by snatching. If they find someone to be weak, they do not hesitate from wickedness also. But when we are working for your rights, you are not even helping us . . .[7]

He turns to the layers and layers of castes in Madras Presidency. Hindu society has not been split just into four sections, he points out, but into hundreds of splinters. Untouchables are not one block; they too have hundreds of subdivisions among them. One has but to get to know of them, and one is driven to vomit. It is *adharma* (unrighteousness) to join two *jaties* (castes), but it is dharma to go on splintering them without end. The incense holder falls from someone's hand. It is pronounced to be a sin. He is turned out of the caste. All who support him are also turned out of the caste. They become a new caste . . . such are the histories of caste formation. Every caste has others below it: even the shadow of a person from a lower caste pollutes one . . . to find the caste that is at the lowest rung among these will require an instrument that can fathom the innards of the earth. . . The customs that have congealed are strange indeed. If a Brahmin accidentally touches a *Huliya*, the former considers himself polluted and does penance. If a Brahmin accidentally steps into a *Huliya basti*, it is the *basti* (village) which considers itself polluted and the residents go through a ritual of purifying it. In the case of some of these untouchable castes, not just their touch or shadow pollutes one, even seeing them from afar or the sound of their voice reaching one's ears pollutes one, and one has to bathe . . . woebegone! In these circumstances, how will there be unity among us? It will not be enough to abolish untouchability. We have to get rid of the root of this poison tree—the caste differentiation based on birth. So long as this caste differentiation continues, no enemy need kill us, we are killing

---

[7] *Savarkar, Samagra,* Volume VII, after 312–13.

ourselves. We will not be able to live as a Hindu rashtra, as one dharma until we get rid of this—there is no other remedy . . .[8]

Another Religion?

The one thing that is *not* a solution to this curse is for untouchables to convert to another religion, he wrote time and again—with mounting anger as Ambedkar began announcing that he would lead his followers to embrace some other religion. It is not a solution either for individuals or groups, Savarkar told them repeatedly. When and where your rights are denied—for instance, where you are not allowed to draw water from a public pond—a peaceful satyagraha is perfectly justified, he wrote in an essay addressed to 'our untouchable brothers-in-religion'. How can anyone justify that you will be kept away from a pond from which Muslims and Christians are allowed to take water? On what reasoning can anyone prove that your drawing water will pollute the pond and sprinkling cow urine will purify it? . . . Why are you telling the higher castes, 'If you do not open public places to us, if you do not give us jobs, if you do not give us our rights, we will join another religion'? Are you guests in the Hindu dharma? Your forbears have contributed as much to our tradition as members of other castes. Moreover, the *anuloma–pratiloma* (marriages) between persons of higher and lower caste categories themselves testify that the blood of all castes has been mixed for generations, indicating that their ancestors were the same. . .

Stand firm like the co-owner of a house, declaring that your ancestors too have contributed to the dharma. Speak plainly to the higher castes: 'Hindu dharma is mine. Who are you to tell me to give it up?' Campaigns for common meals are necessary, but not for inter-caste marriages. The decision to marry should be that of the bride and groom. Our duty is to see that if a high-caste man or woman has

---

[8] Ibid, pp. 92–99.

married a person from among the untouchables, they will be accepted and our relations with them will be of the same kind as if they were all from the higher caste . . .[9]

If the argument is that Hindu dharma does not pass muster on the touchstone of rationalism, then no religion does. Islam and Christianity are as full of false and made-up stories. It would be another thing, if you were to set up a rationalists' sangh, and persuaded your followers to join it. Second, in various ways, the problem of untouchability is on the way to getting solved. It will be erased in ten or so years. Third, only ten in a lakh of untouchables and Mahars will leave Hindu dharma along with Ambedkar. It is not that all Mahars live in one place. There are ten–twelve Mahar families in each village. Once you leave Hinduism, you will be completely isolated in your villages. Fourth, untouchability and caste distinctions survive in Islam and Christianity. In Bengal, quarrels between the untouchable Mussalmaans (halal) and the touchable ones (ashraf) became so intense that in the Bengal Assembly, to save themselves from the assaults of touchable Mussalmaans, the untouchable Mussalmaans sought protected seats. In Travancore, the untouchable Christians have sought representation independent of that granted to other Christians in the Travancore Assembly. Has Dr Ambedkar heard of these instances? Fifth, in any case, even if you leave Hindu dharma at the moment, remember the doors of shuddhi will be open for you to return . . .[10]

Savarkar's campaigns continued, despite opposition from several upper-caste men in Ratnagiri. At last, on 22 February 1933, at a big gathering, and with the enthusiastic approval of all, the effigy of untouchability was burnt . . .

---

[9] Essay 9, 'Warning to our "untouchable" brothers-in-religion', *Savarkar Samagra*, Volume VII, pp. 150–57.

[10] Ibid, pp. 161–65.

An Invitation to Ambedkar

On 13 November 1935, Savarkar wrote to Ambedkar, inviting him to visit Ratnagiri and see the work that was being done. He set out the work: mixed marriages, common meals, the Patit Pavan Temple. He invited Ambedkar to share the common meal with all others, and, if possible, to give a speech also. He explained that such functions were being held regularly. He listed the conditions that were being observed, including the fact that the names of all who attended the functions and shared the common meal were being published. No one who had attended the functions had been banished from his caste as a result, Savarkar pointed out. Ambedkar replied: 'I am happy to learn of the work that you are doing in Ratnagiri. I regret that because of preoccupation with the Law College here, I am not able to take advantage of your invitation.'[11]

As Ambedkar's announcements became more menacing, Savarkar's criticism of Ambedkar's move became sharper.

Decision of the Constituent Assembly

Savarkar expressed great happiness when the Constituent Assembly adopted the Article abolishing untouchability. It has not just abolished untouchability, Savarkar noted, it has made the practice of untouchability a punishable crime in law. He pointed out that this had been done by an Assembly in which the overwhelming majority consisted of the touchable classes, emphasizing that it was done of our own volition and not due to any external pressure, and that many, including Congressmen, had worked toward it over the decades. The few members from the formerly untouchable classes also supported the Article, which, Savarkar stressed, indicated their acceptance of not practicing untouchability towards the subcastes they regarded lower than themselves. The fact that this change

---

[11] Ibid, pp. 165–68.

has been brought about shows that Hindu rashtra retains the capacity to rejuvenate itself, Savarkar wrote, like a snake that sheds its faded skin and shines again in its newly formed skin . . .

Now we must translate this enormous change into our daily practice—at every well, along every path, in every temple and shop. That will be the real test, he wrote. This work will be easier now: formerly those desiring the end of the practice had to change people's conduct only by persuading them that it was harmful, unjustified, that it was not in accord with the spirit of our religion, etc. Now they can invoke the force of law. Correspondingly, the one from the higher castes who decides not to treat others as untouchable will not have to fear that his caste or community will excommunicate him. He urged a spirited campaign across the country to abolish this evil within ten years of the announcement—a concerted campaign by the State machinery as well as organizations devoted to reform. Do not care for opposition here and there, he said. Try to persuade people first. If they still do not change their conduct, use the full force of law, the courts, the machinery of State to bring about the total abolition.

When eight–ten months had passed since the announcement, Savarkar listed items from newspapers to indicate the actual situation regarding temple entry, etc. He also listed and supported the work of organizations and individuals in Maharashtra that were continuing to persuade people, and in the event of failure had been taking recourse to the law, courts and the State machinery to spur the change. The work, though exemplary, is as yet inadequate, he said: *vednaa pahaad ki aur davaai seep bhar—aisi stithi hai*—it is as if the pain was of a mountain and the medicine given was for a seashell. Savarkar listed the additional measures that should be taken. In addition to abolishing untouchability, we must take positive steps to lift the Dalits, he wrote—with common access to schools we have to provide help with textbooks, nutrition, books, tuition, fees, etc. For all this to be done, create an independent department in government to see that the constitutional provision is fulfilled.

Such steps, he said, not special privileges. He concluded one of his series by quoting a passage from the speech by 'Shri Gavai'. There had been a conference of the Dalit leaders of Vidarbha on 21 September 1950. Gavai had presided. Savarkar remarked, 'Every word of the speech that Shri Gavai delivered is worth lakhs and lakhs.' And he reproduced a passage from Gavai's speech. Gavai had said:

> I myself do not derive any happiness by availing of jobs or facilities under reservations. Because by doing so, the mentality of our *heentaa* (our destitution), and low ambition are kindled, and so is the sentiment of our being distinct from the Hindu samaj, which is injurious. We should completely forget that we are untouchables and should not depend on concessions. And we should organise and put our strength in accomplishing social and political tasks.[12]

The Raakshas

The 'greatest curse on India.'[13] The *raakshas*.[14] '*Dhakoslaa*[15] packed with foolishness.'[16] The restrictions—like the prohibition against eating together—that flow from it: 'communal lunacy',[17] 'suicidal blindness'. That is Savarkar writing and speaking about the caste system.

There is nothing God-given about it, he emphasized again and again. It has been just a way of organizing our affairs. There is nothing *sanatani*— eternal or unchanging—about it. As circumstances have changed, as our needs have changed, the arrangements made in its name have changed. Many Shudras became Brahmins by their conduct and *tapasya*—Kaathin

---

[12] For the foregoing, *Savarkar Samagra,* Volume VII, pp. 239–57.

[13] *Letters from Andamans,* www.savarkar.org, Letter 4, 9 March 1915

[14] The demon.

[15] Hypocrisy.

[16] Veer Savarkar, *Hamari Samasyaein,* Rajpal and Sons, Delhi, no date, pp. 16–29.

[17] Ibid.

muni, Vashishtha the son of Urvashi, Narad. Manu himself lists how by doing this or that one's caste changes—one who takes water or food from a Shudra woman becomes a Shudra in this life and is born as a dog in the next life. So, it is entirely wrong to say that once born a Brahmin, always a Brahmin. The same applies to Kshatriyas.[18] In recent times, Brahmins have taken to so many occupations that are far away from the occupations that were prescribed for them—notice that the Shankaracharyas do not speak against this violation of the prohibitions, Savarkar pointed out with much jollity. 'They easily and plainly forget that occupational prohibitions were the very foundation of *jati-bhed* (caste distinction),' Savarkar pointed out, 'and the Brahmin who first uprooted it was the foremost in being guilty of the sin of destroying the fortress of *jati-bhed*—and of religion. The stomach of the Brahmin was not getting filled by his performing his work as prescribed in the shastras. And so, he began adopting whatever occupations he found convenient . . .' Such changes have been happening through the centuries. Sanatan Dharma did not collapse because of these changes.

Even if we confine ourselves to four castes, there is no unanimity about who falls in which of the four categories. From Shivaji to the Somvanshi Mahars, several jatis have been straining to establish their Kshatriyahood, Savarkar reminds us.

The reality is that the four castes are just nominal categories. Each caste has been splintered into hundreds of subcastes. Moreover, among persons who nominally belong to one caste—say Brahmin—there are vast differences: the Punjabi Brahmin is viewed very differently from the Tamil Brahmin. And within a province, such as Bengal, the Vaishnav, Baahayo, Shaiv, Shakta Brahmins differ from each other. From varna to varna in this province or that; within the province, the sect; within the sect, the occupation—but then comes the difference of whether the person or his family is vegetarian or non-vegetarian. Among the non-vegetarians,

---

[18] *Savarkar Samagra*, Volume VII, pp. 113–14.

those who eat fish, those who eat chicken and mutton. The Kannaujia Brahmin is incensed at the fish-eating habits of other Brahmin groups and restricts himself to eating lamb, considering this practice to be in line with the Vaidik religion. Savarkar lists these endless subdivisions with much relish. The attitudes towards members of another subgroup and the restrictions on relationships with them are just as stern as those between the main four castes.

With the rapid advancement of technology, numerous new professions have emerged and continue to do so constantly. How are these to be accommodated?

Restrictions like the prohibition on marriage across castes, Savarkar surmises, must have been assumed to be necessary because it was thought that traits are determined by heredity. But one must remember that, just as good physical traits are passed from parents to children, so are many hereditary diseases through those very genes.[19] Moreover, Savarkar taught his readers that traits are not determined by genes alone: the environment in which the child grows up is as potent in determining what the child will grow up to be. All the more so in regard to emotional and other traits. How different brothers can be, even twins! If this is true for individuals, how can one claim that people in large groups, such as a caste or a sub-caste, share the same traits? Today, Brahmins are cooks, businessmen, farmers, shopkeepers, and many of them are unlettered, Savarkar said. On the other hand, among Mahars, there have been saints like Chokha Mela and learned men like Dr Ambedkar. Banias are appearing for the ICS. A Jat is looked down upon by Rajputs so that if he sits on a horse, he is beaten and turned out of the caste. But if that very Jat becomes a Sikh, he becomes a high category Rajput. Have his traits suddenly changed? Kayasthas are regarded as 'Shudra', yet Vivekananda, Aurobindo, Pal, Ghosh and Bose far surpassed Bengali Brahmins in learning, Savarkar wrote. The Commander-in-Chief

---

[19] *Savarkar Samagra,* Volume VII, p. 64.

at Panipat, Bhau, was a Brahmin; Tukaram a foremost saint, on the other hand, was of the *'yaatishudra vansh'*.[20]

In any case, the castes that we see today—say, the Brahmins or Kshatriyas—are not 'pure' by any means. Nor are these admixtures just recent phenomena.[21] Even texts like Manusmriti, which prescribed

---

[20] *Savarkar Samagra*, Volume VII, pp. 76–77.

[21] Savarkar gave an example that is as conclusive as it is delectable. As an illustration, let us look at the Pandava clan, he said:

> Protectors of religion, the best amongst the Aryas, descendants of Emperor Bharat himself—this [the Pandava] is not some lowly, unfortunate clan. Moreover, this was the time when Krishna himself had declared *'chaturvarnyam maya srishtam'*, ['I have created the system of four varnas'] and had promised to protect *chaturvarnya*. No one can say about that period that 'The Muslims have spoilt everything' or that 'Everything has got spoilt because of Buddha's hypocritical teachings'. That was not the era when religion had been harmed. Yet in that era, the sand-dam of pure *chaturvarnya* was broken and our life-stream was flowing.
>
> Pratip told Shantanu, 'O king, marry this woman, do not ask "Who is this woman, where does she come from, to which caste does she belong?"' After this conversation, Shantanu married Ganga whose caste was not known. Her son Bhishma became a Kshatriya through consecration. After that, Shantanu married a fisherman's daughter, Satyavati, whose caste was known, and made her his principal queen (*patraani*). Even so, Shantanu's caste remained unchanged. Not only this, the sons of this fisherman's daughter, Chitrangada and Vichitravirya, both became kings in accordance with the shastras. Vichitravirya, the son of the same fisherman's daughter, then married Ambika and Ambalika, two kshatriya girls. But he died without any children. Accordingly, their mother-in-law, Satyavati, the same daughter of a fisherman, invited Shri Vyas so that they could have children through *niyog* (having a child through a man other than the husband).
>
> Who is Vyas? The son of the pre-eminent brahmin, Parashar. And who is this pre-eminent brahmin, Parashar? *'Shwapakachcha Parasharah'*—the son of the untouchable Shwapaak. The son of the untouchable Shwapaak was recognized as a pre-eminent brahmin. The son born to this pre-eminent brahmin, Parashar, and the unmarried daughter of the fisherman was Vyas, the learned scholar and the creator of Mahabharat.
>
> It is good that the pre-eminent brahmin Parashar muni was the son of Shwapaak and not of a brahmin or a kshatriya. It is also good that Parashar did not have relations with any girl of brahmin, kshatriya or vaishya caste. In that case, the world would have remained without an exceptional person like Vyas . . . A union that yields such a son is actually a *shaastriya* marriage/a marriage conforming to the scriptures. And a marriage that yields deficient progeny is a hybrid one, be it among the . . .
>
> Through niyog unions with kshatriya queens, Maharishi Vyas gave birth to Pandu and Dhritrashtra, and through their Shudra maid, he gave birth to Vidur.

prohibitions, recognize *anuloma* and *pratiloma* marriages—inter-caste marriages. The fact that the dharmashastras had to establish rules about them indicates that such marriages must have been quite numerous. Rules or no rules, Savarkar wrote, '*rakhney ke liye hum apni pothi-pustakon ki cheen jaisi diwaar bhi banaayein to bhi usey laanghkar sankar, yaun aakarshand ke pushpak vimaan se kilaaband antehpur mein utarey binaa naheen ruktaa*'—even if we raise a Chinese Wall by piling our *shastras*, the flower-airplane of sexual attraction will not stop till it has got into the innermost recesses of the seraglio![22]

How can anyone maintain that the caste system is *sanatan*—eternal, unchanging—when the original four have become hundreds, each insisting that it is different from the others, and strictly enforcing regulations about dos and don'ts? They came to be formed not for any scientific reason or rational consideration, not after any microscopic examination of blood types or traits. So many of them have originated, or been formed by sheer accidents, by focussing on the pettiest of differences, by misconstruing the facts at hand, on laughable considerations, Savarkar showed in essay after essay. Castes have been splintered on whether you eat meat or fish or neither, whether you are a Shaivite or Vaishnavite, whether you spin sitting or standing . . . Among the Kumhaar of Cuttack, Savarkar points out, some turn the potter's wheel while sitting—the wheel is smaller—and some turn it standing. With just this slight difference in the way they work, there is jealously guarded *jati-bhed* among the two sub-sub-subcategories. Some *gvaalaas* (milkmen) churn butter from unboiled milk, others heat

---

These three used to live as brothers in that household. Following the instructions of Pandu, his two wives, Kunti and Madri, through five unknown men, conceived the five Pandavas. Earlier, before she was married, Kunti had given birth to Karna. Duryodhan told Karna that the principal mark of Kshatriyas is not their family but valour, and with this, he made Karna the ruler of Angdesh. Bhim married Hidimba of the *Raakshas* clan. Sri Krishna also married Jambuvanti and Kubja. Arjuna entered into a Gandharva marriage with Nagkanya. But none of them lost his caste as a result . . . [*Savarkar Samagra*, Volume VII, pp. 62–64.]

[22] *Savarkar Samagra*, Volume VII, p. 58.

the milk before doing so. Just from this . . . among fishermen, those who weave the net from right to left and others who weave it from left to right . . . And between these splinters, those restrictions—on eating together, on marriage—are all strictly enforced.

This is *vaahiyaatpanaa* (idiocy), Savarkar says—conduct taken to the limit of foolishness. No more appropriate word will be found for this, he writes.[23] As an illustration, he recalls the tragi-farcical way the subcaste of Kancholey Prabhu originated. About 150 years ago, Savarkar writes, a wedding was to take place in the Paathaarey Prabhu caste. All the prominent persons of the caste had gathered on the *mandap* (ceremonial platform). A young boy was given the task of applying *chandan* (sandalwood paste) on the foreheads of the guests. The young boy looked up and down, but he couldn't make out who should be the one on whom he should apply the chandan first. Confused, he applied it on the forehead of one person. The others flew into a rage. He has insulted all of us, they shouted. Instead of applying it on the head of our clan, this boy has deliberately applied it on . . . thus belittling all of us. The argument turned into a quarrel. The quarrel became a war. Someone grabbed the little earthen dish on which the chandan was and threw it to the ground. The dish broke. As a punishment, the boy was excommunicated. Not just the boy, but his entire family. Not just that family, but the entire clan to which they belonged. Henceforth, they could not find partners for marriages of their children. They had to marry among themselves. And that is how the Kanchole Prabhu caste came to be formed. In another instance, someone stepped on an egg, and the caste got split in two.[24] The result? 'Four thousand jatis from four varnas.'[25]

---

[23] *Savarkar Samagra*, Volume VII, p. 101.

[24] *Savarkar Samagra*, Volume VII, pp. 102–03, 106–07.

[25] The title of one of his essays listing the 'reasons' that led to the multiplication of castes. *Savarkar Samagra*, Volume VII, pp. 38–43.

The Gossip and Fabrications in the Puranas

The accounts given in the Puranas about the formation of castes are worse. They are all just 'gaappein, kapol, kalpit kathaaen'—just gossip, fabricated and imaginary tales, says Savarkar. The reasons for the formation of castes they adduce are, if anything, flimsier and more comical than the ones that have been seen in recent times. The Puranic accounts are 'jhoot kaa aisaa pulindaa'—such a bundle of falsehoods—that compared to them the incidents which triggered the formation of castes later on are, if not foolish, at least true. One instance will have to suffice: the origin of the Bhandari caste. You really should read the two pages in *Savarkar Samagra* to see both the farcical and laughable story narrated in the text and also to see how well Savarkar tells it. *Bhaand* means a large boat. Bhandaries were the ones who operated them—from Mauryan times to those of the Peshwas. The secondary occupation of the Bhandaries has been coconut cultivation. Some imaginative author of the Puranas wove a story joining the two occupations and used it to explain how the caste came to be![26] And then he takes up the account given in regard to *darjis* (tailors)[27] . . . It is nothing but 'paakhand' (villainy), he says, to say that the castes, subcastes, atomic subcastes have been formed as the result of any scientific examination.

Pothi-Jat

In a word, there is no defensible basis for the castes that have come to exist. The system is certainly not *janma-jat* (based on birth), it is nothing but pothi-jat based on some volume. An incident occurs. Quarrels ensue. Some are cast out. They have perforce to form themselves into a separate caste—enforcing everything that will distinguish them from others, in particular from those who had been closest to them till the other day. The new group comes to be accepted as a caste in its own right. It makes it into

---

[26] Ibid, pp. 103–05.

[27] Ibid, pp. 105–06.

some pothi. To make their authority felt, some pronounce that the new subcaste is sanatan—primordial, that it has always been there.

The Swadeshi Shackles

This endless splintering was accompanied by more and more prohibitions being added. Savarkar campaigned against what he called the seven *bandies,* the seven shackles. Prohibitions regarding reading the Vedas; restrictions on occupations—such as who could or could not be priests; rules concerning touch; regulations about drinking water; restrictions on eating food cooked by, touched by, or shared with an untouchable; limitations on marriage; and prohibitions against crossing the seas. And what came to be another prohibition—that of converting persons from another religion, as well as the prohibition against reconverting someone who had adopted another religion.

No one had imposed these prohibitions on us, Savarkar pointed out. They were entirely our own doing. 'Swadeshi bandiyaan', Savarkar called them.[28]

Savarkar wrote extensively about the disastrous consequences of these prohibitions. They splintered the rashtra. Several factors would have kept the Rajputs from coming to the aid of the Marathas as the latter fought to overthrow the Mughal empire. The fact of what would today be called 'othering'—that the Marathas were a different caste—would have exacerbated the other factors. Similarly, the prohibition against crossing the seas, in fact even the Sindhu over land, put an end to our trade and our empires abroad, Savarkar wrote, even as it left others free to come into India and conquer it. And this consequence for trade and empires,

---

[28] Later he put the blame for the prohibition against crossing the Sindhu on the establishment of Islamic power in the west up to the Hindukush mountains and blame for the ban on crossing the seas on its establishment in southeast Asia. Crossing these limits, it was presumed, risked being converted to Islam—forcibly or otherwise. *Six Glorious Epochs of Indian History,* Abhishek Publications, Chandigarh, 2022, paras 519–537, pp. 180–87.

in turn, had consequences for the Hindu rashtra at home. For one thing, anyone chasing Mahmud Ghazni across the Sindhu would lose his caste, but the thousands who stood by and watched him pillage the country did not, Savarkar pointed out with much exasperation. Savarkar returned time and again to what the Hindu Zamorin of Malabar did. As Hindus stopped crossing the seas, to prevent trade from drying up all together, he decreed that each family would make one of its sons Muslim: as a Muslim, he would be able to cross the seas and thereby trade would continue in a fashion.

As is invariably the case, once a restriction was introduced, it became more and more constrictive. To say nothing of going to other countries, according to the Manusmriti, crossing even the Himalayas or Vindhyas came to be forbidden, Savarkar pointed out. A Brahmin, Kshatriya and a Vaishya were strictly prohibited from going even to Bharatiya provinces like Konkan and Andhra, he wrote. One had to perform penance even if one merely visited these places.

Within the country, the prohibitions gave rise to inhuman hardships. Savarkar would often pick up incidents reported in local papers and point to both the foolishness as well as the burdens that ensued. Chamars are not allowed to take water from a well that is used by others. The chamars repeatedly become sick by using brackish water. At last, they are allowed to dig another well. It turns out to have sweet water. The higher castes usurp this new well, and the chamars are excluded from this one also . . . A Jat groom is proceeding to his wedding on a horse. He is pulled down and thrashed by the Rajputs. But the Jats have sat even on a throne, Savarkar pointed out. In any case, the moment he becomes a Sikh, your attitude to him changes at once . . .

Consequences of Trying to Preserve 'Purity'

The obsession with preserving the presumed 'purity' of each caste, Savarkar said, became an insuperable obstacle to converting persons of another religion to Hinduism or reconverting Hindus who had been converted to Islam or Christianity. But this is just one of the handicaps that Hindus have imposed on themselves in relation to other religions, Savarkar pointed out. He pointed to a caste in which girls are married when they are still children. A girl who is not married by the time she is twelve is given over to the Muslims. He wrote of another caste in which children born out of wedlock are being given over to Muslims.

Just Because a Horse Was Useful During Shivaji's Time . . .

The system may have served some purpose at some stage, Savarkar said, but that is no reason to allow it to continue now. Just because a horse was useful in battles during Shivaji's time does not mean that it should be relied upon in the day of tanks. By now, the caste system has become so disastrous in the injustices and other consequences it inflicts that this 'saddi hui' (rotten) institution should be erased all together, Savarkar said. Teach every child that he has only one caste—Hindu. Make sure that the child never gets to feel that one caste is higher or lower than another. Educate people to the consequences of the system. Educate them to how the castes and sub-castes came to be formed . . . Without so much as a thought we pat a pet dog, but if we touch a fellow Hindu, we lose our caste. The same sort of irrationality underlies every other shackle. Therefore, we must completely uproot all the seven shackles. Everyone must be allowed to study the Vedas, follow any profession they want and decide about whom to marry without any interference.

And yet, Savarkar continued to participate in functions of caste organizations. His rationale was that ordinary persons were members of these organizations, they were loyal to and active on behalf of such organizations, they identify with the organizations. If one appeals for funds to finance scholarships for the poor, he said, the response is paltry. But if you ask people to donate money to the Mahar Sangh to provide scholarships for Mahars, they will donate as much as they can. The same goes for religious functions and festivals: a Ganesh festival in which all castes participate becomes a vehicle for social reform. Excess of rationalism is fanaticism, Savarkar said. Breaking idols is fanaticism. But so is cursing and abusing idols. [29]

Pothivaad

At the root of our continuing to believe in irrational rituals, untouchability, the caste system, Savarkar wrote, is our veneration for pothies. All books are man-made, he maintained as any rationalist would. It is evident from the texts that they were not written by one person, at one time. Manusmriti, for instance, itself states that it is the product of and affirmed by several authorities. All texts have interpolations, revisions, contradictions. Manusmriti, as we have it today, is a *'khichdi'* (a hotch-potch), Savarkar showed. Moreover, interpretations of even the most venerated books have differed—among equally learned sages and over time.

Of course, we are to be justly proud of the fact that our ancestors wrote such treatises at a time when other people were wallowing in ignorance. And we must be eternally grateful to them for having bequeathed such a rich heritage to us. But times have changed. The texts reflect what was known at the time they were composed. Many of the premises on which they were based are clearly outdated, especially considering the advance of knowledge. The texts reflect what the sages thought would be best for organizing our affairs at that time. Centuries and centuries having passed, our needs have changed, our norms have changed. The result is that several of the prescriptions that must have seemed so current then are an embarrassment today—Savarkar illustrates this by setting out what Manusmriti provides for and about women.[30]

In a word, the scriptures are 'fossils', palimpsests. They are historical documents—they tell us how things were at that time. In some cases, such as the successive provisions in Manusmriti on a single matter, the

---

[29] Godbole, *Rationalism of Savarkar,* op. cit., pp. 600–07, ePub.

[30] Cf., *Savarkar Samagra,* Volume IV, pp. 415–59.

original passage and the later verses that directly contradict what the original passage had prescribed help us decipher how our society was at the time and how it evolved over the centuries. In deciding what in them we should follow today, we must examine every prescription against the anvil of contemporary knowledge, science, reason and evidence available to us, including the experience that we have gained from living by it. And we must do so by the methods of inquiry and analysis which science has devised and found useful, not by *shaastraartha* (scriptural debates).

The sole test has to be: is the prescription, is the text beneficial in the circumstances as they prevail today?

A Conclusion, and Two Questions

On occasion, while describing several turns in his life, Savarkar invoked 'God'. Even so, in regard to matters such as beliefs and rituals, untouchability and caste, on scriptures, Savarkar was a rationalist. And he was a rationalist not just in a formal sense. What he said was based on a close study of the texts that he was lampooning. What he said about the conduct of castes— 'low' as well as 'high'—was based on intimate knowledge about their practices and beliefs. Moreover, he spoke frankly to all of them, and when some denounced him for having 'offended their religious sentiments', he did not resile one bit. He told them frankly that for them to say that he had 'offended their religious sentiments' was no argument at all. They had to answer his criticisms on the basis of evidence, of logic, of our historical experience.[31] It will be well worth their while for students to study his writings on these matters.

Two questions arise.

What part of Savarkar's writings on these subjects are those who are appropriating him today prepared to accept? How does what they are

---

[31] See, for instance, his spirited essays, '*Hamari dharmabhaavanaa ko mat dukhaayo,*' *Savarkar Samagra,* Volume VII, pp 540-48.

doing compare with what he advocated? For instance, he berates the caste system no end. Our rulers, on the other hand, are fanning that very system day in and day out.

And second, what about Savarkar himself? How come he was such a staunch rationalist in these matters and yet went completely off the rails on others? The answer lies in the philosopher's question: 'Who is it who has not been ruined by his own nature?'

The first question needs no answer: it is writ on every deed of the appropriators. As for the second, a good part of the answer lies in one aspect of Savarkar's nature—Savarkar's image of himself and the ruinous consequences it spawned, a matter to which we will turn in a while.

Much Not to Learn

History Is Made-Up

'Kavi Govind ke shabdon mein—binaa yudh ke Swatantrataa kisko mili hai? Is par jinkaa vishwaas thaa, unhonein balidaan ki paraakaashthaa ki.'

'In the words of Kavi Govind—who has ever attained Freedom without waging war? Those who believed in this made the supreme sacrifice.'

Pause for a moment, and go to:

https://www.youtube.com/watch?v=0HycHbirkTY

It is Atal Behari Vajpayee speaking at a function to commemorate Savarkar. Vajpayee continues:

Savarkar maainey tej	Savarkar—that is, power/force/lustre
Savarkar maainey tyaag	Savarkar—that is, renunciation
Savarkar maainey tap	Savarkar—that is, austerity/fire
Savarkar maainey tatva	Savarkar—that is, truth
Savarkar maainey tark	Savarkar—that is, reasoning
Savarkar maainey taarundya	Savarkar—that is, youthfulness
Savarkar maainey teer	Savarkar—that is, an arrow
Savarkar maainey talwaar	Savarkar—that is, a sword

Savarkar maainey tilmilaahat	Savarkar—that is, restless with rage
Saagaraa praand tadmadalaa [1]	Search the mystery of the soul in torment
Tilmilhati hui atma	The restless, raging soul
Savarkar maainey titikshaa	Savarkar—that is, fortitude
Savarkar maainey teekhaapan	Savarkar—that is, sharpness
Savarkar mahandjey teekhat	Savarkar meaning sharpness
Kaisaa bahurangi vyaktitva . . .	What a multicoloured personality

Even if one gives the poet his licence . . . A while later:

Voh jis tareh jahaaz sey	
saagar mein kood padey,	The way he jumped into the sea
swatantrata ke liye	
chhalaang lagaa di	He jumped for freedom.
Uttaal saagar ki tarangey,	The waves of that stormy sea
anant saagar,	The infinite ocean
athaa jalraashi	Limitless water
kahaan kinaaraa hai,	Where is the shore
kaun saa thikaanaa mileygaa,	Where will I end up
iskaa bharosaa . . .	The trust in this . . .
magar antehkarand mein	
ek sankalp	But in the inner-being, a vow
mein paraadheentaa svikaar	
naheen karoongaa	I will not accept subjection
Aisaa sankalp,	A vow such as this
aisaa paraakram,	Such valour
aisaa paurush	Such manliness

---

[1] The title of one of Savarkar's well-known poems. For his account of it, *Savarkar Samagra*, Volume VII, pp. 362–66.

Saagar se do-do haath

karney kaa faislaa   The decision to take on the ocean

Aur phir unhein saagar ke kinaarey kaaley paani ki sazaa mili

. . . And then, that he should be punished next to the sea at

Andamans . . .

Even if you make allowances for poetic licence, by the time Vajpayee has given this account of Savarkar jumping into the sea for freedom, the infinite sea, the limitless water, his battling the waves of the stormy sea and his not being able to see where the shore is, you'd think that Savarkar had swum miles to reach the shore and freedom.

What Had Happened

What had happened was as follows. The Magistrate at Nasik, A.M.T. Jackson had been shot to death in December 1909.[2] The pistol that had been used to kill him was one of twenty that had been smuggled into India. Savarkar, then in England, was said to have been instrumental in arranging for the pistols to be smuggled. He was arrested in England and was being taken back to India aboard the steamer, SS *Morea*. Two Englishmen and two Indian sepoys had been assigned to accompany him. The ship had started from Tilbury on 1 July 1910. It reached Marseilles on 7 July and was moored alongside the quay in the dock for 'coaling'. Around 6.15 the next morning, Savarkar had asked to be taken to the lavatory. He had jumped into the water through the porthole. He had got to the shore and started running. A French policeman saw him running and heard shouts from the ship. He thought that the man had stolen something or done some other wrong and was trying to escape. In the meanwhile, the two Indian

---

[2] This too figures as a revolutionary act. Ironically, Jackson was a scholar, an Indologist, a historian, one who was so learned in and so loved Sanskrit, our culture, our history and had such high regard for them that, as you will see from accounts of the period, he was known as 'Pandit Jackson'.

policemen ran down to chase him. Together, the French policeman and these two chased Savarkar, and caught him. The chase extended to about 200 yards.

Even the slightest reflection would have shown that the ship was not far out at sea.

A steamship, it had stopped for 'coaling'—it had stopped to replenish its stock of coal. Now, coal was not going to be carried in small boats to a ship far out at sea. The ship was berthed alongside the quay. The distance of the ship from land was *ten to twelve feet*.

Second, if Savarkar had battled the stormy waves, the two policemen from India would also have done so. Nobody has ever said that they did so. They ran down the gangway. To see how they would actually have run down to the shore, we can go to YouTube again and ask to see Gandhiji getting down in England for the Round Table Conferences. We see a gangway that has been extended from the ground to the ship, and Gandhiji walks down the walkway with a host of others.[3] The two policemen would have run down a structure of this very kind. And taken Savarkar back on the same gangway.

Of course, the jump out of the porthole was a daring attempt at escape. But swimming across the stormy ocean, battling waves . . .? Nor are the details difficult to access. They are in a report that was prepared at that very time by questioning the four policemen who had been deputed to escort Savarkar to India. And that account is available in a collection published not by some enemy of Hindutva in distant London but by the Government of Bombay![4]

And yet the myth:

---

[3] The *Pathe* newsreel is at https://www.youtube.com/watch?v=P6njRwz_dMw. Snippets of film from the National Film Archive are at https://www.youtube.com/watch?v=HFtLGX3xhqY

[4] Cf., *Source Material for A History of The Freedom Movement in India, Collected from Bombay Government Records,* Volume II, 1885–1920, Government Central Press, Bombay, 1958, pp. 448–50. As this book is being finalized I chance upon Dhaval S. Kulkarni, 'How Veer Savarkar's escape bid at Marseille port is debated even 113 years later', *India Today,*

Voh jis tareh jahaaz sey saagar mein kood padey, swatantrataa ke liye chhalaang lagaa di. Uttaal saagar ki tarangey, anant saagar, athaa jalraashi—kahaan kinaaraa hai, kaun saa thikaanaa mileygaa, iskaa bharosaa . . . Saagar se do-do haath karney kaa faislaa . . .

In fact, even Savarkar had not flown that far away from facts.

What Savarkar Himself Had Said About This

In *My Transportation for Life,* Savarkar reports his journey back from Andamans. He is brought to Alipore Jail. He is narrating the myths about Gandhiji, himself and others that are being swallowed by our gullible people. He reports the following exchange with a guard at Alipore Jail:

> Another sepoy asked me, 'How many days and nights were you swimming in the sea?' Of course, he meant at Marseilles. I answered, 'What of days and nights? I swam, only for ten minutes before I reached the shore across.' This reply gave a rude shock to his admiration for me, and to the miraculous powers he attributed to me. If I had bragged and lied to him, he would not have received any shock, but the barest truth that I told him seemed to put him out. My habit of reporting correctly what happened at Marseilles had lost me many friendships in life and their reverence for me.[5]

In this instance, Savarkar had been closer to the truth—though the actual minutes may have been considerably less than ten.

'In this instance, Savarkar had been closer to the truth,' I typed. I should have clarified that the *'in this instance'* refers to that paragraph in

---

17 July 2023, and realize that the myth is being corrected in the mass media also. At least now, the myth should be cast out to sea.

[5] V.D. Savarkar, *My Transportation for Life,* Abhishek Publications, Chandigarh, 2022, p. 515.

My Transportation, not to the attempted escape. For Savarkar, or his alter-ego, as Chitragupta had been among the first to have fed that myth.

A Book

But first a word about a slim book, Chitragupta's *Life of Barrister Savarkar.* It was published in December 1926. Said to be the first biography of Savarkar in English, it was exceptionally laudatory of him—it pictured him as burning with patriotism from the time he was a child, of having been alert to the deadly designs of Muslims even when he was but a boy, of having been the inspiration, the kingpin, the guide of revolutionary groups across continents, a revolutionary and strategist of uncommon foresight who foresaw many things and devised ways to put them to use. A second edition was published by the Veer Savarkar Prakashan in 1987.[6] The 'Publishers Preface' suggests more than once that 'Chitragupta' was none other than Savarkar himself! That is the singular reason for attaching importance to what is said in the book. 'Who was this "Chitragupta", the author of "Life of Barrister Savarkar",' the editor–publisher Ravindra Vaman Ramdas asks, and answers, '[From] The pen-picture of Paris [it] appears that "Chitragupta" is none other than Veer Savarkar . . . However, why Savarkar has not disclosed it even after Independence will ever remain a mystery.' Not really a mystery: if a person out to manufacture a myth about himself writes such hyperbolic stuff himself, he would hardly want to puncture the myth by declaring later that the author of the book was none other than himself. Drawing attention to the portion in the text that

---

[6] Chitragupta, *The Life of Barrister Savarkar,* Veer Savarkar Prakashan, Bombay, 1987. The book is full of spelling and grammatical mistakes. Some of these will inevitably find their way into the text when sentences from the volume are reproduced. In his scholarly study, *Hindutva and Violence, V.D. Savarkar and the Politics of History,* [Permanent Black, Delhi, State University of New York Press, Albany, 2022] Vinayak Chaturvedi, gives several additional, and decisive reasons to conclude that Chitragupta was none other than Savarkar himself. See in particular pp. 282–301 of Chaturvedi's book.

reports an exchange of Savarkar with a fellow passenger on the ship that was taking them to England, the very next paragraph reads, 'Veer Savarkar explains to his fellow-passenger . . .' Two pages later, drawing attention to another part of the book, Ramdas says, 'Veer Savarkar aptly sums up the contribution of Abhinav Bharat to India's struggle for freedom,' and proceeds to cite a passage in the book.[7]

Seeding the Myth

An entire chapter in *The Life of Barrister Savarkar* is devoted to the attempted escape from the SS Morea. And it has all the ingredients of the myth. The two Englishmen and two Indian sepoys who have been deputed to keep guard over him multiply: 'ten picked and armed officers and men and hundreds of European passengers guarded him'. Even as he is trying to get through the porthole, the guard notices what is happening: 'The guard shouted, "Treachery" . . .'

> . . . Mr Savarkar had managed to slip half his body out of the porthole and jumped into the sea. Mr Savarkar heard a pistol shot, thought they were shooting at him and dived under the water . . . a number of persons including some officers of the steamer threw the drawbridge and landed on the shore. In the mean while Mr Savarkar was swimming for his very life, now diving, now riding the waves. He reached the shore first, but to his dismay found a steep dock-wall facing him . . . All this did not take a minute: just then the chase was on him . . . He was exhausted by the swimming and the scaling and the nervous strain of the marvellous venture. But he ran on. Not less than a mile the hunt continued . . .[8]

---

[7] Ibid, pp. ii, v.

[8] Chitragupta, *Life of Barrister Savarkar*, second edition, Veer Savarkar Prakashan, Bombay, 1987, pp. 95–112, at pp. 100, 104–05.

That they had thrown the drawbridge on to the land . . . that the chase had begun within a minute of Savarkar reaching the shore. Even the slightest reflection would have shown that, even by this pseudonymous Chitragupta's account, the steamer was berthed next to the quay. The two British officers and two Indian policemen assigned to guard over him become 'ten picked and armed officers and men and hundreds of European passengers guarded him'. Ten to twelve feet of water between the ship and the quay as against 'swimming for his very life, now diving, now riding the waves'. About 200 yards as against 'not less than a mile the hunt continued . . .'

In any case, swimming all of ten to twelve feet would not have required ten minutes. So, even the 'in this instance' referring to the passage in *My Transportation for Life* that I typed is not warranted: even that account is a substantial exaggeration.

By the time the poet puts his pen to the attempt, it has become an epic.

Savarkar, Subhas Chandra Bose and the INA

India has become independent. Gandhiji has been assassinated. Savarkar is among those who are accused of this heinous crime. He is acquitted. He decides to wind up the organization, Abhinav Bharat, that he had set up to bring about an armed revolution in India. He explains that as we now have freedom, as we have our own government, an organization devoted to violent revolution does not have a role. Accordingly, in May 1952, a three-day function is organized in Poona to mark the winding up. Savarkar speaks at length on each day. Thousands, one day over a lakh come to hear him, the editors write.[9]

During his lecture on the second day, Savarkar talks of the strategy he had devised and the steps he had taken to overthrow the British. He says,

---

[9] The functions and Savarkar's lectures are described in *Savarkar Samagra,* Volume VIII, pp. 669–739.

Getting thousands and thousands of patriotic young men to be recruited into the army during the Second World War, and then, when the moment was right to have lit the fuse for revolt . . . Ajit Singh in Italy, Rashbehari in Japan, and, *acting on my soochnaa/counsel/ information—meri soochnaa par amal kartey huey, Subhas Chandra Bose escaped from Bharat, went to Germany* and after his herculean efforts the army of sixty thousand armed revolutionaries, seasoned in war, roared into Sinhpur [Singapore], with the cry, '*Chalo-Dilli, Chalo-Dilli*'/'*To Delhi, To Delhi*' . . . The Hindi[10] navy rose in revolt. The fire of revolt began simmering in the air force . . . The once powerful Britain softened . . .[11]

Thus, '*acting on*' the information that he gives to Bose, Bose escapes from India for Germany. Events have been set afoot. 'The army of sixty thousand armed revolutionaries, seasoned in war' roars into Singapore, across Burma. The Navy mutinies . . . embers of revolt simmer in the Indian air force . . . the British soften . . . they leave. But this mention on the second day is just a passing allusion to the crucial first ignition.

His lecture on the third and final day spells out in much greater detail what transpired in 'The sudden'—*achaanak*—'meeting with Subhash Chandra Bose'.

'By a coincidence on this very occasion, on 22 June 1940, the pride of the country at that time and the current Netaji suddenly arrived at "Savarkar Bhavan" and met me,' Savarkar tells the audience. 'A few of my close associates knew about this meeting but it is the first time today that I am mentioning it . . .' Savarkar says, adding an air of mystery to it, though the fact that they had met was well known.

Bose tells him—Savarkar says—that he is coming directly from Jinnah's residence. Jinnah has asked Bose on whose behalf he has come to talk of

---

[10] His word for Hindu-Indian.

[11] Ibid, pp. 688–89.

an agreement between Hindus and Muslims. Bose replies, 'The Congress.' 'But the Congress has expelled you,' Jinnah retorts. Bose switches and says he is the authorised leader of the Forward Bloc, and so he can speak on its behalf. But does the Bloc say it is a Hindu organization? Jinnah asks. No, Bose admits, and adds, 'In that case, I want to talk about Hindu–Mussalmaan agreement as a Hindu.' On that, Jinnah said, says Savarkar, 'Then go and talk to Savarkar. He alone can represent the Hindus. Friend, what is the point of talking to anyone? Were Savarkar to come, then we shall discuss.' And so, 'I had but to leave Jinnah's house and I have come to you.' Saying this, Savarkar continues, Subhashbabu rolled with laughter. 'In any case, this time I just had to come to you.' We have learnt one thing already: although Hindu voters have shown time and again that they do not think so, Jinnah certainly is of the view that Savarkar is the only one who can represent the Hindus and speak on their behalf.

Lays Out the Entire Blueprint

Savarkar says that he and Bose talked about Hindu–Muslim unity, but then he told Bose, 'Leave all this aside. Tell me, at the time the Great War is raging, what is the sense in agitating to get the statue of Holwell removed from some roadside in Calcutta and then rotting in a British jail?'[12] 'In a slightly disappointed tone, Subhashbabu said, "We shall have to keep the spirit of opposing the British simmering in the people by doing something or the other. Else, what should be done?" '

'I said,' Savarkar told the audience, 'I can understand your faith. But I ask you again, at a time when thousands of British tyrants are ruling over

---

[12] The Holwell monument had been set up in Calcutta to commemorate the Black Hole deaths in 1756. A [disputed] number of soldiers and civilians had been packed into a small enclosure. A [disputed] number of them had died. John Holwell had been one of the prisoners. Nationalists had begun to question the figures, some even claiming that the incident had never occurred. They had been agitating to get the monument removed. Bose was scheduled to lead another agitation for this purpose.

Hindusthan,[13] will the public anger, which will be expended in getting the statue of a dead Holwell removed, not be meaningless? And is it right for a leader like you to be rotting in a jail, isn't that what the enemy wants? Real statecraft is one that puts the enemy in jail, not one that gets oneself thrown into the jail. Subhashbabu, I ask you clearly: yes, you are not active in the work of armed revolutionaries, but you maintain contacts with them. You are one who can keep secrets. Even before this, when you were the President of the Congress, we had met confidentially. With the same faith and taking up that very thread, I want to request you that the campaign I have launched throughout the country, and which is touching the peaks of success for recruiting the maximum number of Hindus into the Hindi [sic.] army is in essence a revolutionary programme. I know that you are carrying out propaganda against it. You thought that like the Congress leaders I too am supporting the British in strengthening their manpower. But the fact is, listen . . .'

Here, Savarkar continues, 'I gave an account of how during the First War, under the equivalent of a friendship agreement, the revolutionary army was set up from among the soldiers of the British Hindi army that had fallen into the hands of the Germans'—remember that the First World War started in 1914, and Savarkar was interred in the Cellular Jail from 1911. On Savarkar's own account of the jail, it would not have been possible for him to remain in touch with persons outside, certainly not on the mainland, and help set up or guide the setting up of the 'revolutionary army'. Presumably, the army, if it had been set up, must have been set up by others. And then, Savarkar told the audience, he drew Bose's attention to the fresh letter that he had received from Rash Behari Bose.[14] 'From this it

---

[13] Is this what Savarkar felt or did the letters that he had been writing to the Viceroy, and which we will come to soon reflect what he really felt?

[14] Rash Behari Bose had settled in Japan, and had developed access to the higher circles there. He propagated the cause of Indian independence. He is said to have been one of the organizers of the INA, and was among those who eventually persuaded Subhas Bose to lead it.

appears that in this very year Japan will declare war. If this comes to pass, then the kind of golden opportunity which has never before arisen would have arisen of invading Hindusthan with ultra-modern Japanese weapons and Hindi soldiers who have been hardened by war.'

'At such a time, for a leader of your kind to have himself incarcerated forcibly and to be rotting in jail will be very harmful,' Savarkar said, as he counselled Bose. 'Before arresting any persons from the Congress, the Government is on the lookout for the opportunity to arrest us. At such a time, just as Rash Behari Bose and other revolutionary leaders have hoodwinked the authorities and escaped from Hindusthan, you and I too should give them the slip and escape.' Having escaped, 'take over the leadership of thousands of Hindi soldiers who are in the hands of Germany and Italy. Declare the complete independence of Hindusthan, and the moment Japan jumps into the war, attack British power in Bharat via the Bay of Bengal or Brahmadesh,[15] whichever is possible. Without such an armed and courageous manoeuvre, we cannot liberate Hindusthan. Only two–three persons have the courage and can accomplish such a plan. You are one of them. That is why my gaze is on you.'

That is,

- Escape
- Form an army out of Indian soldiers who are in the hands of Germany and Japan
- Launch an invasion via the Bay of Bengal or Burma
- We will have primed the soldiers I am getting recruited into the army: they will refuse to fire at your soldiers
- We will have ignited the people here so that, as you approach, they will rise in revolt
- The British will be caught and will have no alternative except to leave

---

[15] Savarkar's name for Burma.

In a word, the exact and entire strategic plan for Bose to follow. And follow, Bose did.

Savarkar continued:

Having said this much, I stopped. Lowering his head, still, as someone lost in thoughts . . . He said, 'I will first go to Calcutta, see what happens there, and then I will decide my next programme. If I come this side, I will definitely come for your darshan.' I did not seek further clarification, and he did not provide more . . .

After a few days, Subhashbabu went to Calcutta and on just reaching there, he was arrested in the affair of that statue—this happening was expected.

In prison, he set aside all those small projects—Hindu–Muslim unity, Holwell's statue, etc.—and focussed exclusively on escaping towards Germany and Japan.

And then 'the agreements with Italy and Germany . . . the Hindi soldiers they had captured . . . the 50,000 Hindi soldiers through Rash Behari Bose in Japan . . . this Hindi sena of 50–60,000, equipped with ultra-modern weapons that Subhashbabu raised, became possible only because of the campaign that we had conducted for getting thousands enlisted in the British Army—this Subhashbabu himself explicitly acknowledged . . .'

Naturally, events took the course Savarkar's plan had laid out. The INA revolutionaries attacked the British, Savarkar said. Even some of the so-called non-violent Congressmen realized that Independence could not be attained through satyagrahas and going to prison, he said. They too took to the way that had been set out by the revolutionaries. 'In this way, the British administration was caught in the scissors of the armed revolutionaries within the Congress and the assault of the vast army of revolutionaries from outside . . .'

In the final lecture, Savarkar proceeds to say:

In writing the true history, attention should be paid to the fact that in both World Wars, the collective efforts of the Bharatiya revolutionary organizations alone made possible the assaults that were launched from foreign lands like Germany and Japan. Assaults of this kind and mobilisation of help from foreign powers were impossible for the arms-less Congress, Home Rule League, etc. to organize . . .

This account has been swallowed whole. As expected, the claims by Savarkar have been built upon by his admirers so much so that one budding historian claims that the meeting between Netaji and Savarkar 'proved to be a turning point in the events of Indian history', and that he does not know what turn Indian history would have taken if that meeting had not taken place . . .

A Few Facts

First, Netaji Subhas Bose himself described that meeting. In *The Indian Struggle*, Bose described how he met Jinnah, Gandhiji, Pandit Nehru and others to discuss what should be done to take advantage of the outbreak of the War in Europe. Jinnah was 'thinking only of how to realize his plan of Pakistan (division of India) with the help of the British,' Bose wrote. 'The idea of putting up a joint fight with the Congress, for Indian independence, did not appeal to him at all, though the writer [that is, Bose] suggested that in the event of such a united fight taking place, Mr. Jinnah would be the first Prime Minister of Free India.' As for Savarkar, Bose noted,

Mr. Savarkar seemed to be oblivious of the international situation and was only thinking of how Hindus could secure military training by entering Britain's army in India. From these interviews, the writer was forced to the conclusion that nothing could be expected from either the Muslim League or the Hindu Mahasabha.[16]

---

[16] Subhas Chandra Bose, *The Indian Struggle, 1920–42*, Netaji Research Bureau, Calcutta, Asia Publishing House, Bombay, 1964, pp. 343–44.

And that is all.

Not quite the impression that you would form from Savarkar's account.

Second, as you would have noticed, Savarkar talked of assaults on India by Germany and Japan, assaults that he said became possible only because of the work done by Indian revolutionaries. Which were the assaults that Germany executed against India—in either the First or the Second World War?

Third, as for his advice, or insight that Bose should seek an alliance with Hitler's Germany, Savarkar had turned a blind eye to Hitler's utter contempt for India and Indians, in particular for Indian 'revolutionaries' who had been strutting about in Europe. A single extract from *Mein Kampf* will bring this home. Even though it is a bit long, do read it—all the while keeping in mind the image that Savarkar conjured up in his lectures.

Hitler on Indian 'Revolutionaries', India, Indians

In *Mein Kampf,* Hitler recorded:

As early as 1920-1921, the young National-Socialist movement was slowly brought into the forefront on the political horizon and was, to some degree, considered as a German movement for independence. Our Party was approached by various sides who attempted to establish a relationship between their people and the independence movements of other countries. This was actually quite similar to the widely advocated League of 'Oppressed' Nations proposed at the time which mainly consisted of representatives from certain Balkan states and those of Egypt and India. To me, they all seemed like pompous windbags without any actual experience. There were many Germans, especially among the nationalists, who allowed themselves to be dazzled by these proud Orientals. They immediately believed any worthless student was a 'representative' of India or Egypt. These fools failed to realize that not only did most of these 'representatives' have no support, but they had not been authorized by anyone to decide on any kind of treaty with anyone.

Therefore, the practical result of all relations with these people was zero. I have always resisted these kinds of pointless dealings. I not only had better things to do with my time than to waste weeks on such fruitless 'discussions', but even if these representatives had been authorized by their respective nations, I would have considered the whole thing to be pointless or even harmful . . .

The Germany of today is like the drowning person who grasps at every straw. They may otherwise be very intelligent, but just as soon as a ray of hope can be seen, no matter how elusive, these people immediately run to catch the ghost. No matter whether it is a League of 'Oppressed' Nations, a real League of Nations, or any other kind of fantastic invention, it will, nevertheless, find many thousands of souls who are willing to believe.

I still remember the childish and incomprehensible hopes that suddenly arose in 1920–1921 in nationalist circles that England was supposed to be on the verge of collapse in India. Some Asian impostors, or for all I care perhaps even real 'fighters for the independence of India' who were loitering about in Europe at the time, had successfully filled the heads of otherwise sensible people with the mistaken idea that the British World Empire was about to collapse in the very part of India where she had her central cardinal position. Of course, it never occurred to them that their own desire had fathered all of their ideas. Nor did they see the paradox of their own hopes. How could they expect that the collapse of English rule in India would somehow lead to the end of the British World Empire and British power? They admitted that India was of the greatest importance to England, so if the Empire was not ended then why would she abandon India so easily? The native German prophet may consider this vital question as the deepest secret known to man, but it is, presumably, known by those who guide the history of England. It is childish to assume that England does not realize the value of the Indian Empire to the British World Union. It is another negative indicator of our absolute refusal to learn a lesson from the First World War when we blindly misunderstand the strong Anglo-Saxon determination, and we let ourselves think that England would let India go without doing everything possible to prevent it. Furthermore, it is proof that Germans do not understand the methods used by the British in their penetration and administration of the Indian Empire. England will only lose India if she falls prey to racial breakdown through her own administrative machine, something that is unlikely in India at this time, or if she is conquered by the sword of a powerful enemy. Indian rebels will certainly never successfully conquer her. We Germans know from experience how difficult it is to conquer England. Apart from this, I, as a member of the Germanic race, would prefer to see India under English rule than under the control of any other nation. . .

It is impossible to successfully attack a powerful state that is firmly determined to risk its last drop of blood for the sake of its existence and especially foolish to launch such an attack with a coalition of cripples. As a nationalist who knows how to evaluate humanity based on its racial foundations, I cannot link the fate of my own nation with that of the so-called 'Oppressed Nations', which I can see are racially inferior.[17]

Later, during his 'Table-talk', he often held up, as an example, how just two hundred and fifty thousand Englishmen with just 50,000 soldiers were able to hold down four hundred million ignorant, backward

---

[17] Adolf Hitler, *Mein Kampf*, Hurst and Blackett, London, 1939, pp, 535–36. For the text, I have used the Ford translation available online.

Indians, and how this success in holding India was the root of English confidence. This occupation of and rule over backward people, and the ways by which these were accomplished must be the example that Germany ought to follow in occupying and ruling lands to the east, that is Russia. They should serve as a negative example also, as an example of what not to do: how one must keep people like the Indians backward, how the great mistake of the English had been that they sent Indians to universities, etc.[18]

And Hitler was neither unique nor original in holding such views. On the contrary: he became just the most visible symbol of an entire line of thinkers and propagandists for whom race was the root of everything, and the Aryan race was the top of the tree. And Indians were certainly *not* among the Aryans on their reckoning![19]

What Bose Experienced

While Savarkar painted a picture of Germans ever so enthusiastic to help Indian revolutionaries, once he reached Germany, it took Bose one year of waiting to even get a meeting with Hitler, and, photos apart, Hitler's operational advice, his decision was to pack Bose off in a German U-boat

---

[18] Cf., *Hitler's Table Talk, 1941-1944, His private conversations,* translated by Norman Cameron and R.H. Stevens, Introduced and with a new Preface by H.R. Trevor-Roper, Enigma Books, New York, 1953/2000, pp. 15–16, 23–24, 33, 42, 188, 198–99, 202–03, 354–55. See also the four indispensable volumes, Max Domarus, *The Complete Hitler, A digital desktop reference to His Speeches and Proclamations, 1932–1945,* Bolchazy-Carducci Publishers, Mary Fran Golbert [tr.], 1962, 1990. Note also the editor's comments about Indian 'mountebanks'—one of Hitler's words for our freedom fighters who were roaming Europe asking for help in what they said was their struggle against the British.

[19] For a telling account of the racial contempt that Hitler and other Nazis had towards Indians, Vaibhav Purandare, *Hitler and India: The untold story of his hatred for the country and its people,* Westland, 2021.

to Japan, and ask him to raise an army there from among the POWs in Japan's hands.[20]

And while shipping Bose off to the Japanese, Hitler was, in fact, distressed at the rapid advances that Japan had made in the east. The reason? Hitler felt that if Japan continued to advance, it is the white race that would have lost: 'As Japan had made swift advances, Hitler had bemoaned in front of one of his generals, Gause, that "it means the loss of a whole continent, and one must regret it, for it's the white race which is the loser." Goebbels, too, recorded in his diary that Hitler "profoundly regrets the heavy losses sustained by the white race in East Asia".'[21] Not just that, as Purandare records, 'Bose was told to join Japan so that Indian aims could be achieved, and [at the same time] the Japanese [Hitler's allies at the time] were counselled to proceed, not towards India but in the opposite direction, with their eyes fixed on Australia and New Zealand.'[22]

Planning Campaigns That Would Collide

Fourth, recall that Savarkar was on 'whirlwind tours' to recruit soldiers for the British Army. Whatever Savarkar may have thought would come to be in 'three or thirty years' time that the war was supposed to last, the one result of his recruitment drive, to the extent that it yielded soldiers, would have been to fortify British power, especially in India. Bose, on the other hand, was toiling for 'the extermination of British power in India'. He felt that the masses in India were fed up with Britain, that they would rise in revolt. He felt, especially after the fall of Singapore, that Britain was

---

[20] On the attitude of Hitler towards Indians in general and towards these proposals of Bose, and for what Bose had to put up with in Germany, see Vaibhav Purandare, *Hitler and India, The untold story of his hatred for the country and its people*, Westland, Chennai, 2021, pp. 180–99. See also, Romain Hayes, *Bose in Nazi Germany,* Random House India, NOIDA, 2011.

[21] Purandare, op. cit., p. 199.

[22] Ibid, p. 200.

likely to get defeated. He realized that Britain would try its utmost to retain India. But he felt that a revolt in the armed forces could be organized. For all this to transpire, he was trying to persuade the Germans to help set up a communication centre in Afghanistan; to recognize a Government of Free India; to provide money; and, as the uprising commences in India, to have fifty thousand Axis troops on the borders of India . . .[23] And to what end was Savarkar working? The very opposite, as we shall see.

Assume that both had succeeded in their stratagems. What would have been the result? Indian soldiers would have been killing Indian soldiers in Burma and in Afghanistan. Savarkar claimed that those enlisting because of his campaign would refuse to fire on Indian soldiers and instead turn their guns on the British. We will soon see what actually happened when Indian soldiers in the British–Indian Army came face-to-face with Japanese soldiers and those in the INA.

Whose Blueprint?

Fifth, what about the claim that Savarkar is the one who put the idea of taking advantage of British difficulties, in particular of escaping from India, of seeking help from Germany and Japan, of forming an army from Indian soldiers in the hands of Germans and Japanese, a claim that continues to be advanced repeatedly to this day? In his authoritative account *Brothers Against the Raj,* Leonard Gordon writes that Subhas Chandra Bose had felt that the troubles in Europe, and in particular the troubles in which UK found itself embroiled, must be used to advance India's interests, and that he must make his way to Europe for this purpose:

Days and months passed by, and Subhas Chandra Bose was still detained in the Presidency Jail. From fragments of written and oral

---

[23] See his memoranda to the Axis Governments: *The Indian Struggle,* op. cit., pp. 419–33; and his 'Secret message to comrades in India,' May 1941: Ibid, pp. 434–37.

testimony, it is hard to know just when he determined to flee India and work for her independence from outside. But in the months after war broke out in Europe, the idea was certainly alive in him. As he had been suggesting in many speeches during the pre-war and war period, Indian nationalists had to take advantage of Britain's hour of weakness. This meant getting assistance from her enemies if nationalist resources did not suffice.

Gordon notes that several have 'claimed foreknowledge and even credit for the whole idea'. But the fact is that

Bose had been trying to make contacts with foreign governments for almost a decade and had spoken to officials of the Italian, German, Japanese and other nations. . . through R. Palme Dutt and Indian communists, he had made every effort to contact Soviet officials. There is no published evidence that he was given any positive feedback by the Soviets. They were probably wary of him and not at war with Britain. They had no reason to be particularly unfriendly—indeed Indian communists had helped Bose to reach Kabul—but they also were not especially encouraging to him.[24]

To compound matters, based on her excellent archival research Marzia Casolari reports, 'Bose was in constant contact with Mussolini from 1933 to 1944 . . .'[25]

Gordon had noted that credit for the idea of escaping, etc. had also been claimed for Savarkar. I inquired from him whether he had come across any evidence in this regard. His reply on this point:

[24] For the foregoing, Leonard Gordon, *Brothers Against the Raj, A biography of Indian nationalists Sarat and Subhas Chandra Bose*, Columbia University Press, 1990, pp. 383–85, 406–07, 415, 421.

[25] Marzia Casolari, *Under the Shadow of the Swastika, The relationships between Indian Radical Nationalism, Italian Fascism and Nazism*, Routledge, London, 2020, p. xii.

I finished this book about 35 years ago. I tried to be as accurate as I could. There was nothing that I saw or read that indicated that this plan—working from outside, building an army, connecting to Indians rising inside India—to drive the British out was formulated by Savarkar or anyone else. It was Subhas Bose's plan. He had a fascination with the military from college days and then was GOC at the 1928 Calcutta Congress. I have tracked this in my book because it led to the INA. The plan, the invasion as part of a much larger Japanese force, and the failures were all his.[26]

The Tasks That Were Assigned to POWs

Sixth, true, Indian soldiers who were in the hands of the Germans and the Japanese were as good as and as brave as others. The question that arises from Savarkar's account is a different one: what were the tasks that were assigned to them, what were they allowed to do by the Germans and Japanese and what did they actually get to do? This is no reflection on the captured soldiers who eventually became the INA. It is about the judgment and decisions of those whose captives they were. Assume the soldiers were the bravest of the brave. If they had continued to be kept in the POW camps; or, even if let out, if they were kept away from actual combat duties, or they were assigned duties such as ferrying supplies, they would hardly have come into combat with soldiers of the British Indian Army. None of the things that Savarkar had 'foreseen', so to say—the refusal of Indian soldiers to fire on the INA soldiers, large-scale desertions from the Indian Army to the ranks of the INA—could have taken place. So, what happened? What roles were assigned to the INA soldiers?

---

[26] Email from Leonard Gordon, 27 February, 2023.

INA and the Rest

INA was not formed in the way, nor did it do what the Savarkar mythmakers have made us believe. The first collection to be formed was the Free India Legion—from a few volunteers and from a few more POWs that the Germans had captured. There was great hesitation among Germans in giving it combat roles—in part because of the difficulty of integrating them with German forces, and in part because the Germans did not think much of the combat abilities of Indians. After he was eventually able to get himself listened to in Berlin, the Soviets having been indifferent to his requests for help in liberating India from the British—Subhas Chandra Bose tried to breathe some life into the Legion. Hitler remained dismissive. In his classic study on foreign legions at Hitler's disposal, David Littlejohn wrote:

> After completion of training, it [the Free India Legion] was sent on guard duty to the Bay of Biscay area of Occupied France. Following the D-Day landings (June 1944), the Indians saw some action against the local resistance in the south of France, but were withdrawn to Holland in the autumn. On 8 August 1944, Indian Infantry Regiment 950 became *Indische Legion der Waffen S.S.* It had at this time a strength of around 2,300 men. Its three battalions were equipped only with rifles and machine pistols. There was an anti-tank company with six guns. Transport comprised 81 major vehicles and 700 horses. Hitler is reputed to have said, 'The Indian Legion is a joke.' He ordered that its weapons be handed over to the newly created 18th 'Horst Wessel' Division of the S.S. . . .
>
> Subhas Chandra Bose was killed in an air crash in the closing days of the war. The 'Free India' Movement disappeared with his death. The British elected not to institute legal proceedings against former members of the Indian Legion, partly as a gesture of conciliation to Indian anti-imperialism, partly, one may conjecture, because

they regarded the whole Indian flirtation with Hitler as too absurd
to merit serious concern. Bose's 'Free India' seems to have left one
lasting legacy—a large number of Vienna manufactured medals and
decorations.[27]

INA

Netaji Subhas Bose boarded the German U-Boat for travelling to Japan
in February 1943. The formation of the INA, Srinath Raghavan informs
us, had been going on by fits and starts from the fall of Jitra in northwest Malay in December 1941.[28] Formal recruitment from among the
POWs began in April 1942. The first division of 16,000 men was raised
on 1 September 1942. The main actors at that stage were a Japanese Major,
Fujiwara Iwaichi, an Indian, Giani Pritam Singh and a POW, Captain
Mohan Singh. There is no record of any of them having been inspired by
or having been in touch with Savarkar.

Nor are there recorded instances of serving soldiers of the British
Indian Army surrendering to or joining up with the INA as Savarkar's
plan had envisaged and he maintained would happen. The opposite did
happen though! In fact, in the very few instances when INA units were
operationally deployed, the Indian Army hit them as hard as it hit the
Japanese. The reason that the instances were few was that, as Srinath
Raghavan notes in his authoritative account, the Japanese did not give
combat roles to INA units, and that was because the Japanese did not
have confidence in the fighting capabilities of these units. Srinath
Raghavan writes,

---

[27] David Littlejohn, *Foreign Legions of the Third Reich*, Volume 4, James Bender, San Jose,
California, 1987/1994, p. 127.

[28] For the following about the INA, the authoritative study, Srinath Raghavan, *India's
War, The making of modern South Asia 1939–1945*, Penguin, Gurgaon, 2016, pp. 280–90,
424–25.

Thus, the Bose Brigade was deployed in the Chin Hills—a relatively inactive sector. Then, too, the men under Shahnawaz Khan were used to repair lines of communication and fetch fresh supplies for the Japanese troops...Nor could the INA's field espionage and propaganda units suborn the loyalty of Indian troops as they had done in 1942. The fundamental difference, of course, was the operational context. With the Indian army gaining the upper hand over the Japanese, the INA's propaganda had little impact . . .

Shahnawaz protested to Bose. At last, the INA were given the responsibility of raiding an airfield. 'The strike force [of 300] took the Indian army initially by surprise,' writes Raghavan, 'but was swiftly beaten back.'

In mid-May, the Bose Brigade was redeployed to Kohima. Its most successful act was to plant an Indian flag in the town—even as the battle was going against the Japanese. In the subsequent offensives launched by the Fourteenth Army, the INA suffered heavily alongside the Japanese . . . the British continued to regard Bose as a political threat, but as a fighting force the INA was no match for the Indian army.

Contrast this with what Savarkar had claimed. *Six Glorious Epochs of Indian History* is the last book he wrote. As one would expect, when he concludes his book, there is not a mention of Gandhiji or others involved in the Freedom Struggle. Credit is given to those who resorted to violence—Subhas Chandra Bose, Savarkar's followers, the 'revolutionaries', and, hold your breath, Hitler and Tojo, who were the only ones to offer them support, Savarkar says:

1126. If we have received any real and effective help from any nation it was from Hitler, the dictator of Germany, and General Tojo, the militant leader of the Japanese! It is these countries, Germany and Japan, which gave substantial help in up to date arms and ammunition for the army, navy and air force, to the revolutionary party from the very beginning, that is from the violent agitation in Europe by the Abhinav Bharat Samstha to the declaration of war against the British by Netaji Subhas Chandra Bose in the second World War. That is why an army of hardly forty to fifty thousand strong could rise in revolt against the British near Malaya and Singapore and could march against India under Netaji Subhashbabu to free it with the war-cry 'Chalo Delhi'. [29]

The 'revolutionary party' had an army, navy *and airforce*? 'An army, navy, air force' equipped, to boot, with 'up to date arms and ammunition'? The 'army' in Southeast Asia 'could rise in revolt against the British near Malaya and Singapore and could march against India'?

In any case, far from breaking away from the Army under the British and joining the INA in accordance with Savarkar's plan, Indian Army soldiers dealt with the INA soldiers in the very same way that they dealt with the Japanese, that is with the same sledgehammer.[30]

After the war, of course, there was a groundswell of sympathy in the ranks of the Army for INA soldiers and the remnants of the Free India Legion—they too had been captured and repatriated back to India—especially when it seemed that thousands would be tried for treason, the punishment for which could be the death penalty. Panditji himself led the defence team. The charges were dropped, the sentences commuted, the trial abandoned. But there was no support for reintegrating the INA soldiers or those of the India Legion into the Indian Army.

The Moral

Such claims in Savarkar's accounts can be multiplied—and we will come across quite a few of them. The moral in each case turns out to be the same: nothing survives scrutiny.

---

[29] V.D. Savarkar, *Six Glorious Epochs of Indian History*, Abhishek Publications, Chandigarh, 2022, pp. 470–71.

[30] For the foregoing on the INA, Srinath Raghavan, *India's War*, op. cit., pp. 280–90, 424–25.

Twin Dangers

One of the principal aims today is to erase Gandhiji. There are twin reasons behind this. First, he is universally hailed to have led the Indian struggle for freedom. As a result, he is a stinging reproach to those who did little during that struggle, even more so to those who actively collaborated with the British. The second reason is what with his emphasis on the purity of means, on ethical conduct, on a mode of living that is the exact opposite of the one into which our country is being hurled, on religion being an inner-directed search, not a political banner—every particle of his teaching and of his life is a reproach to the standard-bearers today. Thus, Gandhiji is a pain. One task, therefore, is to make out that the movement he led was not what actually got us freedom. Many other things were going on. Among these, armed struggle by the revolutionaries was the crucial factor that brought India its independence. Their role has not been acknowledged, so the thesis goes, in part because the Congress and its lackeys took power after 1947, and they moulded history-writing to focus exclusively on themselves. Part of the reason the contributions of the revolutionaries have remained obscure is that they were, by definition, secret.

Now, there can be no doubt that martyrs like Bhagat Singh, who believed in armed struggle, were brave as they come. They were patriots of the highest rank. To the extent that their role has not been fully highlighted, a corrective is certainly in order. There can also be no doubt that the assassination of officials, a bomb thrown into a legislature, a raid on an armoury, the eventual unrest in the naval units stationed in Bombay—all these must have played a part in convincing the British that they could not hold on to India. The new publications about the role of 'revolutionaries' make several points:

- They were many
- As, by definition, they had to operate under utmost secrecy, how many they were cannot be estimated, but they were many

- Their acts were not isolated acts of individuals or tiny groups On the contrary, the revolutionaries formed close networks, they assisted each other, they inspired each other
- Their acts, their daring, their courage inspired many, in particular, many who were formally enrolled in the British Army in India
- In addition, a well thought out effort was made to sow disaffection and disloyalty among Indian soldiers and officers. In the penultimate years, this campaign and the inspiring deeds of the revolutionaries sparked mutinies in the army and Navy
- The assassinations that occurred on occasion, and in the end the Naval Mutiny convinced the British that they could not rely on the armed forces. They decided to leave, and India got its independence

Savarkar often berated writers, and even more so the rulers for obscuring the role of the 'revolutionaries'. Since then, narrations of various kinds have bent the other way. If one goes by some of these, Gandhiji was just one of many figures. In some narratives, and Savarkar's writings would certainly fit the case, Gandhiji was, in fact, an obstacle. But for him, the assertions run, India would have attained Independence much sooner. It would have emerged much stronger. In particular, the country would not have been partitioned.

In all likelihood, everything worked together: the avalanche of a movement led by Gandhiji and the occasional wounds inflicted by the 'revolutionaries'. Even the way Hitler's and Tojo's wars weakened Britain must have contributed to the British realizing that they could not afford to keep the colonies, certainly not such a large one as India. Indeed, Mughal rule never recovered from the blow that Nadir Shah dealt to Mughal finances, to the Mughal military and to Mughal authority. He demonstrated for all to see how hollowed out and weak the Mughal empire had become—and this emboldened the Sikhs, Marathas and others to carve it up into kingdoms of their own. Nor was the message lost on

Europeans: they too saw that they could defeat the Mughals, surely a step in the direction of India becoming independent, eventually. But for that reason, neither Nadir Shah nor Hitler becomes one who fought for India's independence. Moreover, we will not quite know whether the fact that Gandhiji had mobilized millions or the occasional assassination weighed more on the minds of British till we are able to get into the minds of British administrators and military officers in India, and the rulers in Britain.

There is no doubt that we must always remember and be grateful to all the brave women and men who gave their lives so that we may live free. For that reason, and several others no doubt, the new volumes that recount the deeds of these brave women and men are a necessary corrective. But there is a danger we must be wary of.

Many an organization or group that did nothing for the freedom of the country can tomorrow claim that, contrary to all available evidence, its members were totally involved in the freedom struggle. In fact, they were behind both—the mass movements of Gandhi, as well as the violent acts of the armed revolutionaries. It is just that because they operated in secret, available records do not reflect what they were doing.

Savarkar himself had pressed this line of argument and often repeated it. A spate of violent incidents that included assassinations and attempts at assassinations had led the government to set up the Sedition Committee.[31] After recounting the assassinations and attempts at assassination in the Bombay Presidency, the Committee observed:

The Savarkar conspiracy, in so far as it was not Chitpavan, was negligible. Few names from any other community are to be found in the records of political crime in Western India. The conspiracy and its offshoots were therefore within a fairly manageable compass and

---

[31] The Committee was headed by Sidney Rowlatt, and is therefore often referred to as the Rowlatt Committee. It resulted in the Anarchical and Revolutionary Crimes Act, 1919. Gandhiji launched a major movement demanding the repeal of this Act.

there are no indications of contact with any criminal conspiracy in Bengal or other parts of India. The only outside group of conspirators who were in any way responsible for the Nasik murders were the Indian plotters in Paris who furnished Savarkar with the pistols with which the murderers were armed. There is reason to believe that the Paris group also instigated the Tinnevelly murder . . .[32]

Savarkar was proud of the fact that he had been singled out in the report, but perhaps was also put off, feeling that it had underrated his role. In his comments on the report, he listed what he said were inaccuracies in the Report and said that such mistakes are strewn across the Report. 'One gets as surprised and as proud by such blunders,' he wrote:

Pride because the principal reason for this deficiency in the Rowlatt Report was this very thing that the information which the intelligence agencies of the British Government sent the Rowlatt Committee about the activities of the revolutionaries, that information shows, that the revolutionaries had been able to throw dust in the eyes of the vast network and resources of the agencies, and carry out their secret projects. From Khudiram, Madanlal Dhingra, Kanhare, Bhagat Singh, etc. to Udham Singh[33] who carried out the killing of Dyer in London in 1940, the revolutionaries carried out their secret plans successfully. But the vast and world famous Scotland [Yard] could not find out

---

[32] For the foregoing on the INA, Srinath Raghavan, *India's War*, op. cit.

[33] Savarkar, as we shall see, was to imply, and his followers and admirers more than imply that all these had been inspired by, some directly motivated and directed by Savarkar. For instance, Godbole, the compiler of *Rationalism of Veer Savarkar*, writes, '*Due to Savarkar's efforts*, there arose a succession of revolutionaries. For example, Khudiram Bose (1908), Madanlal Dhingra (1909), Anant Kanhere, Karve and Deshpande (1910), Bal Mukund, Avadhabihari, Amirchand and Vasant Vishwas (1915), Bhagat Singh, Rajguru and Sukhdev (1931), Udham Singh (1940) and many more.' Cf., *Rationalism of Veer Savarkar*, V.S. Godbole, Compiler, Itihas Patrika Prakashan, Pune, 2004, pp. 36–37.

these conspiracies. Who will not be proud of the secret conspiracies of our Bharatiya revolutionaries![34]

This veil of secrecy can be the alibi for many. We were fully involved in the freedom struggle, those who weren't can insist, we were the ones who opposed the Emergency. To do the work, we had to remain free. To remain free, we had to work in utmost secrecy. You do not know all that we did precisely because we operated in total secrecy. That you do not know and that there is no trace of what we did is exactly what proves how skilful we were in our work . . . Abhinav Bharat was the first to proclaim Complete Political Independence as the goal, we did so in our *secret* meetings . . . The *secret* contacts that our revolutionaries established with the governments of Russia and other countries, their *secret* activities in Siam, Canada, America, Europe . . .[35]

Believing the Myths One Conjures Up

Conjuring myths, especially about oneself, comes at a cost. The conjuror is always nervous that the audience will see through them. The greater cost arises when the one fabricating myths about himself comes to believe them. Savarkar created myths, of course—and that is a part of the problem: so many just go by what he said and wrote about himself and events of which he was the centre. But the sheer number of the myths, as well as the conviction with which he promoted them, point to something more: he believed the myths he put out.

Acolytes and devotees, and now those capitalizing on his name have, of course, further inflated them. There is a lemma in that: the more inflated the myth, the more the creators are apprehensive that they will be found out. Hence, their utter touchiness. You have but to ask the slightest

---

[34] *Savarkar Samagra*, Volume I, pp. 443–44.

[35] Savarkar's accounts, for instance *My Transportation for Life*, are peppered with such statements.

question about a fabrication, and they fly into a rage: 'anti-Hindu', 'anti-national', 'perverse', 'prejudiced', 'brain-washed by the West', the 'colonial slave mentality'.

A much-favoured device is to attribute the myth to someone else—especially to someone who, not being a *bhakt,* would in the normal course not be expected to manufacture myths about the beneficiary. We have come across the 'biography', *The Life of Barrister Savarkar,* and we saw that there are good reasons to believe that Savarkar himself wrote this 'biography' of himself. But here is what an admirer floats:

> Shree Rajagopalachari (Rajaji), the only Indian to become the Governor General of divided India had openly admitted in 1937 that it was the life of Veer Savarkar that inspired him to join in the freedom struggle. In fact, he wrote a book in 1924 entitled 'Life of Barrister Savarkar' under the pseudonym Chitragupta.[36]

There is just no way that Rajaji—whose writings are a model of lucidity, succinctness, accuracy—could have written such a shoddy book. Moreover, he was poles apart from everything that Savarkar is known for. To make doubly sure, I asked Rajmohan Gandhi, the distinguished writer and historian, who has written biographies of, among others, both Gandhiji and Rajaji. And the two were his paternal and maternal grandfathers respectively. He knows every little thing there is to know about each of them. His reply: 'An utterly baseless claim of course. Predictably enough, the claim is made long after Rajaji's death (December 1972).' If the acolytes actually believed that Rajaji had written the book, he wondered, why had no reader of the book or follower of Savarkar thanked Rajaji for writing

---

[36] *Rationalism of Veer Savarkar,* V. S. Godbole, Compiler, Itihas Patrika Prakashan, Pune, 2004, p. 26 of the e-version.

the book [or even mentioned the book, we may add] while the latter was alive?[37]

'Hindu Rashtrapati Savarkar' [38]

There is a difference that becomes a cause, the difference between a great man and one who is so convinced that he is great that he preens himself as great. How well the poet put it:

Sarkash hain voh darakht	The trees that stick out their heads high
Jin par samar nahin	Have no fruit on them [think of the Eucalyptus]
Pur samar hain jo darakht	Trees that are laden with fruit [think of the tree laden with mangos in summer]
Uthaatey voh sar nahin	Do not raise their heads

---

[37] Email, 28 December 2023.

[38] This is one of the ways in which editors of his collected works refer to him: *Savarkar Samagra,* Volume VIII, p. 545.

Self-Image and Its Consequences

Savarkar was a piercing polemicist and an even better writer. His songs are still sung in Maharashtra today. Some of his books are preserved as prized possessions in the state by families you would least expect to be revering books. Of course, these days the light is being shone on him. But even before this, he had been a household name in Maharashtra.

He writes *Six Glorious Epochs* in his eightieth year. Illness has confined him to bed. Time and again, he states that he lacks the energy to write in detail about the issue at hand. He mentions the event or subject, expresses his inability to describe it in detail and asks the reader to turn to his earlier book, *Hindu Pad-padshahi*. An instance is the 'Hindu war of Independence', the century-long struggle of the Marathas to overthrow Muslim power. He says that he does not have the time or energy to describe the struggle, and that the reader will have to remain content with the *Hindu Pad-padshahi*. This is how he describes that book:

My book, *Hindu Pad-padshahi*, is really the golden temple of the survey and appraisal of that great war—an enthralling piece of sculpture in colour and solidity, of the Goddess of that great war, like any in the caves of Ajantha . . . Under such circumstances, therefore, my book *Hindu Pad-padshahi* estimating this great Hindu-Muslim War through the Hindu national angle of vision is the only one of its kind. That is why I recommend it Wholeheartedly to every Hindu nationalist.[1]

That is quite the pattern.

Mazzini and Garibaldi

Savarkar is sixteen or so. Plague carries off relatives, including his father, and several close acquaintances. The family is compelled to leave their village, Bhogur, and go to Nasik. Here they find a place to stay in a lane of Tilbhandeshwar. He writes of it:

> In the future, this lane was going to acquire the distinction of being the birthplace of the revolutionary organisation that spread across the entire country; and every man, every woman residing in that lane would—according to their capacity and bearing some hardship or the other—became a helper in organising a centre of some revolutionary activity that would shock even the government. Even though no one would have believed such a thing even in his dreams at that time, but now it is the truth . . .[2]

And now, see the parallel. Years later, Savarkar is in Marseilles. He asks the guide who is showing him around the city, where Mazzini lived for many years. The guide doesn't know. Savarkar remarks:

> I said to myself, 'After all, this man is merely making a living. How would he know the detailed history?' I suggested that he should

---

[1] V.D. Savarkar, *Six Glorious Epochs of Indian History,* Bal Savarkar, Savarkar Sadan, Bombay, 1971. pp. 411–12.

[2] V.D. Savarkar, *Autobiography, Savarkar Samagra,* Volume I, p. 208.

contact a newspaper editor or a local teacher. Luckily, we came across the office of a newspaper. My guide went inside and made some enquiries. When he came out, he said—The editor says, 'We do not know the house where Mazzini of Italy once lived. Please make enquiries in Italy. Perhaps the Italians would know the place.'

I laughed and said to myself, 'When Mazzini came to Marseilles some sixty or seventy years ago, hardly a single Frenchman knew him. Today hundreds of passengers from many nations are coming here. No one is bothered about me—an Indian revolutionary. Similarly, when a few Italian revolutionaries were once wandering the streets of this town the Frenchmen hardly bothered. When Mazzini founded his secret society here, the position and strength of that society was no different to our Abhinav Bharat.

. . . No one would have imagined the turmoil that was to come in just four years' time. Today, no Frenchman knows me here. And yet in four years' time many Frenchmen would ask—who is this man Savarkar? The issue of Indian freedom struggle would be discussed throughout Europe. And as a coincidence, the name of Marseilles will make headlines throughout the world at least for one year. No one had the slightest idea that this will happen.[3]

And this comes to pass in less than no time. Savarkar jumps out of the porthole. He is captured. The French demand that he be handed back to them as he was arrested on French soil. The British refuse to do so, on the plea that he is wanted for trial in India on the charge of abetting murder. The case goes for arbitration to the Hague. 'The names Marseilles and Savarkar were in the headlines throughout the World for at least one year,'

---

[3] Veer Savarkar, *Inside the Enemy Camp,* www.savarkar.org, Veer Savarkar Prakashan, Mumbai, 1993, pp. 18–19.

writes Savarkar.[4] He continued to point to the significance of the event. Thus, in *My Transportation for Life,* we find him reminding readers, '. . . my hazardous attempt to escape at Marseilles and the many international issues it had raised, made our movement, its hopes and ambitions, and the sacrifices we had made in its behalf, the topic of discussion all over Europe . . .'[5]

He is reminded of the similarity with Mazzini not just on this but on many occasions, and this gives him heart. 'As I studied Mazzini's works I realized that the revolutionary tactics that I had preached to my friends, were remarkably similar to those proposed by Mazzini for Italian Revolutionaries,' Savarkar recalls. He summarizes what Mazzini had prescribed about the way revolutionary groups must be organized and how they must work, and observes, 'I was surprised to find that Mazzini had followed the same path for liberation of his country.' This fact 'bolstered my confidence [a] hundred times.'[6] And not just Mazzini, Garibaldi too:

In 1906, I and my colleagues in Abhinav Bharat were hardly twenty to twenty-two years of age. Our leaders, both Moderates and Militants dismissed our activities as 'childish'. They were the leaders of our society at that time. But then Mazzini and his fellow revolutionaries were similarly ridiculed as 'childish' and 'absurd' by contemporary elders in Italian society in 1830s. Mazzini had replied to such ridicule in his articles. The funny thing was that in 1906 persons like Mazzini and Garibaldi were regarded as 'great patriots' by Indian leaders without realizing that in their days Mazzini and Garibaldi too were being branded as 'foolhardy' and 'childish'.[7]

---

[4] Ibid, p. 19.

[5] V.D. Savarkar, *My Transportation for Life, op. cit.,* p. 185.

[6] *Inside the Enemy Camp,* op. cit., p. 67.

[7] Ibid, p. 67.

Pseudonymously

To get a glimpse of the opinion Savarkar had of himself, let us start with the 'biography' of Savarkar which, as we have seen, there are good reasons to believe Savarkar wrote himself under the pseudonym 'Chitragupta'— *Life of Barrister Savarkar*.[8] Hero after hero, fighter after fighter is born into the Chitpavan caste, we are told: the first Peshwa Balaji Vishwanath, Bajirao 'one of the foremost generals India ever produced', Nana Fadnavis, Vasudev Balwant who revolts against the British, the Chapekar brothers and Ranade who are hanged by the British, Gopal Krishna Gokhale, Justice Ranade, Tilak . . . 'No wonder then that destiny should have chosen this particular caste to bring forth and nestle the child which [sic.] was to be, to quote Valentine Chirol, one of the most brilliant of modern Indian revolutionists.'[9]

Ever Since His Childhood

'Vinayak ever since his childhood was given to lofty aspirations and was marked out by all those who came in contact with him as an exceptionally gifted child . . .'[10]

He is ten or twelve years old. There are Hindu–Muslim riots. Descriptions of these 'fired the blood of young Vinayak. He could not rest without wreaking some vengeance or other on the Moslems for the outrages they had inflicted on his co-religionists in Bombay and other places in India. He summons 'a council of urgency of his young schoolmates'. They decide to attack a nearby mosque. They 'advanced stealthily but

---

[8] Cf., Vinayak Chaturvedi's scholarly *Hindutva and Violence, V.D. Savarkar and the Politics of History*, Permanent Black, Delhi, State University of New York Press, Albany, 2022, for a fuller discussion on the subject.

[9] Chitragupta, *Life of Barrister Savarkar*, Acharya Balarao Savarkar, Veer Savarkar Prakashan, Bombay, 1987, pp. 1–2.

[10] Ibid, p. 2.

unfortunately met no foes'. 'Was it because the mosque was a deserted and dilapidated structure scarcely visited by any one at that hour or was it out of fear that the foe fled away before he dared even to desert us? Anyway, all that we now have to do is to take possession of the mosque, enjoy our occupation for a while, to romp and dig up a plod or two, pull down a peg here and a nail there and take to our heels before any of the foes scented it all.' 'Cawardice?' [sic.] 'Rat!—even Shivaji used to take to his heels when necessary.' A fight ensues; the Muslim boys are worsted as 'commander' Vinayak has already equipped his troops with the arsenal required for such school battles.[11]

To teach his schoolmates to fight, he divides his classmates into two groups: 'one party of the lads personated English men or Muslims and other the Hindu forces.' In each mock-battle the Hindus are to win, 'If not always through their pluck then at least for the simple reason that those who took the Hindu side must be patriotically permitted to win by us who personated the Aliens!'[12]

He sits 'for hours and hours' in front of an image of Durga, 'at times so completely lost in communion as to loose [sic.] all outward consciousness'. His mother dies when he is just ten years old. He doesn't miss her 'for to him the image of Durga had grown into a living and loving and as real a mother as any incorporated human being could be'.[13]

Everyone naturally wants to hear him and learn from him what is happening.[14]

He is still not thirteen. He is inspired by the assassinations of British officers on the Diamond Jubilee of Queen Victoria. He takes a vow in front of the image of Durga to complete the mission of those executed for the assassinations and dedicate his life to the country. In that resolve, Abhinav

---

[11] Ibid, pp. 2–3.

[12] Ibid, p. 6.

[13] Ibid, pp. 6–7.

[14] Ibid. p. 8.

Bharat is born 'which, later on, was destined to be a force to be counted within Indian politics'.[15]

'An Irresistible Influence'

He enters Fergusson College. There his 'early erudition and oratorical powers' exercise 'an irresistible influence on the minds of his colleagues' in the college. All 'leading students' associations and societies c[o]me soon to be dominated by the 'Savarkar camp.' His lectures 'would long be remembered by those who had once heard them as best samples of Marathi eloquence and revolutionary literature . . .'[16]

To inspire people, he proposes that all foreign cloth and clothes be burnt. 'The idea seemed so extreme that even Lok[manya] Tilak expressed misgivings as to its practicability.' Savarkar presses ahead nonetheless. The response is immense. 'The crowd swelled and swelled till the great leader Lok[manya] Tilak, not in any way dissatisfied to see his misgiving falsified, came out to lead the people . . .'[17]

And that too was to become the pattern in the future: Savarkar and his small band began to do what the indomitable and fearless Tilak, 'because he was a leader', could not. They became his Sappers and Miners, clearing the way for him to do what was in his heart:

Proceeding on his public ideals—Suraaj, Home Rule, Swaraj—we climbed on to his real ideal, independence. What he said in his mind, we proclaimed aloud. Where he stopped, we would advance from that very point. He was a leader, he stayed one step ahead of the country. But so that he may walk the next steps unhindered, we attempted to do what Sappers and Miners do—we tried to walk and clear a hundred

---

[15] Ibid, pp. 9–10; p. 13 for his age at the time.

[16] Ibid, pp. 19–21.

[17] Ibid, pp. 23–24.

steps ahead. Where his means clogged, at that very place suddenly we would melt those very means and forge weapons. We would make the clogged, flow. For this reason we were truly his devoted followers; because, walking ahead, we devoted ourselves to attaining what was in his heart. He was the handle of the sword, we were the blade. The handle of the sword can never be the blade, but the blade dances in battle on the signal of the handle. The blade gives form to the thought of the handle.18

He Changes People's Ways—of Looking, of Living

Savarkar's uncle asks him to teach wrestling to the youngsters in Kothur village. Savarkar recalls what happened as a consequence:

My uncle placed on me the responsibility of teaching wrestling to the youth. Because of his *prabhaav*/influence and love, I too received a great deal of affection in the village. Wherever I would go, my political ideas would get propagated. My age was just 17 or 18 years, but in just a while wherever I went my influence would spread. The older persons too would talk to me and, listening to my lofty ideas they would get attracted to me. I would sing the composition on the Chapekars[19] in several houses . . . There was a public lecture of mine also in the village. From that the esteem in which I was held increased . . .

People used to while away their time, Savarkar recalls. A few newspapers would come, but they would be read as entertainment. That one's heart should stir for the country was not in anyone's mind. But things changed:

---

[18] Ibid, p. 181.

[19] A poem he had composed.

The Lokmanya's *swadeshi* movement had spread the awareness of swadesh in village after village. In an atmosphere like this, my clear, *bhavya aur divya* (grand and cativating) message awakened reverence for and the desire to serve our nation not only among the elderly but even among the youth.[20]

He enters the tenth class. He begins to read publications on history and other subjects. He begins keeping a diary. He prepares notes summarizing what he has read. Seeing my habits, my disciplined life, other boys also changed their ways, Savarkar writes. Their learning comes to depend on him:

> I also gave lectures on 'Moro Pant and the science of rhetoric'. I used to get special delight from speaking on such sweet subjects. The opportunity I got of distributing every week among my friends in 'Mitra Mela' what I had learnt like this had a very salutary effect on my learning and capacity. The learning of my friends in Mitra Mela was all in all dependent on the growth of my learning. I was fully aware of this. As a result, I used to be on the lookout for what I should read and speak about to ensure the growth of that organisation.[21]

He goes to a wedding in another village, Tryamkeshwar:

> No sooner had I got the opportunity of spending extended time with Annaa,[22] I sowed the seeds of *deshbhakti* in that young man. He decided to participate in our brave programmes. I made him take the oath of sacrificing even his life for the country. Gradually, several young men came under my influence and became revolution-minded.[23]

---

[20] V.D. Savarkar, *Autobiography, Savarkar Samagra,* Volume I, pp. 238–40.

[21] Ibid, p. 248. Moro Pant was a Marathi poet.

[22] A relative on whom the responsibility of carrying on the responsibilities of an extended family had fallen.

[23] *Autobiography*, p. 254.

The village is sunk in tradition, in casteism, in fights among castes and subcastes. Sanskrit learning is alive, but the pandits have no notion at all about the world. The local poet recites some verses he has composed in which the British King is spoken of as *maa-baap*, as Bhagwan, Prithvipati, etc. He asks for Savarkar's opinion. Savarkar tells him that his verses are pearls thrown before swine. You look upon the King-Emperor of England as *Dev-avtar*, as *maa-baap*, and proclaim him to be the Lord of the Earth, the young Savarkar tells the poet and the audience. The king of another country, one that is holding us down by force, cannot be our king, he instructs them. '*Merey is saahsik vidhaan ki aur merei samvaad-pratibhaa ko dekh kar Tryamkeshwar ke praudh log mujhse prabhaavit huey . . .*' (The elders of Tryamkeshwar were influenced by this courageous and vivid way in which I put the points across).[24]

His poems were great hits, he writes. He came to be known as the one whose speeches were the most awe-inspiring and inspirational.[25]

The Trust and Bhakti Others Have Towards Him

Contact with him, acquaintance with him, Savarkar says, changed the direction of the lives, indeed the very lives of others:

> The effect that used to come about on persons from close acquaintance with me happened in little time on Bhau also, and, in accordance with rules, after being commended by two or three members and on my recommendation, he joined 'Mitra mandal' . . .
>
> He was among my followers/*anuyaayi* who at that time had surrendered all, but he joined national work only after coming in contact with me. When I went far away our contact ceased and so did the direction of his work for the country. In Andamans I heard that

---

[24] Ibid, p. 255.

[25] For instance, the *Autobiography*, op. cit., p. 227.

he had joined a drama troupe and used to perform comic routines. The affection that persons whom I have mentioned in this part as well as several others had for me was not because of my being the head of their institution but because of their personal affection for me. I dealt with them—the educated and the uneducated equally—in an open way. I used to give equal respect/consideration/*sammaan* to them and used to sit along with these persons who used to repose the faith in me that they would in a guru . . . Most of them—young as well as grown up—used to have such trust in and such bhakti/devotion towards me that they used to consider my counsel to be *Vedvaakya*. They did not have the same sort of regard for what even their parents or wives and children said as they had for my word. If they had to tell them anything, the parents and wives would come and request me to tell the persons as they knew from experience that the latter would listen to me . . . Even at that age, hundreds of workers and grown-ups used to have affection for and bhakti towards me. I would not consider anyone to be my follower/anuyaayi. I used to treat everyone equally and have equal affection for all . . .

. . . People would always gather around me. I too would be absorbed in them, but occasionally the wave of solitude would touch me . . .[26]

Not Since the War of 1857

He reaches England. Dadabhai Naoroji, Lala Lajpat Rai and others have been pressing for reforms. But in a puerile way and to little effect, he tells us. He is the one who proclaims the great goal, he is the one who lifts politics, strategic planning, organization to an altogether higher level. Contact with him transforms the lives of the youth in London.

Till his arrival, the young men were in a pitiable state, he says. He saw the latent spark in them, he says. And he lit it:

---

[26] Ibid, pp. 268, 270–71, 273.

... even more bereft of self-respect, even more encoiled in self-interest, regarding British rule as the incarnation of Vishnu, than the youngmen who had come abroad and looked impoverished politically, were many pandit *dharmaguru* and countless bootlickers back in Hindusthan ... It is not possible to give a description of all the ones whom we and I were able to convert through discussions . . . During the work of Abhinav Bharat I had already drawn up the entire sheaf of responses for dealing with the apprehensions and doubts of these persons bereft of self-respect, these worshippers of the British—like the *Rambaand/* panacea that a Vaidyaraj would devise for different ailments. With this experience gathered in Maharashtra, when I reached London I saw that it will be possible in the majority of British-worshipping students to awaken not just patriotism but also to an extent what had seemed impossible—the consciousness of armed revolution. This I saw for certain, and therefore I began extensive efforts for this purpose.[27]

Their nature, their very lives are transformed because of him:

Mr. Savarkar, when he thus left England in 1910, was nearly 26. He had arrived there when 22 years old. Within the short span of these four years he had transformed the crowd of nerveless ninnies and unprincipled dandies, that the Indian students in England were before [sic.] generally reputed to be, into a band of patriots who, apart from their dreadful methods and questionable tactics, did undoubtedly display a heroic fortitude, a reckless spirit of sacrifice in the interests of the motherland and did indeed win esteem and enlist the moral sympathy of all European nations in favour of the cause of Indian Freedom. Before that the European actually expressed his contempt as [at] the sight of an Indian as a slave, and, worse, as a willing slave. Thenceforth, they looked upon them as men who could retaliate and dare and die for their nation.[28]

---

[27] *Autobiography,* op. cit., pp. 412–13.

[28] *Life of Barrister Savarkar,* op. cit., p. 98.

Till he arrived, Savarkar says, no one had stirred passion in them:

'This Bharatbhoomi is your Motherland, which by force these Britishers have made their maidservant. Therefore, these Britishers are your enemies.' Had anyone addressed them in such spirited language? Had anyone made them understand this? No!! Just no one had spoken to them about the noble purpose of life. No one had brought to the darkness of their hearts the ray of such lofty aspirations instead of narrow, self-centered desire . . .[29]

No one had proclaimed the goal of Absolute Political Independence till then, he says[30] . . . 'In other words, from the available information it is clear that in the interval between the revolution of 1857 and the time I reached London, no organised work for a revolution had begun.' Though he does add, 'If further information becomes available in the future, it is another thing.'[31]

'The Foremost Topic in the World Press'

He escapes through the porthole of the lavatory. He is caught and brought back to the steamer. The British refuse to hand him back to the French. The case goes to the International Court at the Hague. He is compared to great revolutionaries. The attempt to escape and the case draw everyone's attention to India and its struggle for freedom:

For the time being his romantic adventure and a diplomatic complication formed the foremost topic in the world press. That naturally made all inquire into India's struggle for freedom . . . From the remotest China to Egypt, all the world over, Mr. Savarkar's life and

---

[29] *Autobiography,* op. cit., p. 411.

[30] Ibid, pp. 415–16.

[31] Ibid, p. 416.

doings and photos were in demand and the papers, openly comparing him with Mazzini and Kossuth and Prince Kropotkin . . .[32]

That remains for years how he looks back at the effect of that attempt: ' . . . my hazardous attempt to escape at Marseilles and the many international issues it had raised, made our movement, its hopes and ambitions, and the sacrifices we had made in its behalf, the topic of discussion all over Europe.'[33]

'The foremost topic in the world press'? 'The topic of discussion all over Europe'?

'Attracts the Attention of All the Educated World to It'

Savarkar is back in India. He is charged with abetment to murder. The trial takes place in Nasik: ' . . . The trial was a memorable one. The figure of Mr. Savarkar attracted the attention of all the educated world to it . . .' As he enters the dock of the prisoners, he is cheered . . .[34]

The Original Idea

Someone reading his accounts will conclude that the idea of armed revolution came to him before anyone else, and it came to him from within. The fact is that within a few years of the suppression of the 1857 uprising, the idea of getting rid of the British by all means, including and specially violence, was being proclaimed time and again, at festivals, at meetings. This can be gleaned from the opening pages of the Rowlatt report itself. The Committee itself had been appointed precisely because violence, assassinations, etc. were in the air.[35] When Savarkar reached

[32] *Life of Barrister Savarkar*, op. cit., pp. 114–15.

[33] *My Transportation for Life*, op. cit., p. 185.

[34] *Life of Barrister Savarkar*, op. cit., p. 117.

[35] *Sedition Committee, 1918, Report*, Bengal Secretariat Press, Calcutta, 1919, pp. 1–3.

England, armed overthrow of governments, of entire systems—the politics, economics, social relations of countries—was the staple of discourse throughout Europe: in Russia, in France and in Germany. The claim that surfaces again and again in Savarkar's accounts does not square with his own description of the influence that Mazzini and Garibaldi had on freedom fighters of that time, including and especially himself.

His articles, even when they are written anonymously, increase the fame and circulation of the paper, Savarkar wrote. Here, he is commenting on the mistakes that mark the Rowlatt Committee's report:

> . . . After getting introduced to me, its [the paper *Vihari*'s] first editor, Shri Chiploondkar became a member of Abhinav Bharat . . . Following his example, I began to write anonymous articles in *Vihari*. Because of my anonymous writings, the paper's fame and circulation increased across Maharashtra. And the surprising thing is that I was running the paper anonymously. The Rowlatt inquiry did not know even this much . . .[36]

The rumour that a book by Savarkar is going to be printed ignites a rush of orders. Savarkar recounts how he wrote the 300-page book containing Mazzini's autobiography and writings and his own introduction in two/ two and a half months, how he sent the Marathi manuscript to his brother. And then writes, 'The moment people came to know that a book written by Savarkar is going to be published soon, a crowd of customers gathered, they sent money and booked copies.'[37]

To And in the Andamans

Savarkar has been brought back to India. He is convicted for having enabled the murder of Jackson and is now in the train from Bombay to Madras

---

[36] *Autobiography*, op. cit., p. 443.

[37] Ibid, p. 455.

from where he will be sent to the Andamans. Windows of his cabin are shut at every station, he writes.

> The train started, but at every station, where it stopped in the journey, I found the shutters of my window put down. Since the time I had left England, I was never allowed to travel in any compartment with windows up. But the Officer with me in this compartment had, as if by prearrangement, kept the window shutters up so that the European visitors should have a full look of me. A large crowd of them had come near my compartment. Some of these men had lifted up their women-folk on their shoulders that they might see me clearly. One beckoned on to me to stand up. 'There is he; that is Savarkar,' went up the cry from all sides as I stood up . . .[38]

He is being taken in a boat to the steamer that will ferry him to Andamans:

> The boat touched the steamer *Maharaja* which had come from the Andamans. I was lifted up, with handcuffs on, the ladder of the steamer and taken on the deck. While I was climbing up, a whole crowd had gathered around to watch the scene. All the passengers on board the ship, all Officers, all men in the boats around her, and other spectators, had come out to see me. They saw me entering the steamer. They riveted their eyes on me, as we witness a corpse being tied on the bier. With eager eyes and bare-faced shame they kept on gazing.[39]

Officers Take Off Their Hats 'To Show Reverence' to Him

He is taken aboard the steamer:

> A gentleman came up to me, while this was going on, and broached the topic of my escape at Marseilles and my arrest thereafter. In my

---

[38] *Autobiography*, op. cit., p. 443.

[39] Ibid, p. 33.

turn, I spoke to him frankly on the subject. Thereafter, he said, 'We have deliberately come here to see you. May God grant that you return safe and back to your motherland. That is all our prayer to Him, and a very sincere wish, we assure you.' And the European gentleman and other Officers left the steamer bidding me good-bye and showing me reverence by taking off their hats. There was only one person among them who seemed to be displeased by their behaviour to a miscreant and convict like me. He despised me altogether as unworthy of this courtesy. He looked at me full of scorn, and went away without wishing me.[40]

Savarkar is now in the steamer:

The travellers and some of the Indian Officers on board the ship desired to express their feeling of reverence for me by doing me service of one kind or another. They often used to pay me a casual visit. Some of the European soldiers treated me very politely. I was given some English newspapers to read as also some magazines. We got on with nothing else to eat but fried grams and peas. But the Officers insisted that I should have something better. I did not know what special things I should ask for and it was difficult for them to make an exception in my case. As a result, some philanthropic merchants on board that steamer arranged a dinner for all of us with the permission of the Captain. It consisted of rice, fish and pickles and several other preparations. The whole of the prison-world in that steamer welcomed it with joy after two days of practical fasting and I was the cause of it. They were duly grateful to me for it . . .[41]

---

[40] Ibid, p. 34.

[41] Ibid, p. 37.

During the journey:

> From the ordinary sailor to the highest Officer of the ship, from the prisoner right up to the soldier I had become an instrument of political discussion all round. Some of them heard things that they had never heard before. What had never suggested itself to them up to that time did suggest itself to them now. And conviction came to them on matters of which they were never convinced previously.[42]

He is lodged in the horrible cell:

> Next morning these wardens presented themselves before my room and announced that the Sahib was coming and I was to stand up. I came to the door, which was nothing but a barred entrance into my room. Mr. Barrie[43] had come up with his European friends. He had acquired a special importance with them since my arrival in this gaol. The Europeans in the locality, men and women, were naturally curious to see me and talk to me. And for that purpose they had to burn incense before the demi-god, Mr. Barrie. Mr. Barrie pretended that he was taking them to my room under great risk, and they had to request him, again and again, before he would accede to their importunities . . .[44]

Fellow-prisoners are reverential:

> While I was turning the oil-mill, one or two of the political prisoners, my neighbours, who could slip in unnoticed, always came to help me from time to time. Some of them washed my clothes, even with my

---

[42] Ibid, p. 37.

[43] The terror of the jail.

[44] *My Transportation,* op. cit., p. 54.

protests to the contrary, though they had more than enough of their own hardships to bear. And they cleaned and washed my drinking pot and my dining plate as well. The petty officer and the Jamadar often reproved them for it, and even beat them occasionally; but like true friends they helped me on in my daily work. I tried many times to stop them. I washed their clothes without their knowledge, which, when they learnt, gave them exceeding pain. They literally went down on their knees and besought me to refrain from it. When I realised that my not allowing them to do my work, and my doing their work on the sly, both harassed their mind, I thought it the better part to let them do what they liked. On the whole, I found all of them affectionately disposed towards me. Their selfless devotion for me touched my heart. Sometimes, there was a regular rivalry among them to serve me, and it went the length of making them jealous of one another. Then I had to let them wash my clothes by turn. My heart still goes out in gratitude to these political prisoners when I recall their unstinted generosity and their deep friendship for me . . .[45]

Gokhale's Reverence

The distinguished Gopal Krishna Gokhale passes away. Barrie, perhaps with some malicious glee, brings Savarkar the news. He starts by telling Savarkar what he has heard of the differences between Gokhale and him and how the two disapproved of each other:

I answered promptly, 'Do not, please, believe in such hear-say reports. It is no use. We had intimate talks with each other and we cherished deep affection and reverence for each other. And this can be borne out by those who were present on the occasion . . .[46]

---

[45] Ibid, p. 82.

[46] Ibid, p. 104.

War is raging in Europe. Another contingent of prisoners arrives in the jail:

> Though I knew only Professor Parmanand among them, most of
> them knew me. They had read my contributions to the press; they
> had studied my books. Their reverence for me made them eager to
> see me as soon as they had stepped into the prison . . .[47]

One after the other, they tell him how reading his articles changed the direction of their lives.

Not Joining the Strike

Savarkar becomes the beacon for the prisoners. They look to him for guidance. His interventions make them change course—even to abandon their decision to shed their lives. Government personnel and delegations seek to interview him. He strives on behalf of the prisoners. The prisoners go on strike. He guides them through it. But he does not join them.

He goes to great length in his account of his years in the Cellular Jail to explain why he decided not to join the strike: he would not be able to write letters to his brother, that would mean that the cause of the prisoners would not get the publicity which was essential if they were ever to get some relief; the authorities would get even more incensed with him, that would mean that he would not be able to intercede on behalf of the prisoners; he had taken great pains to ensure that his conduct as a prisoner had been above reproach, joining the strike would mean that the conditions in which he was would worsen and his stay would become even longer than it might otherwise be.[48]

At least some of these reasons would have applied to others also. In any case, they did not convince several of his co-prisoners. Trailokya Nath

---

[47] Ibid, p. 202–03.

[48] For Savarkar's explanation for not joining the strike which he had spurred others to launch, *My Transportation for Life*, op. cit., pp. 212–15.

Chakraborty was a renowned revolutionary from Bengal. He spent thirty years in jails. He was in the Cellular Jail in Andamans from 1916 to 1921 and was subjected to all but one of the horrible punishments that the jailers inflicted.[49] In his memoir, he wrote:

> . . . From Government report, it may be learnt that in the Cellular Jails of Andamans on average three prisoners had committed suicide each month. Human beings do not commit suicide so easily but the prisoners over there would be persecuted in such a way that it would exceed the limit of toleration and as such they would make an end of their lives to free themselves from the grip of such persecution. The political prisoners of Cellular Jail resolved to find redress for the same . . . And on this issue we became divided into two groups— the moderates and the extremists. The Savarkar brothers and Barin Babu[50] and a few others who had come earlier, had suffered much persecution and they had obtained a few redresses for themselves.
>
> Now they were found [sic.] [fond?] favourites of the Jailor or Superintendent. They were not prepared to forego those concessions and join us in the proposed movement.
>
> . . . the extremists decided to go ahead and begin their protest by defying regulations and rules imposed by the jail administration . . .

That Savarkar and a few of the other prominent prisoners had refrained from joining the strike served the Government's convenience admirably.

---

[49] 'I was one of those who earned fame by launching agitation in the Andamans. Excepting whipping punishment, I received all of the rest. Starting from cross-bar-fetters, being chained to rods, being shackled, handcuff on vertical-hand, back handcuff, night handcuff, penal diet, cell-confinement, etc. all inflicted on me. We had fought for our redress continuously for three years. A scar-mark was left on our ankle due to constant ankle-chaining.' Trailokya Nath Chakraborty, *Thirty Years in Prison, Sensational confessions of [a] revolutionary,* Enlarged English edition, Alpha-Beta Publications, Calcutta, 1963, p. 143.

[50] Brother of Sri Aurobindo.

Questions about the strike and the suffering of the prisoners were raised in the Bengali press as well as in the Legislative Assembly.

> . . . The Government replied that a few notorious persons were creating these troubles and the political leaders in the Andamans had not participated in the same. These news began to pour in gradually.

That Savarkar had instigated, or if you prefer encouraged others but had stayed away was not at all unusual: recall Madan Lal Dhingra and others. Chakraborty observed,

> The Savarkar brothers used to encourage us secretly but when we asked them to join us openly, they refrained. But the strike continued . . .[51]

The Government announced concessions. Savarkar's account now speaks in terms of 'we', of 'us', and how 'we' and 'us' had wrested the concessions:

> Except our demand for equal rights with political prisoners in England, the Indian Government agreed to grant us all the demands in the statement submitted by us before going on strike. We secured the right to send long letters home; we secured the right of sweet water for bathing; of soap and oil for the Sikhs; of better food for prisoners; and last, of light work as our daily routine.[52]

Two Glimpses From Two Footnotes

Even that has a footnote—in fact, two! R.C. Majumdar, the distinguished historian, thought very highly of Savarkar. He wrote an appreciative introduction to *Hindu Pad-padshahi*. In his eminently informative work,

---

[51] Trailokya Nath Chakraborty, *Thirty Years in Prison, Sensational confessions of [a] revolutionary,* Enlarged English edition, Alpha-Beta Publications, Calcutta, 1963, pp. 125–39.

[52] *My Transportation for Life,* op. cit., pp. 243–44.

Penal Settlement in Andamans, Majumdar referred to Savarkar as 'one of the greatest revolutionary leaders of India whose whole life is a continuous story of suffering and sacrifice for his country . . .' He wrote of Savarkar as '. . . the great patriotic leader.' He took Savarkar's account of his years in the Cellular Jail at face value and reproduced substantial sections from it. But even he found reason to censure Savarkar ever so politely on two counts— each displaying a trait: reviling others and, second, claiming more than was warranted. After recounting the course of the strike, Majumdar recalled what Savarkar had enumerated as concessions that the Government had been forced to make in response to the strike—the prisoners will be allowed in batches to cook their own food; and some of them will work in the printing press, in the Library, and on map-drawing, etc. Majumdar went on to recall what Savarkar had insinuated,

> Savarkar and his brother did not in any way benefit from these concessions, but, he [Savarkar] adds, many of those who did (most of whom were obviously Bengali prisoners for only very few non-Bengalis were left in the Andamans among political prisoners) were so gratified by this monthly pay—'like beggars turned millionaires'— that they 'were at their beck and call for anything they needed'. 'In other words these political prisoners because [became?] very subservient—not to put it more bluntly—to the authorities.'[53]

This did not go down well with Majumdar. He remarked,

> This is a very serious insinuation against these political prisoners and we have no means to determine how far Savarkar was justified in this assumption. He does not give any evidence or practical illustration.[54]

---

[53] R.C. Majumdar, *Penal Settlement in Andamans,* Gazetteers Unit, Ministry of Education and Social Welfare, Government of India, New Delhi, 1975, p. 232.

[54] Ibid. Elsewhere, Majumdar censured Chakraborty: 'Chakravarti [sic.] says in his memoir that the Savarkar brothers secretly encouraged us but when asked to join us they refused.

The second footnote is about the concessions that Savarkar said had been won by the striking prisoners. 'From the concessions granted in the notification it is easy to realise that many of them had confirmed to [conformed to?] the demands made by the strikers', Savarkar had written.

Majumdar's comment was a bit muted, but it is enough to draw attention to a trait in much of Savarkar's writing:

> Savarkar and his fellow-prisoners had deluded themselves into the belief that their strike was a great success as concessions granted by the Notification, mentioned above, conformed to the demands made by them. But little did they know that the major concessions, namely items 1 and 2 mentioned above by Savarkar[55] were due to a change in the policy of the Government of India which was under consideration for a long time even before the visit of Craddock[56] to the Andamans.

And Majumdar had proceeded to cite notings on files that concerned proposals for changes in policy—so extensively had the changes been deliberated upon and over so many rounds that the notings cover twelve pages of Majumdar's book.[57]

This and similar remarks of Chakravarti mentioned above cast very uncharitable aspersions against notable revolutionary leaders like Savarkar and Barin Ghose.' Ibid, p. 241.

[55] These were: '(1) All the prisoners who were sentenced to a definite period of time, short of life-sentence shall be sent back to their respective prison in India, where the remission of their sentences will be duly considered and followed. (2) Prisoners on life-sentence shall be detained in this prison for a continuous period of fourteen years, whereafter they will be set free for some labour of a light character. This shall operate only in the case of those prisoners who give proof of good behaviour during their period of incarceration.'

[56] R.H. Craddock, the then Home Member of the Governor General's Council. He had visited the Andamans to ascertain the conditions at Cellular Jail, and had met Savarkar, among others.

[57] For the foregoing, *Penal Settlement in Andamans,* op. cit., pp. 218–31.

And Thus

Savarkar believed that the Maharashtrians were the ones who had shattered the Mughal Empire—we will come across this claim as we proceed. And that, therefore, they were the true legatees of that Empire. And suddenly another power—the British—had come and 'slyly' usurped that Empire. Among the Maharashtrians, the Chitpavans were the ones who had produced a long line of heroes and martyrs, right up to Lokmanya Tilak. He, Savarkar, was their legatee. He was the heir to Tilak. But, again, while he was confined in the Andamans, suddenly another outsider had come and carried off the prize. Gandhi, with his sanctimonious talk of ahimsa, with his pretensions of Mahatmahood, this 'walking plague'—a typical phrase of Savarkar for Gandhiji—had carried away his personal legacy. But the wheel had moved. The Viceroy was meeting him, corresponding with him. His men had been inducted into the Viceroy's Executive Council, they were members of the Viceroy's War Committee. He was being invited to conferences where the constitutional future of the country was being decided. But now the people, particularly the Hindus, had become the problem. They kept voting for the very persons who, on Savarkar's telling, were betraying their interests day and night. Worse, while he is the one who had staked his all on Hindutva as the founding idea for a Hindu Rashtra, the Hindus kept looking at that pretender, Gandhi, as the embodiment of Hinduness ... And now, the Viceroys too were distancing themselves. He was not being called for those discussions. It was as if all that exertion, all those 'whirlwind propagandistic tours' had been for nothing ...

And all this had come down on a man who had the sort of high opinion of himself that we have seen. His erudition. His eloquence. The one mere contact with whom changed lives. The first one to proclaim the Great Goal. The one who devised and proclaimed the only path to reach it. The one who had himself trudged that path. The one who had borne unspeakable hardships for doing so. And here was this pretender carrying off acclaim and everything else . . .

The disappointment mutated into frustration, that into a sullen gloom, that into bitterness, that putrefied into hatred.

And the hatred, as we shall see, came to centre on one man—Gandhi.

A Revolutionary Writes

A Revolutionary Writes

I am ready to serve the Government in any capacity they like, for as my conversion is conscientious so I hope my future conduct would be. By keeping me in jail nothing can be got in comparison to what would be otherwise. The Mighty alone can afford to be merciful and therefore where else can the prodigal son return but to the parental doors of the Government? Hoping your Honour will kindly take into notion these points.

And what was the conversion to?

The latest development of the Indian politics and the conciliating policy of the Government have thrown open the constitutional line once more. Now no man having the good of India and Humanity at heart will blindly step on the thorny paths which in the excited and hopeless situation of India in 1906-1907 beguiled us from the path of peace and progress. Therefore if the government in their manifold beneficence and mercy release me, I for one cannot but be the staunchest advocate of constitutional progress and loyalty to the English government which is the foremost condition of that progress.[1]

---

[1] For the complete text of the 'mercy petition', R.C. Majumdar, *Penal Settlement in Andamans*, Gazetteers Unit, Department of Culture, Ministry of Education and Social Welfare, New Delhi, 1975, pp. 212–13.

And yet again:

> So far from believing in the militant school of the Bakunin type that
> I do not contribute even to the peaceful and philosophical anarchism
> of a Kropotkin or a Tolstoy. And as to my Revolutionary tendencies of
> the past: it is not only now for the object of sharing the clemency but
> years before this I have informed of and written to the Government
> in my petitions (1918, 1914) about my firm intention to abide by the
> constitution and stand by it as soon as a beginning was made to prove
> it by Mr. Montagu. Since that the Reforms and then the Proclamation
> have only confirmed me in my views and recently I have publicly
> avowed my faith in and readiness to stand by the side of orderly
> and constitutional development. The danger that is threatening our
> country from the North at the hands of the fanatic hoards of Asia who
> had been the curse of India in the past when they came as foes, and
> who are more likely to be so in the future now that they want to come
> as friends, makes me convinced that every intelligent lover of India
> would heartily and loyally cooperate with the British people in the
> interests of India herself. That is why I offered myself as a volunteer
> in 1914 to Government when the War broke out and German-Turko-
> Afghan invasion of India became imminent. Whether you believe it
> or not, I am sincere in expressing my earnest intention of treading the
> constitutional path and trying my humble best to render the hands of
> the British Dominions a Bond of Love and Respect and of Mutual help
> and such an empire as is foreshadowed in the Proclamation with my
> hearty adherence. For verily I hate no race or creed or people simply
> because they are not Indians, (b) but if Government wants a further
> security from me then I and my brother are perfectly willing to give
> a pledge of not participating in politics for a definite and reasonable
> period that the Government would indicate. For even without such

a pledge my failing health and the sweet blessings of Home that have
been denied to me by myself make me so desirous of leading a quiet
and retired life for years to come that nothing would induce me to
dabble in active politics now. (c) This or any pledge, e.g. of remaining
in a particular province or reporting our movements to the police for
a definite period after our release—any such reasonable conditions
meant genuinely to ensure the safety of the State would be gladly
accepted by me and my brother . . .

Yet again, to be of service in the face of this grave and imminent danger:

On all these grounds I believe that the Government hearing my
readiness to enter into any sensible pledge and the fact that the
Reforms, present and promised, joined to the common danger from
the North of Turko-Afghan fanatics have made me a sincere advocate
of loyal cooperation in the interests of both our nations, would
release me and win my personal gratitude.

Magnanimity, Sir:

The brilliant prospects of my early life all but too soon blighted have
constituted so painful a source of regret to me that a release would be
a new birth and would touch my heart, sensitive and submissive to
kindness so deeply as to render me personally attached and politically
useful in future. For often magnanimity wins where might fails.[2]

Savarkar filed his first petition in 1911, just about two months into his
incarceration in the Cellular Jail at Andamans. The second in October

---

[2] From the petition of 30 March 1920. For the complete text, https://counterviewfiles.
files.wordpress.com/2019/05/savarkar2-converted.pdf

1912. The third, a year later, in November 1913. Another one in 1914. The next one in October 1917. One in 1918. In May–June 1919, he appealed that he be granted remission of his sentence. Later in the year, he appealed that he and his brother be released in accordance with the general amnesty that had been announced in the Royal Proclamation. Savarkar filed two more petitions in January and March 1920. In addition, petitions were filed by his wife and younger brother, Narayan, and the wife of his elder brother, Ganesh.

The petitions have drawn a good deal of attention during the last few years, in part, because they had not been openly acknowledged either by Savarkar or his devotees. And, in part, because of the shock people felt when they saw what he had actually written.

Let us start with the contents of Savarkar's petitions. One way to gauge why they caused such a shock is to compare them with the statements of others—Madan Lal Dhingra or Bhagat Singh for instance. As you read what these others did and say, keep thinking back to what Savarkar wrote.

The Statement That He Is Said to Have Written Himself

We have come across the case of Madan Lal Dhingra earlier. He was an understudy of Savarkar in London. Sir Curzon Wyllie was the political aide to the Secretary of State for India. He had served in various capacities in India. His crime seems to have been that as the Political Agent in Baroda, he had come in the way of Shyamji Krishnavarma, the person who had set up India House, being appointed the Diwan of the state.[3]

A meeting over tea had been organized by Indians. Britishers too were invited. As Curzon Wyllie was coming in, Dhingra shot him at point-blank range. A Parsi doctor, Cawas Lalcaca, who was visiting from Shanghai, tried to shield the victim. Dhingra killed him too but was soon overpowered. During the trial, he acknowledged that, yes, he had indeed done what he

---

[3] Cf, *Savarkar Samagra*, Volume I, p. 376.

was accused of having done. He asked that a statement he had written be taken on record. It read as follows:

I admit the other day I attempted to shed English blood as a humble revenge for the inhuman hangings and deportation of patriotic Indian youths. In this I have consulted none but my own duty. I believe that a country held down by foreign bayonets is in a perpetual state of war. Since open battle is rendered impossible to an unarmed race, I drew forth my pistol and fired.

As a Hindu, I feel that wrong done to my country is an insult to God. Her cause is the cause of Sri Ram. Her service is the service of Sri Krishna. Poor in wealth and in intellect, a son like myself has nothing else to offer to the Mother but his own blood and so I have sacrificed the same on her altar. The only lesson required in India is to learn how to die and the only way to teach it is by dying ourselves; therefore I die and glory in my martyrdom.

My only prayer is that I may be reborn of the same Mother and I may re-die in the same cause till the cause is successful, and She stands free for the good of humanity and the glory of God. *Bande Matram*.[4]

Dhingra was twenty-five at the time. The statement was widely distributed and became famous. Both Lloyd George and Churchill are said to have

---

[4] Cf., Leena Dhingra, *Exhumation, The life and death of Madan Lal Dhingra*, HopeRoad Publishing, London, 2021, pp. 325–26. A brief account of the trial proceedings and the statement that Dhingra read out in court is at:
https://www.oldbaileyonline.org/browse.jsp?div=t19090719-55
MADAN LAL DHINGRA,.
Killing: murder.
19th July 1909

Reference Number	t19090719-55
Verdict	Guilty > unknown
Sentence	Death

remarked to one of their friends that it was 'among the finest ever made in the name of patriotism.'[5]

What did Savarkar himself think about Dhingra's deed and statement? At the time, Savarkar used to send home a 'newsletter' for being printed. His newsletter written on 6 August 1909 after the killing of Curzon Wyllie was bubbling with enthusiasm for Dhingra's deed and the statement. Savarkar wrote that one shot from the pistol of Chapekar had sparked more attention in England than hundreds of resolutions and petitions, and thousands of lectures of Gokhale; that now every newspaper in London is full of news about the killing, about Dhingra. He wrote that newspaper sellers are shouting Dhingra's name . . . 'That day, on the lips of everyone in the British Isles only one word could be heard, "Hindusthan, Hindusthan". From that day to this, no other subject has got any place in the newspapers. Discussion even about Cricket has stopped, what to say of other topics?'[6] Concluding the newsletter, Savarkar wrote,

---

[5] W.S. Blunt, *My Diaries,* Part 2, Alfred A. Knopf, 1921, the entry for 3 October 1909, pp. 277–78:

> Again we sat up till late. Among the many memorable things Churchill said was this: Talking of Dhingra, he said that there had been much discussion in the Cabinet about him. Lloyd George had expressed to him his highest admiration of Dhingra's attitude as a patriot, in which he (Churchill) shared. He will be remembered 2,000 years hence, as we remember Regulus and Caractacus and Plutarch's heroes, and Churchill quoted with admiration Dhingra's last words as the finest ever made in the name of patriotism. All the same, he says that he was strongly in favour of the law taking its course, even to the extent of refusing to give back the body of the hanged man to his friends for their funeral rites. He quite agreed that it would have been an additional torture to have commuted the sentence.

Blunt reproduced as an Appendix to his Volume, the statement of Dhingra as reported in the *Daily News* of 18 August 1909. Cf., Ibid, Appendix III, pp. 443–44.

[6] *Savarkar Samagra,* Volume I, p. 596. Savarkar was much enamoured of the sensational effects of assassinations. In *Inside the Enemy Camp,* he again emphasized that the speeches of Dadabhai Naoroji had drawn no reaction from the British, but 'the whole country was

Last week, Dhingra was handed over to the Session [Court]. That evening, all over London, the topic of discussion was Dhingra's reply. In that vast city, on every shop the name of Dhingra was visible. Dhingra's reply was *adbhut*/astonishing/wonderful. He says, my countrymen will in any case avenge my death. I am a patriot, Dhingra says about himself. Dhingra is dying for the rebirth of Hindusthan. These words printed in large type in one line in all newspapers and handbills and posters were hanging all over England. What the killing could not accomplish this courageous reply of his in court did. I will give news when the case proceeds. Dhingra will be hanged in any case. He wants that because day before yesterday at the end of his reply he said, 'I made the statement not because I wished to plead for mercy or anything of that kind. I wish that the English people should sentence me to death for in that case the vengeance of my countrymen will be all the keener. I put forward this statement to show the justice of my cause to the outside world, specially to our sympathisers in America and Germany.'[7]

It was widely believed that Savarkar had written the statement. The police had discovered it in a pocket of Dhingra and seized it. Dhingra was locked up in prison. Savarkar applied for permission to meet him and did so. Dhingra was not allowed to read the statement in court. But copies of it started circulating. One theory was that it had been smuggled out of prison by someone who had met Dhingra. The other theory was that a copy of it had been at India House where it was written and had been used to make and distribute copies.[8]

---

shattered' by the shots of the Chaphekar brothers in distant Poona: Cf., Veer Savarkar, *Inside the Enemy Camp*, www.savarkar.org, Mumbai, 1993, pp. 33–34.

[7] *Savarkar Samagra*, Volume I, pp. 598–99.

[8] In *The Life of Barrister Savarkar*, Savarkar or his alter ego wrote, 'The publishing of the "Challenge" [Dhingra's statement] was a mystery which the London Police could scarcely solve. It was thickly rumoured that the writer of that challenge was Savarkar and when

Now, having read what Dhingra said, or what Savarkar had him say, please go back and read what Savarkar wrote in his petitions.

What Did Bhagat Singh Ask For?

Consider next, the petition that Bhagat Singh wrote. It should be particularly instructive as accounts by some of Savarkar's devotees suggest that he also had been inspired by Savarkar's example.

A superintendent of police, James Scott was said to have ordered the lathicharge in which Lala Lajpat Rai received head injuries. That great leader died two and a half weeks later. Bhagat Singh and Shivaram Rajguru set out to avenge the death. They mistook a probationer, John Saunders, to be Scott, and killed him. They ran. A head constable chased them. Chandrashekhar Azad killed the head constable. A few months later, Bhagat Singh and an associate, Batukeshwar Dutt, threw bombs into the Central Legislative Assembly. This time, they did not try to escape. The trial stirred the country, especially Punjab. In jail, Bhagat Singh and Jatin Das went on a hunger strike demanding better conditions for prisoners. Das died.

Bhagat Singh was hanged. He was twenty-three years old at the time.

He also wrote a petition, to the Governor of Punjab. Do read it. Here is a young man owning what he and his associates have done. And notice what he asks for.

---

the original that was found on Dhingra's person was suppressed, the Abhinav Bharat got that copy of it which they had in their possession published only to humiliate and frustrate the Scotland Yard machinations. This rumour along with the fact that Mr. Savarkar had boldly sought for and obtained an interview with Mr. Dhingra, lay him open to serious charges against him of being a party to that dreadful affair . . .': Chitragupta, *Life of Barrister Savarkar,* Veer Savarkar Prakashan, Bombay, 2nd edition, 1987, p. 68. Savarkar continued to laud this statement over the years. See for instance, the third lecture he gave at the winding-up functions of Abhinav Bharat during which he read out the statement: *Savarkar Samagra,* Volume 8, pp. 686–88

He says that he and his associates have been held guilty of waging war against the King. Going by the judgment, we are prisoners of war, he tells the Governor. Well,

. . .The war shall continue.

It may assume different shapes at different times. It may become now open, now hidden, now purely agitational, now fierce life and death struggle.

The choice of the course, whether bloody or comparatively peaceful, which it should adopt rests with you. Choose whichever you like. But that war shall be incessantly waged without taking into consideration the petty (illegible) and the meaningless ethical ideologies.

It shall be waged ever with new vigour, greater audacity and unflinching determination till the Socialist Republic is established and the present social order is completely replaced by a new social order, based on social prosperity and thus every sort of exploitation is put to an end and humanity is ushered into the era of genuine and permanent peace.

In the very near future the final battle shall be fought and final settlement arrived at.

The days of capitalist and imperialist exploitation are numbered. The war neither began with us nor is it going to end with our lives. It is the inevitable consequence of the historic events and the existing environments.

Our humble sacrifices shall be only a link in the chain that has very accurately been beautified by the unparalleled sacrifice of [Jatin] Das and most tragic but noblest sacrifice of Comrade Bhagawati Charan and the glorious death of our dear warrior [Chandrashekhar] Azad.

As to the question of our fates, please allow us to say that when you have decided to put us to death, you will certainly do it.

You have got the power in your hands and power is the greatest justification in this world.

We know that the maxim 'Might is right' serves as your guiding motto. The whole of our trial was just a proof of that.

We wanted to point out that according to the verdict of your court we had waged war and were therefore war prisoners. And we claim to be treated as such, i.e. we claim to be shot dead instead of to be hanged.

It rests with you to prove that you really meant what your court has said.

We request and hope that you will very kindly order the military department to send its detachment to perform our execution.

Yours,

Bhagat Singh[9]

He is to be executed on 23 March 1931. On the day before his execution, he writes a letter to his comrades. It is the last letter he writes:

Comrades!

It is natural that the desire to live should be in me as well, I don't want to hide it. But I can stay alive on one condition that I don't wish to live in imprisonment or with any binding.

My name has become a symbol of Hindustani revolution, and the ideals and sacrifices of the revolutionary party have lifted me very high—so high that I can certainly not be higher in the condition of being alive.

Today my weaknesses are not visible to the people. If I escape the noose, they will become evident and the symbol of revolution will be tarnished, or possibly be obliterated. But to go to the gallows with courage will make Hindustani mothers aspire to have children who

---

[9] Translated by the Shaheed Bhagat Singh Research Committee, *shahidbhagatsingh.org*

are like Bhagat Singh and the number of those who will sacrifice their lives for the country will go up so much that it will not be possible for imperialistic powers or all the demoniac powers to contain the revolution.

And yes, one thought occurs to me even today—that I have not been able to fulfil even one thousandth part of the aspirations that were in my heart to do something for my country and humanity. If I could have stayed alive and free, then I may have got the opportunity to accomplish those and I would have fulfilled my desires. Apart from this, no temptation to escape the noose has ever come to me. Who can be more fortunate than me? These days, I feel very proud of myself. Now I await the final test with great eagerness. I pray that it should draw closer.

Your comrade
Bhagat Singh[10]

Again, having read Bhagat Singh's petition and letter, please go back and read what Savarkar wrote in his petitions. Of course, there will be explanations. There always are. Savarkar's own writings are full of them. Dhingra and Bhagat Singh knew that they were going to be hanged, it will be said, so they could write anything. Savarkar's plan was to live to fight another day. And yet, the contrast is too vivid to be explained away.

Life in Andamans

Without a shred of doubt, incarceration in the Cellular Jail in Andamans was an ordeal of the worst kind. The dungeon-like cells. The solitary confinement. The anaemic food. The cruel warders and jailor, and the extreme maltreatment by them. The beatings. The all-too-frequent caning.

---

[10] The original letter is in Urdu. *The Bhagat Singh Reader*, Chaman Lal (Ed.), Harper India, NOIDA, 2019, Item 48.

The daily abuse and humiliation. The punishments: the already scanty ration cut to starvation level; being placed in chains and handcuffs for six months at a time; being made to stand for two weeks at a time with iron fetters on one's legs and around one's feet; being locked in a cage. Like others, Savarkar was subjected to them—solitary confinement, to stand for a week with handcuffs; chain-fetters; crossbar fetters . . . 'work', diabolically designed to break the prisoner—pounding coir, extracting oil as the bullock does by pushing the shaft round and round the 'oil mill' to the point one fainted yoked to the 'mill' . . . Many died of exhaustion, from hunger and malnutrition, from overwork, from chronic dysentery, tuberculosis, asthma, phthisis, malaria and unbearable pain. Some went mad. Chakraborty was to recall that on the average three inmates committed suicide every month. About 400 of the prisoners were hanged or shot. Worse than even these, was the daily abuse, the sheer helplessness to which one was driven. And there was no appeal—the perpetrators were the judges. Savarkar's health broke down. He spent almost a year and a half in the jail's hospital. Even as he was dissuading others from committing suicide, at one point, he says, he himself thought of killing himself. That someone should do everything that he could to get out of the place is perfectly understandable.

Why then have the petitions attracted so much censure and derision?

Reasons That Have Ignited Censure

The first, of course, is the contrast with what Bhagat Singh and others said as they faced execution. Recall Ram Prasad Bismil mounting the gallows with Bismil Azimabadi's *Sarfaroshi ki tammana ab hamaare dil mein hai* [11] on his lips.

The second is the halo that has been stuck around Savarkar. When people read the petitions, they naturally wonder whether a 'Veer' would plead in this way.

---

[11] The longing to sacrifice our heads now rages in our hearts.

Third, Savarkar himself did not seem to have been comfortable with the fact that he had submitted the petitions. He certainly did not own up to them. In the letters that he wrote to his family, and in his copious *My Transportation for Life*, he does mention the sort of grounds on which he has asked the Government to reduce his sentence, to transfer him back to a jail on the mainland, to give him a chance to work in constitutional ways. But in those accounts, it is as if an equal is talking to equals, almost as if a Barrister is arguing in court. There is none of the beseeching that we have encountered above. No hint that he has offered to be of service to the Government in whatever capacity they deem fit. No hint of the conditions he has told the Government he is ready to accept.

Next, there is the reaction of his own associates and admirers when they heard that he had accepted conditions for being released. We get a glimpse of it in a report that the Home Secretary of the Bombay Government writes to the Home Secretary in Delhi about happenings in the province. During this survey, he touches on Savarkar and his circle:

Secretary (Home) Bombay Government on Vallabhbhai's Activities in connection with Borsad Satyagraha

Home (Political) 19 January 1924

My dear Crerar,
I am desired to submit my report for the fortnight ending the 15th January 1924. . . .

. . . The news of the remission of the unexpired portion of the sentence of transportation for life passed upon Vinayak Damodar Savarkar and of his release was received very quietly, any tendency to make political capital out of it having been forestalled by the conditions which he agreed to and even more by his full acknowledgment of the justice of his trial and sentence. This acknowledgement has roused some anger in extremist circles and has been described by some of the papers as a 'shocking admission'. It is reported that Kelkar and some of his other friends in Poona, whom he visited on release, intend trying to get the conditions imposed upon him removed after he has had complete rest for six months.[12]

And the conditions that embarrassed them were nothing compared to what he had pledged to accept, and the language in which he had pledged to accept them in his earlier petitions.

The Image He Had Created of Himself

Then there is the image of an uncompromising, fiery, ready-for-death image that Savarkar himself had built of himself. His autobiography, his newsletters from England, his *My Transportation for Life,* his *Samagra,* the pseudonymous *Life of Barrister Savarkar* are all full of passages that lead one to think of him as one prepared to run any risk, to face any hardship, to stare death in its face, to die. A little volume can be filled with those passages.

Savarkar and his friends have set up the *Mitra Mandal,* a fledgling group that it will be said gave birth to revolutionaries and revolutionary organizations. Savarkar and his friends think much of their secret meetings. They feel that they are sowing the seeds of mass upheaval. And, therefore, are under the constant watch of the Government and its agents. Queen Victoria has died. Some of Savarkar's friends, he says, urge that they hold a memorial meeting and pass a condolence resolution so as to allay suspicion about them and their activities. Savarkar as good as scolds them:

---

[12] *The Collected Works of Sardar Patel,* P.N. Chopra (Chief Editor), Volume I, 1918–1925, Item 48, Konark Publishers, Delhi, 1990, p. 222. The report figures in the volume as it dealt in part with the Sardar's role in the Borsad satyagraha. J. Crerar was Secretary, Home, Government of India.

Our country alone is our Emperor. We do not know any other Emperor. This is a golden opportunity to show that there is at least one institution that will proclaim this radiant truth. We should not become afraid ourselves and lose this opportunity. If this organisation is closed down for this reason, we will have to take its life to have been successful. Whenever it wants, the British Government jails even those who write with great circumspection. Then, why should we not speak the truth? Let us unfurl that resplendent emblem of independence openly. Even if we are able to do so for a moment and in the next moment we are killed by a bullet, no reason to worry. Because the cremation pyre of persons who die thus sends out sparks, and the palaces of foreign rulers are reduced to ashes in the fire that these sparks light. Those who say that those who make such attempts are hanged, well let them say what they will. We also know that much. The hanging of Chapekar gave birth to us, our hanging will give birth to others, and this lineage shall remain intact. Having lived many years, lakhs of oldies are striving to work for the welfare of the country. The task for us now is to show how consequential is the death of those who embrace untimely death. If dying by being hanged on the gallows is untimely, what is dying from plague, epidemic and famine? Life or freedom? We have already asked this question of ourselves. We have taken a step only after taking the vow, 'Whether my life goes or not, freedom must be won . . .'

'My speech along these lines had but to finish that everyone was filled with enthusiasm,' Savarkar wrote . . .[13]

In another typical piece, we have him proclaim once again that there is no way to attain independence other than armed revolution. We have to break the weapons and power of the enemy by better weapons and greater power, he says. In no case in history, has independence been won except

---

[13] Autobiography, *op. cit.*, pp. 243–44.

by triumphing in a violent, armed fight. If people are not up to this, he says, then they cannot have freedom. This is as unalterable a law as laws of nature. We have to proceed by the teachings of Guru Ramdas: 'Even while dying, kill the enemy,' 'Kill, go on killing and acquire your kingdom.' We were not for violence out of fondness, but because there was no other way. We realized that even saying that this is our way was liable to invite the wrath of the rulers. To act on it was . . . We were children. Chapekar and Ranade had been hanged before our eyes. They were thrashed before being put on the gallows. We had seen the oppression that had been unleashed on the whole of Maharashtra, how everyone was trembling with fear just because of those two–three bullets. We had seen all this with our own eyes. If tomorrow we converted the whole country into a revolutionary war, we would see convulsions a lakh times greater and of many kinds. Then the sacrifice of lives, the rain of bullets, general slaughter will be the play every day. Lakhs of mothers will lose their sons, lakhs of children will be orphaned, bangles will be broken in home after home, cities after cities will become deserted, and before all that comes to pass, only our ashes and those of our families will remain. 'This we, at least I knew,' Savarkar says.[14]

It is from such passages—and even the ones of which the preceding are a summary, much longer and more colourful—that his image of a revolutionary was embossed on people's minds. Naturally, when the contents of the petitions burst into view, many were nonplussed.

Those Appropriating Him

None more so than those who are appropriating him. So much so that they have put forth the strangest and all together farcical alibi. They say that Savarkar had written the mercy petitions at the urging of none other than Gandhiji—that he wrote the petitions 'Gandhiji ke kehney par' !

---

[14] *Savarkar Samagra*, Volume I, pp. 298–99.

Those advancing the alibi must have been hard-pressed by embarrassment for no one can imagine that even they could have been so innocent of facts.

'Unthinkable, Absurd Beyond Description, Laughable'

After all, Savarkar submitted his first petition in 1911. At the time, Gandhiji was in South Africa. There was no way a person leading agitations against the rulers there could have been even in touch with a high-security prisoner in the Cellular Jail of Andamans. Prisoners were allowed to write one letter a year to their families. All letters went through the jail authorities. The petition was submitted within two months of Savarkar entering the jail. He wouldn't have been allowed to write the letter. Gandhiji would not have written on his own—he was no knight-errant for such causes. As we shall see, after his discussions with Indian youth in England he had come to the view that the course they were championing would spell disaster for India—that if their strategy of murder were to succeed, it would hand the country over to murderers. In any case, during those years, Gandhiji was involved in agitations against the South African government, agitations that led to not just him but even Kasturba being arrested. He returned to India in 1915. By this time, Savarkar had already filed three mercy petitions— including the 1913 one in which he pledged to 'serve the Government in any capacity they like, for as my conversion is conscientious, so I hope my future conduct would be,' in which he asked, 'The Mighty alone can afford to be merciful and therefore where else can the prodigal son return but to the parental doors of the Government.' And he had written his 1914 petition to be released and enlisted to fight in the war on behalf of the British. Soon, after his arrival, Gandhiji was involved in directing the Champaran Satyagraha against the Government—in 1917. In 1918, the Satyagraha at Kheda had begun. In 1919, he was fighting the government through the anti-Rowlatt Act agitation. As part of each of these agitations, people following him were filling jails. Is it at all possible that in such circumstances, he was going to ask Savarkar to plead for mercy?

The historian, biographer of, among others, Gandhiji, and his grandson, Rajmohan Gandhi was asked about the assertion that Savarkar had written his mercy petition *'Gandhiji ke kehney par'*. He called the assertion 'ridiculous, unthinkable, absurd beyond description, laughable.' Yes, Gandhiji did write to Savarkar's younger brother in 1920 saying that Savarkar should send a brief petition setting out the facts of the case and pointing out that his offence was purely political. This was in response to a letter from Narayan Savarkar asking Gandhiji for advice as to what Savarkar and his brother, Ganesh, should do to secure release. And Gandhiji wrote this letter in January 1920—Savarkar had begun filing his petitions nine years earlier.[15]

Rajmohan made another telling point. The Jallianwala massacre had taken place in April 1919. The massacre had been compounded by the notorious 'crawling order' by which all Indians were required to crawl in a lane in which an elderly British missionary lady was assaulted by some Indians. This order, Rajmohan pointed out, had shaken Gandhiji to the core. India had been humiliated, he felt. From September that year, he was touring district after district of Punjab—exhorting people to shed fear, to stand up for their honour and rights, to contribute funds for a memorial to those who had been shot dead. In such a situation, could Gandhiji have advised Savarkar to go down on his knees before the British?[16] Gandhiji did write an article some months later arguing the case for releasing the Savarkar brothers. Their case fell within the Royal Proclamation of December 1919, he argued. And they had pledged that they no longer believed in violence and that they were *not* for India becoming independent:

---

[15] Narayan Savarkar's letter to Gandhiji and the latter's reply are available in *Collected Works of Mahatma Gandhi,* Volume 19, p. 348.

[16] Rajmohan Gandhi's interview with Karan Thapar can be accessed at https://www.youtube.com/watch?v=f03ZCN5ba58. See also, G.N. Devy, 'Gandhi, Savarkar, history', *Indian Express,* 18 October 2021.

Both these brothers have declared their political opinions and both have stated that they do not entertain any revolutionary ideas and that if they were set free they would like to work under the Reforms Act, for they consider that the Reforms enable one to work thereunder so as to achieve political responsibility for India. *They both state unequivocally that they do not desire independence from the British connection. On the contrary, they feel that India's destiny can be best worked out in association with the British.*[17]

How desperate the appropriators must be to snatch Savarkar as one of their own, how embarrassed they must be at the petitions, how bereft of even elementary facts they must be to make out that Savarkar filed them at the asking of Gandhiji—*'Gandhiji ke kehney par.'*

A Precedent Citing Which is Disingenuous

It is said that in writing the mercy petitions, in agreeing to conditions for his release, Savarkar was acting to a plan. Without mentioning the petitions or conditions, through historical allusions, Savarkar himself often implied as much. We have already come across the dictum of Guru Ramdas—that one should not just sacrifice oneself, one should kill the enemy even as one is dying, and, having killed all, establish one's kingdom. Savarkar recalled this dictum time and again—often contrasting it with Gandhiji's *jail bharo* programmes. Our strategy must be not to land ourselves in jail but to throw the enemy into jails, he would say. While lauding the techniques of warfare that the Marathas devised, he tells us in *Hindu Pad-padshahi*, 'Sacrifice was adorable only when it was, directly or remotely, but reasonably, felt to be indispensable for success. Sacrifice that leads not to ultimate success

---

[17] Gandhiji's article appeared in *Young India* of 26 May 1920. It is available in *Collected Works of Mahatma Gandhi*, Volume 20, pp. 368–71. The lines quoted are at p. 370.

is suicidal and had no place in the tactics of Maratha warfare.'[18] It was for that very reason, he says in *My Transportation for Life,* that when the general amnesty was declared and prisoners were to be released provided they signed a pledge, he urged fellow-prisoners to sign the pledge, accept the conditions that the government was prescribing and somehow get out of the jail in Andamans so that they may return to the mainland and work for the Motherland once again.[19] His attitude about himself was the same, it would seem from his conversations with Murray who had succeeded Barrie as Superintendent of the Jail in Andamans and was later posted as Inspector at the Yervada Jail in Poona. Murray would ask Savarkar what he proposed to do if he were released. Savarkar would say that he would plunge into politics. When asked, 'What kind of politics?' Savarkar's

---

[18] *Hindu Pad-padshahi, Or a Review of the Hindu Empire of Maharashtra,* B.G. Paul & Co, Madras, 1925, p. 257.

[19] Recalling the instance, Savarkar wrote,

> All these discharged prisoners had to sign a pledge that they would abstain from politics and revolutionary activity for a certain number of years. And, if again they were tried and found guilty of treason, they would come back to the Andamans to serve the remainder of their life-sentence.
>
> Since the receipt of the wire to which I have already referred on a previous page, a hot discussion went on among us whether we should at all sign such a pledge for procuring our release. My advice to my friends was that there was nothing wrong in it as it referred to a future contingency and was in the best national interest. I quoted to them instances from the life of Shivaji. Of his dealing with Jai Singh and Afzal Khan; I told them of Guru Govind and his flight after the incident of Chamkore; nay I drew upon the life of Lord Krishna himself, in order to convince them of the correctness of the step they were taking. The most obstinately proud among them would not be persuaded even by these parallels from the past. This stubbornness of theirs on the subject, after all that they had suffered for the cause, inspired me with great hope for the future of my country. But at last I could convince them of my point of view, and they all signed the pledge without demur, and thus broke open the lock of the jail in the Andaman. [*My Transportation for Life,* op. cit., pp. 451–53.]

reply would be that it would depend on the circumstances in which he was released:

> If the reforms were to bear good fruit and naturally led to the further enlargement of powers granted to the people, I would be for responsive cooperation and work out my goal through the path of peace and constructive constitutional work. If a ban were put on me not to participate in politics for a few years, I would spend the years in other fields of work open to me. I told Major Murray that it was my duty as a follower of responsive cooperation, to accept such conditions as would enable me to do better and larger work for my country than I was able to do during the years of imprisonment. I would be free thus to serve my mother country, and I would regard it as a social duty.[20]

Too Lofty a Precedent to Invoke

The example that he invoked most often was that of Shivaji. When Shivaji had to get his father released; when he apprehended that the areas which he had captured from Adilshahi were going to be made back to that ruler as a result of a treaty between him and the Mughals; when he wanted to delay a confrontation; when he wanted to get control over some land which was in the hands of the Mughals; when he was held in Agra—in all such circumstances, Shivaji wrote placatory letters to the local governor, to Aurangzeb, etc. He sent emissaries to convey his promises in person. He begged to be pardoned for his transgressions, for having broken his earlier promises. He promised loyalty and devotion. He promised to help the Mughal rulers in their campaigns. He almost sought a rank—a subordinate rank—in the hierarchy of Mughal subordinates.

---

[20] *My Transportation for Life,* op. cit., p. 534.

Jadunath Sarkar published one of these letters in May 1927. Savarkar flew into a rage. His article on the matter is truly worth reading. It is as if someone has published one of his mercy petitions. If you just substitute 'Savarkar' for 'Shivaji', the outburst seems to be about persons who are asking how a revolutionary like him pleaded for clemency.

Shivaji wrote the letter in question after he had disposed of Shaista Khan, Savarkar said. 'But those who could not see the future deeds of Shivaji or whose base and ungrateful minds did not remember the valorous deeds that this lion-of-a-man had done in the past, his unequalled courage, his splendorous vigour, such persons began speaking against Shivaji', Savarkar wrote. 'Those who could not dare to even look at Afzal Khan, whose knees had rubbed off from kneeling before the Mussalmaans, those who, out of fright of Mussalmaans, could not even close their nostrils while passing butchers on the way from Bijapur to Delhi, such cowards, enemies of the country and the servants of maidservants, turning up their noses said, "*Chhi*, he has got frightened. Instead of writing this letter, it would have been better if Shivaji had died" . . .'

'Fools . . .', Savarkar fumed. 'Shivaji wrote this letter after putting Shaista to flight, after tormenting all the five rulers, so that, at an appropriate time later, these five rulers and the power of the Mughals in the south could be thrown into the dust.' 'If you too had humbled Shaista, if you too had confronted each of these five Muslim powers, and even then, had not written such a letter, may be then someone would support your childish prattle', Savarkar said. 'On the one hand you say that it would have been better if Shivaji had died, and, on the other, you are not prepared to shed even one drop of blood for your country. Not just that, you have seen your bravery in rendering life-long service to the enemies of the country. You do not have the guts to take part in the *dharmayuddha,* and if someone else wants to attack the country's enemy, you, on merely hearing the roar of that enemy shake in fright, you bolt the doors of your houses, wear bangles and go and sit next to the *choolah*.[21] Such is your condition and you laugh at the cowardice of Shivaji, you laugh at your peril. History will definitely say that it cares not a bit for the laughter of lakhs of such people, nor for whether they live or die.' Summoned to his court by Aurangzeb, Shivaji swallowed the insult of being made to stand in one of the rows meant for lower subordinates of the empire. He made his way humbly to the house to which he was directed. There he tried to ingratiate himself with the guards, distributing baskets of sweets. And one day, as they lay in a stupor from the opium-drenched sweets, he escaped by squeezing himself in one of the very same baskets. 'If any guard had checked the basket, he would have been caught, and Aurangzeb would have exclaimed, "Without a doubt, he is a mountain rat. See, how he is hiding himself, sitting as a rat."' 'But at that time,' Savarkar said, drawing the moral he wants to stress, 'being like a rat was valour, at that time to roar like a lion would have been the height of foolishness . . .'

That is the moral: 'If the goal is pure, then whatever is shown—bravery or softness, fighting or seeking refuge—both are pure. For attaining a pure objective, the use of whatever means are necessary is pure.'

Savarkar concludes in the first person:

If through the resurgence of Hindu religion, it is just to attain *swarajya*, if it is dharma, if it is the benediction of godly wealth, then I will even place my hand in the mouth of the lion and count his teeth. But if the valour is going to harm the cause, I will with equal gravity even play a flute to bewitch the frightening cobra. For the fulfilment of that objective, for the God-given task, for the welfare of the people, I will become the *Vaamanmurti* [22] that looks feeble to 'Bali', I will

[21] Hearth.

[22] Idol of the dwarf-incarnation of Vishnu.

never do the foolishness of going through the great gate of city of Jaraasandh beating the triumphal drum. I will disappear in front of the *Kaalayvan,* I will hide in the cave of Muchukund, I will become a cook like Bhim, but when the moment comes, I will suddenly somersault, and with the anger with which Sri Rama pounced on Ravana, with that very anger I will pounce on the enemy. I will take a grave form like Narasimha. With no thought of victory, I will like Abhimanyu enter the *vyhu,*[23] even if I am killed thereafter.

The core of the glorious statecraft of Shivaji, Savarkar wrote, was that cowardice, rather the show of cowardice is merely a stratagem. Valour is the most appropriate deed. Like the ocean, it is what leads to victory and defeat. 'It is by following this rule that Shivaji was able to establish swarajya,' Savarkar concluded. 'It is by following this very rule that Shivaji became Shivaji.'[24]

It really is as if someone had chanced upon Savarkar's mercy petitions and murmured something against him for having submitted them.

A Crucial Difference

The angry prose glosses over a crucial difference. In a sense that is embedded in Savarkar's fusillade. 'But those who could not see *the future deeds of Shivaji . . .*,' Savarkar wrote. Indeed, the difference is in what Shivaji used to do the moment the peril had passed, and what those who like Savarkar invoke his example did after their petitions had been accepted by that 'beneficent Government'. The moment Shivaji was out of the clutches, he would resume his struggle to establish an independent kingdom, a

---

[23] Formation.

[24] '*Shivaji Maharaj ki yashasvi rajniti kaa ek sutra,*' May 1927, in *Savarkar Samagra,* Volume VI, pp. 466–73.

kingdom at the expense of the Mughal empire. These feints and somersaults drove even the ordinarily unflappable Aurangzeb up the wall.[25]

---

[25] Shivaji promises to live up to his pledges. Aurangzeb sees advantage in being conciliatory. The moment the corner is turned, Shivaji is again raiding Mughal territories. Aurangzeb to his lieutenants: 'Evict those persons who have raised the dust of revolt in the Ahmednagar area without any loss of time and proceed speedily to Junnar. Invade that ill-fated person's [i.e. Shivaji's] territory, and do not hesitate in plundering, slaughtering and taking captives. Observing this situation, he will be so worried about his own territory that he will become unable to implement his aforementioned plans.' Shivaji reaches out to the local commander and is again humility personified. The commander delays the assault. Shivaji gains another swath. Aurangzeb to his commander: 'It is necessary that the accursed Shivaji should be punished for his audacity and insolence. As such, execute the orders we have time and again issued to you. In conjunction with Rao Karna, Hoshdar, Abdul Munim and Khan Jahan's detachment, invade, plunder and lay waste, without any fear or apprehension, the territory belonging to that ill-fated one [i.e. Shivaji], and plunder and do everything in your power. Invade and despoil his territory as far as your hand can reach. If he steps forward for a conflict, deflate his ego with your sword and punish him suitably.' Shivaji bends. The wheel turns again. Aurangzeb to his commander: 'That ill-fated one must be completely uprooted, and having rebelled thus, he cannot entertain even the thought of receiving any assurance or pledge of peace and goodwill from us.' But he wants the door to negotiations kept open. Only to repent: he is driven to direct his generals to root out this 'son of a . . .' You will find fulsome accounts of these twists and turns in Sir Jadunath Sarkar, *Shivaji and His Times*, S.C. Sarkar and Sons, Calcutta, 1929, and the expression to which Aurangzeb was driven—for instance p. 54; and in Sir Jadunath Sarkar, *House of Shivaji*, Studies and Documents on Maratha History: Royal Period, 3rd Edition, M.C. Sarkar and Sons, Calcutta, 1955. In greater detail in the more recent Gajanan Bhaskar Mehendale, *Shivaji: His Life and Times*, 1st Edition ISBN No.: 978-0-9891538-0-5. We get a glimpse of the exasperation to which Shivaji drove Mughals and other Muslim rulers from a passage from *Tarikh-i-Ali [Adilshah]* that Mehendale quotes to describe one of several instances:

When the late King [Muhammad Adilshah] fell ill, the banished infidel Shivaji Bhosale, who was the virtual mentor of malevolent Satan in trickery and deceitfulness, plundered the entire province of Konkan and captured the fort of Rahir [Rayri]. When the King died, that malicious infidel [Shivaji] regarded that news as more joyous than the tidings of one's victory and captured [some more] forts in that province [Konkan]. He was extending the hand of repression and injustice like a greedy and hungry dog, that does not feel satisfied with the bone it gets and wants more, and was oppressing the faithful [Muslims] who were engrossed in prayers to God.

That is the crucial difference. The moment he got out of the corner, Shivaji resumed his struggle. Savarkar, on the other hand, did what he had pledged to do—that is, to be of use to the British. He formulated the two-nation theory—which was ever so convenient for the British. He denounced the Congress at every turn—which was ever so convenient for the British. He hurled pejoratives at Gandhiji—which was ever so convenient for the British. He poured scorn at the 'Quit India' movement—which was ever so convenient for the British. As we shall see in subsequent chapters, he supported the British in their war effort—which was ever so convenient for the British.[26]

Before one invokes Shivaji as an alibi one should be at least a 25-paise Shivaji.

Another Test

Savarkar himself had provided another good test. While recalling how he argued his friends out of holding that memorial meeting for Queen Victoria, on his account he told them,

> When to mislead an enemy we take some delusory form, we must examine whether the enemy is getting deluded or we ourselves are getting deluded. If there are greater chances of the enemy getting deluded, then only would it be right to sing the song of loyalty to the rulers, to make a show of fear and trembling before the attack on Afzal Khan . . .[27]

The British were not fooled. They released Savarkar when they knew that he would strive to be useful to them. And he did strive.

Then there is the other point.

------

[26] Cf., chapters 6 to 10 below.

[27] *Autobiography*, op. cit., p. 242.

Another Word That is Used Loosely

'Bhagwan', 'God-man', 'Saint', 'Jagadguru', 'Sri Sri . . . 108', even 'Paramhans'—we anoint so many persons with such words. 'Revolutionary' is another word in the same category. If we go along with his acquittal in the Gandhi-assassination case, the one 'revolutionary' act that Savarkar did in his entire life was that he once organized the smuggling of twenty pistols into India, and one of these was used to kill Jackson. Yes, he talked 'revolution', he wrote articles advocating violence. Should one be deemed to be a 'revolutionary' just because one believes and writes essays asserting that an objective—in the present case, the independence of our country—can be achieved only through violence? And in the next breath concludes that large scale violence is not possible, that, therefore, the only way is assassination? And then is careful not to undertake any such task oneself, and just exhorts others to carry out the assassinations?

Two other traits mark some of our 'revolutionaries'. They always know what is going to happen. Savarkar is in the Cellular Jail. He hears that war has broken out in Europe. His reaction is that it is the war he had prophesied years ago. Years pass. A contingent of Sikh prisoners are brought to the Jail. Savarkar's reaction is, 'they have come here at last as I had predicted.'[28]

Often, they know that what they are planning is not going to happen, yet they go on planning as if it will. Savarkar plans to squeeze the British out of India with a pincer: an attack by German and Italian forces from the west, and an attack by Japanese and INA from the east. As these twin attacks take place, the legions he has inspired will commence a revolt within the country. Nothing comes of these plans. Traversing the landmass from Europe to India in the 1940s is no easier than it was during the First

---

[28] *My Transportation for Life,* op. cit., p. 321 and p. 351.

World War. Savarkar says that this was known to the revolutionaries. They planned nonetheless. In any case, they did not lose heart.[29]

An allied feature is that the revolutionaries draw up elaborate plans but, at the last moment, something happens, and the plans cannot be put into effect. In his sympathetic account of the revolutionaries and their plans, R.C. Majumdar writes of an episode that did not take place. The revolutionaries set up centres in the US and Germany, he writes. Germany promises to supply arms through their embassy in the US. The revolutionaries set up centres in Japan, China, Philippines, Siam, Java, and other places also. 'It was decided that the Germans in Siam, along with the Indians there, will attack Burma through Moulmein, and the Germans in China will be divided into two groups, one joining the party in Siam and the other attacking Burma through Bhamo with the exiled King of Burma as their head . . . It was also planned that three ships, full of arms, would be sent to India. One with 500 German officers and 100 soldiers to proceed to Andamans, release the political prisoners, and then go to Calcutta. The second will go to some other place in Bengal, and the third will go to the western coast. As soon as Burma is attacked, there will be revolutionary outbreaks in the Punjab and Bengal and an attempt will be made to invade India through Afghanistan and Baluchistan . . .' As these invasions burst forth, there will be simultaneous uprisings all over India, led by Indian troops.

What happened? 'Unfortunately, the German arms did not reach India and the date for the general rising all over India was communicated to the Government by a police informer, Kripal Singh, who had managed to enrol himself as a member of the conspiracy . . .' The only result was that a large number of persons were arrested. Several of them ended up

---

[29] Cf., R.C. Majumdar, *Penal Settlement in the Andamans,* Gazeteers Unit, Department of Culture, Ministry of Education and Social Welfare, 1975, pp. 235–36; and Savarkar's third lecture at the functions winding up Abhinav Bharat, *Savarkar Samagra,* Volume VIII, 701–02, 707–11, and, in particular, pp. 711–12.

in the Andamans—the number of prisoners in the Cellular Jail rose to about 150.[30]

Playing 'Revolution, Revolution'

Their zeal must have been burning hot. Their idealism was of the highest order. But the plans they made seem at times to be the plans of *sheikhchillies*. It is almost as if they were not carrying out a revolution, they were playing at a revolution. There is a telling figure that Savarkar himself gives which illustrates this. He writes about 'the war-strategy' that he and his friends in Abhinav Bharat devised for the coming two years: raids, an armed revolution, the works. For this, they would carry out revolutionary propaganda in the police and the army, they would launch secret enrolment of revolutionaries, they would establish contacts with Russia and other countries, they would unleash frequent raids on centres of British power, they would store weapons in countries bordering Bharat, they would wait for the opportunity to enter the country, they would conduct big and small revolts in the interval, and through these they would impart education to the country about revolution, they would inspire it to drink the *ghutti*[31] of dying, to awaken to the fact of death . . . In these ways, they would make it more and more difficult for the enemy to rule. And when Britain got involved in a war against some powerful enemy and its forces were weakened, they would take full advantage and launch a revolution and wrest freedom. If the attempt runs into difficulties, they would resume the struggle—organize the same kind of revolt, each would go on fighting and killing till he is killed. This was the picture of our policy, Savarkar says.

---

[30] R..C. Majumdar, *Penal Settlement in Andamans,* Gazetteers Unit, Department of Culture, Ministry of Education and Social Welfare, New Delhi, 1975, pp. 235–36. Also, R.C. Majumdar, *History of the Freedom Movement in India,* Volume II, K.L. Mukhopadhyay, Calcutta, 1963, pp. 407–08.

[31] Imbibed from infancy.

Contrary to what is said, they were realists, it would seem. We never believed that we could get the British to run away just by killing five–ten Englishmen, he says. But we were also convinced that the thirty crore people of this country had never joined a war or a struggle and will never do so. Even so, if two lakh persons of an organization devoted to raids and revolution kept fighting without let, irrepressibly, ceaselessly, we will be able to wrest freedom, he writes.

Fine. Two lakh engaged in raids and revolution. How many young men were at hand for the task? Savarkar says that at that time we were *fifty to a hundred boys, we did not have even that many knives,* and we had to fight the great power of England . . . No matter. Similes take over. We were a matchstick, he says, and, falling on a heap of explosives, a matchstick can set off a conflagration . . . We would be the compass that shows the way for a great ship . . . The programme is accordingly pruned. We decided, Savarkar says, that in the first three years we would devote such strength as we had to spread awareness of the goal of political independence and of the need for and of the instruments for an armed revolution, we would bring about a mental revolution in the country . . .[32]

Savarkar says twice that they were fifty to a hundred boys.[33] Fifty to one hundred on his own telling compared to the two lakh that were on his own estimate required. But if you read their 'war-strategy', the whole country would have been on fire.

In actual fact, one has to search hard for revolutionary acts that can be traced back to Savarkar. Majumdar recalls the long deliberations that preceded the decision of the Government to repatriate several of the political prisoners from the Cellular Jail to jails on the mainland. He notes that the repatriations took place from May 1914 to September 1914. But this policy shift had to be given up within two years, he records: 'This was due to the fresh outbreak of revolutionary activities in India during the

---

[32] *Savarkar Samagra,* Volume I, pp. 302–08.

[33] Ibid, p. 303 and p. 308.

First World War. *Compared with these, the previous revolutionary activities in India almost sink into insignificance . . .*' Surely, Savarkar could not have participated in, organized or directed any of the revolutionary activities during the First World War as he was in the Cellular Jail from 1911. The ones he might have participated in or instigated before the war were such, according to a historian who thinks very highly of him, as to 'almost sink into insignificance'.

Nonetheless, he is, according to the same historian, 'one of the greatest revolutionary leaders of India'.[34] And if you do not believe this with all your heart and soul, you are not just wrong, you are a traitor to Hindutva.

---

[34] R.C. Majumdar, *Penal Settlement in Andamans*, op. cit., pp. 235, 241, 242.

A Revolutionary Acts

A Revolutionary Sees the Way

1938: Europe is galloping into an abyss. Hitler enlarges his demands at every turn. He compels Austria to include more Nazis in their government. A month later, in March, German forces annex Austria. The Germans keep enlarging their demands over Sudetenland on the borders of Czechoslovakia. Having assured Czechoslovakia that they would not allow it to be taken over by Hitler, France and others cave in. Mussolini is flexing his own biceps: he gets the British to recognize Italy's hegemony over Ethiopia. Concentration camps begin to be constructed— in Mauthausen in Upper Austria; six months later another one, this one near Hamburg, begins operations. Britain under Chamberlain, and France under Daladier capitulate to Hitler's annexation of Sudetenland and then of Czechoslovakia. Jews begin to be driven out of Germany. Their synagogues, shops and businesses are burnt . . .

B.S. Moonje who has been head of the Hindu Mahasabha for ten years, till 1937, has visited Italy. He has come to admire Mussolini and has become convinced that organizations akin to the ones that Mussolini has set up and through which he controls Italy and Italians have to be built up in India. He urges Hedgewar to mould the RSS along those lines. Savarkar is no less struck by Mussolini.[1]

In the June 1936 issue of *Stree,* he writes an article on three women— the wife of Chiang Kaishek, the wife of the ruler of Abyssinia, and Rachel,

---

[1] In her telling book, *In the Shadow of the Swastika, The relationships between Indian Radical Nationalism, Italian Fascism and Nazism,* Routledge, London, 2020, Marzia Casolari provides arresting accounts of the fascination and connections.

the wife of Mussolini.[2] He lauds Rachel for her utter simplicity—she continues to stay in a small township away from Rome, she goes every morning to fetch vegetables, she never attends official functions as the First Lady, she devotes herself entirely to the care of the family, etc.[3] The article takes eleven printed pages of the *Savarkar Samagra*. In the four pages devoted to Mussolini's wife, Savarkar uses the following words to preface mention of Mussolini himself:

- *Digvijayi*, thrice in less than two pages: the world-conqueror
- *Rajyadhurandar:* master of the Kingdom
- *Diggaj:* high and majestic—one of the eight elephants that support the earth
- *Mussolini, jinhein sampoorand Europe ko apney anupam saahas se daanton taley dabaaney ke liye baadhya kiyaa thaa*: Mussolini who by his incomparable courage compelled the whole of Europe to get squashed between his teeth
- 'Germany has every right to Nazism, Italy to Fascism'

In 1938, Moonje hands over the reins of the Hindu Mahasabha to Savarkar. Savarkar, according to an account by an admirer, is addressing 'a mammoth gathering at Poona attended by more than twenty thousand'. He speaks on 'India's foreign policy'. He 'strongly deprecated the tendency on the part of some of the Congress leaders to denounce Germany and other powerful Nations in the world on account of the particular political "isms" they contributed to,' the account says. 'Indian foreign policy must not depend on "isms",' he declares. He gives several reasons. First, 'Germany has every right to resort to Nazism and Italy to Fascism,' and second, 'events have testified that those "isms" and forms of governments

---

[2] *Savarkar Samagra*, Volume IV, pp. 514–25.

[3] The editors of Savarkar's writings note within parenthesis that Savarkar's wife, Shrimati Mai Savarkar, was also of the same temperament.

were imperative and beneficial to them under the conditions that obtained there. Bolshevism might have suited Russia and Democracy, as it obtained in Britain, the British. The sound principle of politics lays down that no form of government or political "ism" is absolutely good or bad under all circumstances to all people alike.' Third, 'Who are we to dictate to Germany and Japan or Italy or Russia to choose a particular form of policy of government simply because we woo it out of academical attractions? Surely Hitler knows better than Pandit Nehru does what suits Germany best.' And look at the results: 'The very fact that Germany or Italy has so wonderfully recovered and grown so powerful as never before at the touch of the Nazi or Fascist magical wand is enough to prove that those political "isms" were the most congenial tonics their health demanded. India may choose or reject a particular form of government, in accordance with her political requirements . . .'

Savarkar turns to the annexation of Sudetenland. 'So far as the Czechoslovakia question was concerned the Hindu Sangathanists in India hold that Germany was perfectly justified in uniting the Austrian and Sudeten Germans under the German Flag,' he declares. Now it is democracy that provides the rationale: 'Democracy itself demands that the will of the people must prevail in choosing their own Government. Germany demanded plebiscite, the Germans under the Czechs wanted to join their kith and kin in Germany. It was the Czechs who were acting against the principle of Democracy in holding the Germans under a foreign sway against their will.' 'England's pretension that they sided with the Czechs because Democracy was in danger was thus a mere eye wash, and a stunt,' he says. 'Had the cry raised by England of "Democracy in Danger" been sincere she should have first withdrawn her army of occupation from India and left Indians free to organise themselves into a free and democratic state . . . The fact is that when Germany was weak, they partitioned it piecemeal. Now that Germany is strong, why should she not strike to unite all Germans and consolidate them into a pan-German

State and realise the political dream which generations of German people have cherished?'

'The Hindu sangathanists maintain a neutral attitude with regard to all nations in the world,' he says. The account puts the sentences that follow in capital letters: 'Any nation who helps India or is friendly towards her struggle for freedom is our friend. Any nation which opposes us or pursues a policy enemical [sic.] to us, is our foe. Towards those who do neither, Indian must maintain an attitude of perfect neutrality refusing to poke her nose unnecessarily into their internal or external policy.' And he adds, 'The same rule holds good with our attitude towards England in so far as our free activity is concerned. It is for England to choose.'[4]

The Realist Strategist

Chamberlain signs the Munich Agreement with Hitler on 19 September 1938. Savarkar and others are fortified in, to use words they would have liked, their strategic assessment that England is going to sink further and further into quicksand, that the future lies with Germany, that, therefore, Indians should befriend Germany, and through such an alliance kick the British out of India. And in the East, Japan has invaded China. It will soon be at India's borders. We should ally with it also, and thus deliver a kick to the British from the East also.

On 11 October 1938, soon after the Munich Agreement, Savarkar gives another speech in Poona. Yes, Japan has invaded China, he tells his followers. Indians are blaming Japan. But think for a moment. A hundred years ago, China was powerful. She expanded her empire—it even came

---

[4] *Vinayak Damodar Savarkar's Whirlwind Propaganda Tours: Statements, Messages and Extracts from the President's Diary of His Propagandistic Tours, Interviews from December 1937 to October 1941*, A.S. Bhide [ed.], Bombay, 1941, pp. 50–53. Passages from the speeches are also available in V.S. Godbole, *Rationalism of Veer Savarkar*, Itihas Patrika Prakashan, 2004. And, of course, in *Savarkar Samagra*. In particular, Volume IV. All reports in this chapter of Savarkar's speeches are taken from these books.

and took Nepal. Today, Japan is powerful. It is expanding its empire. 'Under these circumstances we should not discuss who was moral, China or Japan,' he declares. 'We should only consider which country of these two would help us gain our independence. That should be the criterion. If in the present struggle Japan would become enemy of England and help us, we should be friendly with Japan.'

'Today Germany has annexed Czechoslovakia and still England has kept quiet,' he reminds his followers. 'Our enemy is England. Others are neither friends nor enemies. It is not in our interest to be hostile to Germany on account of Czechoslovakia. We should look at international affairs from the point of view of our interests.' The same goes for Japan: 'It is true that Japanese attack on China is deplorable. But how could the western nations blame Japan for that? They are all thieves. If Japan had not attacked China, western European nations themselves would have conquered parts of China.'

And so, why should India unnecessarily get involved in condemning Japan? That does not help China, but we become enemies of Japan 'for nothing'. 'Instead,' he says, 'we should realise that after China, Japan would naturally want to invade India. We should consider how we could take advantage of England's difficulties and of Japan's designs and become independent.'

The Outreach to German Agents

Having researched primary material with minute diligence, Marzia Casolari notes that during these months Savarkar is reaching out to German agents in India:

> While there is no archival evidence of any contacts between Savarkar and the Italian Consulate or Consulate officials, plenty of records are available, showing Savarkar's connections with German agents. From November 1938 on, Savarkar had been writing to two

German agents, G. L. Lesczczynski—representative of the German News Agencies—and a certain P. Pazze. The latter was fronting as a manager of a company based in Bombay, but he was involved in propaganda activities orchestrated by the German Consulate. These two fellows arranged the publication of Savarkar's speech in the *Volkischer Beobachter*. However, before going ahead with the publication, Lesczczynski wanted to know how big was the party headed by Savarkar, in order to know 'exactly what amount of influence the Hindu Mahasabha wields in the country, the strength of its membership, etc.' On 22nd November, the party headquarters promptly informed Lesczczynski that:

So far as the Hindu Mahasabha is concerned it is an All India organisation representing Hindus just as the Moslem League represents the Moslems. Its membership runs [sic] several thousands.

Over the next few months, the relations between Germany and the Mahasabha increased. In early December, Malekar sent Leszczynski a copy of an article published in an unspecified 'Marathi leading Daily', in which Germany's conduct over the Jewish question was described in favourable terms. Two days later, Leszczynski sent Savarkar a complimentary copy of *Mein Kampf*. [5]

20 February 1939: Savarkar is in Calcutta. He repeats his *'real politik'* speech. There is no such thing as morality in relations between countries, he tells the audience. Words like truth and non-violence may be nice to the ear, but they are 'utterly useless' in determining foreign policy. China was an imperialist power when it was strong. Now it has been defeated by Japan. Had Japan not invaded China, Russia and England would have captured parts of it and divided the parts among themselves. Some Indians

---

[5] Marzia Casolari, *In the Shadow of the Swastika, The relationships between Indian radical nationalism, Italian Fascism and Nazism,* Routledge, London, 2020, p. 94.

condemn Japan on moral grounds. They have also sent a team of medical personnel to China. What is the end result? We have made an enemy of Japan.

'As I said earlier,' he continued,

India had unnecessarily created enmity with Germany over Czechoslovakia, which was created by the treaty of Versailles with a view to establish a buffer state between Germany and Austria. Germany was disintegrated. Therefore, Hitler is perfectly within his right to re-unite Germany. England used strong language against Hitler. But when she saw that Hitler would not budge, the British Prime Minister did something, which no one did before. Chamberlain, the British Prime Minister dared to go outside Britain and meet Hitler. Chamberlain completely forgot what assurances he had given to Czechoslovakia just a few days before and agreed to Hitler's annexation of Czechoslovakia. We must remember that Hitler is not a Gandhi who constantly pleads for Hindu-Muslim unity. So, what lay behind British policy? Self-preservation!!

The same principle applied in the case of Abyssinia. Under the leadership of Mussolini, Italy became strong and conquered Abyssinia. Indian newspapers launched bitter attacks on Italy. Unfortunately, Mussolini does not read Indian newspapers. England too condemned Italy's action. But when they saw its futility, they agreed to Italy's rule over Abyssinia. Italy wanted to expand her territories and she achieved her objective.

'You may call it brutal, but self-preservation is the law of nature,' Savarkar says. 'Morality is found only in textbooks. It does not exist in international relations.' 'Words like "moral force", "moral persuasion" however pleasant to hear they may be, are utterly useless in practice. And who is going to put moral pressure on England? Is it going to be France? Italy? Germany?

Or America? But these nations themselves are up to their neck in their evil deeds of theft, deception, and dacoitry.'[6]

We Have to be 'Super-Brutes' and 'Super-Cheats'

Therefore, we must become strong. 'As long as the tiger has powerful toenails, a cow must die. She can be very brave or perform a Satyagraha and say, "It is not in my blood to fight. That is violence!" But a cow has to succumb to a tiger. That is the law of God. I say it again, might is right.' 'Tiny state of Italy is determined to re-establish Roman Empire and Germany is sending shivers down spines all over the world. On what basis? They are fervent nationalists and had taken to arms. Even a five-year-old Italian boy does his drill with a toy gun. We must remember that in the world today, the sword commands more respect than poetry . . . We must undergo military training. . . Once our rifle matches the English rifle and we learn to become as crafty as them, they will have no alternative but to leave India. There is no doubt about it . . .'

And the same holds good for affairs at home. 'It is pointless cursing that the Muslims are naturally hawkish and the English are crafty,' Savarkar said. 'We have got to overcome those deficiencies in ourselves. At times we have to surpass our enemies in these areas. To a brute we have to be super-brute, to a cheat we have to be super-cheat. Only then will we be able to survive . . .'[7]

---

[6] *Rationalism of Veer Savarkar,* V.S. Godbole (Compiler), Itihas Patrika Prakashan, Pune, 2004, Internet Archive, pp. 461–64, 867–74.

[7] Casolari records, Although the sanghatanists continued to show a great deal of interest in Fascism, by the spring of 1939, Germany became the main point of reference of the Hindu Mahasabha, at the international level. On 25th March 1939, the party spokesman stated:

Germany's solemn idea of the revival of the Aryan culture, the glorification of the Swastika, her patronage of Vedic learning and the ardent championship of the tradition of Indo-Germanic civilization are welcomed by the religious and sensible Hindus of India with a jubilant hope. Only a few socialists headed by Pandit J. Nehru have created a bubble of resentment against the present Government of Germany, but their activities are far from having any significance in India. The vain imprecations of Mahatma Gandhi

The Example for Hindusthan

The more Hitler seems unstoppable, the more news about what is being done to the Jews in Germany comes out, the more fulsome does Savarkar's acclaim become—for Germany, in particular for Hitler, most of all for what is being done to the Jews. 30 July 1939, the Poona *shaakhaa* of the RSS is celebrating *Gurupurnima*. Savarkar is the Chief Guest. He lauds Hitler and says in effect that Hedgewar is doing in India what Hitler has accomplished in Germany. He tells the assembled *swayamsewaks*:

> One has to be aware of what is happening in the world. It is in Hitler's autobiography—how the Nazi party grew in Germany. He started his organisation with just 10–12 persons. At that time Germany was lost in clouds of despondence. . . Reflecting on this situation, a foggy idea of how Germany will be brought out of this situation began forming in Hitler's mind. And he decided to give it a solid form. In the beginning ten–fifteen persons joined him. But he, without faltering, advanced his project.

And look at the result:

> What do we see there today? The idea about the unification of Austria is four–five hundred years old. It could not be materialised till now. But through his valour, Hitler has proved that idea to be true and realised it. Truly, he deserves praise for that. He has preserved this great longing—that people speaking German and belonging to German culture should be united, they should be gathered together.

---

against Germany's indispensible [sic] vigour in matters of internal policy obtain but little regard in so far as they are uttered by a man who has always betrayed and confused the country with an affected mysticism. I think that Germany's crusade against the enemies of Aryan culture will bring all the Aryan nations of the World to their senses and awaken the Indian Hindus for the restoration of their lost glory. [The statement, in *Auswartiges Amt-Politischen Archiv* (AA-PA, Bonn)/Pol.VII], Marzia Casolari, op. cit., p. 95.]

And that is the example for Hindusthan, that is the way to weld a nation, that is how we should treat the Muslims:

> Therefore, racially there is no reason to criticise Hindus. All countries the world over are doing this very thing. Assume that there are some Muslims in England. They demand some special rights for themselves and in these days of democracy it is right too. Even so, do you think Britain will give them these rights happily? If you think so, then you are mistaken. You should pay attention to this fact—that democracy is only for the English people. We will just have to accept that a person who proclaims that he belongs to a particular race actually belongs to that particular race. The Germans are proud of German culture. Jews have been staying and flourishing there for centuries. Even so, in their hearts the Germans do not feel one with them.

That is the central point: just because people have been living together does not make them one, it does not make them love each other:

> Reflect on this: what is the root of this? Brothers, love scarcely sprouts by living close to each other. Hindus and Mussalmaans have been living in Hyderabad for centuries. Yet, what do we see there today? The two have become sworn enemies of each other. Muslims face that small Arabistan. I am not surprised in the least by this. In Europe also nations are getting formed on this consideration. If people smell racialism in this, no matter. In the map of the world, Germany for the Germans, England for the English, Italy for the Italians, in this way every corner of the world is reserved. In the same way in world history, this country of Hindus is for the Hindus. Whatever be the view of persons belonging to different political factions about nationality, it is my firm belief that Hindusthan is of the Hindus. It is on this very

feeling of nationhood that the Sangh is working. That its work should succeed fully and the longing of Bharat should fructify—this must be the thought of everyone.[8]

It would therefore be a grave error to look upon Savarkar's advocacy during 1938–39 of possible arrangements with Germany, Italy, Japan as having arisen merely from his 'strategic thought'—that as Germany is becoming the enemy of England, and is manifestly stronger we should ally with it, and, jointly, deal a blow to England and thereby free ourselves. When we come to consider the kind of State that is to be fashioned, we will see that the admiration for Hitler's Germany and Mussolini's Italy was not superficial. There was an 'organic' affinity between what they were doing and what he thought ought to be done.

As various things are about to happen one after another, as various somersaults are going to be executed within months, do bear in mind that this speech was delivered at *the end of July 1939*. Bear in mind that the setting up of concentration camps was being reported in newspapers— and that with photographs of communists and Jews being lined up for them and in them—from *April–May 1933*.[9] All other measures—removal of Jews from government services, removal of Jewish judges, lawyers, doctors, professors, the boycott of Jewish firms and shops, thrashings in streets—were also on parade in every street and neighbourhood. Their 'successes' were hailed in newspapers.

---

[8] *Savarkar Samagra*, Volume VII, pp. 334–35.

[9] See, for instance, Robert Gellately, *Backing Hitler, Consent and Coercion in Nazi Germany*, Oxford University Press, 2001.

Onwards and Upwards to 'Wholehearted Cooperation'

Over the preceding five years, while the Nazis are consolidating their control over Germany and pushing Europe, there has been much activity in India. After much foot-dragging, steps have been taken towards Provincial Autonomy through the passage of the Government of India Act in 1935. Elections are held in April 1937. The Congress wins in seven provinces, and forms governments. Hindu Mahasabha has come a cropper: it gets 3 out of around 1,585 seats in provincial elections—two in Bengal and one in CP & Berar. Things come to a boil in Europe in 1939. The latter half of the year yields *fleur de mal,* the fruits of appeasement:

1 September 1939: Hitler invades Poland

3 September: Britain and France declare war against Germany

17 September: Soviet Union invades Poland to grab some of its territory

27 September: Germans capture Warsaw

6 October: Poland surrenders to Hitler

When Britain declares that it is at war with Germany, India is automatically declared also to be at war. The Congress has been saying that India can be made party to the war only in consultation with the people of India—in practice, in consultation with the elected governments. The Viceroy invites Gandhiji for a meeting in Simla. Gandhiji says that his sympathies are with

England, but 'If there is to be any understanding, it would be between the Congress and the Government.'

The matter gains further urgency. The Congress Working Committee meets on 9 and 10 August. It declares that 'In this world crisis the sympathies of the Working Committee are entirely with the people who stand for democracy and freedom and Congress has repeatedly condemned fascist aggression in Europe.' But later in the same statement, it adds, 'The Congress has further enunciated its policy in the event of war and declared its determination to oppose all attempts to impose a war on India.' It requests Provincial Governments *not* to assist war preparations by the British Government.

The Congress Working Committee meets again from the 8–14 September and declares that the issue of war and peace for India must be decided by the people of India; that cooperation must be between equals, that it must be by mutual consent, and it has to be for a cause which both consider to be worthy. Each clause is a condition: 'decided by the people of India'—not by the Government in London or Delhi; 'between equals'—that means it cannot be between Britain and India so long as Britain is the occupying power and India is the occupied colony; 'mutual consent'; and if the cause is 'freedom and democracy', then it must mean freedom and democracy for India also. On the 15th, Gandhiji issues a statement: 'I was sorry to find myself alone in thinking that whatever support was to be given to the British should be given unconditionally.'

Gandhiji goes back to Simla, meets the Viceroy again, and, having felt the fervour of other members, of other Congress leaders, presses him that the British Government declare unambiguously that at the conclusion of the War, India shall have absolute freedom, and that it should be given a share in power in India immediately. These are what will ensure willing participation by Indians in the war effort, he tells the Viceroy.

As the Government moves unilaterally to declare India to be at war, in October–November 1939, the Congress ministries resign on the ground, among others, that Britain has not taken the consent of Indians or their representatives, that it has not clarified its 'war aims'—in particular what it would pledge to do regarding India on the cessation of the war. Savarkar sees the opportunity.

The Opportunity

Linlithgow, the Viceroy overseeing India, has to win over leaders and parties. He has been 'hard at work', he writes in his regular letter—this one of 7 October 1939—to the Marquess of Zetland, the Secretary of State for India in London.[1] Given the fast pace of events, and the desperate need to get India on a war-footing, he is meeting persons across the board—Gandhiji, Jinnah, Sikander Hyatt Khan, Ambedkar, Jam Saheb, 'the redoubtable Subhas Bose', Cowasjee Jehangir, Chimanlal Setalvad, Savarkar . . . In the letter, Linlithgow gives a detailed account of each meeting.

What He Sought

The account is invaluable for us as we get to know what Savarkar tells the Viceroy in private. I will reproduce the portion of Linlithgow's letter that reports the meeting with Savarkar. Four things stand out:

- While in public till just a while ago Savarkar has been declaiming that India should remain neutral, that what Hitler and Mussolini are doing in their own countries is no concern of ours; while he has been saying in other fora and to other persons that India should take advantage of the difficulties in which Britain is caught and team up with the Germans; that it should not offend the Japanese or Italians; he is telling the Viceroy that the interests of Britain and

---

[1] IOR, Mss Eur F125/8.

Hindus have never been as aligned with each other as they are now; and that the Viceroy can more or less count on support of the Hindu Mahasabha.[2]

- He tells the Viceroy that he and the Hindu Mahasabha will work to dislodge the Congress in the Provinces.

- As you will notice, both these things are exactly what he had pledged to do in the conditions that he had accepted for his release—that is, to be as helpful to the British Government as he possibly can.

- He—and I am using the word that Linlithgow uses twice to describe how Savarkar put the request—'begs' the Viceroy to consider inducting Hindu Mahasabha nominees into responsible positions in Government in place of Congressmen.

In a postscript to the lengthy letter, here is what Linlithgow reports to the Secretary of State about his exchanges with Savarkar:

P.S.– Since dictating the above I have had a series of interviews with Nawab Ismail Khan, President of the United Provinces Muslim League, with Mr. Savarkar, President of the Hindu Mahasabha, and Dr. Ambedkar and it is perhaps worthwhile to add to this letter an account of what passed . . .

. . . I passed from the Nawab to the company of Mr. Savarkar, whose somewhat lurid record and whose alleged connection with the murder of Sir Curzon Wylie will be sufficiently familiar to you. I found him a not very attractive type of little man, but he was

---

[2] The Working Committee of the Mahasabha had just passed a resolution in which it had proclaimed that it 'does not believe in claims of any power among belligerent nations engaged in present war in Europe some of which are themselves imperialistic in character and outlook to the effect that it has been actuated solely by moral and altruistic considerations apart from its national self-interest.' But had proceeded to say that 'as task of defending India from any military attack is of common concern to British Government as well as ourselves and as we are unfortunately not in a position today to carry out that responsibility unaided there is ample room for wholehearted cooperation between India and England.'

definitely interesting and we had a very friendly talk. The situation, he said, was that His Majesty's Government must now turn to the Hindus and work with their support. After all, though we and the Hindus had had a good deal of difficulty with one another in the past, that was equally true of the relations between Great Britain and the French and, as recent events had shown, of relations between Russia and Germany. Our interests were now the same and we must therefore work together. Even though now the most moderate of men, he had himself been in the past an adherent of a revolutionary party, as possibly, I might be aware. (I confirmed that I was). But now that our interests were so closely bound together the essential thing was for Hinduism and Great Britain to be friends; and the old antagonism was no longer necessary.

The Offer on Behalf of Hindus, and What Those Making It Are Really After

And then came an offer that would have been music to Linlithgow:

The Hindu Mahasabha, he went on to say, favoured an unambiguous undertaking of Dominion Status at the end of the war. It was true, at the same time, that they challenged the Congress claim to represent anything but themselves. Congress had accepted office under false pretences and on the understanding that they were doing so in order to wreck the constitution. *But 'we Hindus' were waiting for them.* There was a very great deal of the Congress policy which it had been impossible for the Mahasabha to oppose, because it was essentially a Hindu policy, *but for all that the Mahasabha were determined to have them out. If it could, he could produce much better men to fill the places so vacated.* He went on to urge the importance of military training for Hindus and the repeal of the Arms Act; of a national militia; of compulsory military training for the educated youth of the Hindu community, and the readjustment of the plan of recruitment for the ordinary Indian Army in favour of Hindu classes at present without a real chance of securing admission to the Army. It was of the utmost importance, he said, that we should chastise the frontier tribes now. He could only think that we had some arrangement with Afghans which prevented us from taking a stronger line with them. But the chastisement must be with Hindu troops, the only troops on which we could rely!

I asked him for his views as regards effective implementation of any declaration that might be made, *to which he immediately replied that the Mahasabha had a list of possible members of a Cabinet in the event of our declaration taking that form.* Without much delay he reverted to the communal problem. Pakistan, he said, was an idea wholly abominable, but it was very important that we should not minimize its significance from a Muslim point of view or the depth of Muslim feeling in support of it, which he believed to be growing all the time. I told him that so far as the future was concerned it was no good our having patched up peace at the top without a corresponding reaction in the Provinces but he replied that the communal position in the Provinces would remain in its present condition whatever we might say or do.

Pleading for Positions for His Men

Even Linlithgow must have been struck by what followed: Savarkar seemed to be already dreaming of the kind of governments his men would get, and the powers they would wield. Linlithgow's account continues:

The conversation then took a very interesting turn. What, he said, would happen if the Congress were to go out and if a Section 93 situation were to result? I said that in that event obviously the Governor would try to govern by himself, with a majority Ministry if possible, but that there could be no question of an election. He asked who would be in charge in a Section 93 situation, to which I replied that it would be the Governor under my direction. But who, said he, would be his counsellors? I temporized and advised him to wait and see. He proceeded to press me as to whether we contemplated that they should include no Indians, to which I refused to give any answer, telling him that I could not deal with hypothetical questions, but suggesting that it would be extremely unfair to promising Indian politicians of the future to ask them to accept responsibility in such circumstances.

And then 'he begged':

He said, rather to my amusement, that he begged that the Mahasabha should be left to take the risks of such damage to the careers of individuals if they desired to do so. With the Congress out of the way and the general governmental situation in a state of dissolution, they might be able to produce some extremely good advisers. But could I tell him whether we thought of taking on any number of Muslim advisers? I refused to answer beyond saying that he would realise as well as I did that the post-war position mattered a good deal more in certain ways than the war position, and that he might judge for himself of the likelihood of our basing our arrangements on a one-sided communal panel.

Bad-Mouthing Congress to the British

Finally, the assurance that he and the Mahasabha would do in the Congress, the organization that was synonymous with the National Movement at that time:

His last words were to beg me not to inflate Congress too much. It was true that they were no end of a nuisance, and had the best fighting organisation in India, but very many of their supporters had come in on the Hindu ticket and the Mahasabha intended to have them out. I found the little man quite interesting and very ready to talk frankly. I will not trouble you with the observations he addressed to me about the communal award and its iniquities and the appropriate franchise basis for popular representation, on both of which topics you can imagine his views. But when I asked him, as we parted, whether I could look for some general support from the Mahasabha in relation to whatever might be done at the Centre, without asking public opinion he was disposed to think that the answer would be 'Yes', once the Mahasabha knew our scheme.

'The Parliamentary System Will Not Do'

An aside is in order. After this meeting, Linlithgow met Ambedkar. We learn that Ambedkar had by then concluded that 'the parliamentary system will not do in India.' And that 'He was 100 per cent opposed to self-government at the Centre'—the very object that the National Movement was pressing for at the time—'and would resist it in any possible way.' Here is Linlithgow's account of what Ambedkar said:

From the President of the Mahasabha, I turned appropriately to Dr. Ambedkar, who remains in my judgment as impressive a figure as in the past. I do not know that I need trouble you with any very lengthy account of our conversation, which lasted the best part of an hour. He told me that the depressed classes had never suffered more than they were suffering now from the Congress, and that there was now in his judgment an organised persecution designed to drive his community politically so far as possible into the Congress camp. He and I had seen something of one another in 1934–35; but he had had time to think since then, and the general conclusion which he had in the result reached was that the parliamentary system would not do in India. I asked him whether he would say that in public, to which he replied that he would be perfectly ready to do so, with the utmost emphasis. He was 100 per cent opposed to self-government at the Centre and would resist it in any possible way. As regards liaison at the Centre, he favoured a consultative group but was very strongly opposed to an All-Parties meeting on the ground that there would be no hope whatever of our being able to do business at one, owing to the dissensions that would arise. He was equally opposed to an expanded Executive Council which he thought would never work together, and he begged that no responsibility should be given at the Centre but that whatever organisation we might devise should be consultative in character only. His last words were to beg for some consideration for the Depressed Classes in connection with nominations to the Indian Civil Service and to remark rather acidly that they had had no help, from Gandhi, as regards Scheduled Caste representation in Provincial Cabinets, save in Madras, where, owing to the fact that the Scheduled Castes had 30 members in the Assembly, they were in a position in fact more or less to insist on consideration.[3]

Hitler's armies continue racing through Europe, grabbing one country after another. The British have been anxious to get Indian political leaders to endorse the war effort. The Congress has taken a rigid stand: you cannot commit India to the War without consulting the country. The Government is keen to get public men to counter the impression created

---

[3] Savarkar's views were no different. Bhide's volume reports a speech that Savarkar delivered in Shimoga on 8 May 1943. During this speech, Savarkar told the audience: 'Today everybody is praising democracy. That type of government is suitable where the voters are well educated and know how the democratic government machinery works. But in India where the voters are ignorant and do not know whom to vote and the elected representatives are also selfish it would bring about the ruin of Hindus. Therefore I would support any other form of government that would suit the interests of the Hindu nation.' Cf., *Vinayak Damodar Savarkar's Whirlwind Propaganda Tours: Statements, Messages and Extracts from the President's Diary of His Propagandistic Tours, Interviews from December 1937 to October 1941*, A.S. Bhide [ed.], Bombay, 1941, 1040.

by the Congress. Savarkar, as we noticed, is grabbing at what he sees is the opportunity of a lifetime. But he has a twofold task. On the one hand, he has to convince the Government that he will truly be what he promised in his mercy petitions to be: a most valuable asset of the British Government. On the other, he has to persuade his followers about the somersault this involves from what he had been telling them till the other day. He executes both with his customary certitude.

Suddenly 'Much More Sensible and Realist'

Savarkar meets the Viceroy, Linlithgow, on 5 July 1940. Linlithgow cables a detailed account of what transpired to the Secretary of State in London.

What Savarkar said in private to the Viceroy and his demeanour were very different from the uncompromising tone he adopted in public. Mahasabha was 'quite content with Dominion Status, since they recognized that nothing else was practicable'. Government should set a time limit—a year after the cessation of the war. If Indians could not agree on the constitutional provisions, 'he recognised that His Majesty's Government must come in and settle the issue. But he begged that we should not rub in, if we did decide to say anything, that agreement between Hindus and Moslems was essential as a preliminary as this would upset everything.'

Savarkar then added something that would have surprised Linlithgow: 'He and his friends were uncertain whether, if His Majesty's Government were to drop out of control in this country, it would be possible to get through without a civil war which in fact they were disposed to anticipate, and *in these circumstances they were strongly in favour of a scheme which would retain His Majesty's Government as an effective element.*' As things stood in India, a 'National Government' would be 'meaningless'. The only way forward was to expand the Viceroy's Executive Council—with one member each for Congress, the Muslim League and the Hindu Mahasabha. They had 'preserved their position' by continuing the ban on their organizations joining war Committees and civic guards, *but they had got around this by allowing their members to join as individuals.* And would drop the ban on associate organizations of the Mahasabha from joining the activities. Linlithgow had naturally expressed his 'appreciation' at this!

Linlithgow's overall impression was surely that Savarkar was eager to join hands: 'He was much more sensible and realist than I had altogether anticipated,' Linlithgow concluded. And this, as he noted in the end, even though 'I gave him no indication as to whether or not any declaration might be expected of us.'

Here is Linlithgow's account of the meeting[4]:

Allotted to P. & J. Dept.

Circulated and copy to Sir V. Dawson.

DECYPHER OF TELEGRAM

From   Governor General to Secy. Of State for India

Date   Simla, 13.15 hours, 6th July, 1940.

Received   18.30 hours, 6th July 1940.

IMPORTANT.

1263-S. I saw Savarkar yesterday for an hour and a half. He told me that Mahasabha were quite content with Dominion Status, since they recognised that nothing else was practicable. He was silent about their being appointed to provincial adviserships, and I did not raise the point. The great thing, he said, in any declaration was to get a time limit even if His Majesty's Government took a chance in giving one, and he suggested that we should undertake to get machinery going immediately after the war and add that His Majesty's Government would spare no effort to implement Dominion Status within a year from commencement of deliberations. If there was no agreement

---

[4] IOR, L/P&J/8/507.

between parties, he recognised that His Majesty's Government must come in and settle the issue. But he begged that we should not rub in, if we did decide to say anything, that agreement between Hindus and Moslems was essential as a preliminary as this would upset everything. He and his friends were uncertain whether, if His Majesty's Government were to drop out of control in this country, it would be possible to get through without a civil war which in fact they were disposed to anticipate, and in these circumstances they were strongly in favour of a scheme which would retain His Majesty's Government as an effective element.

2. He asked if I would give an immediate (? pledge) of unification of Central Government. I said certainly not: that whole constitutional future was in terms already stated by His Majesty's Government to be open for examination after the war. If agreement between parties proved impracticable we should have to consider any question in issue on merits. He then asked whether, if parties failed to agree, His Majesty's Government could be relied on to go for unified Central Government. I said that His Majesty's Government would have to consider all possibilities – unified Government, partition, etc. He begged me suggest, if opportunity occurred in connection with any statement, that in so far as parties might fail to agree His Majesty's Government would try to contribute to bring about a settlement. He again urged Congress-Moslem agreement should not be made essential pre-requisite of Dominion Status as in that event the position of Mahasabha would be most difficult.

3. He and Mahasabha entirely accepted the necessity for special arrangements for covering Defence, External Affairs, Commercial discrimination, etc. to be dealt with apart from any general discussion. He urged, however, that any safeguard that might be introduced (e.g. for religious liberty) must be for majorities as well as for minorities.

4. The Mahasabha had now no longer any objection to coalition ministries so long as responsibility, once Ministries had been formed, was collective.

5. He agreed that term 'National Government' of (sic) meaningless in the present conditions in India and did not represent a practical ideal until conclusions had emerged from the post-war enquiries into constitutional position. The only practicable arrangement which he himself saw in present circumstances was expansion of Governor-General's Council. Sounded as to scale he had in view, he replied 'by addition of 1 Moslem, 1 Hindu Mahasabha and 1 Congress'. Spontaneously, he volunteered that his organisation would if invited be prepared to submit a panel of say 3 names from which I could choose their representative.

6. I expressed appreciation of decision of Mahasabha to allow their members to join war Committees and civic guards individually. He thanked me and said that they had of course preserved their position by declining to allow their organisation as such to associate itself with these activities, but that if there were to be an expansion of my Council and Mahasabha to be included, they would drop that ban on associate organisations and lend fullest support as an organisation to civic guard and district war committees.

7. He ended by saying danger from Japan to India was greater, in his judgement, than any danger from Europe.

Could it be that the British were totally unaware of his 'war-plans'—of having Japan invade from the east, with the participation of Indians who Rash Behari Bose was saying he had mobilized? Or were they aware of these 'plans' and listened to the double-talk so as to assess how reliable Savarkar was? Linlithgow's account of what Savarkar said continued:

We must abandon idea of recruitment from martial classes only, and spread our net wide. The Japanese might be here in three years' time, and we could not decently deny Indians of all classes the right to defend themselves. It was important, therefore, that we should go ahead with military preparations on that basis and make India a military nation, or else she would go down.

8. He was much more sensible and realist than I had altogether anticipated. I gave him no indication as to whether or not any declaration might be expected from us.

Even as He is Asking for Seats in Government, He Calls Congress 'Heroic Beggars'

Just five days after this meeting with Linlithgow, and 'begging' him, Savarkar writes a piece, 'Heroic beggars'. He ridicules the Congress for welcoming 'by the sanction of the British Government' the proposal to set up a 'National Government' as 'an intermediate step' and as a 'transitory measure'. 'Thus even heroic beggars cannot long hide their begging bowl,' he taunts the Congress. A paragraph later, he is opening an aperture for getting the goodies in his own hands. He says that the Hindu Mahasabha would be open to the idea of a 'National Government' provided it is not constituted only out of members of the existing legislatures, and provided the share of Hindus in the Government is the same as they are of the population.[5]

'... It is Far Less Dishonourable Than ...'

2 August 1940: Savarkar makes a public speech in Poona. The disquiet among the public that he has to work around comes through. We are concerned with World War II only so far as it affects the defence of India, he says, and for that purpose we can make a treaty with Britain. 'One cannot solve practical problems by reading textbooks,' he tells the audience. 'If someone was our enemy yesterday that does not mean he will remain an enemy today, or that yesterday's friend will remain a friend today. As long as we are careful, cautious and vigilant, there is no objection to making

---

[5] 'Heroic beggars', 10 July 1940, *Vinayak Damodar Savarkar's Whirlwind Propaganda Tours: Statements, Messages and Extracts from the President's Diary of His Propagandistic Tours, Interviews from December 1937 to October 1941*, A.S. Bhide [ed.], Bombay, 1941, pp. 220–23.

friends with anyone. Italy was an ally of France in the previous World War, but today they are enemies, are they not? In 1935, Hitler regarded Russia as a rogue state, but today, on the question of Poland, did he not become a friend of Russia overnight on 23 August 1939?'

But you have been berating the Congress for not demanding complete independence, the people must have wondered. Why are you settling for Dominion Status now? 'Hindu Mahasabha has demanded that we must be granted Dominion Status immediately after the war. Some may ask, "Is it not disgraceful for you who had been clamouring for complete independence?" I say that there is a difference between ideal and reality.' In any case, there is the alibi of what the Congress itself did by forming ministries in the provinces that it won: 'And if our demand is disgraceful,' he says, 'it is far less dishonourable than taking oath of allegiance to the British Crown and accepting their ministerships.' But wouldn't members of the Hindu Mahasabha be doing precisely that if they were given seats in the Viceroy's Executive Council that Savarkar has been pleading for? Naturally, he doesn't address the question. Tarnish and run.

Look at the advantages of cooperating with the British, Savarkar says: 'I say quite bluntly, Britain is allowing the growth of industries and imparting military training to our youth in their interest. We are doing the same to protect our interests.' There is a reason for explaining all this: 'I have to say this explicitly because there are many misconceptions about cooperating with the British. Some say that there can be no common interest between Britain and India. And it is the Congress leaders, who took the oath of allegiance to the British Crown not long ago, that are now opposing us (in cooperating with the British) because it allows us the militarisation of our youth.' In any case, we should not allow them to lead us astray: 'But we should not deflect from our path. Russia and Germany are both powerful nations. And yet they decided to cooperate for their mutual interest. Why can't we do the same? Anyone who always fears that others might deceive him is indeed worth being deceived. Have confidence that we will match the British in diplomacy too and cooperate with them where essential and inevitable, but for our self-interest.'[6]

The Bait

The Viceroy would naturally have been keenly following what each party and public figure is saying. He was shrewd enough to see the portent: that Savarkar is being forced to defend his new prescription against the positions that he has been advocating so vehemently till the other day. On 5 August 1940, three days after Savarkar's speech defending his new position, the Viceroy writes to Savarkar.[7] He refers to their discussion and tells Savarkar that he has 'reported our conversation on that matter' [the 'general political situation'] to Government in London. He has been authorized to issue a statement. What is more important, 'they have authorised me to invite a certain number of representative Indians to join my Executive Council, and they have authorised me further to establish a War Advisory Council which would meet at regular intervals and which would contain representatives of the Indian States and of other interests in the national life of India as a whole.' Then comes the bait: 'I trust sincerely,' the Viceroy says, 'that you and the organisation of which you are the President, will be prepared to join with me in the Central Government and in the War Advisory Council.' He invites Savarkar to meet him again on 13 August 'to clear the ground for your formal reply'. 'I would only add that I am anxious that the names of the expanded Executive Council should appear not later than the end of August, and those of the War Advisory Council by the middle of September latest, and if possible earlier than that date.'

Savarkar is suffering from sciatica pain, and is unable to meet the Viceroy during the latter's visit to Bombay. Instead, he writes Linlithgow a letter.[8]

---

[6] *Rationalism of Veer Savarkar*, V.S. Godbole (Compiler), op. cit., pp. 881–86.

[7] IOR, Mss.Eur.F.125/122 item 138.

[8] IOR, Mss.Eur.F.125/122 item119a.

intellect than the Muslim League can hope to do, in organizing the defence of India, on modern scientific lines. Besides, the inherent loyalty of the Moslems, based on the conceptions of their religion, for Muslim countries outside India which may, at any time in the course of the war, join hands with the enemies of the British Empire, is always a standing potential danger. In contrast with this fundamental fact, the loyalty of the Hindus to their own Sacred Land, Hindusthan, surrounded as it is on the North-Western Frontier by its traditional enemies of the last more than one thousand years, is the one stable factor in its choice of its allies for its permanent safety and prosperity. It will naturally lead the Hindus to look up to Britain, in spite of its quarrels with it for constitutional powers, however bitter at times they may be. Thus Hindusthan and Britain are allied together in unshakeable bond of union for long years to come. Thus this fundamental contrast between the two loyalties, the Hindu and the Moslem, is the chief pivot of the situation which should never be allowed to fade away from Your Excellency's mind.

Demands That 'Can Automatically Be Eliminated'

On 25 September 1940, Savarkar also has written again to, Viceroy.[14] He also forwards the two resolutions that the Working Committee of the Hindu Mahasabha has passed. He draws particular attention of the Viceroy to the change in the Hindu Mahasabha approach. 'The Mahasabha has maintained up to this time according to its previous resolution a policy of organizational aloofness from the Government regarding war efforts,' Savarkar points out, 'though individual members were allowed to join the War Committee . . . provided nothing detrimental to Hindu interests was expected of them.' But now, 'I urge upon Your Excellency to note first of all the italicized sentences in the first resolution in which the Mahasabha

---

[14] IOR, Mss.Eur.F.125/122 item 154.

He expresses his regret at the fact that he cannot go over to meet the Viceroy as he is forbidden by doctors to move out of the house. Could you please come by my house, he suggests. Red tape may come in your way, but, and notice the presumption here, the entire Hindu nation will be grateful for the human gesture shown by you.

'But if Your Excellency finds it inconvenient or inadvisable to be pleased to call upon me on any of the two or three days during your stay in Bombay,' he continues, 'I shall nevertheless write to Your Excellency a detailed letter regarding the Viceregal announcement, after seeing the deputation of the Working Committee of the Hindu Mahasabha with its resolutions at Nagpur which they have decided to send to me during this week. Your Excellency will get my letter before the 21st of August 1940 in any case as desired by you.'

But the Viceroy need have no apprehension about what the Mahasabha will do:

I may in a general way foretell this much that after your announcement the Hindu Mahasabha party will in all probabilities meet Your Excellency's wishes if but some explanations and one or two additions are generously made by Your Excellency to what you have already said. And with the Hindu Mahasabha party, I hope, I shall be able to pull up a number of important parties in the Land in trying our level best to push on the war efforts so far as they are directly connected with the question of Indian defence.

I beg to remain,
Your Excellency's most obedient servant,
V.D. Savarkar,
President, Hindu Mahasabha

Linlithgow receives the letter at night and replies immediately. '. . . I have read with much interest what you tell me in Section III of your letter, and I note that I may hope for an early reply from you.' As for going over to

Savarkar's house, he says '. . . I take your invitation in the friendly spirit in which it is made, but I fear that I cannot manage to accept it. I do however hope that you may soon be out of pain.' He invites Savarkar to meet him in Delhi on the 20th or 21st.

The Government's High Table

Savarkar is still unable to travel. He writes to the Viceroy again.[9]

From V.D. SAVARKAR, Esq., President, All-India Hindu Mahasabha

Savarkar Sadan,
Keluskar Road,
Dadar, Bombay-14,
August 19th, 1940

I. The Deputation, sent by the Nagpur Working Committee of the Hindu Mahasabha to acquaint me their decisions, saw me. They had kindly permitted me to take final decision in my own discretion after going through all their diverse instructions and views.

II. The millions on millions of Hindu Sanghatanists throughout the Land have appreciated the recognition on the part of the Government of the fact that the Hindu Mahasabha represented the interests peculiar to Hindus as Hindus and the Congress represented but the Congressites. This recognition was brought out in Your Excellency's speech beyond cavil or criticism. Although you must have noticed that Mr Amery has not yet forgotten the old category summing up Indian World 'as the Congress and the Muslim League' more out of routine than intention. Your Excellency will kindly impress upon Mr Amery's attention that it is the Hindu Mahasabha

---

[9] IOR, Mss.Eur.F.125/122 item 125.

now, that represents the special interests of the Hindus in India and the Congress has definitely forfeited its claim to that.

Was Savarkar assuming too much about the status that his Mahasabha had been accorded? Or was the Viceroy, having found a convenient instrument for undermining the Congress, boosting him up? In any case, the real thing Savarkar had his eyes on was getting seats at the Government's high table:

> III. The extension of the Advisory Council is looked upon by the Hindu Mahasabha as a step in the right direction taken together as the Government's promise to grant the Dominion Status immediately after the war. In accordance with the seasoned policy of the Hindu Mahasabha of responsive cooperation, of occupying every point of vantage with a view to march on further or at any rate to stop the vantage points from being abused in the hands of inepts and anti-Hindus, the Hindu Mahasabha has decided to participate in and utilise every war effort on the part of the Government which is genuinely calculated to contribute to Indian Defence and to further, in the long run, Hindu interests.

The Advance Tip

He proceeds to list seven names for the Viceroy to choose from, and then adds:

> If Your Excellency wishes to add or to substitute any names of any of these prominent Hindu Sabhaites you will kindly wire to me to that effect. The Hindu Mahasabhaites as a body are all of one mind in participating in the extended Council. I shall accept any two or three names which Your Excellency selects out of this panel or proposes anyone in addition to this.[10]

---

[10] In a subsequent letter, Savarkar added an eighth name to the list—that of Gokul Chand Narang for either Council.

Choose whom you will, he is telling the Viceroy, just give me an advance tip—when I read this request, and its being repeated twice, I was reminded of what a 'godman' was to tell me decades later about his—the godman's—*modus operandi*. But to continue with Savarkar:

> I hope you will let me know, telegraphically if necessary, the names you select or any new names you propose from Mahasabha platform in advance of the final announcement. Any name of the Hindu Mahasabha representative, of course Your Excellency will please note, should have a formal acceptance on my part as the President of the Hindu Mahasabha. I do not mind whom you select from the other parties.
>
> V. So far as Your Excellency's proposal regarding the War Committee is concerned, it is also fully appreciated by me and the Mahasabha has decided to participate in it, as Wholeheartedly as possible, to render the question of Indian Military Defence effective. I suggest that those prominent Hindu Sabhaites who have already joined the War Committees in different Provinces should form the panel.

Even more so in regard to the Central War Committee:

> Anyhow on the Central War Committee Your Excellency should have some of these gentlemen so that the committee may have the moral support of the Hindu Mahasabha party as such.

And that request again:

> Your Excellency will of course let me know beforehand, telegraphically if necessary, whom you select.

Please choose whom you will, but let the stamp be mine!

The Dilution to Crown Dilutions

What about the demand for complete independence? If it is to be Dominion Status, what about the demand that a declaration be made here and now that India will be given this status the moment the War ends? Under cover of obfuscation, Savarkar dilutes:

> VI. So far as the promise of granting Dominion Status is concerned, I for one am satisfied—and am going to issue a public statement to that effect—that the phrases used by Your Excellency and by Mr Amery are as convincing as any other sentences could have been. To me it is not now the question of the clarity of words. It is now only a question of sincerity with which the words are carried into effect and that could only be judged by the result.

'The beginning is well made,' he concludes. 'I hope the end will not falsify the hopes.'

From the British Point of View, a Big Step Forward

From Linlithgow's point of view, this was a big step forward. In the resolution that it had passed just weeks earlier—on 19 May 1940—the Working Committee of the Mahasabha had used language that seemed uncompromising:

> . . . That in accordance with the resolution passed by the Working Committee last February at Delhi, the Government should immediately announce that Dominion Status under the Statute of Westminster will be granted to India immediately on the cessation of the War, guaranteeing the indivisibility of India as a political unit and a Central Government strong enough to maintain it. This grant of Dominion Status should not be made conditional on any Hindu-Moslem pact as an indispensable prerequisite, nor

should the future constitution of India be based on the present Communal Award.

The Working Committee reiterates that it is prepared to accept Dominion Status as the immediate step towards the attainment of its goal of absolute political independence.

Savarkar is now saying that 'I for one am satisfied' with the statements that have already been made, that intention is what matters and sincerity in the steps to be taken in the future.

The Matter He Will Pursue, Nominally

Savarkar then turns to a matter that he will stress again and again—but which too will have an unflattering *denouement*. He writes about the atrocities that continue to be heaped on Hindus in Sindh, Bengal, Punjab and the NWFP, adding,

> But I leave the discussion for the future and only note in this short letter that any attempt to cut at the root the indivisibility of India as a political unit from Indus to the Seas and with a strong Central Government to maintain it cannot fail to evoke an undying opposition from Hinduism as a whole.
>
> The Muslims or the Government have not now to count with the colourless Congressites or their Pseudo-Nationalistic enuendos [sic.] but with the organic racial forces of genuine Hindudom for whom India, this Hindusthan, constitutes not only an indivisible Father Land but an Indivisible Holy Land too.

Seeing how Savarkar had diluted his public statements and the Mahasabha's resolutions, would the Viceroy have quaked at this 'fire and brimstone' warning?

In any case, the ending is placatory:

IX. In the end I thank Your Excellency for the ship-yard, the aeroplane factories, the increased output of up-to-date ammunitions, the increase in the recruitment in the Military, Naval and Aerial [sic.] to which Indians are allowed without any distinction of religion or caste, etc.

The beginning is well-made, though halting. But I hope everything will be put right as the Central War Committee sits shaping day-by-day on straightening and intensifying these war efforts.

I beg to remain,

Your Excellency's most obedient servant,

V.D. SAVARKAR

Linlithgow seizes the opportunity. He replies on 24 August from Simla.[11] He is 'greatly obliged for the letter of 19 August,' he tells Savarkar, '. . . which I have read with great interest and close attention.' '. . . and I am very glad to learn from it of the readiness of the Hindu Mahasabha to work with me in the Central Government and in the War Advisory Council. I have taken note of the names which you have been good enough to let me have for consideration, and I will not fail to let you have a further communication in the near future.'

What Weight the Viceroy Really Placed

Linlithgow's real assessment of what is in Savarkar's mind, about how far Savarkar is now prepared to go, of what Savarkar wants in the immediate future and how granting that is 'of course out of the question' is evident from Linlithgow's encrypted telegram to the Secretary of State[12]:

---

[11] IOR, Mss.Eur.F.125/122 item 153.

[12] Mss Eur F125/19.

Allotted to P. & J. Department.

Copy Circulated, Copy to Sir V. Dawson.

DECYPHER OF TELEGRAM

From	Governor General to Secretary of State for India
Date	Simla, 14.50 hours, 25th August, 1940.
Recd.	15.00 hours, 26th August 1940.

1696-S. Constitutional position. I have now received Mahasabha reply. They are prepared to cooperate and make no embarrassing demands, though Savarkar's letter makes it clear that there are a number of issues on which they are not wholly satisfied. Savarkar adds that so far as promise of granting Dominion Status is concerned 'I for one am satisfied, and am going to issue a public statement to that effect, that phrases used by Your Excellency and by Mr. Amery are as convince (?ing as) any other sentences could have been. To me it is not now question of clarity of words. It is now only a question of sincerity with which the words are carried into effect, and that could only be judged by result. The beginning is well made. I hope the end will not falsify the hopes.'

2. His letter suggests that Mahasabha may hope for two or three seats in my Council. That is of course out of the question. But I do not propose to argue the point with Savarkar, and will in due course, and after consultation with you, let him know the name of the [person] we contemplate for the Executive Council and names (probably two, I think) to be selected for the War Advisory Council.

Longing Is the Mother of Rationalization

The Working Committee of the Mahasabha meets in Bombay on 21 and 22 September 1940. In view of Savarkar's indisposition, Moonje directs affairs. The discussion revolves around the prospect of the Viceroy expanding his

Executive Council and some persons from the Mahasabha joining it, as well as the proposed Military Advisory Council. The Working Committee passes two resolutions. Longing is the mother of rationalization. 'In view of opportunity that the present war offers for general militarisation of Hindus and organization of system of India on sound modern lines so that India may be converted into a self-contained defence unit, Mahasabha is prepared whole heartedly to work out schemes of expansion of the Executive Council and the War Advisory Council but on honourable terms of equity and justice,' the resolution declares. The 'honourable terms' are two. First, the Government must make a clear and definite statement that it has not approved or accepted any demand entailing the partition of the country. Second, in view of the understanding that the Viceroy is reported to have reached with the Moslem League of giving them two seats in the Executive Council and five seats in the War Advisory Council, Hindus should get six seats in the Executive Council and fifteen in the War Advisory Council. Of the six seats, one should be given to the Sikhs, one to Scheduled Castes and four to nominees of the Mahasabha.

The 'Honourable Terms' Explained Away

On 26 September 1940, Moonje writes to the Viceroy enclosing the resolutions.[13] These 'would appear to be rather a lengthy document', he tells the Viceroy, but the matter is 'very simple', and the length has been occasioned by the complications that Jinnah has created. Moonje states his central point, and his central argument for Wholehearted cooperation of the Hindus and the British thus:

I may repeat here my conviction that between the two communities, the Hindu Mahasabha, which represents the Hindus, will be in a position to give immensely large help both in men, material and

---

[13] IOR, Mss.Eur.F.125/122 item157

states definitely that "the Hindu Mahasabha is prepared Wholeheartedly to work out the schemes of the extension of the Viceroy's Executive Council and the War Advisory Council".

All this while the Mahasabha has been proclaiming to the public that it has laid down a series of conditions which the Government must meet before the Mahasabha will join the war effort. In this private letter, Savarkar tells the Viceroy not to attach importance to those conditions! 'Of course, I quite expect it that Your Excellency will at the first glance find the conditions laid down in the first resolution rather impracticable inasmuch as the Extended Executive Council was never expected to be of such a large dimension as to include so many members claimed by different parties in India.' 'But,' the word that buries what has gone before, 'I assure you that the Mahasabha has not laid down these conditions in any obstructionist spirit.' Savarkar tells the Viceroy that 'The only fact that compelled the Mahasabha to lay down these large number of seats was the preposterous demands made by the Muslim League that they should get 50 per cent seats and the fact that Your Excellency had promised them two seats already. Mahasabha is not particular about the number of seats but it is determined to see that the preposterous claim of 50 per cent seats for the Muslims is not conceded to them.' All that the Government has to aim for, he says, is that the Hindus [including Sikhs] shall have two-third of the total seats and the Muslims will have just one-third.

'Similarly,' he says in the give-away sentence, 'nearly every other demand is but a counter-demand to checkmate the aggressive demands of the Muslim League. If but these aggressive League demands are not conceded to, the counter-demands of the Mahasabha can automatically be eliminated . . .'

And what were these other demands in the Mahasabha resolution which Savarkar was now waving away? The first was:

In view of the declaration made by the Muslim League of its 'determination, firm resolve and faith' that the partition of India is the only solution of Indian future constitution, the Hindu Mahasabha urges upon His Excellency the Viceroy to make a clear and definite declaration that the Government has not approved or accepted any such proposal or scheme.

That Savarkar was as good as his word—that the Viceroy could just as well disregard the demand, this one asking the British to affirm that the country would not be partitioned—will be evident from the fact that the British made no such declaration and yet Savarkar continued to press that his men be inducted into the Central Executive and War Councils.

The backtracking that he is doing in private becomes even more galling when we consider the points made in the next resolution:

1. Resolved that the statement made recently by His Excellency the Viceroy and the Secretary of State for India are highly unsatisfactory and disappointing: in that they make no reference to India's right to Independence which has been declared to be the goal of Hindu Mahasabha; reference made to the grant of Dominion Status as an immediate step in constitutional advance is vague and uncertain. Hindu Mahasabha claims Dominion Status of the Westminster type within a definite time-limit not exceeding a year after the war.

2. That the statement made to the effect that the British government will not agree to hand over Indian Administration of a system of Government which will not be acceptable to large and powerful elements of Indian life, requires clarification, as it is capable of the interpretation that if Muslim League, the Princes or other vested interests oppose the recognition of the legitimate rights of the majority in India, the further constitutional advance will be held up or the rights of the majority will be surrendered to them which will mean the negation of principle of Democracy and incitement to minorities to obstruct and revolt.

The language on such matters in these resolutions was uncompromising, minatory. In the resolution it passed during its meeting on 21 to 23 September 1940, the Working Committee, after characterizing the statements of the Viceroy and the Secretary of State on further constitutional progress as 'highly unsatisfactory and disappointing', etc. declared:

> The Hindu Mahasabha notes with regret and disappointment that the British Government even at this crisis is not prepared to give up its old Imperialistic policy and states that its latest proposal is hardly of a nature to satisfy the demands of the Indian people. In the Mahasabha's opinion a great opportunity has been lost by the Government. The Mahasabha makes it clear to the people of India and particularly to the Hindus that in all its actions and activities it will be guided by a policy whereby the Hindu interests will be furthered and no element will be permitted to dominate the public life of India to the detriment of the Hindus. The Hindu Mahasabha is determined to fight every inch of ground both inside and outside the Government to achieve the above subject. The Hindu Mahasabha will accept any reasonable and honourable offer made by the Government only if it will stimulate and advance the Hindu cause and prevent any encroachment being made on the rights of the Hindus by reactionary elements in the country. But this acceptance of the offer will not be considered to constitute a bar against Hindu Mahasabha carrying on agitation for the further advancement of the Hindu cause and interest.

Manifestly, these declarations also were only for public consumption—to announce that the Mahasabha was standing up firmly for the country remaining united, that it was opposing resolutely proposals that would give a veto to the Muslim League. In his speeches, Savarkar was proclaiming again and again that his Mahasabha was the only one that was standing firm on these points. And in the letter to the Viceroy?

The second demand—this too had been put forward in the resolution that the Working Committee had passed unanimously in its meeting held on 21st to 23rd September 1940—was that as the Viceroy had promised two seats in the enlarged Executive Council to the Muslim League, the Hindus must, on the basis of their share in the country's population, be given six seats. One of these should be given to the Sikhs and one to the Scheduled Castes. All the remaining four should be given to nominees of the Hindu Mahasabha. And the Hindu Mahasabha must be given fifteen seats in the War Advisory Council.

These demands having been tom-tommed in public as irreducibles, in this private letter Savarkar is telling the Viceroy that these had been projected only as a counter to the Muslim League's demands!

Decades Later, a Godman

'The best way will be,' Savarkar tells the Viceroy, 'that Your Excellency should immediately inform me definitely of the scheme which you have decided to put in operation with regard to the Extended Executive Council and the War Advisory Council and the distribution of number of seats you have fixed for different parties so that instead of dealing with alarming and vague press reports or the bombastic claims of the Muslim League, the Hindu public and the Hindu Mahasabha will have something tangible and authoritative to deal with and the lot of unnecessary and vague "ifs and buts" may be eliminated at a stroke.' This request merits a moment's notice. In letter after letter, Savarkar tells the Viceroy to decide what he deems fit but to just give him—Savarkar—information in advance about what he has decided and is going to announce.

Years later, I was to come across a godman with several *chelas* in the government at the time. He told me that he never told his men to award the contract to the wrong person. All he told them to do was to inform him two–three days in advance who it was they had selected. He would then tell the businessman how he was working to get him the contract, but there were so many obstacles . . . 'Did I do anything wrong?' he would ask me. 'The officers selected the right man. I got the credit and the *dakshina*.[15] But this was nothing compared to what I really got: everyone began to think that I had tremendous influence, that I was the one through whom things could be obtained from this Government. So, what I got was—the next businessman. The queues outside this ashram became longer and longer!'

'As soon as I hear of these definite proposals,' Savarkar says, the Hindu Mahasabha 'will meet to consider them and arrive at a final decision.' Lest the Viceroy think that he is holding on to any conditions, Savarkar adds that if only the Government does not grant half the seats to Muslims, 'in all likelihood' the Working Committee of the Mahasabha will not just endorse the Viceroy's scheme, it will take the next step and forthwith nominate Hindu Mahasabha members for both the Councils.

He ends on a hopeful note: 'Hoping confidently that all difficulties will be surmounted by the tactful and conciliatory attitude which Your Excellency has been maintaining throughout our negotiation and will enable the Hindu Mahasabha to participate honourably in both the Councils and all other war activities which are so essential in our common interest.'

Difficulties Removed

Muslim League has demanded that Muslim soldiers should not be compelled to fight any Muslim invaders. The Viceroy naturally turns this down. Savarkar latches on to this as the 'news-peg' so to say. He sends a new letter to the Viceroy on 2 October 1940.[16] In this new letter he writes,

---

[15] Gift or fee given to a Brahmin for services performed.

[16] IOR, Mss.Eur.F.125/122 item 166.

I regret that I should still be confined to bed and unable to walk or work. Nevertheless I hasten to thank Your Excellency for the firmness with which you have turned down some of the unjust, unreasonable and even treacherous demands such as the one which dictated that Muslim forces in the Indian Army should not be compelled to fight with alien Muslim invaders, advanced by the Muslim League. Your correspondence with Mr Jinnah which the latter has released to the press will no doubt remove a number of misgivings which the press reports and the pompous speeches of the League leaders had raised in the mind of the Hindu public.

The turning down of these League demands has consequently removed a number of difficulties which up to this time stood in the way of an amicable understanding between the Hindu Mahasabha and the Government regarding the proposed extension of the Executive Council and the War Council.

Savarkar and the Mahasabha had been projecting the demands to show how firmly they were standing up for Hindu interests, how they were standing against the Muslim League, and, in contrast to the Congress and other lackeys of the British, against the partitioning of the country. These demands, he now tells the Viceroy, were only meant to serve as a mere 'counter-check' to the League and which 'are now automatically eliminated by your rejection of some of the Muslim demands':

Your Excellency's clear statement made in your letter to Mr Jinnah dated the 6th of July to the effect 'that any Council so expanded would cooperate [sic.] as a whole and as a single Government of India. It is not a case of striking a balance between the different interests or of preserving the proportions between the important parties . . . There are parties other than either the Congress or the Muslim League who may fairly claim to be considered for inclusion,' gives altogether a new and welcome view-point, and it was precisely from this very viewpoint that the Hindu Mahasabha framed its original and substantial demands. It was only later that the aggressive demands trotted out by the League compelled the Hindu Mahasabha to add a number of counter-demands which were in fact meant to serve as a mere counter-check to the League and which are now automatically eliminated by your rejection of some of the Muslim demands.

So, Now Don't Hold Up the Fruit

Now that the ground 'is more or less cleared up,' Savarkar writes, 'I urge upon Your Excellency to lose no time in framing and forwarding to me a definite proposal regarding the constitution of both the Councils and intimation of your readiness to put the proposal into execution as early as possible. No time should now be lost in merely beating about the bush.' Is he putting on airs? the Viceroy would have wondered—that the Viceroy should '. . . lose no time in framing and forwarding to me a definite proposal regarding the constitution of both the Councils and intimation of your readiness to put the proposal into execution as early as possible'!

Savarkar assures the Viceroy that as soon as he receives the 'definite proposal and the number finally allotted to the Hindu Mahasabha, the Depressed Classes and the Sikhs or other Hindu or non-Hindu parties, I shall place the definite proposal before the Working Committee to be considered as a whole so that it may arrive at a final conclusion in the spirit of responsive cooperation of which the Working Committee of the Hindu Mahasabha at Bombay last month had assured Your Excellency.'

The critical phrases are 'responsive cooperation' of which the Viceroy has already been assured, and the proposal 'to be considered as a whole'—an assurance that Savarkar would not allow any reservations on individual points to stand in the way of endorsement.

Savarkar ends the letter with a wedded partner's words:

> ... as under the present circumstances and on these given points at any rate the political interests of the Hindus are on the whole allied with the British interests as never before, and a hearty alliance between them can but conduce to their mutual political benefit and strength.

Another Argument

The next day, Moonje sends another letter adding further arguments in favour of considering the Mahasabha's case for inclusion into the Councils: the Princes.[17] They 'are obliged to be dumb and perhaps even deaf publicly,' Moonje writes, 'but that is all the more reason to attach overwhelming importance to what they say when they break their silence in complete confidence within closed doors.' '... from this vital point of view the status and importance of the Hindu Mahasabha in relation to the work in hand, is immeasurably greater than that of the Congress,' he tells the Viceroy. The Princes can provide significant help in the war effort, and it is the Hindu Mahasabha which is close to the Hindu Princes.

In a word, the demands in the resolutions, that business about Direct Action: not worth the attention. The main point is:

> The Hindu Mahasabha has, I feel sure, taking the whole situation into consideration, wisely committed itself to work out Your Excellency's schemes Wholeheartedly, but on honourable terms of equity and justice. Your Excellency, therefore, should have no doubt, whatsoever, even under the present changed circumstances, about the attitude of the Hindu Mahasabha in this vital matter of Self-Defence.

---

[17] IOR, Mss.Eur.F.125/122 item 167.

'Awaiting Anxiously'

Impatient to seal the matter, ten days later Savarkar sends the Viceroy a telegram:[18]

> Dr V.D. Savarkar to Viceroy
>
> Telegram, 12th October 1940
>
> Awaiting anxiously Your Excellency's definite reply extension Executive Council. Now no difficulty regarding numerical proportion or other serious impediments. Consequently Your Excellency's proposal may meet requirements, namely, one representative of Hindu Mahasabha, one Scheduled and one Sikh and other men Hindus. Mahasabha prepared to work out any equitable scheme. I fervently hope this opportunity of enlisting goodwill and active participation of millions of Hindu Sanghatanists in the common cause of Indian Defence will not be lost. Expecting reply.

So, we have, 'the political interests of the Hindus are on the whole allied with the British interests as never before', to striving for a 'hearty alliance between them', and now 'the common cause of Indian defence'.

Savarkar had ended his preceding letter with, 'Expecting to receive Your Excellency's definite and detailed out proposal as soon as possible.' Not having got the reply that will enable him to tell his associates not just that the decisions have been taken with his concurrence but that he is so close to the Viceroy that the latter shares information with him in advance of announcing things in public, Savarkar has to end the telegram also with, 'Expecting reply.'

---

[18] IOR, Mss.Eur.F.125/122 item 176.

'Exaggerated', 'Absurd', 'Unacceptable'

The government had put forward proposals on 8 August 1940 for ensuring greater participation by Indians in governing the country and in planning and carrying through the war effort. This would be achieved through an expansion of the Viceroy's Executive Council and the setting up of a War Advisory Council. The Congress and Muslim League both declared that they would not participate.

As a result, the general position, Linlithgow wrote on 13 October 1940 to Roger Lumley, the Governor of Bombay 'is one for the moment of very considerable awkwardness'.[1] The Congress is threatening civil disobedience and the Muslim League will come on board on terms, 'which we cannot concede to them consistently with our obligations to other parties and communities'. To compound matters, Jinnah has so established his control that neither Punjab under Sikandar Hyat Khan or Khizr Hayat Tiwana nor Bengal under Fazlul Haq can break from his line.

'The Rump'

The Mahasabha, 'frightened of course by the Muslim League, have advanced exaggerated demands for representation both on my Council if expanded, and in the War Advisory Council, though I can see now, from letters and a telegram I have had from Savarkar in the last few days, that they realise they may have prejudiced their chances by taking this line, and

---

[1] For the following, Linlithgow to Roger Lumley, Governor of Bombay, 13 October 1940, IOR Mss. Eur.F.125/54.

that they are very ready to come in on the terms originally offered to them now that they are satisfied that the Muslims are going to stay out.'

'On the other side,' he informed Lumley, 'I know that Aney is prepared to serve; so is Ambedkar; and the Sikhs are thirsting to be given representation both in the expanded Council and in the War Advisory Council.' But 'By no stretch of imagination could the resultant government be regarded as representative, and it is equally out of the question to hope that it could look for a majority or anything approaching a majority in the Central Assembly.' And what if Congress and League team up to discredit the expanded Executive Council—which, Linlithgow wrote, he had been warned 'from certain Muslim quarters such as [the Nawab of] Chhatri,' they might do?

With the expansion of the Executive Council gone, the setting up of the War Council too must go, the Viceroy said. Congress and Muslim League will not participate; Jinnah will not allow any other Muslims to join, 'and I am not prepared to consider giving the Mahasabha 15 seats, or whatever absurd demand they have put forward for representation. The rump would hardly be worth getting together'.

'Both Amery and I have taken the line that if we cannot get those to work with us whom we want, we shall work with those whom we can find,' the Viceroy explained. But a government opposed by the Congress and the League, and consisting of Hindu Mahasabha, Ambedkar and the Sikhs would not be taken as representative. On the other side, abandoning the proposal would, of course, involve a loss of face. It would also setback constitutional progress as it would demonstrate the inability of Indian parties to get together for governing their own country.

Arguments on both sides are finely balanced, Linlithgow noted, but concluded that 'I am, with the utmost reluctance, forced to the conclusion that the wiser course would be to put our scheme into cold storage and to carry on as present, making it clear that we had not abandoned our scheme, which remained our settled policy, and from which we would not resile, but that before it could be implemented we must be able to rely on some greater degree of general support for it.' 'It is lamentable that things should have taken this turn,' Linlithgow said, 'but we can, I think, reasonably claim that we are blameless. Equally, we can, and must, I feel, bring out so far as world publicity is concerned, that we have made a very extensive move indeed, and that our intentions have been frustrated by circumstances essentially Indian and entirely beyond our control.'

Thus, while Savarkar and his associates were feeling that circumstances had turned so much in their favour that seats in the Viceroy's Executive Council were at hand and they could pitch for fifteen seats in the War Council, the Viceroy thought their demands to be 'exaggerated', 'absurd', 'unacceptable'. While Savarkar was projecting the Mahasabha as the true representative of Hindus, one whose influence was spreading by leaps and bounds, the Viceroy knew that a government consisting of the Mahasabha and the rest of 'the rump' could 'by no stretch of imagination . . . be regarded as representative.' While Savarkar was 'Expecting reply' impatiently, the Viceroy had concluded that the whole scheme had to be put in the cold storage for now.

God, Someone Is Actually Reading the Resolutions

To get back to Savarkar's letter and what followed. Linlithgow has actually already sent his reply to Savarkar on 11 October.[2] The assurances that Savarkar is giving are in private. The resolutions are in public. Linlithgow presses the point. In his reply, Linlithgow tells Savarkar, 'I had already received from Dr Moonje the full text of the resolutions passed by the Hindu Mahasabha.' The next sentence is ominous: 'These I have not failed to communicate to His Majesty's Government, and the position will of course have to be considered in the light of them.'

---

[2] IOR, Mss.Eur.F.125/122 item 206.

Savarkar has been drawing up lists of people who he would get into the Government, and here is the Viceroy paying heed to resolutions that are meant only for public consumption. It 'is the very point to correct which I am hastening to write this letter', Savarkar explains. He can't let his dream of seeing his men in the British Government turn into a mirage. And so, Savarkar is at pains to reiterate that no importance needs to be attached to the demands that have been made in the resolutions. In his letter of 22 October 1940,[3] Savarkar assures the Viceroy,

> A number of events have happened since the Resolutions were passed which have given a favourable turn to Political situation from the Hindu Mahasabha point of view. Your firm reply to the League and refusal to grant a number of aggressive demands forwarded by the League such as 'the 50 per cent Ratio' or that 'the Government should get itself definitely committed to the Pakistan proposal,' etc. etc. — your firm refusal has automatically eliminated a number of counter-demands which the Hindu Mahasabha had to make in its Resolutions. Consequently, now, those Resolutions must be considered not 'by themselves' alone but in the light of and in connection with this favourable turn events have taken . . . Now, the position is simple. . . the Hindu Mahasabha is firmly of the opinion that the proposal of the extension of the Executive Council must in no case be abandoned . . .

And he gives up yet another demand—that all the seats set aside for Hindus should be given to nominees of the Hindu Mahasabha because, going by the Government's own announcements, the Mahasabha alone represents the Hindus, the Congress representing only the members of the Congress. He says that the situation has changed, and so

> Now even if the original proposal which Your Excellency had referred to during our interviews is definitely announced reserving one seat

---

[3] IOR, Mss.Eur.F.125/122 item 189.

for the Hindu Mahasabha; one for the Scheduled classes; one for the Sikh or any other Hindu party and the remaining one for the Muslim or any other non-Hindu if necessary, taking for granted that only four members are to be added, such a proposal will meet the requirements of the situation and enable the Hindu Mahasabha to participate in the Council inasmuch as this scheme too does naturally meet the just contention of the Hindu Mahasabha that the representation the Hindus get must be in the proportion of their population.

Members of the Hindu Mahasabha have already joined the War Committees in several parts of the country, Savarkar writes, and 'are extending whatever cooperation is possible and advisable in pressing the war effort'. If the Mahasabha is not given representation on the enlarged Councils 'on equitable terms', 'it will necessarily have an alienating effect on all these Hindu Sabhaites who are holding such prominent positions on most leading War Committees . . .'. On the other hand, 'if the Hindu Mahasabha is enabled to send its representatives on the extended Councils, such a step on the part of the Government will doubtless encourage these Hindu Sangathanists all over the country and cement further the alliance between the Government and the Hindu Mahasabha which it is my aim to bring about in the prosecution of the common cause of defending India against aggression from outside or from anarchy at home.'

Danger of the Mirage Dissolving, and the Dilemmas That Poses

All this is fine when stated in private, but the lunge for supporting the British Government has tightened the bind in which Savarkar and the Mahasabha are. The Congress has been caught in a dilemma also. On the one side, there is the strong view that the country should support every effort to defeat the Axis Powers, and on the other, there is the view held with equal conviction that the difficulties of the British should be used to hasten Independence. A Gandhian via media is agreed upon: register opposition to the country having been taken into the War without consultation but do it in such a

way that the British war effort is not hampered. Designated individuals are
to break a designated law—peacefully and one at a time, and thereby court
imprisonment. The Government comes down heavily on the protestors.
The public is outraged. The Mahasabha is on a cleft stick: it is supporting
the British, the Congress is opposing the British. Its Working Committee
meets and passes a Resolution—condemning everyone.

It castigates the Government for having unleashed repression, for not
having won the hearts of Indians by 'the immediate and actual grant of
Dominion Status' and thereby to win them over to join the war effort. But
in view of public anger at the arrests of even the tallest national leaders,
this is clearly not enough. So, the Resolution proceeds to say,

> The Working Committee feels aggrieved at the suffering of those
> patriotic Indians, to whatever parties they may have belonged who
> had to face imprisonment under the Defence of India Act or otherwise
> for activities and issues which were actuated with patriotic motives

But this would put it on the side of the Congress, and against the
Government. So, it adds,

> even though the Working Committee may not have believed in the
> wisdom or utility of many of those activities and issues in themselves.

But this will not be enough for the Government. So, the resolution launches
the familiar attack on Gandhiji for using the occasion to preach absolute
non-violence once again.

> But in spite of this sympathy with their suffering and appreciation
> of their patriotic motives, the Working Committee cannot but
> condemn the issues which the Congress has raised of preaching the
> principles of absolute non-violence which as interpreted by Gandhiji
> denounces all armed resistance even to incorrigible aggression under

all circumstances as a moral sin, and a crime. The Hindu Mahasabha holds that constituted as the world is, absolute non-violence as thus interpreted is absolutely impracticable in action and immoral in theory. Such absolute non-violence can only lead a nation to annihilation which again being an act of self-violence cannot but constitute violence just the same. Moreover, an absolute non-violence is under certain circumstances as great a crime as aggressive violence. In realistic political life, in particular, the armed strength of a nation does not only provide the acid test of its fitness to survive but constitutes as well the only guarantee of it. Consequently, the Hindu Sanghatanists have to dissociate themselves from the Civil Disobedience Campaign which the Congress has started on the issue of preaching this vicious principle of absolute non-violence sterilising the very martial instinct of our nation.

But such denunciation—especially when so many Congressmen have been thrown into prisons—will anger the people and confirm the public impression that the Mahasabha is doing the Government's bidding. And so, the resolution adds,

> But if any movement be started based on any definitely political issue, not detrimental to Hindu interests, the Hindu Mahasabha may consider the question of joining hands in a common struggle.

To dispel the impression further, and to shift the focus from the demands it has been proclaiming and which have been 'automatically eliminated', the resolution advocates an 'immediate programme' for members of the Mahasabha:

(a) To secure entry for as many Hindu recruits as possible into the Army, Navy and Air Forces.
(b) To utilize all facilities that are being thrown open to get our people trained into military mechanics and manufacture of up-to-date materials.

(c) To try to make military training compulsory in colleges and high schools.

(d) To intensify the organization of the Ram Sena.

(e) To join the Civic Guard movement with a view to enable to defend our own people against foreign invasion or internal anarchy provided always that the Civic Guards are not used against any patriotic political movement in India or in any activities detrimental to the legitimate interests of the Hindus.

(f) To start new industries on large scales to capture the market where foreign competition is found eliminated.

(g) To boycott foreign articles and defeat the entry of new foreign competitors.

(h) To set on foot an all-India movement to secure the correct registration, in the coming census, of the popular strength of the Hindus including Tribal Hindus such as Santhals, Gonds, Bhils, etc. and to secure their enlistment as Hindus instead of as Animists or Hill Tribes and by taking every other step necessary to secure the object in view.

All angles covered, Savarkar sends another letter on 25 November 1940 to the Viceroy 'for favour of personal perusal and needed action'.[4] He encloses the two resolutions.

Harmonizing the Resolutions

The two resolutions have given ammunition to critics. Which part of the resolution on the 'War Situation' is meant to be taken seriously? More than that, of the two resolutions which is to take precedence—the general essay on the 'War Situation' or the one listing specific points as the 'Immediate

---

[4] IOR, Mss.Eur.F.125/122 item 207.

Programme'? Savarkar issues a statement trying to harmonize the two resolutions.

The Mahasabha meets in an open session in Madurai on 28–29 December 1940. Public reaction to this convoluted stand forces Savarkar and the Mahasabha to adopt a more strident stand.

New Stance for the New Situation, New Arguments for the New Stance

On 28 December 1940, Savarkar, as their President, tells the audience, 'Under the present circumstances there is no reason for helping England unconditionally. On the contrary, we ought to think how we can turn the war situation to our advantage and for our defence . . .'[5]

'When two powerful countries go to war, it is quite possible for a country enslaved by one of them to resort to armed uprising and seek its independence,' says the revolutionary of yore. 'But at present we are disunited, divided and unarmed . . . Hence that course is not possible.' 'Moreover,' says Savarkar, with his reputation for organizing secret societies and operations, 'it is not right for Hindu Mahasabha or any other political party to discuss such a possibility openly. This is not out of any moral values that armed uprising should not be discussed, but present circumstances preclude that discussion.' And the usual switch to attacking the villain: 'On the other hand, it is absurd to think that only non-violent methods are moral. I just say this much that only relative non-violence is a virtue. The non-violence of Jain and Buddhist kings was quite different from Gandhi's non-violence. Jain and Buddhist scriptures state that those who murder sages (monks) should be killed.'

However, the issue is the about-turn of the Mahasabha. And so, the usual tactic: accuse the villain of doing what actually you are doing. While

---

[5] Like other speeches that Savarkar delivered as its President to the Hindu Mahasabha sessions, the Madurai speech is available in *Hindu Rashtra Darshan,* e-book composed by Chandrashekhar V. Sane.

he is the one who is making a deal with the British, he accuses Gandhiji of doing so. He says,

> But the British are crafty. They do not want the military spirit to be kindled among Hindus. That is why they praise Gandhi. I would not be surprised if Gandhi is allowed to preach his non-violence so long as the war effort of the British is not hindered. I go further and say that there has been a secret deal between the British rulers and Gandhi in which it was agreed that the British would propagate that Gandhi's non-violence became successful. We must condemn such killing of our martial spirit. That is the need of today.

In a word, we have to revive the military spirit among Hindus. The way to do so is military education and enlisting in the armed forces. The British are loathe to allow this. But the war has forced their hand. And so, a rare opportunity has fallen into our hands. To grasp this, we have to join hands with the British and help their war effort. QED:

> So, as I was saying, we should use the opportunities presented by the present situation for the militarisation of our youth and for industrialisation. We should not throw away such a rare opportunity simply because Gandhi cannot visualise it. I must remind you that even the moderates of Tilak's generation had demanded time and again that the Arms Act of 1858 by which Indians were disarmed should be repealed. They were far more wiser than the followers of Gandhi today. The Congress Party came to power in seven major provinces in 1937 and remained in office for 27 months. But they paid no attention to impart military training to our youth. On the contrary, Muslims never bothered about non-violence and their percentage in the Armed Forces is quite high. Dr Moonje and Bhai Paramanand had realised the Muslim game and have been trying to

counter it. Gandhi's obsession with non-violence killed the martial spirit in Hindus.

During the last three years, he has travelled from Punjab to Madras and has been urging all to imbibe military training, he tells the audience. But he could not figure out how this is to be done. 'This war has now provided the solution. Britain, in her self-interest, has decided to impart military training to our youth. Hindu Mahasabha has decided to take full advantage of this opportunity and support the British Administration in this respect. I say to you that after one year, our efforts have been largely successful.'

Don't think we are being fooled: 'I say once again that Britain has decided to militarise our youth and support the growth of new industries in their own self-interest. We have also decided to cooperate with them but in our interest. I have to say this explicitly because many of our people have some wrong ideas in their head about cooperating with the British. Their misgivings and fears need to be repelled . . .' Look at what is happening around the world: 'Russia and Germany are powerful nations. But overnight they came together for their common interest by signing a pact on 23 August 1939. So why should we be afraid of cooperating with Britain on specific issues?' He repeats his dictum: 'Anyone who always fears that his enemy will deceive him deserves to be deceived and get killed. Let us assure ourselves that we will match British craftiness. Let us be confident of ourselves and we will win.'

So, what his critics lack is understanding of world affairs, they are speaking out of fear, out of lack of confidence. He and the Mahasabha have no fear, they have courage that we can be as crafty—of course, they are not looking for anything, certainly not those seats in the Central Executive and War Councils; these are not even mentioned.

The collaboration is already bearing fruit, Savarkar says. Because of the Mahasabha's encouragement, 'thousands of Hindu youth' have enlisted in the armed forces. As a result, Muslims, who constituted 75 per cent of the armed forces, are now just a third. Similarly, many Hindus are overcoming age-old restrictions imposed in the name of religion, and because of encouragement by the Mahasabha are joining the Navy. 'They are rapidly learning the modern technology.' Our youth are learning how to produce rifles, ammunition, explosives, tanks. Licences have been given, factories are being set up to produce ships, aeroplanes, heavy machinery, chemicals. 'Until now they were obstructing such industrial establishments, now they are encouraging them because they have realised the importance of the need for India's self-sufficiency in this matter.' Are we to turn 'down this opportunity simply because some fools say that this amounts to collaborating with the British or that it encourages violence? We will be fools to miss this opportunity . . . This military build-up will provide jobs for millions and provide food, cloth and shelter to their families.'

And there is the other certainty: 'I must warn that if Hindus do not take advantage of this opportunity, Muslims would gladly cooperate with the British. They will gain the training and knowledge of modern warfare. Thus, we would make the folly of helping our other enemy with untold disastrous consequences for our future.'

And what exactly are we worried about? The British have already granted our demands:

I now declare that the British Administration has consented to the demands of Hindu Mahasabha. As we have asked, both the Viceroy and the Secretary of State for India have declared that within one year from the end of war, India will be granted Dominion Status. We asked for a promise, they have given it. At present they call it British Commonwealth. We should call it Indo-British Commonwealth. Our second demand was that there should be no partition of India. The Secretary of State for India has granted that also.

Had they really? The truth will soon be out—when the Viceroy's team make amply clear that they are not giving any specific date by which the British will give Dominion Status to India; when they make clear that to pledge categorically that India will not be partitioned would be to disregard the wishes of sizeable sections of Indian opinion and of those like the Princes towards whom they have treaty obligations.

Savarkar, who has been demanding assurances, turns around and asks his critics: in any case, why should one fight for such assurances? What is the use of such assurances on paper? Who knows when the war will end? Have big powers not made pledges and then just forgotten them? But for now, 'I now declare that the British Administration has consented to the demands of Hindu Mahasabha.'

Has to Explain Repeatedly

Savarkar had to press these arguments repeatedly—as often to audiences of Mahasabha members as to the general public. From this point of view, would it have been right to launch a movement during wartime for changing the method of administering Bharat? he would ask . . . In these circumstances, would it have been right for thousands of persons committed to Hindu Sangathan to rot in jails and part with lakhs of rupees as fines? All right, even if after doing so one got the assurance that within a year after the war ends, we will give such and such rights, will such rights be given to us? In statecraft what is the value of such verbal promises? Hasn't this been established by various events in international affairs? How can one be assured when the war will end? It is said that it will last anywhere from three to thirty years. In that case, should we keep sending members to jails for that many years? What will we secure with so much sacrifice— that we are at par with other dominions within the British Empire? From the point of view of policy, this is foolishness. And from the point of view of tactics, it is suicide. Today, the battlefield is prepared to yield any kind of outcome. Therefore, it is prudent to wait and watch which side will come out on top. Because then we will get to know who stands where . . . Once the war ends, and after seeing how victorious Britain has been, the time would have arrived to examine what kind of parity we can secure. Once that happens, it will be appropriate to put pressure on the Government through an open movement . . .[6]

True Patriotism

Yes, the Hindus too may not understand, Savarkar said. They may not vote for us in the coming elections. So what? We are patriots. What is losing one election against serving the interests of Hindudom? Here is how Savarkar equates the decision to support the British war effort with sacrifice:

I appreciate that many of our party workers are eager to court imprisonment, so that, come elections, they could say that they too have faced imprisonment like the Congressmen. However, what is the purpose of winning elections? Is it not primarily to protect Hindu interests? I am equally anxious to win seats in the next elections. However if, to win elections, we have to sacrifice the 'protection of Hindu interests' then, is it not better that we should not worry about winning elections in the future?

Today, it is our duty to support the militarisation and industrialisation of our country that would naturally follow with our present demand. That is of vital importance to our future. There is a possibility that by following this path, Hindu voters, unable to understand our policy, would not vote for us. But then, is it not

---

[6] Cf., *Savarkar Samagra,* Volume VIII, pp. 556–60.

better not to appeal to the foolhardy Hindu voters than abandon our work of national importance? If the voters realise the sacrifices we have made during our struggle for the legitimate rights of Hindus in Hyderabad, they would know that our workers had suffered far more hardships in Nizam's prisons than what Congressmen had suffered at the hands of the British. If we had been after ministerships alone we could have easily changed overnight and joined the Congress Party. But we are not crazy after power or for public applause but only for their good. Therefore we pay more importance to the militarisation and industrialisation. If by protecting interests of the Hindus we lose forthcoming elections, so be it. That is the true patriotism.

'Direct Action'

Unfortunately, not everyone is swayed. The resolutions take a different tack. Yes, under pressure from the Mahasabha, the session resolves, the Government has recognized that the political situation cannot be satisfactorily dealt with without the cooperation of the Mahasabha. For its part, without abandoning its faith in complete independence for a united India, the Mahasabha is prepared to accept Dominion Status as an immediate step. But even in regard to this, the declarations of the Viceroy and Secretary of State have been vague, inadequate and unsatisfactory. Unless by 31 March 1941 the Government makes an unequivocal statement that Dominion Status will be granted within one year of the ending of the war; unless it states clearly that it shall not countenance the division of India; and unless visible and effective steps are taken to protect Hindu minorities in Sindh, Punjab, NWFP and Bengal, the Mahasabha shall launch Direct Action. The session sets up an eight-member committee to devise and steer the Direct Action programme.

Another Letter is Needed

The two resolutions of the Working Committee and this call to Direct Action make Savarkar's task of playing all sides all the more difficult. On 11 January 1941, he writes to Linlithgow.[7] He downplays portions of and points in the two resolutions, and requests the Viceroy to see what he has emphasized in his statement about the resolutions:

> Your Excellency must have seen in the statement that the Mahasabha wishes the Government to take a special note of the fact that the Hindu Sanghatanists are not only exhorted to join the army, navy and air forces, manufactures for the war materials and all such allied departments as well as the Civic Guards, the A.R.P. organisations, etc. and to that extent participate Wholeheartedly in the war efforts on the part of the Government, — but are all called upon to be amenable and obedient to the discipline of those various organisations and do their duty without fail under their orders so long as they form part of them.

He gives a double guarantee of loyalty to the Government: those who join activities related to the war effort of the Government shall 'be amenable and obedient to the discipline of those various organisations and do their duty without fail under their orders.' And those who are mobilized for other activities shall not participate in war-related organizations. 'Consequently,' he says,

> whatever the other programme or activities of the Hindu Mahasabha be, the Government should entertain no doubt whatsoever as to the sincerity and dutifulness of the Hindu Sanghatanists who participate in these war efforts. The other programme and activities on the part of the Hindu Mahasabha whatever direction they may take cannot involve those Hindu Sanghatanists and Hindus in general who

---

[7] IOR, Mss.Eur.F.125/123 item 5.

join these organisations. The fact that both those resolutions were deliberately passed by the Session—the latter one on the 'Immediate Programme' being passed unanimously—is in itself a sufficient guarantee of the determination of the Mahasabha to maintain this attitude of responsive cooperation within these limits.

A Few 'Verbal Changes' to 'Weather the Storm'

Savarkar then tries to pare down what the War Situation Resolution has proclaimed to the public by condensing it to a few sanitized points. What this exercise is in aid of becomes clear: 'I am sure that if Your Excellency views the resolution in the light of the suggestions I make in this letter, we shall be able to weather the storm quite smoothly.' In a word, the double-talk has created a 'storm' and here is a way to weather it.

First, as for demanding a declaration of Dominion Status being granted within a year of the cessation of the War, all that is needed is a slight verbal change in what the Government has already declared. Not just that. Savarkar assures the Viceroy that 'if owing to some unavoidable delay, the framing of the constitution and its passing into an act require a prolongation of a few months more, no sensible party can fail to acquiesce in it if the reasons for that delay were reasonable.'

Second, as for safeguarding the legitimate rights of minorities in any future constitution, all the Government has to declare is that the legitimate rights of both the minorities and the majority shall be protected. There should be no difficulty in saying this 'Because in any case even such a proposal as this has after all to take for granted that the last word shall remain with the British Parliament unless indeed it renounces all rights of sovereignty over India. The very fact that the statements that the Government shall not accept any constitution unless it is assented to by the minorities do imply that the Government reserves to itself the right of sanctioning or rejecting any part of the draft prepared by Indians in connection with the future constitution. That is, in the last resort, it is the

British Government which accepts the responsibility for the constitutional scheme when they get it passed through the Parliament.' Of course, the constitution so framed 'will be founded on the basic principles of the indivisibility of India as a Nation and a State, a central Government strong enough to maintain this integrity against any attacks from outside or inside and the status of a self-governing co-partnership as contemplated under the Westminster Statute within the Indo-British Commonwealth.'

The British Government made no such announcement. On the contrary, the British Prime Minister, Churchill left no one in any doubt that he was fighting for the indivisibility of the British Empire, that he had not become Prime Minister to preside over the liquidation of the British Empire. Yet, Savarkar led the Hindu Mahasabha into joining hands with the Government 'Wholeheartedly' as he stressed repeatedly.

The third point in the resolutions is easiest to satisfy, Savarkar told the Viceroy: just allow colleges and universities to offer compulsory military education. It will be enough to do this 'on a small scale at any rate, to begin with'. And look at the returns—it will keep the youth from joining the civil resistance programme: 'Such a step if readily taken by the Government cannot fail to appeal to the imagination of the youths, ensure to some extent on that score the belief in the efficacy of the constitutional agitation and restrain them from taking to any civil resistance programme through sheer despair, having every demand slighted.'

The fourth point is one to which we will have to return more than once. It concerns, to use Savarkar's words,

... the most intolerable distress which the Hindu minority in Bengal, Sindh and the Frontier Provinces are forced to face as a consequence of the planned-out anti-Hindu policy of the Muslim Governments there and the failure of the Governors to protect even the life, property and honour of Hindu womanhood. It is painful and humiliating in extreme even to catalogue the sufferings of the Hindus in some districts in

Bengal. The case of Sindh is too notorious to require any emphasis. It is a bit reassuring that the pressure brought by the Governor to bear on the Provincial Government in Sindh has at last resulted in checking to some extent at any rate the financial outrages of the Muslims against the Hindus for the time being. But that is only a haphazard step and in Bengal even that much check has not been put by the Governor of Bengal to the anti-Hindu policy of the Muslim Government there. The Hindu Sabhas in Bengal, Sindh and the North-Western Province can quote chapter and verse to prove these serious charges against the Muslim fanaticism running rampant in those Provinces. I ask Your Excellency whether the solicitude which the Imperial Government has been expressing in their announcements, statements, speeches every now and then about safeguarding the interests of minorities do or do not apply to the Hindu minorities as well?

Government should make a clear announcement asking the concerned governments to stop the atrocities forthwith, failing which the Governors would be authorised to take the governments in their own hands, Savarkar writes.

The final paragraph puts even these four points—'in perspective', one may say. Savarkar concludes with an assurance:

In the end I assure Your Excellency that the Hindu Mahasabha is not in any uncompromising mood. The very Resolution mentions that 'Responsive cooperation has been, is still, and will be the policy of the Mahasabha'; and it has appreciated and recognised some efforts on the part of the Indian and British Government to concede some legitimate demands of the Hindu Mahasabha during the war period. I hope Your Excellency will accept my suggestions made in this letter by me in a very frank and friendly way especially so as they, in general, involve only some verbal and not very drastic improvements in the language and policy which the Indian Government under Your Excellency's lead have already come to adopt.

To what purpose, pray? To 'weather the storm smoothly'—that clearly was Savarkar's purpose:

> If but Your Excellency meets these four important points referred to above as (a), (b), (c), (d) in some such manner as I have explained above, I am sure we shall all be able to weather the storm smoothly and the Hindu Mahasabha will be in a position to continue to participate in war efforts far more effectively than it could do as yet on points where the interests of the Hindus are now identical with the interests of the British.

Left to the Secretary

The Viceroy is camping in Jamnagar. His Secretary replies on 13 January 1941 by telegram:[8] His Excellency desires me to thank you for the letter and documents you sent 'which he has read with interest,' he wires, but adds, 'though he feels sure that you will recognise that it will be impossible for him to accept certain of the statements or criticisms suggested in those documents as in his judgment accurate'.

An Ominous Opening

The Secretary sends a fuller reply on 30 January 1941.[9] The opening paragraph is as ominous as it is cutting:

> His Excellency is greatly obliged to you for your full and clear letter of 11th January, and very much appreciates the pains to which you have

---

[8] IOR, Mss.Eur.F.125/122 item 6.

[9] IOR, Mss.Eur.F.125/122 item 16.

been to put him in possession of your mind on the important points which it covers, and to elucidate the intention of the resolutions passed by the Hindu Mahasabha at their session in Madura. He appreciates also the general tone of your letter, though he asks me to say that he cannot but regret that in their public resolutions the Mahasabha have taken up an attitude so threatening and pugnacious as they have, since they can hardly hope to help their case by taking up in public an attitude which does not apparently reflect their real ideas.

As for the rest, the Secretary says that the points have already been covered, and he refers Savarkar to speeches that Amery, the Secretary of State for India in London, and Linlithgow have made from time to time—except in regard to compulsory military training in schools and colleges: on this, the Secretary says that he will get back later. 'Having regard to the statements referred to, which in his judgment clearly set out the position, His Excellency, while appreciating the reasons for your request, regrets that he is unable to accede to it.'

How You Should Write Your Reply!

Savarkar sends another long letter on 20 February 1941—reiterating his suggestions, but now with a tinge of impatience.[10] He begins by telling the Viceroy how his—the latter's—reply should be written! The Secretary has merely referred to assorted speeches and statements that have been issued, Savarkar says. 'It is very likely that I may miss some sentences you meant to serve as a reply to a particular point at issue,' he tells the Viceroy, 'or on the contrary it is very likely that some of your sentences may seem to me to contain your intended reply on some other point without your meaning it.' 'To avoid this difficulty and possible misunderstanding I think it is very necessary and advisable that Your Excellency should kindly set forth

---

[10] IOR, Mss.Eur.F.125/122 item 26.

definite replies under definite points to which they refer, serially as (a), (b), (c), (d). It matters not if the reply to a point consists only of quotations from your old speeches or statements. But then those quotations should be collected together and laid down as a definite reply to a definite point. This arrangement will also enable me to place before the Working Committee in a well tabulated form these replies to the points (a), (b), (c), (d), <u>serially and with precision.</u>'[11]

Having stood firm on how the Viceroy should write his reply, Savarkar capitulates on the main demand! He and the Hindu Mahasabha have been declaring again and again that nothing short of a categorical commitment that India will be given complete independence/sorry Dominion Status as soon as the war ends will suffice. Savarkar changes this to read as follows:

(a) The Government <u>will try its best</u>[12] to grant Dominion Status to India in such wise as to ensure her free and equal co-partnership in the Indo-British Commonwealth, within a year after the cessation of the war.

'Try its best', and that too underlined—how could the Viceroy have missed the capitulation?

And what is it in pursuit of? Linlithgow is not one to miss that it is in regard to nothing other than the prospect that he himself had held out in the beginning—of the Hindu Mahasabha persons joining the Viceroy's Executive Council and the War Advisory Council. The anxiety shouts through the concluding portions of Savarkar's letter:

Inasmuch as Your Excellency still maintains that the proposal to expand the Executive Council and to form the War Advisory Council is still open, I wish to draw your pointed attention to the fact that

---

[11] Underlining in the original.

[12] Underlining in the original.

the Government can no longer be justified in refusing to give effect to that proposal on their own responsibility by pointing out to the excuse that a party here or there is still refusing to participate in it. If we are to wait till all the parties and persons agree to support any given progressive step, we shall have to wait for ever. Neither in England, nor in France, nor in any country, the Government there are backed by all parties and down to a man. Even today in England there are political parties opposed to the present 'National Government' and several leaders of antagonistic political schools are clapped in jail.

I consequently call upon the Government that –

(e) Now that the Hindu Mahasabha, the Liberal League, the All-India Christian Federation and several other political parties as well as many leaders occupying an outstanding position in the public and who have held responsible positions as Prime Ministers, Ministers, Executive Councillors, &c., have declared themselves openly in favour of an immediate expansion of the Central Executive Council and the establishment of the War Advisory Council, the Indian Government should give effect on their own responsibility to this proposal by nominating outstanding and able Indian leaders on the Executive Council and the War Council and should transfer all important portfolios to such non-official members, taking care to see that the population proportion of the Hindus in general is roughly reflected in any such extended Executive Council as well as the War Council.

'Hoping Fervently'

The malapropism in the next sentence cannot be improved. Savarkar says, 'I exhort Your Excellency to take immediate steps to grant these most reasonable and compromising demands without any further delay which cannot but be dangerous to the peace and progress of the Indian nation as well as to the best interest of the British people.' Lest that, in spite of those 'compromising demands', seem peremptory, Savarkar concludes with a fervent hope:

> Hoping fervently that a sympathetic and wise handling of the situation on the part of Your Excellency will enable us all to arrive at an amicable settlement on the points at issue . . .

The Door Shuts

Apparently, Savarkar's declamations about atrocities being committed against Hindus have had no effect. The Secretary has merely drawn attention to the 'constitutional position' regarding law and order—it is the responsibility of the provincial governments. But the Constitution also empowers the Governors to intervene to protect the interests of minorities, Savarkar points out and asks: Had similar atrocities been committed against English men, women and children, would the Governors not have stepped in? Would they not have dismissed the Ministries? 'Consequently,' Savarkar writes,

> the Indian Government should give a solemn and public assurance to the Hindus that stringent steps will forthwith be taken to protect the life and property of Hindus in Sind and North-West Frontier Province, to inflict condign punishment on the murderous Muslim gangs and tribes and to compel the Muslim Ministries in Punjab and Bengal to give up their anti-Hindu policy and in cases it is found necessary to give effect to this objective to suspend the provincial autonomy in these provinces and to call upon the Governors to resume all governmental powers in their own hands.[1]

Again, it is Linlithgow's Secretary who replies—on 7 March 1941.[2] The letter is firm in rejecting Savarkar's demands and suggestions for verbal

---

[1] IOR, Mss.Eur.F.125/122 item 26.

[2] IOR, Mss.Eur.F.125/122 item 30.

subterfuges. The Secretary again refers to statements that have already been made regarding constitutional progress, etc. and observes,

> He [the Viceroy] feels sure that if the pronouncements on these matters made in the declaration of 8th August, in Mr. Amery's speech in the House of Commons on the 15th August 1940, in His Excellency's speech of 20th November to the Legislature, and in the section of the Viceroy's own speech to the Associated Chambers of Commerce of 18th December, are studied with attention and with full belief in the sincerity of His Majesty's Government, their reassuring character will be apparent to you. You will appreciate at once the impracticability, given the fact that the policy of His Majesty's Government is represented in the carefully considered declaration of 8th August 1940, of making supplementary declarations going substantially beyond the terms of that declaration, such as those for which you ask in your letter.
>
> His Excellency asks me to add in the same connection that while he greatly regrets that the requisite degree of support for the proposals embodied in the statements of 8th August 1940 should still be lacking, he greatly regrets that he cannot accept the suggestion that it would be wise or desirable to give effect to those proposals in the absence of such support, anxious though he has always been and remains today to see an early and generally acceptable solution of the constitutional problem.

So, that door is shut. Worse, on the matter on which several hearts have been racing in anxiety—that of finding places in the Viceroy's Executive Council and the War Advisory Council—the news is most discouraging:

> As regards the request embodied in (e) of your letter of 20th December, he would invite attention to the statement made by him in his speech to the combined Legislature on 20th November 1940 as to the views

of His Majesty's Government and the fact that the proposals which were put forward in August of last year remain open and that His Majesty's Government are still prepared to give effect to them as soon as they are convinced that a sufficient degree of representative support is forthcoming, although as that degree of support 'has evidently not yet manifested itself' His Majesty's Government has decided that the Viceroy would not be justified in proceeding with the expansion of his Executive Council or the establishment of an Advisory Council at the present moment.

Afraid to Wound—Himself

Savarkar is finding it difficult to keep up the pretense of negotiating as an equal, indeed of showing the way to a poor Viceroy. That he feels slighted, or, God forbid, that by now he has reason to believe that he was being played along, shows through his next letter to the Viceroy— that of 27 March 1941.[3] He is moved to strike, but is afraid to wound— himself. He placed the Secretary's reply before his Working Committee, Savarkar informs the Viceroy. The Working Committee gave it a careful consideration and deliberately postponed making any final decision till 31 March 1941, the date which was fixed by the Madura resolution for negotiations to continue. As the Working Committee is still prepared to arrive at an amicable understanding and as some margin was left in Your Excellency's latest letter for further negotiations, it was thought advisable that Your Excellency should be acquainted with the views of the Working Committee in connection with the points touched in your latest communication referred to above and to see if the Government could be persuaded in consequence of those views to meet those outstanding and legitimate demands of the Hindu Mahasabha, which were not satisfactorily met even in your last reply.

---

[3] IOR, Mss.Eur.F.125/122 item 35.

Savarkar largely reiterates what he has been saying. He strains to make out that there has been no dilution in demands. Linlithgow would have seen through the effort. On the crucial question—of constitutional reform, Dominion Status, equality with other members of the Commonwealth, etc. for instance—Savarkar says that the declaration made recently by the British 'meets more or less the demand of the Hindu Mahasabha on this outstanding point'. Of course, some differences remain, 'But these differences may be accommodated later on and conveniently overlooked for the time being'—a giveaway if ever there was one.

Savarkar comes back to the real point—places in the Executive Council and the War Advisory Council:

As to the last of the outstanding demands made by the Hindu Mahasabha in connection with the immediate Indianisation of the Executive Council on the lines suggested in (e) in my last letter, Your Excellency has again assured the Mahasabha in your last reply that the proposal was still open and the Government was prepared to give effect to it as soon as sufficient public support of a representative character was forthcoming.

Now, if the lack of such a support was the real difficulty standing in the way of the Government to take that step, then it could no longer be said that such a difficulty exists still in the face of the co-operation promised by the Hindu Mahasabha on one hand in that respect and the readiness expressed by the recent non-party conference of eminent political leaders held at Bombay on the 13th and 14th instant to do the same on the other hand.

If the Government questions, 'But what of the Congress?' all that I need ask here in reply, 'Has not the Government said more than once that it was prepared to proceed to give effect to the expansion of the Executive Council and the War Advisory Council even if the Congress kept out of it? Or has the Government ever stopped for a minute to function even autocratically because the Congress or any other party in the Land refused to co-operate with it?' Consequently, the Congress can no longer serve as an honest excuse to the Government to postpone all progressive reforms.

The 'non-Party conference' that Savarkar pointed to had been held in Bombay on the 13th and 14th. Eminent men like Sir Tej Bahadur Sapru, M.S. Aney, Pandit Hriday Nath Kunzru, Dr Ambedkar 'and others representing hundreds of thousands of voters and several outstanding leaders of the Hindu Mahasabha commanding the confidence of millions of Hindus' attended the conference, he points out. '. . . can such a conference be ever said to be not sufficiently representative of the principal political elements in India?' he asks. The Hindu Mahasabha itself counts for a lot, Savarkar emphasizes. It has inflicted electoral defeats on the Congress 'in a dozen places in Sind, Bengal and Maharashtra'. This 'renders it impossible for the Government to deny that now at any rate this united strength of so many leaders and parties does constitute public support sufficiently representative to enable the Government to proceed with the Indianization of the Executive Council of the Indian Government as a measure during the war period to serve as an earnest of the post-war constitution.'

The Prime Minister Himself

Savarkar returns to the atrocities being heaped on Hindus:

> . . . Bengal too like Sind is having a blood-bath as an inevitable consequence of the anti-Hindu policy of the Moslem Ministry there where the very Prime Minister Mr Fazlul Haq has openly declared that he would tyrannise the Hindus (*'Hum Hinduon ko satayenge'*).

'No'—Across the Board

The Viceroy's Secretary replies on 4 April 1941.[4] The letter is a comprehensive 'No' couched in politesse. His Excellency 'appreciates the pains you have taken to set out your point of view for his consideration', the Secretary writes, 'and he is glad to observe from your letter that the correspondence which has passed with you has made the position clear in relation to a number of important points raised by you'.

Far from further concessions being made, further statements also are not required, Savarkar is told:

He has very carefully considered, and with every desire to assist you in reaching your conclusions on the matters under discussion, whether there is anything which he can at the present stage usefully add to my previous letters or the public statements which the Secretary of State and he have made on various occasions, and to which particular reference has been made at various stages of our correspondence, and notably in paragraphs 1 and 4 of my letter of 7th March last. After reviewing the correspondence, and the various statements to which I have already referred, he feels, however, that the ground has been so thoroughly covered in our correspondence and in the statements of the Secretary of State and himself that there is nothing fresh that he can profitably add; and in particular on the point discussed in paragraph 4 of your letter he cannot but feel that the statement contained in my letter of the 7th March entirely covers the position. He asks me, however, to thank you again for your very full and detailed exposition of your views, and to say that he trusts that any misunderstandings that there may have been have now been overcome.

And here was Savarkar drafting phrases that the Viceroy and the Secretary of State should use!

---

[4] IOR, Mss.Eur.F.125/122 item 40.er

Jinnah's Contempt

Within days of Savarkar invoking the Bombay Conference to buttress his demand for an expansion of the Executive Council, Jinnah makes light of the Conference: 'He [Jinnah] was frankly contemptuous of Bombay Conference,' Linlithgow informed Secretary of State by telegram of 16 April 1941. 'Given great importance of securing reasonable degree of Moslem support for any compromise, this is material.' And soon Savarkar himself disowned Sapru's statement that the Mahasabha had participated in the Conference.[5]

Dismissive and Firm

Days before the Secretary's reply to Savarkar, in an 'Immediate', encrypted telegram to the Secretary of State, Linlithgow had struck down the demand for Indianization of the Executive Council already. On 30 March 1941, he had given a detailed account of developments in India and of his interactions with various leaders.[6] On the immediate proposal that Savarkar was pressing—the enlargement and Indianization of the Executive Council—and on his invoking the meeting in Bombay to buttress his case, Linlithgow had been as firm as he had been dismissive. He had cabled:

> I need not comment on the fact that (a) the demand put forward by this body goes far beyond the considered (? policy of) His Majesty's Government as set out in the declaration of last August (b) that other objections apart, we could not transfer defence or finance to non-officials or concede Dominion position in Imperial and international relations without hopelessly prejudicing war discussions; it would, too, very definitely close the door to any translations into new scheme of safeguards of Part I of the Act of 1935 (c) that it ignores

---

[5] IOR, Mss.Eur.F.125/20.

[6] IOR, L/P&J/8/508.

difficulties of a communal character which will be concomitant of
transfer of defence portfolio to an Indian and equally extent to which
it is essential for us to maintain existing arrangements (though we
cannot say this publicly) at a time when India is so much the material
center for Eastern Supply Group area, and when there are military
considerations which weigh of extra-Indian importance. Finally,
even if the conference were unanimously in support of its resolution
(which as you will see from para. No. 4 of my telegram of March 19th
they were not) a Government composed of men of this type could
not hope to deliver the goods without support of at least one of major
political parties; would be in a minority in the assembly and could not
be regarded as really meeting demand that India as a whole should
be more closely associated with the Government and (? war) effort
in war-time.

And here was Savarkar, 'I consequently call upon the Government that
. . ', 'I exhort Your Excellency to take immediate steps to meet these most
reasonable and compromising demands without any further delay which
cannot but be dangerous to the peace and progress of the Indian nation
as well as to the best interests of the British people . . ', 'I expect to receive
Your Excellency's reply separately and serially detailed as requested above
to all these points. . .'

Reason for Viceroy's Confidence

Linlithgow was emboldened in waving aside Savarkar's demands and
arguments because he was convinced that Savarkar and the Mahasabha
were panting to join hands with the Government and would not distance
themselves an inch—their demands met or not met. In the telegram, he
informed the Secretary of State:

My correspondence with Hindu Mahasabha continues on friendly
basis. They clearly do not want a real break and letter I have just had

from Savarkar, while demanding full Indianisation of my Council, a guarantee of indivisibility and essential unity of all India and various minor adjustments, is friendly in character. But Mahasabha by themselves cannot tilt the balance.

While Savarkar, and we can presume others, were imagining that they were engaged in, to use Savarkar's oft-repeated word, 'negotiations', the Viceroy was clear that the Government must not move beyond the announcements it had already made in August the previous year. He emphasized this to the Secretary of State:

It remains in my judgment axiomatic that substantial support, i.e. either from Moslem League or from Congress, plus in either event less important elements such as Scheduled Castes, Aney, the Mahasabha, is an essential pre-condition of any workable scheme. I am equally clear that we should not allow ourselves, merely because of impatience here or at home at present stalemate, to be bluffed into going in any degree beyond offer of last August, which I have no doubt whatever represents farthest to which we can wisely go during any transitional period and pending post-war discussions . . .

This was the reality. But the great realist was still dreaming of the mirage.

They Seek Our Intervention, They Depend On Us

Riots have broken out in Dacca. Savarkar sends a telegram to the Secretary of State for India. He says that ten thousand Hindus have been rendered homeless, that they are starving, that the provincial ministry is partially unwilling and wholly incapable of protecting the Hindus. Savarkar urges that the Governor be instructed to dismiss the ministry and take over the administration. On 18 April 1941, the Secretary of State sends the Governor General an encrypted 'Important' telegram.[7] He informs him

---

[7] IOR, L/P&J/8/508.

about Savarkar's telegram and what the latter has urged in it, adding, 'Unless you see any objection will you please acknowledge on my behalf in such manner as seems appropriate.' While Savarkar may have thought that he was putting the British Government on the spot, the Secretary of State sees in Savarkar's telegram and suggestions quite the opposite. He tells Linlithgow, 'I am thinking of quoting this in Debate as showing how instinctively Indians still demand our intervention to solve difficulties and how little direct government is really resented . . .' He adds, '. . . but will not do so or will do so without mentioning name or party if you think it might embarrass you in relation to Savarkar.'

In an encrypted telegram to the Secretary of State on 20 April 1941, Linlithgow says that 'I quite agree as to the attractiveness of idea, but am on the whole a little afraid that it might be turned against us, and am inclined therefore to deprecate.'[8] If, however, the Secretary decides to make a statement, it should be couched 'in very general terms', and should 'avoid any direct association either with Savarkar or the very delicate Dacca situation.'[9]

Another Rollback

Time for further rollbacks. During its open session in Madurai on 29 December 1940, the Mahasabha had resolved that unless by 31 March, 1941, the Government made a definite and clear declaration that India would be granted Dominion Status within one year of the termination of the War, and that the integrity and indivisibility of India would be preserved, the Mahasabha would start 'Direct Action'. It had even set up a committee to chalk out the elements of, and the plan for countrywide Direct Action. A meeting of the All-India Committee of the Mahasabha

---

[8] IOR, L/P&J/8/508.r

[9] Governor General to Secretary of State for India, 20th April, 1941. The reference to Dacca is to the riots that had erupted there.

is scheduled to take place in Calcutta on 14 June 1941. Agitated members draw up a draft resolution to carry forward the Direct Action Plan. Several members, including Savarkar's brothers, sign the draft. It is brought to Savarkar for endorsement. As has been his usual practice—recall the fourth strike in the Andamans—he tells the signatories that personally he is for Direct Action and 'Buy Indian' but, being the President, he cannot take 'a partisan stand' by formally endorsing a draft prepared by some members. He would have to wait for the decision at the meeting.

Of 400 who were to attend, 200 attend. Savarkar presides. He reminds members of the War, that it is approaching both eastern and western frontiers of the country. He reminds them of internal disturbances. It is in the best interest of Hindus, he says, for them to look at the fiasco of the Congress and not imitate its foolish jail-going programme. Moonje moves the main resolution. He explains that the Madurai resolution announcing Direct Action if demands were not met by 31 March was passed with an eye on provincial elections and to show that the Congress did not have the monopoly of sacrifice. In any case, much has been achieved as a result of the Mahasabha's pressure.

The resolution toes this 'positive spin'. The Viceroy has rejected the 'fantastic' demands of the Muslim League in regard to the expansion of the Viceroy's Council, it proclaims. Under pressure of public opinion created by the Hindu Mahasabha, the Secretary of State has criticized Muslim League's demand for Pakistan. As urged by the Mahasabha, the Government has taken action against the Khaksars, though the Government has not yet acted to protect Hindu interests in Sindh, the Frontier province, Punjab and Bengal. In view of the international situation and internal disturbances, the aggression against Hindus, 'and also in view of the fact that the war is rapidly approaching our Motherland on both frontiers', the resolution proposes that the planned Direct Action be postponed. Instead, it urges all to create Hindu solidarity by removing all artificial barriers; to organize Volunteer Dals; to launch a vigorous campaign to enroll at least one crore members before the next All India session; and to launch a 'Buy Hindu' campaign to help Hindu industries and concerns. Members pass it—61 to 10.

The Government notes the large number of abstentions. At the junior level, officers are also anxious about the call to 'Buy Hindu' and about the programme to enroll one crore members. But seniors point out that these are not new, and that, overall, the Mahasabha is anxious not to go beyond what discussions and correspondence with Viceroy would allow. The main outcome is that even though the demands they had been making have not been met, they have decided to postpone Direct Action. Savarkar's special pleading makes this evident to the officers.

The Usual Villain

But the public is another matter. The large number of abstentions also speaks to a disapproval within the Mahasabha—in fact, a disapproval even among these handpicked Mahasabha leaders. Savarkar sees this. He *has* to fortify the rationalizations, and to do so publicly. As is his custom, he blames others for it—members of the Mahasabha as much as of the public who do not understand even such an elementary thing about political life. And the one who has clouded their minds—the usual villain, Gandhi! Savarkar fumes. We do not believe in absolute non-violence, or in filling jails. By 'Direct Action', he says,

the Hindu Mahasabha means resistance to aggression offered in such wise as to inflict a deterrent punishment on the wrong-doer, to make the aggressor suffer more in the long run than their own forces. It never contributed to the general superstition which fancies that going forward must always be an act of bravery or falling backward of cowardice. If your forces, while marching on, find themselves suddenly on the point of a precipice, it cannot be an act of bravery but of criminal foolhardiness to persist still in going forward and furl [sic.] then down into an abysmal depth of destruction. While you are waiting for a frontal attack, if you find all of a sudden that an hostile force appears on your rear to attack you, does not bravery consist in suddenly taking a roundabout turn in falling back and returning the attack? Or does it consist in still maintaining your frontal stand simply for the boorish fear that such a falling back will be stigmatised by some fools or knaves as an act of cowardice? The first principle in politics as well as in warfare lays it down that consistency is to be judged in relation to the ultimate goal and not in relation to the movements and manoeuvres.

And then to the villain:

These are truisms. But the public sense and view have been blurred to such an extent by the fantastic exhibitions of the so-called Gandhist 'Technic' during a couple of decades in the past that even such political truisms require to be retaught as original truths![10]

In any case, the Muslims are always there to help explain away uncomfortable things. Savarkar has throughout been conjuring miasmas about the calamity that the inherent treachery of the Muslims is bound to bring down on the country. As had happened during the Khilafat agitation, he says, treacherous Muslims here, especially in the NWFP may enter into an alliance with foreign Muslim powers to establish a Muslim State from the Frontier up to Delhi:

The tribesmen and the Muslim forces throughout Punjab, Sindh, etc. are very likely to betray the Hindus and rise *en masse* in pursuance

---

[10] 'Direct Action myth exploded,' 24 June 1941, in *Vinayak Damodar Savarkar's Whirlwind Propaganda Tours: Statements, Messages and Extracts from the President's Diary of His Propagandistic Tours, Interviews from December 1937 to October 1941,* A.S. Bhide [ed.], Bombay, 1941, pp. 434–35.

of the pan-Islamic designs to carve out an independent Moslem State
or Federation stretching out from Baluchistan to Kashmir to Delhi
In view of the attitude of many a responsible Moslem Organization
in India as revealed by their resolutions passed in their open sessions
betraying their extra-territorial sympathies it would be nothing short
of a suicidal and purblind step on behalf of the Hindus to make light of
this serious danger threatening them. Under such an emergency they
will have to ally themselves with the British Forces in the common
objective to avert this national calamity.[11]

'One Has to Be a Crook'

Back from the Calcutta gathering, Savarkar continues his speeches—he
has to explain the about-turns to his followers, and at the same time he
has to ensure that the Viceroy continues to believe that he will live up to
his commitment of helping the British. On 13 April 1941, he gives another
speech, in Nagpur. This War presents us with a golden opportunity. We
should take advantage of it. 'Until now, the revolutionaries had to smuggle
pistols and bombs. But now the British authorities are giving them in the
hands of the youth . . . I have never made a secret of the need to undergo
military training,' he says. This is not so much for helping the British as
it is 'with the ultimate aim to achieve our independence,' he says. 'I have
even told the Viceroy that I am encouraging our youth to join the armed
forces for gaining knowledge and then for defending our freedom.' Yes, he
acknowledges that he has said, and the resolutions of the Mahasabha have
emphasized that so long as the Sangathanists are in the armed forces and
in factories producing war material, they must obey orders. But that is as

---

[11] This thesis of Savarkar was repeated in resolutions of the Hindu Mahasabha: Cf., the
resolution of 19 November 1939: *Vinayak Damodar Savarkar's Whirlwind Propaganda:
Extracts from the President's Diary of his Propagandistic Tours and Interviews from
December 1937 to October 1941*, A.S. Bhide (ed.), Bombay, 1941, pp. 166–68.

of now: 'At present we have to obey the orders of the British. I have not guaranteed what would happen in the future.'

'One has to be a crook in politics,' he explains. 'We can make a treaty with the British for our own interest. Therefore I urge you to join the Army, Navy and Air Force. The British are facing danger on all the fronts. Take advantage of that situation.' 'We are not ashamed of going to England to become Barristers. So, why should we be ashamed of approaching the British for military training? They know why I am asking you to enlist, but they are accepting you because they need you.'

On the Other Side There Is the Viceroy to Persuade

Savarkar keeps sending letters to the Viceroy. On 12 July 1941, he tells the Viceroy that the Hindu Mahasabha is prepared to wait 'for a reasonable length of time' for the Government to fulfil the 'promises and assurances given by Your Excellency during the course of our correspondence'; that for its part the Mahasabha has been persuading Hindus to join the armed forces in their own interest.[12] But now the Government 'also must respond to this favourable attitude on the part of the Hindus by indicating Governmental appreciation and by stimulating public enthusiasm.' And the one way to do so is 'to effect some substantial constitutional reform which could be ushered in even during the war time and would consequently serve as an earnest for the promised grant of "The equal co-partnership in the Indo-British Commonwealth during the shortest possible time after the end of the War".'

As for a concrete step, Savarkar is back to recommending the expansion of the Viceroy's Executive Council and the constitution of the War Advisory Council. He has by now realized that the sort of persons he had recommended are not going to be taken in. So, he temporizes: 'The intention of the Government, as reported, to appoint on the War

---

[12] Mss Eur 125/123.

Advisory Council only members from the Central Legislature is not quite objectionable in so far as it goes'—with a caveat: 'But Your Excellency will take a special note of the fact that amongst the members nominated on the War Advisory Council there must be someone possessing the full confidence of the Hindu Mahasabha.' He suggests a name. He now displays similar flexibility for the proposal to confine the selection of additional members for the Viceroy's expanded Executive Council: 'the Mahasabha would not mind much for the present if the choice is restricted only to the members of the Central Legislatures . . .' and he suggests a name.

Quite a climbdown: from all Hindu seats in the expanded Executive Council and fifteen seats in the War Advisory Council to be given to nominees of the Mahasabha, now to 'some*one*'.

He is more emphatic on the next point. In case the Defence portfolio is to be transferred to an Indian, under no circumstances must it be given to a Muslim: 'The Hindus can never be persuaded to entrust Indian Defence, under the present circumstances,[13] to any Moslem member whatever his eminence or party label may be.' 'It is not the question of sentiment alone,' he explains to the Viceroy, 'but the Hindus are convinced and the Government also have reasons to realise that the Hindus are justified in being thus convinced that not only the interests of the Hindus alone but the interests of the Indian Nation and the Indian State as well demand that under the war situation as it prevails in Asia and Europe and in view of the Moslem designs as they are outspokenly and actively pursued in India no Moslem should be entrusted with the portfolio of Indian Defence.' 'I earnestly hope,' Savarkar adds, 'the Government will not deliberately do anything at this time which they can very well avoid doing, to alienate the sympathies of Hindudom as a whole and make them doubt the wisdom of the policy of extending a Wholehearted

---

[13] Underlined in the original.

cooperation to the war efforts of the Government. Your Excellency can easily tide over the difficulty by entrusting any non-Moslem gentleman to that office. There are so many of them as capable to discharge that duty as any Moslem gentleman available.'

This is the point that catches the officials' eyes. The official processing Savarkar's letter remarks on file that it 'inter alia illustrates the difficulties attending the question of giving the "Defence Portfolio" to an Indian'—a good reason not to do anything in the matter.

In his writings and speeches, Savarkar has been claiming thundering response to his appeals and the efforts of the Mahasabha: thousands and thousands have been joining the armed forces as a result. In the letter, he is compelled to defend the outcome. 'In this connection I must put in an emphatic contradiction,' Savarkar writes, 'of the vague impression which some interested parties are spreading about that the Hindus have not contributed to the war efforts as largely as others have done.' Hindu Princes and people have 'contributed immeasurably more both in men and money,' he says. 'The Hindu Princes alone have donated not less than some ninety-five lacs of rupees in addition to an equal sum contributed by the Hindu public in general,' he informs the Viceroy. And the princely states have sent 'large forces to the front'. More to the point, 'The Hindu Mahasabha has given in unambiguous terms a lead to the Hindu people to fight in the cause of Indian Defence in this war. Its leaders are touring throughout India to whip up military enthusiasm and spirit in the Hindu public. It has set up "Hindu Militarisation Mandals" throughout India. Some of these are doing excellent work and thousands of Hindus have already joined the rank and file of the Indian forces in all branches . . .'

The Government would have had a measure of how much of the increase in recruitment had come about because of Savarkar's tours and how much had been caused by other factors—like inflation, scarcity of goods, difficulties in getting jobs, etc.

Denouement

The Muslim League passes the 'Pakistan Resolution' in March 1940 at its session in Lahore. The Congress launches its Civil Disobedience movement. Around 2,000 leaders and members of the Congress are put in jail, and many more in the following weeks. In November, the All-India Congress Committee declares that the apprehensions of the minorities, and of the Princes are no obstacle to constitutional progress, nor to the country's independence. It is the British Government which has been stoking these issues and projecting them as hinderances to their declaring explicitly that it is pledged to grant independence to India. The resolution reaffirms the Congress position that these issues can and will be solved solely by the Constituent Assembly consisting of Indians alone, that India's support for the war effort can be assured only through a 'National Government'. The Congress says it is prepared to endorse the proposal as 'an intermediate step' and as a 'transitory measure'.

Great Minds Think Alike

Savarkar ridicules the idea, exactly, as we shall see in a moment, like Jinnah. This idea reflects nothing but the Congressmen's lust for office, he announces. The Congress, we have seen him declare, has once again shown itself to be what it is—a beggar. In its eagerness to be in office, Congressmen are prepared to participate in a 'National Government' 'by the sanction of the British Government'. 'Thus even heroic beggars cannot long hide their begging bowl.' But a paragraph later, as we have seen, he veers towards accepting a 'National Government' provided it is not constituted out of the present legislatures only. 'The Hindu Mahasabha will of course welcome a National Government as a transitory measure,' he says. 'But for a Government to be truly National, it must include Hindu representatives in proportion to Hindu population who are pledged to protect Hindu interests and consequently possess the confidence of

Hindudom as a whole'—in a word, his nominees. He, of course, is not longing for office, he is only wanting to further Hindu interests![14]

Jinnah meets the Viceroy on 27 June 1940. Linlithgow prepares a full record of the meeting.[15]

As for the proposal for a 'National Government', this is what Linlithgow records Jinnah as saying:

> He would like to tell me that Bose had talked about the need for forming 'a National Government' at the Centre. He, Jinnah, had replied that was in fact nonsense. How could one form a National Government at the Centre unless there was agreement between Indians. And meantime there was no sign of such agreement. Therefore, the only practical step open to those willing to help in government was to go into partnership with the existing Government by accepting places on the Governor-General's Council.

What is of even greater interest is what Jinnah told Linlithgow the next steps should be. Here it is:

> The only hope was to strike at the position of the Working Committee of Congress. That body is immune from any control by public opinion or criticism, an oligarchy utterly intransigent and entirely devoted to the establishment of a purely Hindu system of life and government throughout the sub-continent. That was Mr. Gandhi's lifelong urge, and despite the presence of a few tame Muslims, it permeated all the effective members of the Working Committee. The thing to aim at was to break up the power of the Congress Working Committee. He recognised that my invitations to join my Executive Council must include an invitation to Congress. But if Congress refused

---

[14] 'Heroic beggars,' 10 July, 1940, cited earlier.

[15] Mss Eur F125/122.

to cooperate, surely the time had come to give other parties, more reasonable government. The Muslim League was willing to serve, and he knew of others who were of the same mind. The depressed classes in the person of Dr. Ambedkar; the Hindu Mahasabha (though he did not overweight their substance or importance); also Subhas Bose for the Forward Bloc. Subhas had the reputation of being wild, but he was a man with whom one could do business, and his coming in would put a most powerful twist on Congress. He himself had been in personal contact with Mr. Tara Singh, who had shown himself willing to consider bringing the Akalis into such a coalition.

With Jinnah's unequivocal rejection of the 'National Government' idea, nothing comes of it. But, and there is no wonder in this, the Hindu Mahasabha under Savarkar's control, apart from vigorously campaigning for the British during the war, and continuing its denunciation of the Congress, joins coalition ministries of, hold your breath, the Muslim League in Sindh as well as NWFP. In Bengal, the Ministry is headed by Fazlul Haq. He is the one about whom Savarkar is always complaining to the Viceroy—that Haq and his ministry are trampling on the Hindus by design, that they are doing so as a deliberate anti-Hindu policy, that Haq himself has declared '*hum Hinduon ko satayenge*'. Well, Syama Prasad Mukherjee joins this ministry headed by the very same Fazlul Haq as its finance minister!

But our objective has not changed, Savarkar argues. The reason for opposing Muslim League ministries was to prevent atrocities against Hindus. The reason for joining the Muslim League ministries is to prevent, from within, atrocities against Hindus.

Elation to Disappointment
to a Sullen Gloom

'The Hindu Mahasabha captures the political stage,' proclaims the text. It is 1940. Savarkar is delivering his Presidential Address at the 22nd session of the Hindu Mahasabha.[1] He says that the Hindu Mahasabha has been growing by leaps and bounds, and this has changed the entire complexion of political developments in the country. Till now, '. . . . the Hindu view continued to be ascertained by the Government through the opinion of that very body which indignantly repudiated the advocacy of the Hindu cause,' he tells the delegates. 'Consequently, the Hindus as Hindus not only continued to be unrepresented but were positively misrepresented in all Governmental Constitutional deliberation, All Indian Round Table Conferences, etc.' But now things have changed.

What It Has Got the British to Do

'[T]he *growing prestige, influence and effective activities of the Hindu Mahasabha* did at last impress the Government with the fact that it was no longer possible to look upon the Congress as a representative Hindu body or to refuse to recognize the Hindu Mahasabha as the real representative Hindu body and as such the third indispensable political factor which must be taken into consideration in gauging the Indian opinion in its

---

[1] Savarkar's Presidential Address at the Hindu Mahasabha's 22nd Session, Madura, 1940, *Hindu Rashtra Darshan*, e-book composed by Chandrashekhar V. Sane, pp. 78–110. Italics have been added.

entirety.' The result is that 'The Indian Government have thus unlearnt the old equation, "Congress+ League equals Indian people" and had to learn the new equation, "The Hindu Mahasabha, the League and the Congress equal the sum total of Indian representation."' 'This new equation does really respond to the present political situation in India,' he says, 'and I thank H.E. the Viceroy for having deliberately and decisively recognized the position of the Hindu Mahasabha as, at any rate, the most outstanding representative Hindu body, if not the only one . . .'

And this is going to have far-reaching consequences: '. . . This recognition by the Government of the Hindu Mahasabha as the most outstanding representative of the Hindu view and the consequent consultation which the Viceroy held with its president, is an event which is certain to have far-reaching consequences on the Hindu movement in general because it implies the recognition by the Government of the fact that the Congress does not represent the Hindus as Hindus and that just as to ascertain the Moslem opinion they have to consult the Moslem League or any other such Moslem institution which is independent of the Congress, so also the real Hindu interests, rights and claims could only be ascertained by consulting a representative Hindu body which is independent of and apart from the Congress. Once this principle is admitted as now it is done by the Government itself and Hindudom shakes off the grip that the Congress has tightened round its neck in virtue of no other right but that of an unchallenged usage, the political, social, religious and cultural interests of the Hindus as Hindus could no longer be betrayed by the Congress or go undefended by default . . .'

Of course, one cannot rest on one's laurels, work remains to be done, he says. '. . . In any case, I have no hesitation in expressing my sincere appreciation of the clear attitude which Mr. Amery has taken on the firmness with which the Viceroy turned down a number of the anti-Hindu and aggressive demands which the League had advanced during the recent negotiations in connection with the war committee and the extension of the Executive Council.' This too has happened because of the Hindu Mahasabha, he claims. *'That also could not be but the result of the negotiations carried on, on behalf of and the most legitimate and reasoned out attitude taken up by the Mahasabha in opposing those aggressive Moslem demands.* The Congress had said nothing to denounce them and but for the opposition of the Hindu Mahasabha, in all probabilities the Moslems could have secured a very large portion of the ground which they aggressively claimed [as] their own.'

And not just the rejection of the aggressive demands of Muslims. It is the pressure that the Hindu Mahasabha put on the Government which has compelled the latter to address the question of the integrity of India, he tells the delegates:

It is to be noted in this connection that we admit and emphasize in our own interests that the Indian as well as the British Government have not only recognized the right of the Hindu Mahasabha to represent the Hindu view independently of the Congress but has tried to meet the wishes of the Mahasabha, at least on the vital points affecting the Hindu interests. *It cannot be gainsaid that the important speech which the Secretary of State delivered this month dealing with the question of the political and National integrity of India was chiefly the result of the pressure brought to bear by the Hindu Mahasabha and the Sikh organization on the Government to declare in unambiguous courage [sic., language?] or even contribute tacitly to the mischievous Moslem movement to vivisect the integrity of the Indian Nation, country and State as the Pakistan proposal demanded.* The Moslem League had of course Godfathered the Pakistan scheme. The Congressite leaders of note, including all their Rajajis and Pradhanjis, had made it clear that they would not oppose it if the Moslems insisted on it.

So important is this achievement that he returns to it later in the Address and reminds the audience, 'As I have shown above *under the pressure of the*

Hindu Mahasabha alone, Mr. Amery has made a clear declaration to that effect in his speech on "India First".

A Certificate from the British

Two years later, in 1942, he is delivering his Presidential Address to the 24th session of the Mahasabha, this time at Kanpur. That the Viceroy had been in correspondence with him, that there has been the occasional meeting or at least the willingness to receive him face-to-face has convinced Savarkar that his Hindu Mahasabha has now become a factor to be reckoned with. Speaking in the House of Lords, Lord Devonshire, the Under-secretary of State has referred to the Hindu Mahasabha as 'the second-largest great all-India Hindu organisation', he tells the twenty-fourth session of the Mahasabha in Kanpur in 1942. He invokes this certificate a second time in the Address, but this time a bit defensively. 'If the Congressites were anxious to secure credentials from the Governors,' he says, 'there is no impropriety if we refer incidentally to some references just to know in what light others view our activities.'

A Monkey and Three, or Four, or as Many Cats as He Chooses

What actually lies behind such testimonials is the need of the British. As the war is taking every ounce of their time and energy, they cannot go around crafting advances in constitutional arrangements. And they have had a good excuse thus far: we are determined to advance on the constitutional front, they say, the difficulty is that the Congress and Muslim League do not agree. Having propped up the Hindu Mahasabha, a party that, in the words of Savarkar himself, does no more than 'pass pious resolutions', they can say, 'We are unable to press ahead with constitutional reform because a third party also does not agree.' This is evident from what Devonshire had actually said. The Cripps proposals floundered on the obduracy of the Congress. In the circumstances, nothing further can be done, he said:

To have handed the Government of India over to the Congress ignoring the claims of the various elements which in the aggregate greatly outnumber the Congress, could have led only to chaos. While to form a representative government from the other Indian parties without the Congress would not have provided a satisfactory solution. Even that solution seemed ruled out by the mutually incompatible demands of the *second largest Hindu party* after the Congress the Mahasabha and the Muslim League. Hence the deadlock, a deadlock for which the British Government is most unreasonably being blamed . . .

'Unreasonable indeed!,' the Congress historian, Pattabhi Sitaramayya remarked as he recalled these words. He put the matter aptly—in particular the certificate that had been handed to the Hindu Mahasabha and which Savarkar was holding up for the delegates to see:

First the British make a declaration through Cripps—cutting out the States People from the picture and permitting secession of Provinces from the Indian Union, then blame India that the Congress and the League do not agree, then recognize the Hindu Mahasabha (August 8th, 1940) and then say there is one more body which disagrees with the other Non-Congress bodies, even for a constitution to be attempted without the Congress! This is the story of the monkey and not the proverbial two cats, but three, four or as many as the monkey chooses to bring into the dispute![2]

Savarkar continued to believe, at the least to proclaim that under his leadership the status of the Hindu Mahasabha had soared. In the written

---

[2] Pattabhi Sitaramayya, *History of the Indian National Congress,* Volume II, S. Chand and Co., Delhi, 1969, p. 420.

statement that he submitted to the Court during the trial for Gandhiji's assassination, he proclaimed:

> Hindu Mahasabha kept expanding at speed, and, along with the Congress and the Muslim League, it came to be recognised as a third All-India Bharatiya National Political Party. Its representatives used to be called to the Round Table Conference and other conferences in London. To understand its viewpoint on important questions, the Viceroy and Governors used to invite me as the head of the Hindu Mahasabha. During the Cripps Mission also, at the invitation of the Government, I had led the delegation of its representatives, and at that time, of the three All Bharatiya organisations, it alone opposed and rejected out of hand the whimsical/*man-maani* Cripps plan aimed at striking at the very roots of unity of the Bharatiya rashtra, at breaking Bharat into pieces . . .[3]

Subhas Bose's Assessment

Did these invitations testify to the real strength of Savarkar and his Hindu Mahasabha? Or did they testify to the usual British policy of propping up persons and organizations that could be useful as counters to the freedom movement? Netaji Subhas Bose, who had by then broken away from the Congress and was a strong critic of the Congress as well as of Gandhiji, described the British stratagem well in his *The Indian Struggle*.

'Whenever the Occasion Demands, Leaders are Created Overnight . . .'

Talking of parties like the Muslim League and the Hindu Mahasabha, Bose wrote, 'Besides the above political parties comprising members of

---

[3] *Savarkar Samagra*, Volume II, pp. 592–633, at 594.

all communities, there are communal organisations whose avowed object is to secure loaves and fishes for members of their own community . . .' Repeating this characterization a paragraph later, he remarked,

> While the political parties we first dealt with have a political programme and carry on some sort of agitation against, or opposition towards the Government, the communal parties are more concerned with dividing amongst themselves such of the crumbs that are thrown at them from the official tables. In accordance with the time-worn policy of *divide et imperia,* the Government greatly encourages these parties—just to spite the Indian National Congress and try to weaken its influence. This was clearly exhibited in 1930 and later, when the Indian representatives to the Round Table Conference were not selected by a vote of the Indian people—but were nominated by the British Government and in making these nominations, the communal parties, who have no concern with the fight for political freedom, were given exaggerated importance. As a matter of fact, whenever the occasion demands, leaders are created overnight by the British Government and, thanks to the British Press, their names are made known to the whole world. When the Government of India Act, 1919, was under consideration, Mr. T.M. Nair of Madras, was made a leader in London, in opposition to the Congress leaders at the time. In 1930 and after, Dr. Ambedkar has had leadership thrust on him by a benign British Government, because his services were necessary to embarrass the nationalist leaders.[4]

This is what lay behind Devonshire's reference to the Hindu Mahasabha.

---

[4] Subhas Chandra Bose, *The Indian Struggle, 1920–42,* The Netaji Research Bureau, Calcutta, Asia Publishing House, Bombay, 1964, pp. 30–32.

The Weight They Carried

But even as they propped up such leaders and parties, the British had a good measure of their real strength on the ground. Yes, as Savarkar told the Court, Cripps and his colleagues had received Savarkar and his team— and we will come later to the impression Savarkar made on Cripps. But Savarkar would have soon learnt how much weight, in the assessment of Cripps, etc. they carried. An internal note about the meeting has this to say:

> Further reports received were that Savarkar and some of the non-party people had been offended by being told by Sir Stafford that the Muslim League and the Congress were the people that really counted, and that the effect of this remark might be to drive them into the arms of the Congress.[5]

There was a report to the same effect from the United Provinces—this report was based on what the Governor of the Province had learnt from Sir J.P. Srivastava, a member of high governmental bodies:

> Now that the Cripps mission has ended, I feel it desirable to put before you some of my ideas on the position. I have had a talk with Sir J.P. Srivastava who was up in Delhi lately attending the National Defence Council and he of course is full of stories and rumours. But it is clear that what he and a good many others who have been actively supporting war effort feel is that the whole discussions were conducted with Congress, that Congress was given the predominant position and that other associations were treated with contempt. I need not repeat the stories he told me, but I gather that the Hindu

---

[5] Diary note, 30 March 1942, Mss Eur F 125/141, *Constitutional Relations Between Britain and India, The Transfer Of Power 1942–7, Volume I, The Cripps Mission January–April 1942*, Editor-in-Chief Nicholas Mansergh, Her Majesty's Stationery Office, London, 1970, p. 562.

Mahasabha and the Sikhs were very annoyed. But it is satisfactory that the Sabha have made a definite offer of further cooperation. What Sir J.P. and others also are, I think, apprehensive about is that yet another attempt may be made to conciliate Congress, as has been done in the past.[6]

A trifling matter provides a good glimpse of the actual importance the Mission attached to what Savarkar, and his team said, and it contrasts sharply with what Savarkar was proclaiming to his delegates at that time and what he was to claim during the trial for Gandhiji's assassination. Cripps has finalized his report. The question is what to do with the opinions that have been expressed by organizations that they have met. Cripps sends a 'Most Immediate' cable to Churchill seeking the Prime Minister's concurrence. He says that he is inclined to publish in full the opinions of the Congress and the League, but he does not think it worthwhile to publish the opinions of groups such as the Hindu Mahasabha and the Sikhs—as they are not really material, they have not been decisive in any way in his finalizing the recommendations. But he does think that they should mention that these opinions had been sought, received and considered lest these groups think that 'we pay no attention to what they said'. 'I think therefore that some sort of note should be added explaining that though they were fully considered and taken into account it is not possible from the point of view of paper economy to print them all in full.'[7] 'From the point of view of paper economy'—an exclamation mark is in order.

---

[6] *Constitutional Relations Between Britain and India, The Transfer Of Power 1942–7, Volume I, The Cripps Mission, January–April 1942, op. cit.,* pp. 776–77.

[7] Sir S. Cripps to Mr Churchill (via H.M. Ambassador, Cairo, and Foreign Office) Telegram, L/P&J/10/2: f 133 Most Immediate, 15 April 1942, *Constitutional Relations Between Britain and India, The Transfer of Power, 1942–7,* Volume I, *op. cit.,* pp. 779–80.

The Other Problem

There was also the perpetual problem about Savarkar, and therefore about the organization that he controlled. How far could a man of his background, and whose private and public statements are at such variance, be trusted, in regard, for instance, to professions of supporting the war effort? How far would he cooperate in evolving a scheme for further constitutional arrangements? When the Cripps proposals came out, the Mahasabha passed a strongly worded resolution rejecting them. John Herbert, the then Governor of Bengal, wrote to Linlithgow expressing doubts that went beyond mere rejection of the Cripps recommendations:

> The Hindu Mahasabha appears to have definitely rejected the [Cripps] proposals, and thus emphasised that Party's attitude that it will be content with nothing but Hindu rule. *Information recently received indicates that the Mahasabha would be prepared to go to the length of invoking any outside power to attain their object, and suggests that this Party may prove to be the most strongly pro-Japanese.*

At that time—the first half of 1942—what with adverse developments in the far east and Burma, this, the apprehension that a group may turn towards the Japanese, was a real worry with every officer in-charge of affairs in Bengal. Herbert continued:

> It considers—so this information states—that if Pandit Jawaharlal Nehru were to be placed in charge of the defence of India, that would be regarded as tantamount to a surrender to the British proposals, and that the Mahasabha would have to fight Congress over that issue. There is no pleasing some people.[8]

---

[8] J. Herbert (Bengal) to Linlithgow, MSS. EUR. F. 125/42, *Constitutional Relations Between Britain and India, The Transfer of Power, 1942–7, Volume I, op. cit.,* pp. 696–97.

'Those Whom We Can Find'

Thus, while Savarkar was proclaiming that the British had at last recognized the importance of the Hindu Mahasabha, and that this was going to change the direction of affairs, for the British he was just one of those—M.N. Roy being another good example—who had made themselves available. Linlithgow was to visit Bombay. He thought of meeting Savarkar. The Governor of the Province, Roger Lumley was trying to dissuade the Viceroy from doing so, and thereby giving Savarkar the sort of importance that the latter did not deserve, and should not be given. Linlithgow explained his view: the moment in which they are to work is one 'of very considerable awkwardness,' and so both Amery and he have come to the conclusion that they have to work 'with those whom we can find,' that they cannot confine themselves to those with whom they would want to work.[9]

What a pity that a 'Veer', one so proud and so convinced of his true worth had brought himself to this position. And how much greater the pity that either he was misrepresenting the true situation to his delegates and the people, or, even worse, that he himself believed what he was telling them.

And Who Had to Do the Explaining?

The British did not have to explain using whomever they could find. They had the War to contend with. They had to overcome Congress' opposition. They had to contend with Jinnah's hold over the Muslim League. They had to expand the army at top speed. They had to pacify a population that was being buffeted by soaring prices and scarcities. They had to contend with danger of another sort. Setbacks on the eastern front were triggering all sorts of wishful thinking among many: that the British would lose, and thus have to rush out of India. In a word, they took on board whoever was prepared to work for them. And gave each the paltry thing he wanted:

---

[9] Linlithgow to Roger Lumley (Bombay), 13 October, 1940, IOR, Mss Eur F 125/54.

funds to M.N. Roy, a seat in the Executive Council to Ambedkar, seats for his men in the Executive Council and War Committee and a sense of importance to Savarkar, newsprint to the communists to run their publications.

Having made himself available, Savarkar is the one who had to keep explaining the somersaults—and there were four of these, not just one: joining the Muslim League ministries, teaming up with the British, abandoning the mass agitation that the Mahasabha had resolved to launch, diluting the demand for a declaration here and now in favour of full Independence. Nor had he to explain these about-turns only to a sceptical public. His own followers couldn't see how the new positions were to be harmonized with what they and their leaders had been proclaiming from every platform.

Ministries

The Mahasabha had fared miserably in the 1937 elections—it got only three of 1585 seats in the provincial Legislative Assemblies. In both the provinces in which Hindus were in a majority as well as in provinces in which they were a beleaguered minority, even the Hindus had voted for the Congress rather than the party that was proclaiming to be their sole protector. The 19th session of the Hindu Mahasabha was held in Ahmedabad from 30 December 1937 to 1 January 1938. It passed 12 resolutions. Speakers made the usual speeches. Savarkar who was the President gave a lengthy and fighting speech. But disappointment at the election results was apparent. In its account of the session, *The Indian Annual Register* reported,

> Concluding the session the president, Mr. Vinayak Damodar Savarkar said that the position of the Hindu Mahasabha was similar to the position of the Congress 20 years ago when it passed pious resolutions. If Hindu voters voted at the next election for Hindu

candidates standing on the ticket of the Hindu Mahasabha they would come into power.[10]

But a new situation had arisen. The War had broken out. The Viceroy had announced that India was a belligerent country. The Congress had opposed this: India has been made to join the War without consulting the Indian people. And in protest, the Congress ministries had resigned. Five provinces were already in the hands of the Muslim League. The Government began making efforts to get parties to join hands with the Muslim League and form ministries to fill the void left by the Congress resignations. Here was a golden opportunity. After all, if in these provinces, the Hindu Mahasabha had done miserably in the elections, so had the Muslim League: even in the Muslim constituencies, and looking only at seats that were reserved for Muslims, the Muslim League had received less than five per cent of the votes cast by Muslims. When the League can be forming ministries, why not the Mahasabha? Moreover, the field was clear. Congress leaders were locked up in jail. The British were looking for ones who would oppose and abuse them.

But there was a difficulty. Savarkar's followers had been weaned on hatred for Muslims. The singular aim of Muslims—of *all* Muslims—is to re-establish Islamic rule over India, the Muslim League is the principal enemy, it is hell-bent on breaking the Motherland, Muslims and the Muslim League are behind riots, they are terrorizing and killing Hindus, they regard doing so as their religious duty, they can never be trusted. Such axioms had been drilled into every member of the Mahasabha. And here was Savarkar having his men join League ministries. Here was Savarkar asking his units to form ministries in Hindu-majority provinces by inviting Muslim politicians to join them as ministers. They hesitated, they recoiled at the idea.

---

[10] *The Indian Annual Register,* 1937, Volume 2, July–December 1937, N.N. Mitra (ed.), The Annual Register Office, Calcutta, at p. 422.

The Encyclical

Savarkar issued an encyclical, an exhortation to get over reticence, to forget what he and the Sabha had been proclaiming for years. Look instead at the opportunity. 'Efforts are being made to form Provincial Ministries in several provinces which are still under the Governor's rule,' Savarkar said. 'This movement is not quite unwelcome.' Joining such ministries or, even better, forming them ourselves where we can would be the best way to protect and further Hindu interests—that was his new thesis. Not just that, such ministries can do more: 'Coalition ministries if they are actuated by patriotic and just motives can be an effective process which will train us up in team work, remove the sense of alienation and lead to national consolidation in-spite of racial or credal differences.' This from the very theoretician who has been proclaiming day in and day out that Muslims and Hindus are two nations, that the Muslims are out to and will settle for nothing less than re-establishing Islamic rule over all of India.

And so,

> In the Hindu-minority provinces whenever a Moslem Ministry seems
> inevitable whether it is a League one or otherwise and Hindu interest
> could be served better by joining it, the Hindu Sabhaites in particular
> should try as a matter of right to capture as many seats as possible in
> the Ministry and do the best they could to safeguard the interest of
> the Hindu minority.

I am sure you noticed the 'as a matter of right'. We are not seeking ministries. We are wresting them 'as a matter of right'.

If, disregarding the principle of collective responsibility, Muslim ministers express support for the idea of Pakistan or 'the treacherous principle' of self-determination, Savarkar said, our ministers should also disregard the principle of collective responsibility, and oppose them. Lest anyone expect or demand, or, God forbid, think of doing something more, Savarkar directed,

If the Hindu Ministers are known to have recorded their protest against such steps they should not be asked to resign from the Ministry.

In other words, assume the Muslim League ministers and members of the legislature pass a resolution demanding Pakistan. You issue a press statement opposing their demand. That is enough. As is usual with him, Savarkar raises this to a matter of 'principle':

> The leading principle which must be emphasized is that the boycotting of a Ministry altogether is bound to be more often than not highly detrimental to Hindu interests.

And this is exactly what happened. Mahasabha members joined the Sindh government. The League and non-League Muslim members passed a resolution in favour of creating a separate Pakistan. In fact, the Sindh Assembly was the first to pass a resolution to this effect. The Mahasabha ministers issued statements opposing the demand. And continued in the ministry. As usual, Savarkar had foreseen such a turn, and the embarrassment that it would cause. Accordingly, he had listed another reason—the longer run—for joining the ministries and hanging in:

> Under the present circumstances the Hindu Mahasabha should try to capture as many positions of vantage as possible in order to assert the rights of the Hindu Party as an indispensable constituent factor, apart from the League or the Congress, in any future constitution to be framed after the war.

Nor was this ministry-seeking to be limited to provinces in which the Muslim League had acquired office. On the contrary, it must be pursued in Hindu-majority provinces as well, Savarkar had said. After all, there is parity! In these provinces, the Mahasabha had been wiped out as much as in the Muslim majority provinces! Savarkar instructed 'Mahasabhaites' of these Hindu-majority provinces to 'take the lead to see if it was feasible to form a Coalition Ministry.' But what about the insistence of the League, 'Pakistan and nothing less'? Savarkar prescribed,

> The question of Pakistan or self-determination for the provinces to secede must be entirely left outside the ministerial scope in these provinces as one which could be raised after the war is over.

As was his custom, Savarkar laid down conditions—no one could say that they were hankering after ministries. 'Members of the Muslim League and other Muslims should of course be invited to join the Ministry but their number should not far exceed the proportion of their population in their province...' And, the Chief Minister should be a Hindu, pledged to Hindu interests.

There was no reason to be defensive about all this. The Barrister in Savarkar was ready with a reason. To say nothing of ministries in Hindu-majority provinces, even the ministries in Muslim majority provinces, ministries headed by a Muslim or the majority of whose ministers were from the Muslim League are not 'Muslim League ministries' in any case, he said:

> It is a misnomer to call a Ministry a League one or a Moslem one simply because the chief minister or the majority of the ministers happen to be Leaguers or Moslems. If the Ministry contains Hindu Sabhaites or Hindu ministers it cannot but be recognised as a Coalition ministry.

So, no reason to demur.

He returned to this lawyerly obfuscation time and again:

> ... One point has been emphasised in my statement. So long as Muslim League members are working in a ministry within their rights, the ministry is not that of the League. In Sindh it is a League-Hindusabha ministry; in Bengal it is a League-Hindu ministry; in the Frontier Province it is League-Sikh ministry.

Finally, the exculpatory clause:

> Within the scope of these leading principles the formation of ministries and adjustment to the special circumstances prevailing in each province should be left to the discretion of the respective provincial Hindu Sabha.[11]

As the about-turn continued to be held up as an example of opportunism, as having been instigated by nothing more than craving for office, Savarkar issued statements to explain and justify his decision. The ministries are *not* League ministries, he repeated . . . In any case, in my statements I had left the decision to the local units of the Mahasabha, he repeated. The leaders of the Mahasabha in Sindh have decided that joining the League ministry is the best way to advance Hindu interests, he repeated . . . See, how the courage with which Mahasabha ministers in Sindh have opposed the resolution for Pakisthan, he repeated . . . The objective has remained the same, he said, it has not changed—to protect Hindu interests and Hindus. But the way this can be accomplished varies from province to province: in each province, one has to adopt the policy that is the best instrument for securing that singular objective in that particular province:

> One should adopt varying policies keeping in mind the different circumstances in different provinces, in particular in provinces in which Hindus are in a minority. For instance, [in Bengal] we shall drag the League-led ministry by the neck—if the Bengal Hindu Mahasabha have this much confidence. In the Frontier Province it seems appropriate for the Hindu Mahasabha leaders to fight elections in alliance with the Congress. If the Congress leaders there abide by their promise to protect the interests of Hindus, then the support of Hindu Mahasabha leaders seems to be in line with what has been set

---

[11] For the text of the statement, V.D. Savarkar, *Historic Statements*, S.S. Savarkar, Bombay, 1967, pp. 55–57.

out in my statement. In Sindh, the leaders of the Hindu Sabha have supported the League ministry because they feel that this is the best way by which the interests of Hindus can be protected . . .[12]

In any case, the assessment of whether teaming up with the League will serve Hindu assessments and the final decision about what to do had been left to the provincial units, he repeated. People who are criticizing us have not paid attention to this part of my statement, he said:

> . . . whether Hindu interests will be served through coalition ministries had been left to the reasoning and intelligence [*vivek-buddhi*] of provincial committees of the Hindu Sabhas. Those who criticise with their understanding intact have not paid attention to this . . . In Sindh, the local unit of the Sindh Hindu Sabha decided that the interests of the Hindus can be best safeguarded by supporting the League sabha . . .[13]

And so on.

The explanations did not carry conviction. The League ministries and the League itself continued to behave as they had been doing. In Sindh, the Pakistan resolution was passed. Yes, the Mahasabha people opposed it. But it was opposition so feeble that it seemed it had been put up so that they could claim that they had opposed the resolution.[14] Savarkar himself had to write letter after letter to the Viceroy, as we have seen, drawing attention to the atrocities that continued to be committed on Hindus in Sindh, in Bengal, in Punjab, in NWFP.

---

[12] Cf., 'Why are coalition ministries necessary?,' *Savarkar Samagra,* Volume VIII, pp. 585–89.

[13] *Savarkar Samagra,* Volume VIII, p. 587.

[14] Savarkar, of course, claimed that the opposition they put up has been so consequential and courageous that they deserve congratulations. Ibid. Pattabhi Sitaramayya's assessment was closer to how these maneuvers were perceived. 'The spectacle of five or six provinces run by the League Premiers created an earnest desire among them [the Mahasabha leaders] that in suitable provinces they might run their own ministries, at any rate ministries with

Teaming Up with the British

Switching from admiration for what Mussolini and Hitler had accomplished for their countries, to advocating neutrality, to supporting the British also required explaining. The point that Savarkar pressed on every occasion was that this was the very opportunity that they had been waiting for. After the 1857 war, the British had disarmed Indians. They did not trust us. Therefore, there were the strictest restrictions on possessing arms on the one hand, and, on the other, only a selected lot, in particular the Muslims, were being taken into the Army and the police. But here was a God-sent opportunity—for their own sake, the British had to induct Hindus into the armed forces. For their own sake, they needed our help in governing India. Therefore, join the Army, join the factories where guns and ammunition are made, learn to make and wield them. Specially you from Maharashtra. Let Maharashtra be, once again, the Sword of Bharat.

That much is what Savarkar used to say at every function. But what about the British, and the help we would have rendered them? Pressed, Savarkar would add, '. . . Enter the Army. Learn how to wield guns. In which direction they will point when the time comes, we shall see.' A decade and a half later, he is giving the same explanation. At the three-day function that is held in Poona to mark the winding up of Abhinav Bharat,

---

Mahasabha Premiers, and where that was not possible, coalition ministries, formed by combination with other groups,' Sitaramayya wrote. As a result,

> The Hindu Mahasabha reduced itself to the position of the 'Hindu Edition of the League' as was well said at the time and was abusing the Congress in season and out of season as yielding to the League demands, while all the time it had been trying to share the booty with the League, in the absence of those people whom the Electorate had returned as its true representatives in the Legislature. It is noteworthy that the Hindu Sabha ministers of Sind remained passive spectators to the passing of a resolution in favour of Pakistan by the Sind Legislature, and contented themselves with a protest which remained impotent and unimpressive. [Cf., Pattabhi Sitaramayya, *History of the Indian National Congress,* Volume II, S. Chand and Co., Delhi, 1969, pp. 513–14.]

he explains 'The meaning of militarisation'. He told Hindu Sabhaites to 'enter the military in large numbers,' he says, 'so that when the time comes for armed insurrection, lakhs of soldiers, skilled in the use of weapons and the arts of war, spring upon the British as they had done in 1857 . . . Therefore, with a view to fomenting a revolutionary war against Britain I launched a nation-wide campaign for militarisation . . .'[15]

Information from Multiple Sources

Whether such statements evoked more than applause and knowing laughter from his audiences, they were not lost on the British. After all, they were receiving information from many sources. On the one side, for two years you have been receiving from the Mahasabha leaders protestations of 'responsive cooperation', of 'Wholehearted cooperation', of Hindu and British interests now being intertwined, and, on the other, the Director of the Intelligence Bureau, Denys Pilditch sends you reports such as the following:

Dr B. S. Moonje to a correspondent in Delhi (Extract) MSS. EUR. F. 125/156
NASIK, 21 July 1943
As for the policy of the Hindu Mahasabha, I say as follows:
(1) That we have no faith in and are opposed to Non-Cooperation and Non-Violence, which forms the creed of the Congress.

We believe in what is known as Responsive Cooperation, that is, actual contact and struggle with our opponents. Similarly we believe in violence, organised scientifically on modern European methods, and we also believe that Swaraj will not be attained without violent struggles when the time comes. In short we believe in Responsive

---

[15] *Savarkar Samagra*, Volume VIII, p. 714.

Cooperation which includes all this and also Non-Cooperation when it will suit to achieve our ends.

(2) That thus we are prepared to cooperate with actually the Devil, what to say of Britishers or the Moslems; our only condition is that such cooperation should suit to achieve our ends.

(3) That our cooperation with the Moslems is not of the same kind as that of the Congress. Congress believes that Swaraj cannot be attained without the cooperation of the Moslems. We believe that, when time will come, we can win Swaraj even in spite of the Moslem opposition. The Congress therefore surrenders to the Moslems and its cooperation with the Moslems is merely another word for surrender. Our cooperation is manly and fruitful, though it assumes different colours according to different circumstances in different Moslem-Majority Provinces. I hope I have made my position clear.

The import of this did not escape Linlithgow. In the file, he added in his own hand:

Responsive Cooperation = {Struggle with our opponents; Non-Cooperation; Violence.}
This is worth remembering.
L. 29/7/43[16]

---

[16] *Constitutional Relations Between Britain And India, The Transfer Of Power 1942–7, Volume IV, The Bengal Famine and the New Viceroyalty, 15 June 1943–31 August 1944,* Editor-in-Chief Nicholas Mansergh, Her Majesty's Stationery Office, London, 1973, pp. 112–13. The note was submitted by D. Pilditch: he had been Director of the Intelligence Bureau since 1939.

Independence to Dominion Status to . . .

For decades Savarkar had been priding himself, and he would continue priding himself for decades to come that his Abhinav Bharat had been the very first to declare 'Absolute Political Independence' as the goal. He had been berating leaders from Dadabhai Naoroji on down, he had been vilifying Gandhiji and the Congress for pitching the goal lower, for diluting it over time. But now, he himself was changing from complete/absolute Independence here and now, to an assurance of complete/absolute Independence, to Dominion Status here and now, to an announcement that Dominion Status would be conferred as soon as the War ended, to an announcement that Dominion Status would be conferred as soon as possible after the conclusion of the War. And soon, as we have seen, he was hurling a completely different answer at his critics: what is the use of demanding assurances and announcements, in any case?

And so:

From Direct Action to No Action

It was with much fanfare that the Mahasabha had resolved to commence Direct Action for securing Independence and other goals. It wasn't just dedication to these goals that had been the spur. People had been contrasting the Mahasabha's empty hectoring with the Congress' activism. And now: the Congress programme of going and sitting in jails is plain foolish . . . This is not the time for . . . When this did not convince people, Savarkar and his colleagues argued, but the plan for Direct Action has not been abandoned. It has just been postponed. Whether this convinced the people or not, it certainly deepened apprehensions among British officials about Savarkar's dependability.

There was another, deeper problem—one related personally to Savarkar. The myth of Savarkar had been built not on his proficiency in manufacturing lawyerly arguments. It had been built on his being an uncompromising 'revolutionary'. One who insisted on full and 'absolute' Independence, on how it would never be possible to attain that goal without violence, on the fact that he stirred others to take to violence, on the fact that he had got pistols smuggled into India, on the fact that one of these had been the very weapon by which a British official had been killed, on the fact that he devised strategies for revolutionary war, on the fact that he knew the sacrifices that a revolutionary war would entail and yet had chosen that course. And here was a Barrister giving lawyerly arguments for twists and turns like any other politician, in fact like the very politicians he had been vilifying. Even all these decades later, we can experience the disillusionment people would have felt when they read these explanations and remembered the oath that he had authored, the oath he had taken himself, the oath he used to administer to every new entrant to Abhinav Bharat:

Bande Mataram
In the name of God,
In the name of Bharat Mata,
In the name of all the Martyrs that have shed their blood for
Bharat Mata,
By the Love, innate in all men and women, that I bear to the land of
my birth, wherein lie the sacred ashes of my forefathers, and which
is the cradle of my children,
By the tears of Hindi [sic.] Mothers for their children whom the
Foreigner has enslaved, imprisoned, tortured, and killed,
I, . . .
Convinced that without Absolute Political Independence or
Swarajya my country can never rise to the exalted position among
the nations of the earth which is Her due,
And convinced also that that Swarajya can never be attained except
by the waging of a bloody and relentless war against the Foreigner,

Solemnly and sincerely Swear that I shall from this moment do
everything in my power to fight for Independence and place
the Lotus Crown of Swaraj on the head of my Mother;
And with this object, I join the Abhinav Bharat, the revolutionary
Society of all Hindusthan, and swear that I shall ever be true and
faithful to this my solemn Oath, and that I shall obey the orders of
this body;
If I betray the whole or any part of this solemn Oath, or if I betray
this body or any other body working with a similar object,
May I be doomed to the fate of a perjurer![17]

Even though decades have passed, how does the one contriving lawyerly
arguments compare with the portrait that he had drawn of himself?

The legend had been built on such oaths, on such means to violence,
war, sacrifice, death. Savarkar himself had done much to build that legend.
He continued to reinforce it throughout his life. And here he was—acting
the Barrister.

With this kind of disenchantment having been festering for a decade,
with 'Quit India' having stirred the country, with the wholesale arrests
of Gandhiji, Panditji, the Sardar and all Congress leaders having
angered the people, Savarkar's dalliance with the British led even
members of the Mahasabha to participate in Congress demonstrations
and meetings. This participation was noted by British officials at the
local level, and reported to the higher ups. The higher ups had to pacify
the apprehensions: don't worry, the Mahasabha leadership has nowhere
else to go, they counselled.

But that still left the question open. True, Savarkar and other
leaders at the top had committed themselves too far to immediately

---

[17] Veer Savarkar, *Inside the Enemy Camp,* www.savarkar.org, Veer Savarkar Prakashan,
Mumbai, 1993, p. 16.

reverse course. But will Savarkar be able to hold the ordinary members together, to say nothing of the extent to which his word will count with the public in general? Will he be able to deliver on his promises of recruitment? Will pressure from below cause him to execute another somersault?

A new announcement had been made by the Viceroy that the objective of the Government was to help India achieve Dominion Status 'at the earliest possible moment that circumstances render possible'. The Intelligence Bureau was engaged in gauging the reactions of different political parties and the common man to the announcement. The Congress President, Rajendra Prasad had summoned an urgent meeting at Wardha. Rajaji, Pandit Nehru and Sardar Patel had been asked to come a few days earlier. The usual friends of the Government were busy trying to bring opponents of the Congress—of the National Movement—together. The Director of the Intelligence Bureau drew attention to possibilities, but also to the fact that the influence of the Mahasabha whose leader the Government was cultivating 'is as yet of too little account . . .' During the course of his report dated 13 January 1940, the Director noted,

> What may amount to no more than kite-flying is the appearance in the Press of a report that there is a move on foot to bring together Jinnah and V. D. Savarkar, President of the All-India Hindu Mahasabha, through the good offices of Dr. Ambedkar, in order to explore the possibility of a communal settlement independently of Congress. While the proposal is of considerable interest, the influence of the Mahasabha as a political body is as yet of too little account to give rise to any reasonable hope of such an attempt being immediately fruitful.[18]

---

[18] Weekly report of the Director, Intelligence Bureau, dated 13 January, 1940: IOR:L/P&J/12/482.

'... of too Little Account'

Yes, Savarkar was giving lectures and penning press statements exhorting everyone to join the British Army. Recruitment had indeed swelled. But the British would have had a good idea as to how much of the increase was due to Savarkar's exhortations, how much to their own efforts, and how much to spiralling prices and shortages that made living more onerous. Yes, Savarkar was denouncing Gandhiji and the Congress day in and day out. But was this swaying the people? Every programme, every election answered with a resounding 'No'. Savarkar's influence was confined to Poona and its environment, to some localities in Bombay and to isolated pockets in the rest of Bombay province. The Mahasabha was somewhat stronger in Bengal, but that unit was not entirely in Savarkar's hands. Syama Prasad Mookerjee had greater control over it, and he had several differences with Savarkar. Reports from Bengal referred to the 'feuding' Hindu Mahasabha leaders. Mookerjee was a more flexible leader. He made it a point to be in touch with Congress leaders, even with Muslim leaders—after all, till his resignation he had been a member of Fazlul Haq's cabinet, and had even stood up for Haq when some Muslim Leaguers made attempts to undercut the latter, his 'leader' as he referred to Haq. Then there were Savarkar's illnesses. Moreover, the tide of the War had changed.[19]

The long and short of it was that the Congress remained the main, and formidable vehicle of the National Movement, that even Hindus *qua* Hindus continued to flock to Gandhiji, that the Hindu Mahasabha was 'of too little account' and, therefore, they—the British—would have to contend with the Congress by themselves. The other concern too had abated. Opposition to the war had waned. By now, the British Indian Army was *twenty-five lakh* strong. The soldiers were fighting with the fullest

---

[19] On this, the fine and detailed account in Nandini Gondhalekar and Sanjoy Bhattacharya, 'The All India Hindu Mahasabha and the End of British Rule in India, 1939–1947,' *Social Scientist,* July–August 1999, Vol. 27, No. 7/8, pp. 48–74.

devotion and ardour. Indian officers had fully assimilated to the ways of a British Army. The public was not impeding the war effort. Savarkar was a fading asset.

There were several additional factors that turned the British off Savarkar.

Unappealing

Linlithgow was a patient man. He was the Viceroy for seven years, a tenure longer than that of anyone else. He had the ability to play a long game. He would keep engaging with a person even if the latter was all presumptuousness, on the off chance that the person might be of some use some time in the unseen future. Others were not of that kind. Savarkar did not, to put it mildly, enrapture them.

Savarkar led a delegation to meet Cripps, as we have seen him remind his delegates at Hindu Mahasabha conventions as well as the Court during the trial for Gandhiji's assassination. This is what Cripps wrote about the encounter:

> Note by Sir S. Cripps
> L/P&J/10/4: f 38
> My interview with the Hindu Mahasabha
> 28 March 1942: This delegation was led by Savarkar, who spent most of his time lecturing me upon the principles of majority determination and of the fallacies within the document which I had submitted to him. On the few occasions when I was able to get a word in I tried to point out that . . .

There would be no meeting of minds. The delegation stressed the indivisibility of India. Cripps pointed out that 'the principle of the document was a single unitary India for which purpose a constituent assembly voted by majority would be set up and that it was only in the case of the failure of the Hindus and the Moslems to agree that any question of a second dominion would arise. I am afraid I made little or no impression on him and his colleagues . . .' The delegation opposed the right of non-accession being held out to, say, the Princes, and asked whether they—the Hindu Mahasabha—were at liberty to accept some recommendations of the Mission and reject others. 'I told them that the document must be accepted as a whole or rejected so far as the fundamental parts were concerned and that we regarded the right of non-accession as fundamental. I gathered that they would on this basis reject the document.' These ideas were in accord with the well-known positions of Savarkar and the Mahasabha. The remaining idea was Quixotic:

> They then raised the question of the Defence Minister and said that as they did not trust the Moslems and they imagined they did not trust the Hindus, they would want to have two Defence Advisers, one Hindu and one Moslem, whose advice the Viceroy would undertake to accept.

A horse with one head in the front and one in the rear when the British were fighting for their lives.

> I pointed out that it did not appear to me to be a very practical scheme, but the Viceroy would no doubt get his advice from the Executive Council and not from outside advisers, and it appeared that the advice tendered by the Moslem might not be the same as the Hindu.[20]

That was all.

Linlithgow was succeeded by Field Marshall Wavell. Wavell was a tough, straight-talking soldier. He had been Commander-in-Chief in India from 1941 to1943, and, therefore, would have known enough about

---

[20] *Constitutional Relations Between Britain and India, The Transfer of Power 1942–7, Volume I, The Cripps Mission January–April 1942*, op. cit., pp. 513–14.

Savarkar, the Hindu Mahasabha and their potential. Savarkar sought an appointment. Wavell met him. In his report to the Secretary of State, Amery, Wavell wrote:

> Savarkar, the Mahasabha leader, also asked to see me, and I granted him an interview. I thought him an unpleasant, intolerant little man, full of communal bitterness and with no constructive ideas.
>
>   Conversations of this kind are part of the ordinary routine here, especially during the sessions of the Legislature, and these examples are interesting only because they seem to show how the different parties are thinking . . .[21]

Time and again, events showed up the very restricted reach of the Mahasabha and, within the Mahasabha, of Savarkar. Wavell was thinking of convening a meeting with Indian leaders to consider constitutional alternatives. There was some to and fro about inviting the Hindu Mahasabha, now led by Syama Prasad Mookerjee. Wavell decided against doing so. Others felt that he might as well include the Mahasabha. Eventually, no invitation went.

Savarkar's Replacement

In part this had to do with Syama Prasad Mookerjee. He had replaced Savarkar as the President of the Hindu Mahasabha. He had been part of the Fazlul Haq ministry in Bengal. Even when he was in Government, there had been run-ins with the Bengal Governor and other officials. In July 1942, as it seemed more and more likely that the Congress would launch

---

[21] Wavell to Amery, L\PO\l0\21, Private and Secret, 29 November 1944, *Constitutional Relations Between Britain and India, The Transfer Of Power 1942–7, Volume V, The Simla Conference Background and Proceedings, 1 September 1944–28 July 1945*, Editor-in-Chief Nicholas Mansergh, Her Majesty's Stationery Office, London, 1974, p. 253. In fairness, we must remember that Wavell's assessments of other leaders—from Gandhiji to Panditji to the Sardar, down to Suharawardy—were equally merciless.

a movement, Mookerjee wrote to the Governor, John Herbert, urging him in strong words to crush with a heavy hand the Quit India movement, should it rear its head in Bengal.[22] His letter was also harshly critical of the Governor personally and the clutch of officers around him. In November 1942, he resigned from the Government denouncing, among other things, the suppression of the same Quit India Movement. As a result, while his acumen was recognized, the Governor and his colleagues were wary of him.

By now Mookerjee had seen how much the Mahasabha had lost by its association with the British. His resignation letter struck all the nationalist notes. It was hailed by the public but seen by the British as what would today be called a PR-exercise. His speeches and writings had become increasingly hostile to the British. In an 'Immediate' cable to Amery, Wavell told the Secretary of State,

> Casey has just brought to my notice consistently anti-British and anti-Allies character of articles in Shyama Prasad Mookerjee's paper *Nationalist* which was founded at end of 1944. Mookerjee is bitterly communal as well and would (? ultimately) refuse to cooperate with me or with other leaders. I have therefore decided to drop him. My original plan did not repeat not include invitation to Mahasabha, and I am sure this was right and advice of Council wrong.[23]

In the event, Hindu Mahasabha was not invited for the Simla Conference. Predictably, the Mahasabha denounced not having been invited. In equally strident terms, it denounced Wavell's proposals for constitutional advance. That did not nudge Wavell or his officers. Colville wrote from Bombay,

---

[22] For his letter to the Governor, John Herbert bearing on this topic, Syama Prasad Mookerjee, *Leaves from a Diary*, Oxford University Press, Calcutta, 1993, Appendix II, pp. 175–90.

[23] Wavell to Amery, Telegram, L/P&J/8/322: f 174, Immediate, 9 June 1945, *Constitutional Relations Between Britain and India, The Transfer Of Power 1942–7, Volume V, The Simla Conference Background and Proceedings, 1 September 1944–28 July 1945*, Editor-in-Chief Nicholas Mansergh, Her Majesty's Stationery Office, London, 1974, pp. 1110–11.

'I sent you my report on the Hindu Mahasabha position. I do not think we need be unduly concerned about it. The core of it is here in Poona, and there might be some trouble locally, but with little effect outside. The Mahasabha would of course rejoice if the whole scheme broke down.'[24] In his 'Private and Secret' communication to Amery, Wavell reported,

> The Governors generally advise me that the intemperate resolution of the All-India Committee of the Hindu Mahasabha has had little effect and that the Hindus generally will stand behind Gandhi. The Mahasabha is a curious body; many of its rank and file seem to be Congressmen, and on big political issues will follow Gandhi rather than Shyama Prasad Mookerjee or Savarkar.[25]

Savarkar had faded away. The Hindu Mahasabha had been seen to be a hollow reed.[26]

---

[24] J. Colville (Bombay) to Wavell, Report No. 46, 5 July 1945, L/P&J/5/166: f 110, Ibid, at p. 1200. Colville was the Governor of Bombay from 1943. He had been Acting Governor-General of India during March-June 1945 when Wavell had gone to England.

[25] Wavell to Amery, 'Private and Secret,' L/PO/10/22, 1 July 1945, Ibid, at p. 1182.

[26] Mookerjee had thus far had a round-about career. Son of Sir Ashutosh Mookerjee, Judge of the Calcutta High Court and Vice Chancellor of the Calcutta University, Syama Prasad had been elected to the Bengal Legislative Council in 1929 on a Congress ticket. But soon, the Congress decided to boycott the legislature. He too resigned. He got elected back into the Assembly, this time as an Independent. He had been elected to the Provincial Assembly in the 1937 election, again as an Independent. He served as Finance Minister in the Fazlul Haq ministry in 1941–43, often speaking up in defence of Haq, whom he referred to as 'my leader', when the latter was at loggerheads with the Muslim League. Eventually, the Congress recommended his name for the Constituent Assembly and Panditji included him in the list of names he sent to Mountbatten for being appointed ministers in the new Government. The new Viceroy lauded this. In his 'Top Secret and Personal' report, he wrote,

> It is of course admirable that they should have got an important member of the Hindu Mahasabha to join the Government, and Mukerji is an intelligent man (whom they wanted to remove from Bengal); but Burrows, who knows him well,

I Know the Pain Better than Anyone

Though he invoked God on occasion, Savarkar, as we have seen, was a rationalist. And yet, he had pitched his tent on 'Hindutva'. His speeches and writings, his politics were all about 'Hindudom', about re-establishing the Hindu Rashtra. And his Hindutva was one turned outwards, strident, flexing its muscles, about the here and now. Other things apart, this conception of our religion, culture, history enabled him to scoff at Gandhiji, for instance, and to differentiate his programmes from that of, say, the Congress.

The problem was the people, in particular the Hindus. To his chagrin, they continued to stay away from this conception of their past, culture and religion. Worse, they continued to look upon Gandhiji as the embodiment of the Hindu way. And to the Congress as *the* movement for freedom. They continued to look upon the Congress as *the* party that was fighting for them.

Whether it was a municipal election, an election to provincial legislatures, or a countrywide election, Savarkar would exhort the Hindus to vote for Hindu Mahasabha candidates. He would plead with them. He would warn them not to cast 'even a single vote' for Congress candidates—they are sure to betray the interests of Hindus, he would

---

described him to me recently as being so low that a snake could not crawl under his belly . . .

The Cabinet is still far from being an ideal selection but the requirements of party politics could not entirely be done away with. On the whole, it must be conceded that Congress have been very generous and have included as large a proportion of non-Congressmen as one could possibly expect. Sir Shanmukham Chetty in particular has been a bitter critic of the Congress for a long time . . . [Viceroy's Personal Report No. 16, L/PO/6/123: ff 224-41, 8 August 1947, *Constitutional Relations Between Britain and India, Volume XII, The Mountbatten Viceroyalty, Princes, Partition and Independence, 8 July–15 August 1947,* Editor-in-Chief Nicholas Mansergh, Her Majesty's Stationery Office, London, 1983, at p. 601. At the time, Fredrick J. Burrows was the Governor of Bengal.]

warn. They are ashamed to call themselves Hindus. They oppose Hindu Sangathan and shuddhi. They spread the falsehood that Islam spread only through persuasion. They condemn Hindu patriots like Shivaji and Maharana Pratap as 'misguided patriots'. Cast not a single vote for these Congressmen 'who do not utter a single word condemning the continuous kidnapping of Hindu girls and boys, looting Hindus, desecrating their temples . . . who try to vitiate our Hindi language by letting the high bred [sic.] stream of Urdu words and raise the Bazari Hindusthani to the pedestal of your National tongue. Even the President of the Congress wants to throw out our Nagri script for the simple reason that the Nagri script stinches [sic.] in the nostrils of the Muslims. The Bande Matram song was mutilated to placate Muslim sentiment but the Hindu sentiment in favour of it was trampled underfoot' . . . They do nothing to protect Hindus during riots . . . they insist that there must be no music before mosques and during Moharram . . . but dismiss the demand to ban killing of cows as 'superstitious and communal and against the tenets of civil liberty' and are promising Messers Jinnah, Haq and Co. that Congress will never abolish cow killing in India . . . When the Hindu Mahasabha declared that the reformed Councils Act should be worked to continue further the fight for freedom, the Congress dubbed it as 'Haram' and said that they would never take the oath of allegiance to an alien Government. The very same Congress is now begging you for votes and its ministers are sticking to their ministries 'like so many leeches'. The Muslims with just 14 per cent of the population have captured more than 50 per cent in different government departments . . . 'The only remedy to root-out all this mischief lies in relieving these Congress-minded gentlemen from the responsibility of representing the Hindu Community and the Hindu Electorate and leave them free to act as Nationalists whatever that may mean and to elect only those who would act plainly, publicly and boldly as advocates of the Hindu cause, representatives of the Hindu community in particular and in the main owing to the simple fact that they have been elected by the

Hindu voters as Hindus.' So mighty a fusillade just for a local election in Faizabad—there was a Congress ministry in office in UP at the time.[27]

'The Muslims are represented by the Muslim League which says openly and is committed to safeguarding interests of the Muslims,' Savarkar tells the Hindu voters. 'It therefore takes an uncompromising stand for those interests. The Congress, Forward Bloc, etc. say they stand for the interests of all, and then to prove to the satisfaction of the League that they are *not* parties of the Hindus, that they do *not* represent Hindu interests, they sacrifice these at every turn.' The motives of the leaders of these 'Pseudo-Nationalistic' parties may be higher than their personal interests, they may even be patriotic, but, he warns the voters, 'patriots can also be fooled and betrayed into a suicidal policy.' In any case, 'whether their policy or their ideology be the cause, the results are what matter most to the Hindus who have been victimised and will continue to get victimised so long as the Hindu electorate persists in the suicidal folly of electing candidates who have pledged to the ideology and discipline of these Pseudo-Nationalist bodies.'

And therefore, he urges the electorate fervently, in this and future elections, they should not cast a single vote for the Congress or the Forward Bloc or any other Pseudo-Nationalistic party, that they should cast them only for the Hindu Mahasabha candidate. It is then and then only that 'the claim of the Hindu Mahasabha to represent Hindu interests will be legally and legitimately established'. And it is imperative at this juncture that this happens. 'These elections are a challenge thrown by the Government to the Hindu electorate to prove that the Hindu Mahasabha represents them and the Congress can no longer sign any pacts like the Communal Award or the Pakisthan [sic.] that is threatening to come

---

[27] *Vinayak Damodar Savarkar's Whirlwind Propaganda Tours: Statements, Messages and Extracts from the President's Diary of His Propagandistic Tours, Interviews from December 1937 to October 1941*, A.S. Bhide [ed.], Bombay, 1941, pp. 3–14. See also, *Savarkar Samagra*, Volume IX, pp. 304–05, 312–13, 454–55.

into being to the detriment of the Hindus.' The 'conference to frame the future constitution of India will soon be summoned,' he tells the Hindu voters. 'If the Hindu Mahasabha can pass the acid test at the polls all over India and has its candidates returned by the Hindus as their accredited representatives, the Government will be compelled to recognise the position of the Hindu Mahasabha on par with the Moslem League in this conference. Then no Blank Cheques, no Communal Awards, no Pakisthan Schemes, no weightages can be binding on the Hindus simply because the Congress signs them. The religious, the political and economical [sic.] interests, the culture, the language, the script, the honour and the whole future of the Hindu Nation will be safe in the hands of the Hindu Mahasabha and no constitution or law or understanding can be binding on the Hindus unless and until it is signed by the Hindu Mahasabha. If but the Hindu electorate returns only the Mahasabhait [sic.] representatives to the Legislatures, there will be in almost all provinces Hindu Sangathanist Ministries formed, pledged to safeguard and promote Hindu interest openly and uncompromisingly and even in the Hindu minority provinces powerful Hindu Sangathanist opposition parties will be in a position to exercise an effective check on the Moslem Ministries to defeat their anti-Hindu aggressions.' 'Consequently,' he concludes, 'I call upon Hindus all over India and specially in Bengal to realise the significance of this Pan-Hindu aspect in all future electoral campaigns.'

'If but the Hindu electorates take up a vow at any rate for the next five years to vote for the Hindu Sabhait candidates only and not to cast a single vote to the candidates of any other Pseudo-Nationalistic parties, the Hindus will be able to capture whatever political power there exists at present in India and from that position of vantage Hindudom will be able to defeat all anti-Hindu designs of the Moslem League and even of the Britishers and,' he assures the voters, 'will grow from strength to strength on its forward march to achieve the absolute political Independence of Hindusthan, the land wherein a free and powerful Hindu Nation flourished for ever and ever.'

Nine days later he is reiterating the same points and making the same appeal to Hindus in Sindh. He points out that Congress candidates win on Hindu votes—as the Muslims vote *en bloc* for Muslim League candidates—and then refuse to protect the interests of Hindus. Hindus are voting for candidates who are ashamed even to be known or seen to be working in their interests, Savarkar remarks. 'No sane man will engage an advocate to plead his case who openly pockets the fees paid by that man but refuses to plead his cause and even betrays his case as a Nationalist.'

He repeats the same arguments and the same plea to voters in Assam.[28]

But the stubborn ignoramuses . . . In the 1937 elections, the Mahasabha is as good as wiped out.

The 1945 elections come around. Savarkar issues a statement: 'Return the Hindu Mahasabha victorious'. He asks Hindu Mahasabha members to stand for the elections, and exhorts the voters to ensure their victory. He starts his appeal on a hopeful note. Today, in several Congressmen the belief in the interests of Hindus seems to be awakening, Savarkar says. They clearly realize the mistakes of the Congress. Even so they are sticking to the Congress because they hope that the Congress will reform its ways today or tomorrow. On this delusional faith, he says, thousands of Hindus remain in the Congress because they cannot overcome their greed for the loaves that may fall to them by their association with it. They have even thrown away that ticket which at the time of elections brings *yash* and the people's affection.

They have realized that the current Congress is not the true Indian National Congress of Tilak which used to aspire for the freedom of an unbroken Hindusthan, Savarkar says . . .

'Hence, the forthcoming elections acquire an even greater importance,' he tells the voters. 'The ones who win will get to the Constituent Assembly, and if the *Congressi* Hindus win it will be taken to mean that their view

---

[28] For the foregoing statements to voters, Bhide *op. cit,* pp. 381–82, 383–84, 387–89, 398–403, 448–49. Several of them figure in *Savarkar Samagra* also.

is the view of the majority Hindus . . . The Hindu Mahasabha is the only organisation that can fight the non-Hindu forces. All Hindus should unite under its banner. If you cannot do this, then at the least definitely cast your vote for the Hindu Mahasabha candidates. It alone is competent to protect Hindu interests. No Hindu should cast his vote even in forgetfulness to the Congress.'

And it isn't just that the opportunity for securing our interests would have been lost. 'Bear in mind that if striving for the interests of Hindus, we, who are a minority of Hindus, are defeated, the blame for that will not fall on us but on you. On those thousands and thousands of Hindus who, even as they see the fight that is being put up by a few Hindu fighters, do nothing to help them—the stain of that sin will be pasted on them. If you will do nothing to keep the Hindu banner spotless, the result will be just one—Hindusthan will not remain Hindusthan, it will become Pakisthan.'

As he reaches the concluding part, he seems a bit despondent: 'Even in these discouraging circumstances, I have hope that the people will listen to my call. No person with reason will be able to remain in the Congress now, and none will remain without casting his vote for the Hindu sangathan. If doing so is not possible for someone, then let him not cast a vote. But let no true Hindu give his vote to the Congress.'[29]

But the Ignorant People

But the stubborn ignoramuses . . . In the 1945 elections to the Central Legislative Assembly, the Mahasabha gets only 3.6 per cent of the votes cast—as against around 60 per cent of the Congress, and 28 per cent of the Muslim League. It gets no seat at all. Even of the non-Muhammadan votes cast, it gets only 5.9 per cent: the Congress gets 91.5 per cent.[30] In the

---

[29] Letter of 22 October, 1945, 'Make the Hindu Sabha victorious,' *Savarkar Samagra*, Volume VIII, pp. 622–25.

[30] Of the Muhammadan votes cast, the Congress gets only 1.3 per cent, the Muslim League gets 86.7 per cent. The Mahasabha gets none.

1945/46 elections to the Provincial Legislative Assemblies, the Mahasabha gets only 1.3 per cent of the votes cast—as against 57.2 per cent of the Congress and 21.3 per cent of the Muslim League. It gets just three of 1581 seats. Even in the two provinces in which it is said to have strength, it fares miserably: in Bombay Province, it gets 2.7 per cent of the votes cast, in Bengal it gets 1.4 per cent of the votes cast. It gets one of 175 seats in Bombay Legislative Assembly, and of 250 seats in the Bengal Assembly it wins one, that of Syama Prasad Mukherjee. The third seat it gets is in CP and Berar.[31] And yet it is the Mahasabha and Savarkar who have been hectoring the Congress, Gandhiji and the rest.

As Partition Becomes Inevitable

All too soon, Partition seems to have become inevitable. Savarkar has been holding the Congress responsible for the Partition. He has been threatening that Hindu Sangathanwadies will never allow the Motherland to be partitioned, that they will go to every length to prevent this, that, as we shall soon see, the great Hindu Rashtra of Nepal with its thousands of well-armed, battle-hardened Gurkhas will step in and crush the Muslim conspiracies to break the Motherland. Unfortunately, none of these vows and forecasts comes to pass. Savarkar does the next best thing: he issues a press statement.

Savarkar says that the question of Pakistan is a very fundamental one, that it is going to be a source of turmoil for generations of Hindus. Therefore, no general decision should be taken without obtaining the consent of the *janata*. No one has the moral right to decide it. He demands that the people of India be asked to vote on it, that fresh elections be held.

The lines that follow are full of pathos, of the realization that the very ones in whose name he has been speaking all these years have not been

---

[31] For the foregoing results, *Return Showing the Results of Elections to the Central Legislative Assembly and Provincial Legislatures in 1945–46,* Manager, Publications, Delhi, Government of India, 1948.

listening to him. 'So that no one misunderstands this view of mine and so that no one misrepresents it [*iskaa viparyaas naa karey*],' Savarkar continues, 'let me state clearly that in demanding fresh elections and the consent of all I am not depending even a bit—*rati bhar*—on the wisdom and understanding [*soojh-boojh*] of the Hindu voters. I have more of the painful experience than others of how, turning away from the only Hindu *sangathanvaadi* formation there is, the majority of Hindus will place their faith in the very group which has been creating impediments with a delusionary nationalism, who with their eyes shut will place their faith in and elect the very persons who throughout their lives have been doing the work of putting burning hot coal on Hindu interests, and who will continue to distrust those who have been fighting in the interests of Hindus. To continue to do again and again whatever he can and to continue to struggle, this is the duty of every Hindu *sangathanvaadi*.'[32]

From the fire-emitting dragon to this, '. . . I have more of the painful experience than others of how, turning away from the only Hindu *sangathanvaadi* formation there is, the majority of Hindus will place their faith in the very group which has been . . .'

There was a personal trait, one of the most prominent traits because of which this disappointment mutated into frustration and that transmuted into bitterness and that putrefied into hate.

---

[32] Statement to the press, 19 May 1947, 'Unite, Partition will be averted,' *Savarkar Samagra*, Volume VIII, pp. 635–36.

A Revolutionary Prescribes What to Write and
How to Write It

Made to Order

'Our history should be divided into periods in such a way that the reader should be able to easily make out how the unity of our Hindu race, its spread, its prestige and influence just went on increasing,' Savarkar prescribed.[1] 'The reader should understand this easily. The history of our Hindu rashtra is in fact such that after every external or internal difficulty our Hindu rashtra has emerged with even greater lustre like the sun from an eclipse . . .'

It is not that the reader should merely understand, he must form a definite conviction. 'From the moment we pick up history the sentiment should arise in us that it is the history of our *Akhil* Hindu *jati*. It is not the history of only Brahmins, not only of Jains, Lingayats, Aryans, Dravidians, nor of Bengal, nor Gujarat . . . The small kingdoms and principalities of the past have all not just unified into, but have acquired one life and a "Hindu Rashtra" has emerged.'

Yes, on occasion there were differences, he concedes. The sects and kingdoms may have fought each other also. But look at the so much smaller Britain, he says: the Irish, Welsh, Scots, Anglo-Saxons have been at each other. In our case also, there must have been some contests . . . some struggles between kingdoms, between different sects, some must have

---

[1] *'Hindu sangathankartaa svarashtra kaa itihaas kis tareh likhein aur padhein,'* Savarkar *Samagra,* Volume V, pp. 443–52

attacked each other, Savarkar says, but no one will want to 'dig up corpses from the past' . . .

Notice the '*may* have fought each other', then the tentative, the indefinite 'there *must have been* some contests . . . some *must have* attacked each other'. To narrate those, however, would be to '*dig up corpses*' from days long gone.

He does say at one point in the essay that the history we write should be truthful, that we should not be concerned with what effect it will have on the current situation. We should describe even regrettable events, he says.

But—and this is the theme of not just this essay, it is the theme of Savarkar's entire corpus—the way events are recalled and explained, and the way motives that impelled persons to act as they did are narrated must be such as subserves the main goal, of establishing the conviction that the Hindu rashtra is not the result of some principalities being stitched together. It is, and has been from time immemorial an organic, self-aware whole.

The Way to Narrate the Elimination of Buddhism

An example is how he wants us to treat the elimination of Buddhism from the country. We have to focus much more on the Buddhists' traitorous character rather than on religious differences between Hindus and Buddhists, he says. But as times have changed, he says that we must also acknowledge that they made an invaluable contribution to the growth of the ancient grandeur, vigour, knowledge, and literature of Hindu rashtra.

Two points in that. The good they did was as part of and for the glory of Hindu rashtra. Second, as we shall see when we review what he wrote about Buddhists in *Six Glorious Epochs of Indian History*, that is not the prescription that he himself followed. The reason is manifest. History has to be written for a purpose. And the purpose had changed by the mid-1960s.

In the tussles that took place more from political than religious reasons between Hindus and Buddhists, ultimately the Buddhists lost, he writes. In this way, the national problem that was going to come over the rashtra went away. In the period which followed, by the effort at assimilation, Bhagwan Buddha was acclaimed as the tenth incarnation of Bhagwan Vishnu. Therefore, the Hindu Sangathan worker should read that history from the point of view of *samanvaya,* of assimilation, of concord. Do not find fault with the past wearing the spectacles of today, he says—another prescription that he disregards resolutely. At the time a particular incident took place, the configuration of society was different, the situation was different . . . In the same way, one should determine what should be done today, and what not. Every Hindu Sangathan historian should in the appropriate way alert his readers to this as he concludes his account. That there may have been struggles with some sect in the past, or some persons of some subsect might have taken to condemnable ways, from this to look upon that community or subsect as condemnable for all times is not worthy of support. Only that should be regarded as worth shedding which is wrong or injurious to the rashtra at the present time. That alone is worth being preserved which is in the interest of the rashtra today . . . In the same way, only those deeds and themes should be written which evoke pride in all. Only in an unavoidable situation should the blemishes of our past be mentioned, and then in such a way that no one's sentiments are hurt—that last bit also, as we shall see, is to be observed by lesser mortals, of course, not by Savarkar. And it should be clearly stated that the blunder of the past is being mentioned only so that it is not repeated again. Today we are all Hindus, Savarkar says, we have all merged into the Hindu rashtra, and so that they are never repeated again we have left behind all those impediments.[2]

---

[2] Ibid, in particular, p. 447, pp. 451–52.

An Example

In his *Six Glorious Epochs,* Savarkar narrates an anecdote as it is in circulation about Chanakya, and then prescribes how that anecdote should be presented and understood. Chanakya and Chandragupta have been watching with rising anger the corruption, and even more so the inability and unwillingness of King Mahapadmanand to stand up to the Greeks. The immediate requirement is to get into the inner circle of the King and determine the apertures through which he can be dislodged. Chanakya makes his way into the Grants Department of Mahapadmanand. He becomes its head. One day the King comes to inspect the work of the department. He is incensed at the sight of this toothless, ugly-shaped old man. He orders that Chanakya be turfed out of the palace. Chanakya is enraged. He vows to overthrow Mahapadmanand.

Savarkar says that this would imply that Chanakya revolted against Emperor Nanda merely because he had been insulted personally, and that, 'had he not been thus insulted, he would have remained a loyal servant of Mahapadmanand, that the India-wide revolution that he successfully brought about was not for the sake of freeing the Indian land from the foreign Mlenchcha domination, but only to avenge a personal insult!'

'For this very reason this anecdote is clearly perverted,' Savarkar pronounces.

The logic of made-to-order history: because the anecdote can lead to a conclusion that is prejudicial to the message that we want to convey, it 'is clearly perverted'! May be, the message needs to be looked at again?

To continue with Savarkar:

Therefore, this anecdote should be understood, explained and taught in a different way, Savarkar prescribes. The correct way to present and understand it is the following, Savarkar says. '. . . Mahapadmanand had been receiving secret reports that, availing himself of the weakness of the reigning monarch, Arya Chanakya was busy conspiring against him so as to overthrow the Nanda empire. Therefore, Emperor Nanda insulted him in his royal palace and at that very moment the illustrious Brahmin Arya Chanakya retorted boldly, "If I am a true Chanakya I shall see to it that your tyrannical rule is overthrown so that Bharat might prosper." 'This is how the anecdote should be explained,' Savarkar says.

And as proof, he offers a strange inference. 'A very solid proof for this is available to us in the very *Kautiliya Arthashastra* written by Chanakya himself. While introducing himself Chanakya says, "He who destroyed Nanda and rejuvenated the national armed strength, as also the national scientific advance, which were decaying under the Nanda regime and thus caused the uplift of his Bharatbhoomi," has written this treatise.' Notice, says Savarkar, that 'He [Chanakya] has not used even a single word in these introductory lines to say that he destroyed Nanda to avenge the personal insult. It is for the progress and prosperity of his own nation and motherland that Nanda was destroyed! Chanakya's great treatise itself tells it clearly!'

So, while we do not know what may have triggered Chanakya's wrath, we must narrate the anecdote in such a way that he is seen to have acted out of a lofty motive, and not a mere insult. 'The anecdote which is told in a downright dramatic way perhaps means only this,' Savarkar says, 'that his original nationalistic animus towards Nanda was whetted the more because of this personal insult.'

There is also another reason for presenting the incident in this way, Savarkar says. If we believe that Chanakya decided to work for the overthrow of Mahapadmanand merely out of personal pique, could the same sort of construction not be put on Shivaji's striving to overthrow Aurangzeb and the Mughal rule?

'When as a strategy in politics Shivaji went to Agra accepting the overlordship of Aurangzeb, the latter insulted him,' Savarkar writes, 'and when there was a clash of words, Shivaji was put under arrest.' Shivaji escaped and declared war against Aurangzeb. 'If, after telling this story,' Savarkar tells us, 'some wiseacre were to conclude that it was because he was personally insulted that Shivaji bore a grudge against Aurangzeb and established an independent kingdom for himself, that he had no higher motive in his mind of emancipating his religion and country, it would be the height of absurdity and foolishness.'

'It is not true to say that because of his personal insult Shivaji revolted against Aurangzeb. On the contrary, Aurangzeb had taken a fright that it is to overthrow his alien religious domination that Shivaji had taken up arms, fired as he [Shivaji] was with a glowing fervour for Hindutva. That is why he insulted Shivaji and relegated him to captivity! In a similar way because Mahapadmanand had secret reports that, availing himself of the weakness of the reigning monarch, Arya Chanakya was busy conspiring against him so as to overthrow the Nanda empire, the Emperor Nanda insulted him in his royal palace and at that very moment the illustrious Brahmin Arya Chanakya retorted boldly, "If I am a true Chanakya I shall see to it that your tyrannical rule is overthrown so that Bharat might prosper." This is how the anecdote should be explained.'[3]

In a word, construe the incident to have happened in the way that, construe the motives of the *dramatis personae* to be those which will fortify the main purpose that we must bear in mind—that their singular objective was to revive and strengthen Hindu rashtra.

That is far more than inferring a motive. It is prescribing, indeed imposing a motive.

Reading Savarkar

How then are we to read Savarkar's engrossing account of the 1857 rebellion? On Savarkar's telling, everyone—from Mangal Pandey to rulers of principalities to feudatories of the Mughal Emperor—were all impelled by one burning motive. Not, for instance, to protect the privileges that they enjoyed but to end foreign

---

[3] *Six Glorious Epochs of Indian History,* op. cit., paras 99–104, pp. 37–39

rule—in this instance, *British* rule. What to do about Mughal rule would come later. The account makes for an arresting read. But, given Savarkar's stern prescription of how incidents are to be recounted, about which motives are to be read into the deeds, how much can we trust the account?

In Selecting Sources Too

Not just individual incidents. Not just entire epochs—as in the *Six Glorious Epochs*. Even in regard to a source or a category of sources on which we rely, the purpose we are striving for at that time should determine the weight that we attach to that source or category of sources.

For instance, when he is arguing against castes and the caste system, he scoffs at, and dismisses what is said in the Puranas about, say, their origin.[4] The thousands upon thousands of castes and subcastes and atomic castes have not been created by some scientific method after microscopic analysis of the blood of its members, he points out. And the reasons that have been given in the Puranas about their creation or origin are all gossip, imaginary fabricated tales. Describing some idiotic and cruel consequences of caste-based rules and the continuing fragmentation that have bedevilled Indian society, he refers to these accounts in the Puranas as a bundle of lies—*jhoot kaa pulindaa*—and affirms that compared to them the incidents which have triggered the formation of castes in more recent times are at least true if not foolish.

Consider next the weight he attaches to what is stated in the Puranas when he is talking of something closer to the Hindu rashtra which he wants the reader to believe implicitly. You will recall that Savarkar has a definite map in his mind—his conception of Hindu rashtra incorporates much of what is today Afghanistan, Tibet, Pakistan, Bangladesh, Nepal, Bhutan, Burma, Sri Lanka. The question is how to give this demarcation an

---

[4] *Jaatibandhak Nibandh*, Essay 6: 'Heredity or suicide or *vaahiyaatpanaa*,' *Kirloskar*, the date is not given. *Savarkar Samagra*, Volume VII, pp. 100–07.

ancient provenance. Savarkar invokes the *Bhavishya Purana*. He says that
it says that Shalivahana, the 'great King', the grandson of Vikramaditya,
demarcated the land as that of the Aryans and beyond it as that belonging
to the Mlenchhas. A decree was then issued prohibiting people from
crossing into the Mlenchha lands. And this must have been done, Savarkar
says, not just because the King thought this to be the right regulation but
because the people yearned for it.

We thus have four steps: [i] a decree was issued; [ii] it demarcated the
boundaries of Hindusthan; [iii] the decree was issued by the grandson of
Vikramaditya; [iv] he issued it in response to popular yearning:

> A decree *must have been issued* to this effect, and it *must have been not
> merely* a decree issued by the executive on its own but one that had
> been issued because of strong national imagination and sentiment, in
> response to 'a strong and popular movement.'

Two assumptions become facts in that single sentence. Reiteration
becomes reason:

> This Royal Decree was as all Royal Decrees in Sindhusthan had
> generally been, the mere executive outcome of a strong and popular
> movement. For, the custom of looking upon Attock as the veritable
> Indian land's-end as the very word Attock signifies *could not have
> been* originated and observed so universally and so long, had it not
> been inspired by and appealing to our national imagination. This
> custom that is so tenaciously and reverently observed by millions
> of people, premiers and peasants alike, is a good proof that strongly
> corroborates the fact that *some such royal edict* sanctioning the
> identification of our frontiers with the ancient Sindhu and associating
> the name of our land and nation with it as Sindhusthan had actually
> been issued; and that the highest religious sanctification consecrating

this royal sanction and popular will *must have* enabled this attempt to restore the Vedic name of our country to triumph in the end.

Once the decree had been issued, and that too in deference to popular will, the next step was as inevitable as it was logical—and here we see a third assertion become a fact.

But the word, Sindhusthan, Savarkar tells us, was not just territorial. It signified 'the best nation of the Aryas' as distinct from Mlenchhistan, the land of the foreigners. And the Aryas were, and here comes another crucial invention, those who resided on this side of the Indus and who owned and claimed what Savarkar has decided they did:

> However, it must be clearly pointed out that the definition is not based on any theological hair-splitting or religious fanaticism. The word Arya is expressly stated in the very verses to mean all those who had been incorporated as parts integral in the nation and people that flourished on this our side of the Indus whether Vaidik or Avaidik, Bramhana or Chandal, and *owning and claiming to have inherited a common culture, common blood, common country and common polity*; while Mlenchha also by the very fact of its being put in opposition to Sindhusthan meant foreigners nationally and racially and not necessarily religiously.[5]

Take a step back. It isn't just that we do not know much about the 'decree' and whether or not it was issued in response to popular sentiment, we do not know anything about Shalivahana, the king who is said to have issued it. In one legend he is the grandson of Vikramaditya, in another he is the enemy of Vikramaditya, one who defeats the latter. This victory

---

[5] On this string of assertions and claims, V.D. Savarkar, *Essentials of Hindutva*, V.V. Kelkar, Poona, 1923, in particular, pp. 26–29. The book was originally published under the pen-name, 'A Maratha'.

was so important that the Saka era, the alternative to the Vikramsamvat, is said to commence from it—in another version the Saka era is said to commence from the birth of Shalivahana. In some legends, Shalivahana is the great champion of Hindus. In some, he is an atheist who persecutes them no end. The Brahmins have to appeal to Shiva to rid them of this menace. Shiva has to appeal to Brahma. Shiva himself has to exert himself to finish him—once Shalivahana escapes Shiva's stratagem, it is only on the second attempt that Shiva succeeds. And so on. The *Encyclopaedia of Hinduism* puts the matter succinctly:

> Vikramaditya, son of Gardabhilla, was a great emperor ruling at Ujjayini during the period 58–57 B.C., (according to the Prakrit work *Kalakacarya-kathanaka).* However, no historical or literary evidence is available to prove the existence of Shalivahana.[6]

In a word, we do not know anything definite about Shalivahana. But we must believe that he issued the decree, and that he issued it as a true democrat—in response to public demand. And that decree has since then defined the contours of a living, organic, pulsating Hindusthan.

Why? Because we must project and believe only the version which subserves the objective, the objective of Savarkar being to establish that there has been since times immemorial a Hindusthan as delineated by that king in that decree—from Attock to Cuttack, from Manas Sarovar to Rameshwaram, a Hindusthan that was not just ruled by a great king but was also truly democratic centuries and centuries before Europeans and others.

The country having been delineated, Savarkar proceeds to set out by example what is becoming the new approach to history:

---

[6] Swami Harshananda, *A Concise Encyclopaedia of Hinduism,* Volume 3, Ramakrishna Math, Bangalore, 2008, p. 160.

The verses from *Bhavishya Purana* quoted above *seem to be quite trustworthy so far as their general purport is concerned.* Firstly, *because they record a general tradition* that, unlike dates or individual successions, can easily be remembered longer.

The verses 'seem to be quite trustworthy' because they record a general tradition? Or the tradition must have been a general one and must have been in vogue for long because, see, it is mentioned in the Puranas?

Secondly, independently of that, *the general trend of our history as shown points to some such state of affairs.* Thirdly, *it is not necessary here for our arguments to be very precise either about the date of this Decree or even the king by whom it was issued.* And fourthly, the author does not seem to have been writing about things only haphazardly or to which he is entirely a stranger. For the family table that he gives of the House of Vikramaditya is again given in other parts of the work and the two agree closely with each other. The writer who knows of details about the House is likely to know the *salient* facts of the most distinguished king that belonged to it.

After all, *the main resources of our history had been and must ever be our national traditions remembered or recorded in our ancient puranas, epics and literature. Their details may be challenged, their dates determined and rejected, but on account of discrepancies here or miraculous colouring there which are in fact common to all ancient records of mankind, we cannot dismiss them altogether, especially where the acts recorded have not an impossible or unnatural element in them or when they do not contradict events otherwise proved to be indisputably true.*

As *udankhatolas* are not impossible, as weapons that rain incalculable destruction are not impossible, we must believe that our forefathers had them and wielded them ages ago. Suddenly, doubting this way of assessing sources and endorsing evidence becomes slavishness to foreigners!

The habit of doubting everything in the Puranas till it has been corroborated by some foreign evidence is absurd. The sounder process would be to depend on our works especially where general traditions and events are concerned till they are found to be unreliable in the light of any more weighty and less ambiguous evidence and not simply on account of the airy imaginings of someone to whom it does not seem probable. Take the case of this *Bhavishya Purana* itself: because it contains some inaccuracies and even absurdities—and is Plutarch free from them? Are we to reject the personality of Alexander himself because of the supernatural touches given to the story of his birth? Would it be reasonable to doubt, say the following verse?

[The son of Chandragupta with leanings towards Buddhism then married the Greek daughter of Sulava, Governor of Purus]

In fact, we owe a debt of gratitude to these Puranas and Epics for having preserved all ancient and venerable records of our people through revolutions which had effaced the very traces of whole nations and whole civilizations elsewhere in the world. For after all, these records of our ancient and patriotic Puranas and Histories are at any rate more faithful, more accurate and more reliable than the modern up-to-date western puranas that have such convincing discoveries to their credit as the one which assures us that Ramayan sings of the foundation of Vijayanagar or the other which asserts that Gautam the Buddha was merely the Sun or the Dawn personified!

Now, there are several renditions of, to take the Purana that Savarkar is using, the *Bhavishya Purana*. Parts of it are borrowed from another Purana, others from a Samhita. Some of the 'prophecies', as in the case of Nostradamus, seem to be retrospective prophecies—among these would be structures of

Queen Victoria! Some of the entries are said to date from as recent a period as mid-nineteenth century. The polite expression is that, like other Puranas, and like the Ramayana and Mahabharat, it is a 'living text'—with additions, interpolations, substitutions having been made over the ages as seemed appropriate in the new circumstances. In some parts, the Purana seems to be very similar to the *Manusmriti,* in others to be amending the latter.

In *Six Glorious Epochs,* written as Savarkar records in the book, in his eightieth year when he was bedridden, he takes a somewhat more circumspect view of the Puranas as a source for historical facts. Here are the sort of things he says about relying on Puranas as sources:

- Like that of China, Babylon, Greece and other ancient nations our ancient history, too, is clothed in the poetical garb of mythology. It is replete with anecdotes, folk-lore, and deification of national heroes and heroines, and resorts to supernatural and symbolic description. Yet these ancient mythologies (Puranas) of ours are the pillars supporting the edifice of our ancient history. Just as these extensive Puranic texts of ours are a magnificent treasure of our ancient literature, our knowledge, our glorious deeds and our grandeur and wealth, in a similar way they are a vast store-house of the accounts of our past, desultory, chaotic, even at times, ambiguous though it may be . . .
- Our Puranas, however, are not 'history' pure and unadulterated . . .
- Hence, I propose to set aside the consideration of the 'Puranic times' in the present context. For the 'Glorious Epochs' that I am going to refer to, and dilate upon, belong not so much to the Puranic times, as to the historic periods of our national life.[7]

---

[7] *Six Glorious Epochs of Indian History,* op. cit., pp. 1-2.

For this reason, Savarkar decides to select for the 'Glorious Epochs' that he shall consider the period only from the appearance of Buddha onwards.

Convenience as a Touchstone

Five points to bear in mind about this attitude of convenience towards sources, of what is useful for the purpose at hand. First, as we have seen earlier, Savarkar himself scolds people for basing their lives on, for basing their arguments on texts—the *Manusmriti,* for instance—which have overwriting, interpolations, contradictory statements, which, in a word, are 'living texts'. So, how come he himself takes the Puranas as believable texts? Second, what if we had come across the foregoing paragraphs of Savarkar in the thesis of one of our Marxist 'Eminent Historians'? Would we not have leapt up and proclaimed that with such a cavalier attitude to evidence, one can conjure up anything one wants? Third, the errors of Western scholars are no guarantee that the imagined assertions of Savarkar or his *bhakts* will be sound. In fact, when they commit the same mistakes, when they adopt the same subterfuges, they will end up in the same place as the 'Eminent Historians'. They will inflict the same consequences on their followers, on public discourse, and therefore on the country.

Fourth, recall Savarkar's prescription that we should interpret events in the way which, that we should put those constructions on texts and legends which, in a word that we should write history in the way which would serve the objective of establishing Hindu Rashtra. Does that not give a licence to others to twist facts and impose interpretations that would further *their* objectives, a licence to our 'eminent historians', for instance, to impose constructions that show our history to have been one long march of the conflict between classes which, in turn, were occasioned by the changing means and modes of production? Finally, how does this prescription of Savarkar sit with his insistence that we must live by what science teaches us, that we must go by evidence, that we must adopt the scientific method?

Are we to be rationalists in regard to customs, beliefs, rituals, in regard to life in general but to be propagandists in regard to history?

To Establish Us as a Race

In delineating Hindutva, Savarkar says in several of his writings and especially in *Hindutva*,[8] that the Hindus constitute a race, and that is because we have the same blood. His discussion about our common blood in this context must be distinguished from his discussion about blood in the context of castes. In the former, he is asserting that we are one 'because chiefly' our blood is the same. In his discussion about castes, his concern is to establish that castes are not watertight compartments. And this is so because there have been inter-marriages and extra-marital inter-caste affairs so that the blood of no caste is 'pure'. The blood of each caste is mixed with that of other castes. 'Mixed' doesn't amount to 'common'.

Savarkar says, 'Its name is Bharat and the people are Bharati' is a definition ten times better because truer than that. We, Hindus, are all one and a nation, *because chiefly of our common blood—'Bharati Santati'*.[9] The Hindus are not merely the citizens of the Indian State: 'they are united not only by the bonds of the love they bear to a common Motherland but also by the bonds of *a common blood*,' he states.[10] The expression 'common blood' occurs again and again, like a talisman. Witness the following passage in *Hindutva*:

---

[8] V.D. Savarkar, *Hindutva*, V.V. Kelkar, Poona, 1923. Savarkar wrote this book in 1921–22. It was published under a pen-name, 'A Maratha'. An e-version is available As *Essentials of Hindutva*, published by Himani Savarkar, https://savarkar.org/en/encyc/2017/5/23/2_12_12_04_essentials_of_hindutva.v001.pdf_1.pdf

Unfortunately, the verses and shlokas that appeared in the original are missing; for some of them translations have been given; for some, not. In the following, page numbers refer to the original 1923 edition.

[9] Ibid, p. 34: '*Bharati santati*': Bharati offspring.

[10] Ibid, p. 73.

Some of us were Aryans and some Anaryans; but Ayars or Nayars—
we were all Hindus and *own a common blood*. Some of us are
Brahmans and some Namashudras or Panchamas; but Brahmans
or Chandalas—we are all Hindus and *own a common blood*. Some
of us are Daxinatyas and some Gauds; but Gauds or Saraswats—we
are all Hindus and *own a common blood*. Some of us were Rakshasas
and some Yakshas; but Rakshasas or Yakshas—we are all Hindus and
own a common blood. Some of us were Vanaras and some Kinnaras;
but Vanaras or Naras—we are all Hindus and *own a common blood*.
Some of us are Jains and some Jangamas; but Jains or Jangamas—we
are all Hindus and *own a common blood*. Some of us are monists,
some, pantheists; some theists and some atheists. But monotheists or
atheists—we are all Hindus and *own a common blood* . . .[11]

'We [the Hindus] are not only a Nation but also *a race—jati*.[12] The word
jati derived from the root *jan* to produce, means a brotherhood, *a race*
determined by a common origin—*possessing a common blood*.'[13]

By the very next sentence, 'possessing a common blood' becomes
claiming to have the blood of a mighty race! 'All Hindus *claim to have in
their veins the blood of the mighty race* incorporated with and descended
from the Vedic fathers, the Sindhus.'[14]

---

[11] Ibid, p. 90.

[12] Ibid, p. 73. 'Jati' is race in the early writings, and the core of race is 'blood relationship.'
As race becomes discredited because of the Nazis, and 'blood relationship' becomes
impossible to establish, and, worst of all, as 'blood relationship' would entail that Muslims
too are part of the nation—especially in view of the assertion that very few among them
had come from abroad, that the overwhelming proportion among them are Muslims
because their forefathers were forced or deceived or lured to become Muslim—'Jati'
became caste.

[13] Ibid, p. 73.

[14] Ibid, p. 74.

Notice how things are being conflated: we 'have been born in the same place,' 'joined together by the same blood', and 'the same blood flows in our veins' [. . .] 'claim to have the same blood.'

Even in April 1940 by which time racialism is in bad repute, Savarkar speaks of 'a Hindu who is not a traitor to his own *racial self*', and exhorts 'Let the Hindus who stand by their *racial soul and honour*' leave the Congress. Similarly, 'the *racial dream* of a consolidated, mighty and independent Nation could be realised sooner than they dare to expect'; 'Let every Hindu of Gujarth [sic.] join the Hindu Mahasabha because he is a Hindu first and everything afterwards. His religion, *his Race, his Blood, his Seed* all that he is, is Hindu in substance, in essence. He is an Indian because he is a Hindu. He is not a Hindu because he is an Indian. India to him would [be] but a funeral ground, a Sahara Desert if his Hindutva and Hinduness are annihilated and leave no trace in India. India is dear to him because his Hindutva flourished there and because it is the Fatherland of *the Hindu Race* and the Holy Land of his Hindu Gods.'[15]

A series of problems there:

- Is the claim—that we are all 'descended from the Vedic fathers'— even being made? For instance, by the Tamils so proud of their Dravidian, and emphatically *not* of Vedic-Aryan fathers? Remember in this context, the poetic flights in which Savarkar himself describes the conquest of the land by the Aryans.
- Is a mere *claim*, even if it is being made, sufficient to establish a biological fact?
- What is one to understand by 'common blood'? When you go to donate blood for someone who has been in an accident, you realize that blood type varies from individual to individual. If by 'blood' in this context is meant 'genes', then we have the disconcerting findings of recent research about ancient genes—from fossils,

---

[15] Bhide, *Whirlwind Tours,* op. cit., pp. 189, 258, 259–60.

geography, languages, literature, genetics—that the DNA of Indians is descended from and blended to varying degrees from dissimilar stock.[16]

Savarkar sees the gross infirmity in the assertions. His answer is typical: offence is the best defence, and, better still, offence with a touch of menace:

> We are well aware of the not unoften interested objection that carpingly questions 'but are you really a race ? Can you be said to possess a common blood?' We can only answer by questioning in return, 'Are the English a race? Is there anything as English blood, the French blood, the German blood or the Chinese blood in this world? Do they, who have been freely infusing foreign blood into their race by contracting marriages with other races and peoples possess a common blood and claim to be a race by themselves?' If they do, Hindus also can emphatically do so.[17]

Notice first, the *'if they can say this, then'*. But if they are not saying *that*, what then? Savarkar continues,

> For the very castes, which you owing to your colossal failure to understand and view them in the right perspective, assert to have barred the common flow of blood into our race, have done so more truly and more effectively as regards the foreign blood than our own. Nay is not the very presence of these present castes a standing testimony to a common flow of blood from a Brahman to a Chandal? Even a cursory glance at any of our Smritis would conclusively prove that the *Anuloma* and *Pratiloma* marriage institutions were the order of the day and have given birth to the majority of the castes that obtain amongst us.[18]

---

[16] See, for instance, Tony Joseph's riveting, *Early Indians, The story of our ancestors and where we came from*, Juggernaut, 2018.

[17] *Hindutva*, op. cit., pp. 83–84.

[18] Ibid.

Can one deduce from the examples that Savarkar gives that *anuloma* and *pratiloma* marriages were 'the order of the day'? Or, while decreeing where in the slots the children of such marriages will be placed, did Manu, etc. provide for exceptions? Savarkar's answer is poetry, and a bow to eugenics:

From the Vedic story of Satyakama Jabali to Mahadaji Shinde every page of our history shows that the ancient Ganges of our blood has come down from the altitudes of the sublime Vedic heights to the plains of our modern history fertilizing much, incorporating many a noble stream and purifying many a lost soul, increasing in volume and richness, defying the danger of being lost in bogs and sands and flows to-day refreshed and reinvigorated more than ever. All that the caste system has done is to regulate its noble blood on lines believed– and on the whole rightly believed-by our saintly and patriotic law-givers and kings to contribute most to fertilize and enrich all that was barren and poor, without famishing and debasing all that was flourishing and nobly endowed.[19]

This from the very person who spent so much time and paper to show how castes were oppressing castes, how within individual castes there were and are invidious hierarchies and oppressive practices, how the caste compartments had become ironclad.

In the end, as is usual with so much of Savarkar, it all comes down to an assertion: as 'We *feel* we are a *jati*, a race bound together by the dearest ties of blood, and *therefore* it must be so':

We are not only a nation but a *jati*, a born brotherhood. Nothing else counts, it is after all *a question of heart*. *We feel* that the same ancient blood that coursed through the veins of Ram and Krishna, Buddha and Mahavir, Nanak and Chaitanya, Basava and Madhava, of Rohidas

---

[19] Ibid, pp. 74–75.

and Tiruvelluvar courses throughout Hindudom from vein to vein, pulsates from heart to heart. *We feel we are a JATI,* a race bound together by the dearest ties of blood and *therefore it must be so.*[20]

QED!

In the next breath, the problem is defined away. In any case, we are all humans, Savarkar tells us, and all of us have human blood in our veins:

> After all there is throughout this world so far as man is concerned but a single race—the human race kept alive by one common blood, the human blood. All other talk is at best provisional, a makeshift and only relatively true. Nature is constantly trying to overthrow the artificial barriers you raise between race and race. To try to prevent the commingling of blood is to build on sand. Sexual attraction has proved more powerful than all the commands of all the prophets put together. Even as it is, not even the aborigines of the Andamans are without some sprinkling of the so-called Aryan blood

What did he say? *'so-called* Aryan blood'?

> in their veins and vice versa. Truly speaking all that any one of us can claim, all that history entitles one to claim, is that one has the blood of all mankind in one's veins. The fundamental unity of man from pole to pole is true, all else only relatively so.[21]

But just a while ago Savarkar was saying that a distinctive mark is not one that is common to all. It is one that distinguishes us, that separates us from others. Be it just a name, 'Hindu'. Or, as Savarkar affirms a few paragraphs later, a complex of beliefs and mores—'a common history, common heroes, a common literature, common art, a common law and a common jurisprudence,

---

[20] Ibid, pp. 77–78.

[21] Ibid, pp. 78–79.

common fairs and festivals, rites and rituals, ceremonies and sacraments.' Having enumerated these, Savarkar says, '. . . Not that every Hindu has all these details of the Hindu *sanskriti* down to each syllable common with other Hindus; but that, he has more of it in common with his Hindu brothers than with, say, an Arab or an Englishman. Not that a non-Hindu does not hold any of these details in common with a Hindu but that, he differs more from a Hindu than he agrees with him.'[22] So, if the blood running through the veins of Hindus is just the same—'human blood'—as the blood coursing through the veins of other human beings, then at least 'blood' is *not* a criterion by which we may distinguish Hindus from others. But till now, we were separate because a common blood was flowing through our veins.

All Right, Not Blood, but Two Other Criteria

In the very next paragraph, two further criteria are proclaimed. First, 'all those who love the land that stretches from Sindhu to Sindhu, from the Indus to the seas, as their fathers did, and *consequently claim to inherit* the blood of the race that has evolved . . .' But that leaves things to the wish of individuals and groups. What if the Muslims of Mewar love the land and 'consequently *claim to inherit* the blood of the race that has evolved'? God Forbid!

And so, a second criterion is inserted: 'A Hindu believing in any theoretical or philosophical or social system, orthodox or heterodox, *provided it is unquestionably indigenous and founded by a Hindu* may lose his sect but not his Hindutva—his Hinduness.' Nagas and Mizos and Kukis and Meities, and Marma and Bawm anyone?

Savarkar is alert to the danger of communities such as the Meos of Haryana:

a moment's consideration would show that these two qualifications of one nation and one race—of *a common fatherland and therefore of*

---

[22] Ibid, pp. 87–88.

a common blood—cannot exhaust all the requisites of Hindutva. The majority of the Indian Mohammedans may, if free from the prejudices born of ignorance, come to love our land as their fatherland, as the patriotic and noble-minded amongst them have always been doing. The story of their conversions, forcible in millions of cases, is too recent to make them forget, even if they like to do so, that they inherit Hindu blood in their veins. But can we, who here are concerned with investigating into facts as they are and not as they should be, recognize these Mohammedans as Hindus? Many a Mohammedan community in Kashmir and other parts of India as well as the Christians in South India observe our caste rules to such an extent as to marry generally within the pale of their castes alone; yet, it is clear that though their original Hindu blood is thus almost unaffected by an alien adulteration, yet they cannot be called Hindus in the sense in which that term is actually understood, because we Hindus are bound together not only by the tie of the love we bear to a common fatherland and *by the common blood* that courses through our veins and keeps our hearts throbbing and our affections warm, but also by the tie of the common homage we pay to our great civilization—our Hindu culture, which could not be better rendered than by the word *sanskriti* suggestive as it is of that language, Sanskrit, which has been the chosen means of expression and preservation of that culture, of all that was best and worth preserving in the history of our race. We are one because we are a nation, a race and own a common *sanskriti* (civilization).[23]

That excludes Muslims all right, but it also leaves out the Nagas, Mizos, Meities, Kukis . . . indeed the tribals in general. They would scarcely have

---

[23] Ibid, pp. 79–80.

heard of *'sanskriti'* and Sanskrit. And, if truth be told, their *sanskriti* is very different from what we find in, say, the 'cradle of Aryan civilization', the Gangetic plain, as is that of the people in, say, Kerala.

The Power to Certify Is Handed to or Snatched by Someone Else

And there is the second problem: the key to belonging is now handed over to or snatched away by someone else. *He* will decide what constitutes the *'sanskriti'*. North Indian classical music, for instance, or some of the schools of *Pahari* and Rajasthani painting certainly cannot be part of it, what with so much Islamiyat/Muslimhood in them. And *he* will decide whether you really and truly and genuinely and sincerely and honestly and absolutely and fully and only and exclusively have in your heart-of-hearts veneration for our great civilization.

The Sort of Result That Ensues

That would certainly exclude the one Savarkar excoriates as the 'Hindu hater', as the one 'burning with hatred for Hinduism'; as the one putting out 'extravagant and vulgar remarks on Hindu history'; as the one who is 'berating Hindu Dharma with falsehoods and in filthy language'; as the one who is taking his followers into 'this maze of wrong, unjust, untruthful and Hindu-hatred of his'; as the one who is misleading them into 'the fraud of conversion'; as the one who is fooling them with his *'gup'*, with his *'jaani-boojhi guppon yaa chaturaayi kee batein'*/with clever talk and things he knows are just gossip; as the one who has been 'raining abuse only on Hinduism' but dares not utter a word about Islam or Christianity 'out of fear'; as 'the one-eyed emperor among the blind'; as the one who has been hurling *'gaali-galoch*/abuse through his publications and speeches at what he calls Hindu Dharma and Hindu society' 'in language so vulgar/ *vaahiyaat,* unjust and at places so low that only the Hindu society gripped by the ailment of forbearance could have tolerated it'; in the 'dark well of [whose] mind there lies hidden a grand political ambition that will be fatal to the rashtra, the ambition that, if under his leadership the number of Buddhists becomes large enough then, by joining forces with disruptive forces in Jharkhand, he aims to establish an independent Buddhist land, an independent Naagraaj'. And who is that person who on Savarkar's reckoning can certainly not be said to have veneration for our history, culture, religion, civilization? Each of these remarks of Savarkar is directed at Ambedkar.[24]

Of course, the appropriators, the ones dressing themselves up or covering themselves up in the robes of our religion and civilization have not the slightest compunction in appropriating both!

How the Behaviour of Others Does Not Prove the Point

And then comes the definition of *sanskriti,* of 'civilization' that nails the exclusion further: a common history in that people venerate the same heroes, vilify the same traitors, feel joyous and proud of the same victories and achievements and moan over the same setbacks. 'But what of the internecine wars among Hindus?' Savarkar has his critic ask:

> We answer, what about the Wars of Roses amongst the English? What of the internecine struggle, of state against state, sect against sect, class against class, each invoking foreign help against his own in Italy, in Germany, in France, in America? Are they still a people, a nation and do they possess a common history? If they do, the Hindus do.

---

[24] For the epithets that Savarkar hurled at Ambedkar, see, for instance, *Six Glorious Epochs of Indian History,* op. cit., para 320, pp. 131, para 706, pp. 281–82. And the numerous articles that Savarkar wrote in the wake of Ambedkar's *Annihilation of Caste,* and his announcement that, together with his followers, he would be converting to Buddhism. For instance, *Savarkar Samagra,* Volume VII, pp. 150–65, 169–83, 258–62, 262–71, 272–79.

If the Hindus do not possess a common history, then none in the world does.[25]

But the others are not making the claim. *You* are making it on our behalf. 'If the Hindus do not possess a common history, then none in the world does,' you say. Well, what if no one does? That certainly does not prove that we do. It just means that you have to think again about the criterion you invoked to exclude some.

The same sort of assertions about Sanskrit being the 'mother of all our present tongues', of our having common institutions and laws, feasts and festivals, rites and rituals . . . People of Punjab believe in *rahu-kaalam*? For people in one part of the country, the auspicious time for performing marriages is at night. Among Sikhs, it is during the day. Some Hindus cremate their dead, some bury them . . . Common rites and rituals?

Writ in Stone

Thus, the sources are malleable, as far as daily living is concerned the boundaries are as lines drawn in water, but the exclusion is absolute and writ in stone. And that in two steps. First, the assertion that this land is the land of the Hindus—Savarkar always spells it as Hindu*sthan*. Second, only she or he is a Hindu for whom this land is the *punyabhoomi*, the holy land. Even if the current-day Muslims have been converted by force or deception, once converted the land which they regard as holy becomes Arabia or some portions of what is today Israel. The Sikhs or Jains are Hindus.[26] The Japanese or Chinese may be Buddhists and

---

[25] *Hindutva*, op. cit., pp. 83–84.

[26] Throughout *Six Glorious Epochs of Indian History*, Sikhs are treated as Hindus: Sikh forces, Sikh kingdoms—such as that of Maharaja Ranjit Singh—are treated as Hindu

so this may be the Holy Land for them. But it is not the land of their ancestors. Their language, culture, history are different. Jews, Bohras, Parsis may be from among us but in their mind they have their holy land elsewhere.

Look Closely at What Has Happened Next Door

The first thing to remember is that once this search for purity starts, there is no end. Look at Pakistan. They started persecuting the Ahmediyas. This small, harmless lot, most of them poor were pronounced to be kafirs and *murtads*, heretics. They were prohibited from even calling themselves 'Muslims'. They were forbidden from calling their places of worship 'mosques'. They were prohibited from having any mark not just on their places of worship, not just on themselves or their houses but even on their clothes that might suggest that they were Muslims. And this was decreed when, as Justice Muhammad Munir showed in his incisive report, the ulema could not agree even on who was a 'Muslim', when many of the ulema held Jinnah to be a kafir.[27] Ahmediyas having been cast out, the Sunnis pounced on the Shias. And then disagreements erupted among Sunnis, and these took a violent turn. Various sects among the Sunnis began forming sectarian armies and terrorist outfits. Shouldn't we learn?

But this formula of exclusion was not the end. It was fortified by an assertion, one that went far beyond the claims to 'common blood'. And it is to that we must now turn.

---

rulers and kingdoms. For instance, see *Six Glorious Epochs of Indian History,* op. cit., para 1099, p. 457. And what do the Sikhs say about this appropriation?

[27] *Report of the Court of Inquiry constituted under Punjab Act II of 1954 to enquire into the Punjab Disturbances of 1953,* Superintendent, Government Printing, Lahore, Punjab, 1954.

'The Undying, Unifying Force'

The exclusions which Savarkar's formula was designed to ensure are but a stepping stone to the central claim of Savarkar: that from time immemorial our society, our polity, our people have been animated by, suffused by, soaked in a pan-Hindu consciousness. The others, of course, have viewed us for the Hindus we are, Savarkar said. Their viewing us in this way, their tormenting us for being Hindu has made us all the more conscious of who we are, he maintained. And all our struggles have been to preserve and fortify this Hinduness. That is what Savarkar would have us believe. In the oft-invoked *Hindutva*, for instance, we learn:

> In this prolonged furious conflict, our people became intensely conscious of ourselves as Hindus and were welded into a nation to an extent unknown in our history . . .
>
> The enemies hated us as Hindus and the whole family of peoples and races, of sects and creeds that flourished from Attock to Cuttack was suddenly individualised into a single Being . . . For it was the one great issue to defend the honour and independence of Hindusthan and maintain the cultural unity and civic life of Hindutva and not Hinduism alone, but Hindutva—i.e. Hindudharma that was being fought out on the hundred fields of battle as well as on the floor of the chambers of diplomacy. This one word, Hindutva, ran like a vital spinal cord through our whole body politic and made the Nayars of Malabar weep over the sufferings of the Brahmins of Kashmir. Our

bards bewailed the fall of Hindus, our seers roused the feelings of Hindus, our heroes fought the battles of Hindus, our saints blessed the efforts of Hindus, our statesmen moulded the fate of Hindus, our mothers wept over the wounds and gloried over the triumphs of Hindus.[1]

It is this Pan-Hindu consciousness, according to Savarkar, which spurred Hindus to get together from time to time to throw out foreign invaders. It is this consciousness which held society together in spite of divisions such as caste:

388. The structure of the caste-system was based on the principles of heredity, of the economy based on the division of labour, of social co-existence and of social ethics . . .

In spite of these distinctions and divisions the society and *jati* and *rashtra* held together for thousands of years because of some undying and unifying force with a certain consciousness of its true self.

388-A. This powerful unifying national sentiment which so unmistakably held together these different and apparently autonomous elements of the Hindu society and fused them together was: Hindutva! And Hindu dharma.[2]

It is this consciousness which gave our people a sense of identity and purpose. It is this consciousness which raised our people above their personal and parochial concerns and made them strive for the greater goal. It is this consciousness which, in spite of our being prone to frictions

---

[1] V.D. Savarkar [writing as 'A Maratha'], *Hindutva*, V.V. Kelkar, Poona, 1923, pp. 39–40

[2] *Six Glorious Epochs of Indian History*, op. cit., pp. 158–59.

that are common to all societies, ensured a harmonious life. As we have seen, Savarkar was unsparing in his criticisms of the caste system and the rules associated with it. He was unsparing in his denunciation of what he called the perverted sense of virtues. But, he was emphatic in *Essentials of Hindutva, Hindu Pad-padshahi, Six Glorious Epochs of Indian History,* in his numerous articles and speeches that this pan-Hindu consciousness has pervaded, and has always pervaded our rulers and people, that it has given us through the ups and downs of ages a sense of identity, purpose, unity. Here are some typical passages from the opening pages of *Hindu Pad-padshahi:*

We shall observe how the consciousness of this noble ideal [of setting up a Hindu Empire] animated their efforts from generation to generation, gave to their distant and widely scattered activities a unity of aim and kinship of interests, made them feel that their cause was the cause of their Dharma and their Desh—a mission worthy of the efforts of their saints and soldiers alike—carried the Marathas in triumph from step to step to the gates of Delhi, to the banks of the Indus in the north and the season [sic.] the south; and how it raised the story of their deeds to the grandeur of a great national epic that every Hindu mother can proudly sing to her infant in strains far more triumphant and ennobling than the ballads that tell us how our day was lost, how our banner was torn and how, ultimately, our foes triumphed.

Hindu forces inspired and animated by the ideal of Hindu *Pad-padshahi*—the establishment of an independent Hindu Empire . . .

It was essentially a Hindu movement in the defence of Hindu Dharma for the overthrow of the alien Muhammadan domination, for the establishment of an independent, powerful Hindu Empire. It was not only the leader of the Marathas who was actuated by this patriotic zeal, but it was more or less shared throughout his camp and his country. The people were as fully conscious of the patriotic spirit that actuated the efforts of Shivaji, as he himself was. He was everywhere hailed as a deliverer of the Hindus.

... District after district, and town after town, longed and pressed for the coming of the Marathas under Shivaji and rejoiced to see the Muhammadan flag being torn asunder from its flagstaff and the sacred Geruva of the Marathas rise and wave triumphant in its stead.

... This was felt all over the country as is evident in the poems of Bhushan ...[3]

Pan-Hindu Consciousness?

Our gods are often fighting with, and in the process hurling the most lethal of weapons at each other. Each just to establish his dominance.

The Mahabharata is the great war in which millions of Hindus are said to have killed millions of Hindus—the core fighters are said to have been not just Hindus but of the same caste, Kshatriyas. Indeed, they are said to have been cousins. Both sides are as Hindu as one can get.

The Ramayana culminates in a war between Rama, a Kshatriya and an avatar of Vishnu, and Ravana, a learned Brahmin and devout worshipper of Shiva. Both are as Hindu as one can get.

The Aryans fought and subdued the Dasas and Dasyus. The conflicts covered vast areas, they continued for long. The Rig Veda has allusions to the 'Battle of the Ten Kings'. Our epics, the Puranas, inscriptions on pillars and metal plates, coins, and of course our legends and folklore celebrate the conquests of one Hindu king over other Hindu kings. Literary works in our many languages record wars between Hindu kings and Hindu kings. They sing praises of warriors and their deeds.

Institutions like the *ashwamedha yagya* and the anointing of a king as a 'Chakravarti' mark the fact that one Hindu king has defeated and established dominance over other Hindu kings.

---

[3] *Hindu Pad-padshahi,* op cit., pp. 2–5, 3, 6, 7, 10–11.

Having worsted other Hindu kings, the chakravartis sometimes fight other chakravartis. Harshavardhan ends up fighting the Chalukya king Pulakeshin II. Both were outstanding rulers. Both ruled over vast empires. The former was a devotee of Shiva, the latter a Vaishnavite—both sincere Hindus nonetheless. And the example is particularly interesting because of the almost laughable construction that Savarkar puts on their going to war, a construction to which we will come in a moment.[4]

Pan-Hindu consciousness?

An entire volume can be compiled on the question and should be. After all, the persons who led Mahmud of Ghazni to the Somnath temple were Hindus. The General who led Mughal forces against Maharana Pratap at Haldighati was a Hindu, Man Singh. Among the generals that Aurangzeb sent to lead his forces against Shivaji was a Hindu, Jai Singh. The letter that Shivaji wrote to him is often cited—Shivaji appealed to him to join hands as a Hindu. True. But equally true is the fact that Jai Singh did not do so, and continued in the service of Aurangzeb. Just the names of Hindu rulers who entered into alliances with Mughal Emperors, who became the latter's vassals in effect, of those who occupied high positions in Mughal courts and administration are enough to call into question the claim that a Pan-Hindu consciousness pervaded our entire polity and society. The simple fact is that—and Savarkar himself is acutely aware of it—if such a consciousness, if such conviction of identity, if such sentiment of solidarity had indeed pervaded our society, invaders wouldn't have been able to establish their rule in the first place, and their rule could never have lasted as long as it did.

---

[4] For a fine recapitulation of the evidence on our violent past see Upinder Singh, *Political Violence in Ancient India,* Harvard University Press, Cambridge, Mass., 2017.

One Suggestion and One Thread

A good place to get acquainted with the facts about wars among our Hindu rulers is the volumes published by the Bharatiya Vidya Bhavan on our cultural and political history. There are several reasons for this. Each chapter has been written by a scholar who had thorough knowledge of the period and sources. More importantly, one has just to read the forewords to each volume by K.M. Munshi, the guiding spirit behind the entire project, and the kinship with Savarkar's objective in his histories becomes evident. These volumes also seek to portray the emergence of a Pan-Aryavrata/ Hindu/Indian consciousness rooted in a common 'race memory' and 'race tradition', a consciousness rooted in one religion and culture. And here is how this consciousness is described in the volumes:

> It was based on the faith that Bharatavarsha, in its ideal aspect often referred to as Aryavrata, was the sacred land of Dharma, 'the high road to Heaven and to Salvation'; where 'men were nobler than the Gods themselves'; where all knowledge, thought and worship were rooted in the Vedas, revealed by the Gods themselves; where the Dharmasastras prescribed the fundamental canons of personal life and social relations; where Chaturvarnya, the divinely ordained four- fold order of society, embraced all social groups; where, whatever the dialect of the people, Sanskrit, the language of the Gods, was the supreme medium of high expression . . .[5]

Here too, the Buddhists appear as having an 'unpatriotic character'. In these volumes too India offers 'collective resistance' to Muslim invaders. And 'Aryavrata consciousness, which related dharma to India as a whole, also continue[s] as an effective group sentiment, particularly in north India . . .'

---

[5] For this representative passage, *The History and Culture of the Indian People*, Volume V, *The Struggle for Empire*, R.C. Majumdar, General Editor, Bharatiya Vidya Bhavan, Bombay, 1957/1979, p. viii.

In a word, reliable volumes to assess Savarkar's assertions about a Pan-Hindu consciousness. And what do we find? The chapters dealing with political developments and dynasties in volume after volume—in regard to south India as much as north and central India—describe wars, subjugation, rebellions, intrigues, murders, usurpations, betrayals, shifting alliances . . . the works. All this among and by the most pious of Hindus. Pan-Hindu consciousness? A society in harmony and kingdoms at peace?

As merely listing these will add a hundred pages, let us take up just one thread. Savarkar says repeatedly that of all communities in India, the Maharashtrians were the best qualified to found a Hindu empire—so much so that a Hindu empire had necessarily to be a Maharashtrian empire. So, to get a measure of his assertions let us just stick to the example he holds up to us: the *Hindu Pad-padshahi* based in Maharashtra.

The point is not that Maharashtra or Maharashtrians lacked something that others had. On the contrary. Maharashtra has had great spiritual figures like Sant Gyaneshwar. It has had saints like Sant Tukaram. It has had great teachers like Guru Ramdas. Most of all, it has had the life, deeds and legacy of Shivaji Maharaj, a visionary and creator like no other. On Savarkar's own telling, it is Maharashtra, and Maharashtrians who were suffused with Hindutva, more than any other region or community. So, if what transpired in Maharashtra, if what Maharashtrians did as they rode forth to other regions do not conform to his claim, forget about upholding it, little else is likely to do so.

'A King Among Men'

That is how Jadunath Sarkar describes Shivaji, and his success in founding an independent empire in the face of four great powers of the time—the Mughals, Bijapuris, the Portuguese, and the Abyssinians of Janjira. And there is no doubt that, even though he was tolerant of other religions, even though he appointed Muslims to important posts both in his administration as well as his military, he aimed at and founded a Hindu State. Sarkar put it very well while summing up the account in *Shivaji and His Times*:

> I regard him as the last great constructive genius and nation-builder that the Hindu race has produced. His system was his own creation and, unlike Ranjit Singh, he took no foreign aid in his administration. His army was drilled and commanded by his own people and not by Frenchmen. What he built lasted long; his institutions were looked up to with admiration and emulation even a century later in the palmy days of the Peshwas' rule.

Shivaji's achievements were all the greater because

> Shivaji was illiterate; he learnt nothing by reading. He built up his kingdom and Government before visiting any royal Court, civilized city, or organized camp. He received no help or counsel from any experienced minister or general. But his native genius, alone and unaided, enabled him to found a compact kingdom, an invincible army, and a grand and beneficent system of administration.
>
> Before his rise, the Maratha race was scattered like atoms through many Deccani kingdoms. He welded them into a mighty nation. And he achieved this in the teeth of the opposition of four great Powers like the Mughal empire, Bijapur, Portuguese India, and the Abyssinians of Janjira. No other Hindu has shown such capacity in modern times.[6]

But even in his case, what do we see?

He had to continuously 'unsheathe his sword', to use Savarkar's phrase, against other Maratha, that is Hindu chieftains.

---

[6] Jadunath Sarkar, *Shivaji and His Times,* Third Edition, S.C. Sarkar & Sons, Calcutta, 1929, p. 405.

When the time came for his coronation, an impediment which can only be described as having been born of unimaginable lunacy had to be removed. It was felt that Hindu chieftains could pledge their allegiance to a king only if he was a Kshatriya. But Shivaji was a Maratha. And so, a Brahmin, Gaga Bhatt, well-versed in the texts had to be found and fetched all the way from Banaras. After dogged persuasion, he certified that Shivaji was a thorough Kshatriya, that notions to the contrary had been fabricated. The Brahmin was handsomely rewarded. Imagine: this King among men having to establish himself to be from this caste rather than that.

In spite of all he accomplished, in spite of the veneration in which he came to be held, we learn that neither Shivaji nor his successors could erase or get people to vault over the divisions and endless subdivisions of castes and the walls between them. Indeed,

> Shivaji had, besides, almost to the end of his days, to struggle against the jealousy, scorn, and even opposition of Maratha families, his equals in caste subdivision and once in fortune and social position—whom he had now outdistanced . . . The Bhonsale savants of Vadi, the Yadavas of Sindhkhed, the Mores of Javli, and (to a lesser extent) the Nimbalkars, despised and kept aloof from the upstart grandson of that Maloji whom some old men still living remembered to have seen tilling his fields like a *Kunbi*! Shivaji's own brother Vyankoji fought against him in the invasion of Bijapur in 1666.[7]

'There was no national spirit, no patriotism in the true sense of the term, among the Maratha people to assist Shivaji and hasten his success,' Sarkar noted in an article written about the same time. 'Not to speak of the common people, who patiently and blindly tilled a grudging soil all their lives—many of the higher and middle class families were content to serve

---

[7] Jadunath Sarkar, 'Shivaji's genius and environment,' *The Modern Review*, May 1927, pp. 618–22, at p. 621.

Muslim rulers as mercenaries throughout the Chatrapati or royal period of their history, as their descendants did the English aliens by deserting Baji Rao II.'

And that for a reason: everyone had only his patch of land to cling to in a world being rocked every other year; and so, he who could assure them or take away their land got their allegiance: 'The same clinging to land . . . drew many Deccani families to the Mughal standard against Shivaji and Shambhuji, and kept them faithful to the alien so long as the Mughal Empire did not turn hopelessly bankrupt and weak, as it did after 1707 . . . Shivaji had to build on a loose sandy soil.'[8]

At one stage, his own son went over to the Mughals—in spite of Shivaji entreating him, employing every filial argument, holding out every prospect. It is only a year later that the son came back—repelled as he was by the extreme cruelty with which the Mughal commanders dealt with Maratha prisoners.

Unfortunately, Shivaji's life was cut short just six years into his reign. The very first months foretold the troubles that were to come:

After December 1679, Shivaji's health seems to have declined, and he seems to have had a premonition of the approach of death. This fact made the choice of an heir a live issue, and the plots and counter-plots in his harem and cabinet thickened in consequence.

On 23rd March, 1680, the Rajah was seized with fever and blood dysentery. The illness continued for twelve days. Gradually all hopes of recovery faded away, and then, after giving solemn charges and wise counsels to his nobles and officers, and consoling the weeping assemblage with assurances of the spirit's immortality in spite of the perishableness of the body, the maker of the Maratha nation performed the last rites of his religion and then fell into a trance, which imperceptibly passed into death . . .

---

[8] Ibid, p. 621.

He had not yet completed the 53rd year of his age. The Muslim world ascribed his premature death to the curse of the saint Sayyid Jan Muhammad of Jalna. In Maharashtra there were some whispers of his wife Soyra Bai, the mother of Rajaram, having administered poison to him to prevent his giving the throne to Shambhuji.

. . . Shambhuji on his accession put Soyra Bai to death on the charge of her having poisoned her husband [Shivaji], but it was in all probability a false pretext for wreaking vengeance on his step-mother for her late attempt to crown her own son . . .[9]

An illustration of what was often the case in those times, not exactly an illustration of Pan-Hindu consciousness that Savarkar would have us believe permeated the nation.

The Question at Hand

The force of Shivaji's example was such, the principles on which he had founded the State were such, and fortunately several of those to whom power passed in the ensuing decades and some of the Maratha generals were so proficient that the Maratha empire spread far and wide—so much so that the eighth volume in the Bharatiya Vidya Bhavan series is entitled, *The Maratha Supremacy*.[10] Remarking on their success against Ahmed Shah Abdali, as Savarkar was to note, Antaji Mankeshwar wrote to Raghunath Rao: 'Lahore is taken; the foe driven out and chased beyond the frontiers; our forces reached the Indus. Glad news indeed! It had cowed down all the disaffected elements in the north, Rajas and Raos, Subhadars and Nabobs. Only the Marathas could avenge the wrongs done to our nation. They alone have wreaked the vengeance of all Hindustan on

[9] *Shivaji and His Times*, op. cit., pp. 339–40.

[10] *The History and Culture of the Indian People*, Volume VIII, *The Maratha Supremacy*, *(1707–1818 A.D.)*, R.C. Majumdar, General Editor, Bharatiya Vidya Bhavan, Bombay, 1977/1991.

Abdali. Words fail to convey the fulness of my feelings. Heroic deeds have been done, no less heroic than those of the avatars!' The Mughal empire had been disintegrating. The Mughal emperor became in many ways a dependent of Maratha forces. At one point, Maratha forces were able to plant their standard over Delhi.

But the question before us is not the excellence or otherwise of the Marathas and their forces. The question is about the weight we should attach to Savarkar's repeated assertion that the forces were, that the people at large were suffused with a Pan-Hindu consciousness, with a singular yearning—for *Hindawi Swarajya*. Shivaji died in 1680 and Guru Ramdas in 1681, Savarkar wrote, and added, 'A nation succeeds Shivaji.'

What happened in the ensuing decades?

What the Others Saw and Experienced

The Mughal hand is shaky and infirm. The kingdoms and principalities of Malwa have begun to act on their own. The Marathas move in. Are they fired by Hindu consciousness? Do the rulers and people of the region see them as Hindu liberators?

In his succinct and meticulous *Malwa in Transition*, Raghubir Sinh tells us what actually happened and what the people experienced.[11] The records establish beyond doubt that the Maratha raids, and the over-riding concern subsequently of the Peshwa, the commanders and those who took charge of affairs was to collect money to defray the large debts that the Peshwa and his government had accumulated.[12] Similarly, 'The success of

[11] Raghubir Sinh, *Malwa in Transition, A century of anarchy, 1698–1765*, D.B. Taraporevala, Bombay 1936.

12 Ibid, see in particular page 188 onwards: '. . . the main cause of the invasion was economic. The letters of Baji Rao, Chimaji and other Maratha officers written during the campaign amply prove this point . . . Chimaji having left Poona ahead of him, the Peshwa clearly states the chief aim of the expedition thus, "the sum and substance of the whole thing is to follow a policy by which debts may end and permanent arrangements be made for the future." He advised Chimaji to keep this fact in view and to send money at an

the Maratha forces in Malwa was in no way due to reasons of religious affinity,' Raghubir Sinh says. To ascribe their success to any support from the local landlords and chieftains, even less so from the people at large to Hindu solidarity, etc. would be 'going against historical evidence'. The thorn in the relationship of the locals with the rulers in Delhi and their local factotums had been *jazia*. But this had been abolished and there was no possibility of its being reimposed: 'Under such circumstances there was no inducement to the people of Malwa to welcome the Marathas on religious grounds . . .' The reason Maratha forces prevailed was simpler: the local forces were too weak, their controllers in too much disarray to offer any effective resistance.[13]

For long the Marathas were preoccupied with developments in Delhi and the south. Malwa was left to local chieftains who busied themselves consolidating their own hold over district-sized principalities. In return for being left to do this, they gave varying amounts to the Maratha overseers. Malhar Holkar reasserted Maratha authority with a heavy hand. He died.

---

early date . . . Immediately after Baji Rao had heard of the victory of Chimaji over Girdhar Bahadur, he ordered his brother to make heavy exactions from the city of Ujjain, and after settling the affairs of the province, immediately to hasten to a rich country to collect money and thus to refurnish the army. Lastly, he added that a policy which would result in the defeat of the enemy and the clearing of the debts should be followed. The need for money was greatest at Satara, and in reply to his despatch of victory, Chimaji was asked to give details of the monetary gains in the battle . . . Later, as the details of the victory and further movements of the Maratha army reached the Peshwa, he instructed Chimaji to immediately send money to the Deccan through a banker at Aurangabad. He ordered that the sums due from Nandlal Mandloi in connection with expedition of Ambaji Pant in the year 1725–26, be exacted. He further asked Chimaji to confiscate all the jagir lands belonging to Girdhar Bahadur and then to exact their dues from the same. The one all-absorbing thought with Baji Rao was the clearing of the debts and he definitely wrote to his brother, "Go roaming about wherever you like, but bring money somehow or other' . . . Chimaji himself was involved in debt and the news of his victory only made his creditors press him to pay off their loans.' Ibid, pp. 189–91.

[13] Ibid, pp. 193–94.

New actors cast their shadow over the province. To describe what followed, Sinh quotes Jadunath Sarkar with approval:

> The ambition and aims of the revived Maratha Power in the north were hence-forward cooped up within the barren sands of the Rajputana and the broken, infinitely chequered wilderness of Bundelkhand—all Hindu territory—and their activities there for forty years, 1765–1805, have left a legacy of hatred for the Maratha name in Rajput hearts, which has not yet died out.

With the resounding defeat of the Marathas at Panipat, Rajput princes saw an opportunity to free themselves from 'these looters from the south.' Unfortunately—and here we have another glimpse of whether any section was united by a Pan-Hindu consciousness—in the absence of a dominant leader, the Rajput princes could not fashion a united front. No one seemed to get along with anyone. A minor was pole-vaulted on to the throne here, a weakling scrambled on to one there, their contending controllers—courtiers, commanders, mothers, wives, concubines—flitted on to and off the stage.

With the concurrence of or by the neglect of the Maratha generals, Pindaris entered the arena. These became 'a constant menace to the peace and prosperity of the province and an additional cause for alienating the local princes and zamindars from the Maratha patrons of these predatory bands.'

The result? 'These alienated Rajputs and the bitterly estranged Muslims knew that against any other Indian power the Maratha forces would prove stronger, but when pitted against a foreign power they would not be able to hold their own, and thus when the English entered into the political arena of Malwa they appeared as the redeemers of the harassed princes and the impoverished peasantry.'[14]

---

[14] Ibid, pp. 319–21.

As the over-riding Maratha objective was to collect funds, they did not establish any regular system of governing the province. It came to be 'parceled out into a number of fiefs.' The jostling and rivalry between the Holkars and Sindias affected governance in the region, and, as would be expected, 'their assistants carried the bad relations of their masters to the bitter end.' The military presence in the area was also of a very rudimentary form, Sinh wrote. And 'whenever the Maratha armies encamped there they subsisted by plunder or on dues exacted from the farmers, Rajas or other rich people. The camping of the Maratha army in the province was, hence, considered a calamity.'[15] The economic condition went 'from bad to worse . . .'

The sorry tale continued.[16] Maratha rulers appointed agents and representatives in the courts of Malwa rulers—to see that the amounts due were defrayed, to keep a close watch on the perpetual jostling, to determine which contender they should back, etc.—much as any occupying power would do. The consideration that Malwa princes showed these agents waxed and waned with the waxing and waning of Maratha power. As they did not station a regular military presence, to collect funds the Marathas launched assaults with considerable regularity. The more the Maratha generals focused on extracting the maximum from Malwa the more the local chieftains were, and felt crushed. Even so, Raghubir Sinh wrote, the hunger of the Peshwa and Maratha generals was never satiated. Their conduct and rule became more and more oppressive. The tensions and conflict between the Rajputs and Marathas did not remain merely political, Raghubir Sinh found, they became racial and cultural—*jaatiya evam saanskritik bhi ban gaya.*

The Marathas alone were not responsible for the chaos that ensued. They were taking advantage of a situation that had been created by the

---

[15] Ibid, p. 328.

[16] Cf., Raghubir Sinh, *Poorva Adhunik Rajasthan, 1527–1947*, Rajasthan Vishwavidyapeeth, Udaipur, 1951. In particular, pp. 178–266.

personal ambitions and petty contests of the Rajput princes. Jadunath
Sarkar summed up the matter aptly:

> The imperial Government of Delhi had held together and protected
> all the feudatory States of India. But when the Emperor became a
> lifeless shadow confined within the harem, when the wazir's role was
> pursuit of pleasure varied only by contests with his court rivals, this
> unifying bond and common controlling authority was dissolved. No
> superior power was left to enforce lawful rights and prevent ambitious
> conflicts between one vassal State and another, and between one
> prince and another of the same royal house. All the pent-up personal
> ambitions and inter-State rivalries (hitherto checked) now burst forth
> without fear or check. And Rajputana became a zoological garden
> with the barriers of the cages thrown open and the keepers removed.
> The fiercest animal passions raged throughout the land, redeemed
> only now and then by individual instances of devotion and chivalry
> which had not yet totally disappeared from the human bosom.[17]

In this fertile ground, the Marathas began to interfere in the rivalries
and tussles over succession among the princes, sometimes to the extent
of sending forces to help their preferences prevail. The more bitter the
contest happened to be among Rajput rivals, the higher the price the
Maratha generals exacted. Rival factions approached the Peshwa with
promises of huge sums. The Peshwa's men agreed to support one side, and
then, having been promised more by the rival, switched. This unending
sequence alienated the Marathas further from the local population, and
also from the local factotums on whom they depended for their exactions.
The bitterness and hatred intensified to such a level, Raghubir Sinh noted,

---

[17] Cf., Jadunath Sarkar, *The Fall of the Mughal Empire, 1739–1754,* Volume I, Orient
Longman, Bombay, 3rd edition, 1964, p. 170; also, *The Maratha Supremacy,* op. cit., p. 142.

that realizing their helplessness *vis a vis* the Marathas, the Rajputs, to rid themselves of the Marathas, gladly accepted tutelage of the British.[18]

What in this lamentable sequence shows Hindu solidarity? Where is the Pan-Hindu consciousness that according to Savarkar spurred all?

Nor is it the case that Rajput rulers and society themselves were paragons of Hindu dharma or any other collection of virtues. They had turned to the Marathas—not to fight the Mughals but to fight each other. As Maratha power waned, they turned to the British—again, not for some pan-Hindu ideal, not even for a pan-Rajput goal but to get out of the clutches of the Marathas and to get an advantage over fellow Rajputs. They were drowned in opium, liquor, revelry, and the rest. They had, Raghubir Sinh laments, become 'frogs in a well,' unaware of the way the world was changing. Even their successive defeats at the hands of forces trained in European discipline, equipped with European arms did not shake them out of their stupor. A proud people, they just became pawns in the hands of foreigners, and, as if in stupefied submission, slipped into vassalage.[19]

Pan-Hindu consciousness among the Rajputs any more than in the Marathas who had subdued them?

Bargis in Bengal

A Maratha force led by Bhaskar Pandit has reached Bengal to wrest it from Alivardi Khan.[20] The latter is retreating with his men. '. . . The Marathas cut off his grain supply, one party of them under Bhaskar Pandit keeping up the investment and another party plundering the country for forty miles around . . .' Skirmishes continue. Alivardi Khan breaks through the encirclement and hastens to reach areas where he can

---

[18] *Poorva Adhunik Rajasthan,* op. cit., pp. 179–80.

[19] See the searing pages with which Raghubir Sinh concludes his account of this pen-ultimate phase: Ibid, pp. 213–17.

[20] For the following, Jadunath Sarkar, *The History of Bengal, Volume II, The Muslim Period, 1200 A.D.–1757 A.D.,* B.R. Publishing Co., Delhi, 1943/2003.

secure reinforcements. '. . . During this retreat, whenever the Bengal army halted, the Marathas used to halt likewise, just beyond the range of the long muskets while their roving bands plundered and burnt the village[s] for ten miles on each side of the track . . .'[21] 'All over the country from which the Nawab's authority had disappeared, the roving Maratha bands committed wanton destruction and unspeakable outrage . . .'[22] Sarkar cites what an Englishman and a Frenchman reported. Let us come straight to what Gangaram, an eyewitness, reported:

> Every class of people took flight with their property . . . when suddenly the *bargis*[23] came up and encircled them in the plain. They snatched away gold and silver, rejecting everything else. Of some people they cut off the hand, of some the nose and ears; some they killed outright. They dragged away the beautiful women . . . The *bargis* after thus committing all sinful acts, set these women free. After looting in the open, they entered the villages and set fire to the houses . . . and roamed about on all sides plundering . . . They constantly shouted 'Give us money, give us money, give us money.' When they got no money, they filled their victims' nostrils with water, or drowned them in tanks . . . It was only after crossing the Bhagirathi that the people found safety.

Another eyewitness, Vaneshwar Vidyalankar, the Court pandit of the Maharajah of Bardwan, recorded,

> Shahu Rajah's troops are niggard of pity, slayers of pregnant women and infants, of Brahmans and the poor, fierce of spirit, expert in robbing the property of every one and committing every kind of sinful

---

[21] Sarkar, *History of Bengal, Volume II,* op. cit., pp. 457–58.

[22] Ibid, p. 457.

[23] The name by which the Marathas come to be called.

act . . . Their main strength lies in their marvellously swift horses. If it comes to a battle, they secretly decamp to some other country.[24]

Hindu sensibility? Hindu solidarity? A unified Hindu consciousness?

In all this, the Maratha forces are fighting Alivardi Khan and his men. Within months, the distinguished Peshwa, Balaji Rao and Alivardi Khan have formed an alliance to rein in the Maratha, Raghuji Bhosle, the Raja of Nagpur.

Early in February 1743, the Peshwa entered Bihar . . . with a strong force. His army was irresistible, and 'along his route those who gave blackmail or costly presents, saved their lives and property, while those who attempted defence were killed and their houses were given up to plunder.'[25]

Raghuji Bhosle retreats. The Peshwa with his forces chases him. Gives up the chase and sets out for Poona. Blood, gore continue.

At the beginning of March 1744, Bhaskar Pandit again invaded Bengal by way of Orissa and Medinipur. He was furious at losing all the spoils of his raids in the two previous years, and his disappointment was heightened by the knowledge that his master's rival the Peshwa had cleared twenty-two lakhs of rupees easily by a short campaign in Bengal . . . The sufferings of the innocent people who came in his way were worse than anything undergone by them before . . .[26]

Were they fighting to establish *Hindu Pad-padshahi*?

But how come the Marathas—or at least one faction of them—were back when Alivardi had paid the Peshwa Balaji Rao twenty-two lakhs 'for

---

[24] Ibid, pp. 457–58.

[25] Ibid, p. 459.

[26] Ibid, p. 460.

insuring against all the *bargi* raids in future'? No surprise: Balaji Rao and Raghuji Bhosle had come to an agreement to divide the areas between themselves!

Alivardi Khan then got an Afghan general, Ghulam Mustafa Khan to do an Afzal Khan on Bhaskar Pandit. Pandit was invited for a discussion under a grand tent to settle matters peacefully. 'On entering the tent, the unsuspecting Maratha general and 21 of his captains were all massacred by assassins hidden in the double side-screens . . .'[27]

Soon enough, Mustafa Khan turned against Alivardi Khan and teamed up with Raghuji Bhosle who had fallen out with the Peshwa once again . . . Skirmishes, raids, looting, betrayals, advances and retreats . . . continue. The Marathas acquire Orissa and establish a reign of terror.

> The loss of Orissa to the Mughal empire was the one permanent result of the Maratha invasions. Another was that the *bargis* showed the way for the organized looting of Bengal and Bihar to the Upper India robber bands calling themselves *sanyasis* . . .[28]

The Bharatiya Vidya Bhavan's *The Maratha Supremacy* gives a fuller account. From its chapter on 'Language and Literature in the Eighteenth Century' we learn that 'the memory of [the *bargis*'] oppressions and cruelties has been still preserved in the lullaby songs in Bengal.'[29] After quoting the account of Gangaram, etc. it remarks, 'The view of the Marathas entertained by the Bengalis, and probably also in other parts of India invaded by the Marathas, is certainly not calculated to favour the idea of a political hegemony of Hindu India under the Maratha rule, and

---

[27] Ibid, p. 461.

[28] Ibid, p. 467.

[29] *The Maratha Supremacy,* op. cit., Chapter XIX, at p. 644.

we may understand why the dream of Shivaji of founding a Hindu empire was never realised.'[30]

Back Home

And what was happening back in Maharashtra itself? Several of the generals were outstanding. Several who ascended to the Peshwa's *gaddi* were men of great calibre, astute, far-seeing, nimble. It was because of these few individuals, and because of the disintegration of Mughal governance that the Marathas were able to establish sway over such a large swathe of the country—from Maharashtra to Bengal and Orissa, from Delhi to Seringapatam.

But, almost by definition, such exceptional individuals are, well, exceptional—few and far between. As they aged and passed away, the great edifice that Shivaji had established and which Savarkar celebrates began to crumble like any other structure. It is a heart-searing tale. You can read it in Jadunath Sarkar's *The Fall of the Mughal Empire*,[31] G.S. Sardesai's *New History of the Marathas*,[32] and in the Bhartiya Vidya Bhavan's *The Maratha Supremacy*.[33] A race to the bottom, it sends one into a paralytic's rage. The Mughal Empire was falling apart. The country could have been put on its feet. Shivaji had shown the way. But . . .

The strong men are consumed by rivalries. When they pass away, the intrigues common to courts engulf everything. The rivalry of two dynasties shakes and weakens the entire confederacy. The widows of a strong man complain that their allowances have been cut. They are dragged out of their tents and thrown in prison. A Holkar is caught and trampled under

---

[30] Ibid, p. 645.

[31] Jadunath Sarkar, *Fall of the Mughal Empire*, Volumes I to IV, Orient Longman, New Delhi, 1971/72.

[32] G.S. Sardesai, *New History of the Marathas*, Volumes I to III, Phoenix Publications, Bombay, 1946, 1948, 1949.

[33] *The Maratha Supremacy*, op. cit.

the foot of an elephant. To get out of the control of a minister, a new ruler promises to a fickle ally 'fabulous treasures' that he—the ruler—does not have. The latter asks an underling to recover the amount from the minister and his associates. The man turns out to be 'a monster in human form'. Poona undergoes what Delhi had undergone at the hands of Nadir Shah, we are told. An opportunity opens up beyond Lahore. But the Peshwa directs the generals to return to Delhi as he has huge debts to repay and he wants them to exact the amounts from Delhi and other northern provinces. Another opportunity opens up. But the Maratha generals cannot agree on how to exploit it. Caught in a bind, a general appeals to the ruler to arrange help. The ruler asks the minister who controls affairs to do so. The latter orders two commanders to proceed to help. One reaches *six months later*, the second *a year later*. The rivalries and animosities between the mother of the new, 16-year-old Peshwa and the regent, his uncle and the latter's wife . . . A Peshwa falls out of a window or commits suicide. Another is murdered . . . On the western coast, a formidable admiral controls the naval power of the Marathas. He has kept the British, Portuguese, Dutch at bay. He does not get along with the Peshwa. The latter seeks the help of the British to put down the admiral. 'The British were very glad of this golden opportunity to crush the Maratha naval power completely,' we learn. 'Balaji was blind to this. Thus, one of the greatest achievements of the Marathas and a century-old unique creation of Maratha naval genius was destroyed by the Peshwa with the help of a foreign enemy. It was a suicidal act born of a short-sighted policy.' The highest in the court take to profiteering off supplies to the city, to soldiers . . . Wine, nautch girls . . . Soldiers are not paid . . . The Maratha army comes to consist more and more of mercenaries, under the command of foreigners . . . At critical turns, they go over to the opponent . . . The 'Maratha Machiavelli' is by now 'only a puzzled and ostensible Prime Minister'. In his last days, we read, 'he ruined Maratha national interests by selfishness and want of statesmanlike vision' . . . The son of a nephew of the great Mahadji Sindia is installed as the successor to the great man: 'Dull of intellect and with practically no education, he had fallen in public esteem by his debauchery, vices and frivolous amusements like kite-flying and jackal hunting' . . . On the Holkar side, Tukoji Holkar dies: 'After his death violent quarrels broke out among his two legitimate sons, Kashi Rao Holkar and Malhar Rao Holkar. Kashi Rao was a weak-minded cripple and Malhar Holkar was a ruffian' . . . The third son was 'full of adventure and resourcefulness', the fourth 'trained for no worthy work, took to the predatory way of life' . . . He 'provoked the wrath of the Peshwa by his devastations round Pandharpur. He was captured alive by Bapu Gokhale, given 200 stripes on his body, tied to the foot of an elephant and killed with horrid cruelty. Baji Rao II [the Peshwa] and his favourite Baloji Kunjar gleefully watched the sight' . . . One after the other, each faction turns to the British . . . Baji Rao II alternately seeks the help of the British and plans to finish them. He is defeated. Exiled to Bithur near Kanpur. The Peshwai is abolished . . .

Of course, this is not all there was to the hundred years. There were many victories. Some exceptional generals and statesmen. A home-grown, astute Machiavelli. A pious lady who came to exercise considerable influence. Saints and savants continued to impart ennobling teachings. The main feature of the Maratha Supremacy, however, is that it ended all too soon and for the all-too-familiar reasons.

An Authoritative Summing Up

As they conclude their survey, historians of the Bharatiya Vidya Bhavan volume provide a succinct summary of the factors that led to the disintegration of the Maratha confederacy and the evaporation of Shivaji's dream.[34] Do read it. As you do so, at each paragraph, if not each sentence

---

[34] Lest charges of partisanship are hurled at it, we should bear in mind that the volume, *The Maratha Confederacy*, was prepared under the General Editorship of R.C. Majumdar, an admirer of Savarkar.

ask, 'Where is the pan-Hindu consciousness that Savarkar says suffused the whole country, in particular the rulers and people of Maharashtra?' Reading it will also prepare us to consider the explanations Savarkar gives for such a denouement. And thereby see the perils of wishful history-writing.

Well, here is how the historians sum up the reasons that led to so swift a disintegration of the Maratha empire:

> The Maratha polity dissolved through internal stress. The conflicts between Nana Phadnis and the House of Sindia, between the Peshwa and the Chhatrapatis of Satara and Kolhapur, between Daulat Rao Sindia and Yashwant Rao Holkar, between Malhar Rao Holkar II and Kashi Rao Holkar, between Parsoji, Baka Bai and Appa Saheb, between Tulsa Bai and Ram Din, between Anand Rao Gaikwar and Kanhoji Gaikwar, are some instances of this suicidal schizophrenia.

The Maratha Supremacy

> It is difficult to overstate the evils which originated from the Sindia-Holkar rivalry. Its genesis is to be found in the political psychology of the times. It started as a race for obtaining power in Malwa and ended with a struggle for ascendancy in the Peshwa's Darbar at Poona. The Poona Darbar followed the imbecile policy of maintaining its hold by encouraging this friction. Nana Phadnis made Tukoji Holkar his instrument against Mahadji Sindia. It is tragic indeed that even pious Ahalya Bai Holkar constantly egged on Tukoji Holkar to assert himself on terms of equality with Mahadji Sindia. Surprisingly enough, a point of prestige rather than any substantial material gain was sometimes the cause of this conflict. The Sindia-Holkar rivalry disturbed the peace of the land, bred suspicion, fostered internal dissensions, hampered the establishment of Maratha hegemony in North India, and finally broke up the Maratha coalition against the English.

The internal stress in Maratha State was emphasised by administrative anarchy. Nothing could exceed the state of anarchy which prevailed throughout the country; at the court, bribery, execution and murders; in the provinces violence, rapine and bloodshed . . .

. . . The Maratha chiefs believed that the highest political wisdom consisted in finesse or diplomatic intrigue. But diplomacy in their hands stooped to the low level of playing a waiting game, base treacheries and selfish intrigues. The methods employed by Maratha diplomats were extremely crude. Against this, the diplomacy of the English was remarkable as they were always careful to win over a section of the opponents . . . There was hardly any chief in the Peshwa's services who had not been won over by British money.

The Maratha Supremacy

The military organization of the Marathas was ill-organized, ill-equipped and ill-disciplined. In the army of Peshwa Baji Rao II, the rank of officer was given to men like Qadir Khan who was a butcher. Discipline was lax and the emphasis was on pomp and display. Forbes tells us that the tails of grey horses were frequently dyed red and their manes plated with silk ribands and interspersed with silver roses. At Laswari, Ambaji Ingle's richly caparisoned elephant drew everyone's attention. The Maratha chiefs and soldiers became addicted to the vices of camp-life. In 1800, Daulat Rao Sindia[35] covered the 140 miles between the Tapi and the Narmada in 18 days, whiling away his time in attending to dance and music of dancing-girls, tiger-shooting and kite-flying. Bhosle's troops were imperfectly disciplined. Yashwant Rao Holkar commenced a complete reformation of his army only after his defeat in 1805. Elphinstone described the Maratha army as a 'loose and straggling mass of camels,

---

[35] The son of Mahadji Sindia's nephew, whom we have encountered earlier.

elephants, bullocks, nautch-girls, fakeers and buffoons, lancemen and matchlockmen, banyans and mootasuddis'.

. . . A nation's liberty cannot be preserved only by foreign mercenaries. . . It is remarkable that there was not a single man of the Maratha race in Sindia's infantry and artillery that fought at Laswari. Preference for foreign mercenaries in the Maratha army is obvious from the rates of pay of soldiers. An Arab soldier was paid Rs. 18 a month, a Christian and Portuguese soldier Rs. 15, a Hindustani sepoy Rs. 8 and a Maratha and Deccani soldier Rs. 6.

The Maratha chiefs made a serious mistake in entrusting the defence of their country to foreigners . . . [The historians proceed to list various instances in which the foreign officers passed on vital information to the adversaries.]

There were discordant elements and ignominious betrayers among the Marathas too . . .

The Maratha
Supremacy

Various forms of moral cankers were also eating into the vitals of Maratha society—the popularity of erotic compositions of Anant Phandi and Ram Joshi, the wide-spread belief in witchcraft, the great demand of the services of astrologers, marriages of infant girls. Concrete instances are on record of excessive indulgences in sensual pleasures, drunkenness and frivolous enjoyments of the most degraded type on the part of top-ranking Maratha leaders like Peshwa Baji Rao II, Nana Phadnis, Daulat Rao Sindia and Yashwant Rao Holkar.

The Marathas lacked the corporate spirit so essential for their national independence. To every one in that age his own fief *(watan)* was the only reality. Feudal system fostered individual selfish tendencies. The Maratha chiefs also failed to protect their subjects from excesses of their own armies. Peasants tended to turn towards anyone who could give them protection. The Maratha government was not influenced by the people and so the people did not take any interest in its permanence. The cohesion of the Maratha people was not organic but artificial, accidental and therefore, precarious. The Maratha chiefs could not sink their differences and unite, even in times of common danger, for the service of the State and nation. Nationalism of the 19th century was unknown to them.

Casteism also added to want of social cohesion. . . The partiality towards Brahmins imposed a heavy burden upon the finances of the Government . . .[36]

Did you remember to ask yourself as you finished each paragraph, 'Where was the pan-Hindu consciousness that Savarkar said suffused the entire country, rulers and people alike?' Did you find it anywhere? Did it slow down, to say nothing of arresting the disintegration of the Maratha Empire?

And How Does Savarkar Explain Away This Reality?

How does Savarkar get over this infuriating record? That while Shivaji was risking his life to set up a Hindu State, even in his own immediate circle persons were passionate about advancing their own interest? That even he had to continuously put down several local Maratha local strongmen? That while his vision was a pan-Hindu one, caste continued to divide Hindus, and dogged even him at the acme of his glory? That while the Maratha Empire was certainly enlarged to cover vast portions of the country, the people of other regions did not come to look upon the Maratha forces as liberators? That far from looking after people of the areas they were conquering, the Maratha commanders and soldiery looked upon them merely as herds to be fleeced? That far from that common spirit pervading the people or the soldiery, even persons at the very top, who one would presume were better informed and so more committed to the national identity and cause, continued their fratricidal manoeuvres? That far from

---

[36] *The Maratha Supremacy*, op. cit., pp. 509–16.

devoting themselves to the weal of the *Hindu Pad-padshahi,* so many drenched themselves in dissipation? How can one say that they were fired by one goal and one goal alone—to create and sustain and bring glory to a Hindu kingdom?

Even in One Region

Savarkar's first dodge is simplicity itself: 'Even an essentially provincial movement, whether it be a Rajput or a Sikh, a Maratha or a Madrasi achievement, is bound to reflect its greatness on the history of Hindudom as a whole,' Savarkar declares. 'The achievement of a section necessarily reveals the latent possibilities of the whole race.'[37] In a word, even if a movement is confined to one corner of the country—and remember that on Savarkar's reckoning Hindusthan extends from Afghanistan to Burma, with the Himalayan kingdoms and much of Tibet, certainly up to and including Manas Sarovar as he spells it, within itself, and down to Sri Lanka—and even if its nature is 'essentially provincial', its greatness will get beamed on the 'history of Hindudom as a whole.' But that is not the question. The question is: even if 'an essentially provincial movement' in one corner of the country is permeated with a pan-Hindu consciousness, does it prove that the pan-Hindu spirit pervades the whole? That the achievement of Maharaja Ranjit Singh will in retrospect 'reflect [his] greatness on the history of Hindudom as a whole' is an entirely different matter, and one with an answer—that both Maharaja Ranjit Singh and his kingdom were suffused with a Pan-Hindu consciousness—the Sikhs today may not like—especially if the achievements of Maharaja Ranjit Singh are going to be appropriated by propogandists of Hindudom.

The same holds for the next sentence—'The achievement of a section necessarily reveals the latent possibilities of the whole race.' But that would

---

[37] V.D. Savarkar, *Hindu Pad-padshahi, or A Review of the Hindu Empire of Maharashtra,* B.G. Paul & Co, Madras, 1925, Foreword, pp. viii–ix.

depend on whether in the centuries that follow 'the whole race' builds on the achievements of that section. That a section has achieved something does not in the least guarantee that 'the whole race' will achieve it. The super-intelligent score unthinkable scores on MENSA tests. That does not mean that 'the whole race' will attain those scores. The crucial words in Savarkar's sentence are *latent possibilities*—the fact that a section has been able to achieve something shows that others too *can*. It would be as true to say, 'The achievement of a section of humanity necessarily reveals the latent possibilities of the whole of humanity.' But there is an ocean between a 'possibility' and what transpires in fact. Yes, the Maratha Empire *could have* continued forever. Yes, it *could have* been in the mould of the State that Shivaji set up. Yes, it *could have* replaced the Mughal Empire. But what happened in practice was . . . Perhaps a more congenial example would be: that India has been able to send a rover to the moon shows that Pakistan also *can*. But whether it will . . .

And then in Savarkar's account follow sentences about the Marathas: '. . . the Maratha movement under review transcends the limits of a provincial movement so decisively and so deliberately that it seems pre-eminently entitled to a *Pan-Hindu* importance and treatment. In fact, we will fail to understand its significance altogether unless it is perceived from a Pan-Hindu stand-point.' The assertions are manifestly self-serving. First, the conduct of commanders who led the campaigns in Malwa, in Bengal and the soldiers who were part of them certainly does not show that they were motivated by pan-Hindu feelings.

That bit about those assaults being 'pre-eminently entitled to a *Pan-Hindu* importance and treatment' may be true—in a sense that Savarkar did not intend. The significance and importance of those campaigns from a pan-Hindu standpoint is as 'a negative example': a movement that aims to represent and work for the whole should ensure that its leaders and soldiers do *not* conduct themselves the way these did. The same goes for 'we will fail to understand its [the Maratha movement's] significance altogether unless it is perceived from a Pan-Hindu stand-point.' The significance is that they conquered vast areas and lost them to a foe—the British—to whom many of their own leaders appealed for help for doing in their own relatives and co-religionists. The significance from a pan-Hindu standpoint is that what they did when they ventured out of Maharashtra did not suggest that they were impelled by a pan-Hindu feeling.

We should beware of another meaning that is implicit in the words, 'we will fail to understand its significance altogether unless it is perceived from a Pan-Hindu stand-point.' We encountered Savarkar's prescription that we must understand and present events, motives, policies in ways that serve the main message that has to be conveyed—recall that incident of Chanakya walking out of Mahapadmanand's establishment. Consistent with this dictum of how history ought to be written, Savarkar imposes an interpretation of what the Maratha forces exacted from Malwa and even what they took from Bengal and Orissa. That accords with what he says about writing history in his *India's War of Independence*, in *Hindu Pad-padshahi* as well as in his essays. And that is why we should beware of such pronouncements and prescriptions.

Even For One Day

Maratha forces are advancing under the gallant general Sadashivrao Bhau. Amidst them is the much-loved Vishwasrao, the son of the Peshwa Balaji Baji Rao, and Sadashivrao's nephew. They occupy Delhi and raise the Maratha standard over the fort. Soon they will be on their way to the Battle of Panipat. But the moment in Delhi is the one to savour. Savarkar is lyrical in writing about it:

> Sadashivrao Bhau felt that his dream of the *Hindu-pad-padashahi* was—*be it for a day*—but realized before his eyes. To bring about and render the birth of *even one such day* possible justifies the existence of a nation. Such a day, even in its short span of life, focuses in its rising splendour the activities and achievements, the rejoicings and

sufferings, the trials and tribulations, of centuries of national existence. For, that day proved beyond cavil or criticism that seven centuries of Moslem persecution and power had failed to crush the Hindu spirit or its vital faculty of rejuvenation. They had, not only proved themselves equal to, but had ultimately prevailed over their foes.[38]

Left to himself, Sadashivrao Bhau would have crowned Vishwasrao the emperor of Hindusthan, Savarkar tells us. Lest the Muslims cavil at accepting him, and other Hindu rulers get jealous, he settles for a grand ceremony minus the coronation. But there is no time to rest. They have soon to leave to meet the forces of Ahmed Shah Abdali near Panipat.

There the Marathas fight valiantly. Almost a lakh of them are killed. The youthful Vishwasrao is killed, so is Sadashivrao Bhau. But, on Savarkar's telling, by a series of accidents and because of betrayal by a Muslim contingent among them, they lose.

The facts were more complex. For all his brilliance and courage, Sadashivrao Bhau had not heeded the advice of others to take the Jats as allies, to do a bit more to enlist the reluctant Rajput rulers, to leave behind the huge non-combatant entourage. All this had inflicted a heavy cost. For one thing, Maratha forces had run short of supplies. Much of this gets obscured in Savarkar's telling, for he is celebrating that *one day*, the fleeting period when he sees the dream of establishing *Hindu Pad-padshahi* in Delhi as having been realized.

The brief stay at Delhi is as if a simile for the short life of the Maratha confederacy itself. You can see the significance of Savarkar's emphasis on *'be it for a day . . . even one such day . . .'* He proclaims that that one day proves that pan-Hindu consciousness has withstood the assaults of centuries, 'For, that day proved beyond cavil or criticism that seven centuries of Moslem persecution and power had failed to crush the Hindu spirit or its vital

---

[38] *Hindu Pad-padshahi,* op. cit., p. 105.

faculty of rejuvenation. They had, not only proved themselves equal to, but had ultimately prevailed over their foes . . .'

What holds for that fleeting moment in Delhi holds for the Maratha confederacy itself. Yes, it was gone all too soon. Yes, it was gone for all the usual reasons. But in that brief period, Savarkar's reasoning goes, it showed the *possibilities*, like that one day it showed that pan-Hindu consciousness pervades the land, that it had not been crushed.

Not a good answer.

Jealous, In Spite Of . . .

But what about the Rajputs and Jats? Why did they not team up with the Marathas? Why did they not rush to help even when Maratha forces were in a life-and-death struggle? That is because the success of the Marathas had made these communities jealous says Savarkar. The Rajputs wished the Marathas would be 'utterly crushed', he says.[39] In spite of pan-Hindu consciousness?

The Blame Shifts to an Unexpected Quarter

But what about the Marathas themselves? Several of the chieftains opposed even Shivaji. Even Shivaji had to 'unsheathe his sword' to put them down. Savarkar shifts the blame to an unexpected quarter:

> But in emphasising this national and Pan-Hindu feature of the Maratha movement, facts as revealed by our sketch would not justify us in assuming that therefore all of the actors, at all times, were inspired in their actions by public good or Pan-Hindu interests alone. Civil feuds and civil wars were constantly going on, side by side with the noble activities of the nation in the defence and propagation of the Hindu cause. The fact is that, *as the Marathas were Hindus first and*

---

[39] *Hindu Pad-padshahi,* pp. 113, 133–34.

Marathas afterwards, they therefore naturally shared to some extent the essential virtues and vices, the strength and the weakness of the general and particular temperament of the race they belonged to.[40]

Savarkar presses the blame on to Hindus in general and their past:

. . . With this conviction he and his school made it a point to first consolidate Maharashtra herself and then lead on their forces in a holy war for winning the Independence of all Hindustan and deliver their Rajya and Dharma, the Hindu temple and Hindu throne, from the foreign yoke by subduing all India to a consolidated and powerful Maratha Empire which, being dedicated to the Hindu cause, would serve as a defender of the Hindu Faith and a champion of the Hindu race. But in this attempt *they could not and could not have eradicated at a stroke the denationalising tendencies of the Hindu race entirely either in Maharashtra or of course in Hindustan.*[41]

That is certainly new—'the denationalising tendencies of the Hindu race.' It flies in the face of assertion after assertion in *Essentials of Hindutva*.

Subduing Others

Savarkar moves on to lay the ground for Maratha forces subduing others:

All that they could do was to eradicate them to such an extent as to enable the patriotic impulses of the Hindus of Maharashtra on the whole to hold in check the lower instincts of the people that goaded them on to self-aggrandisement or to sacrifice their national and Pan-Hindu interests to their parochial private ends. That is why we find civil strife breaking every now and then in the Maratha history, but

---

[40] Ibid, pp. 225–26.
[41] Ibid, p. 229.

on the whole the nation as such at many a critical point succeeded in enabling their national, Pan-Hindu and patriotic instincts to have the better of their degrading tendencies and hold them in check if not eradicate them altogether.[42]

Three giveaways there:

> *'on the whole,'*

then

> *'the nation as such'*

and then

> *'at many a critical point'*

Savarkar proceeds to maintain that 'the mighty Hindu Empire' could not but be 'a Maharashtra Empire':[43]

This Pan-Hindu spirit, this longing and capacity to deliver all Hindudom from the bondage of the foreign and unbelieving races, this patriotic fervour that could hold in check the lower selfish and individualistic tendencies of their nature, or make them subserve the cause of their nation and their Faith which the Marathas rapidly developed and displayed, rendered them decidedly superior in all national qualities to the Muhammadans and pre-eminently fitted them amongst all other Hindu people to rear up and sustain *a mighty Hindu Empire which*, for the very reasons above indicated, *could not but be a Maharashtra Empire.*

---

[42] Ibid, pp. 229–30.

[43] Ibid, p. 230.

We must pass over how one faction among them after another entered into agreements with the British—for that was only because they were 'Hindus first' and Marathas later.

Savarkar reinforces his assertions about the Marathas:

For the *Hindu-pad-padshahi* which so indubitably inspired the efforts of the Maratha nation had, to be realisable at all under the circumstances, *necessarily to be a Maharashtra-padshahi too*. The Hindus could not have risen to be a great power and able to repulse the formidable attacks of all the haters of the Hindu cause and maintained their independence unless they got themselves consolidated into a strong and enduring Empire, a Hindu-*pad-padshahi*. And there was, under the circumstances, no centre, no pivot, no mighty lever that could be used as an instrument in this gigantic task of uplifting the Hindu race from the political servitude into which they had sunk, other than the people of Maharashtra. In spite of the fact that they, too, though far more patriotic and public spirited than the Muhammadans and far more united and politically willing and capable to fight the War of Hindu Independence than all other sections of their countrymen and co-religionists, still fell far short of ideal patriotism and public Virtues, say, relatively to the English who therefore beat them in the long run. In spite of this fact the Marathas were right in insisting on keeping the strings of the Hindu movement in their own hands and in assuming themselves the insignia and office of a Hindu-*pad-padshahi*. They dared first, succeeded so well, sacrificed so much, and, judging from the circumstances under which they stood, were naturally justified in aiming to consolidate all Hindustan under their standard, in bringing all the scattered rays of Hindu strength into a focus and by subordinating all the Hindu principalities to their sceptre. They took upon themselves the responsibility of championing the Hindu cause. They must be held justified in doing so from a Pan-Hindu point, for as our sketch would show they proved themselves capable of championing it effectively against all hostile attacks.

Is this the sort of presumption that lay behind the refusal of a formidable general like Sadashirao Bhau to heed the counsel of others to reach out to others, like the Rajputs?

Suddenly, a qualm: 'Have I gone too far?'

Of course, had any other section of our Hindu people dared first and achieved results so mighty and then called upon Maharashtra to pay homage to it and forced her into subordination to their Hindu Empire, they would have, from a Pan-Hindu point, been equally justified. It mattered little whether the Hindu Empire, the Hindu *pad-padshahi*, was a Rajput-*padshahi* or a Sikh or a Tamil or a Bengali or even a Kolarian one: it would have been entitled to equal honour and gratitude from us all so long as it championed the cause of Hindudom so well and so effectively by welding all our people into a grand Hindu Empire even though controlled and led by its own province or caste or community.[44]

Did the Marathas pass Savarkar's test—'so long as it championed the cause of Hindudom so well and so effectively by welding all our people into a grand Hindu Empire'? Did the Marathas 'weld our people into a grand Hindu Empire'? Did they even weld them into one to fight unitedly for that cause? Not if you ask the people of Malwa. Not if you ask the people of Bengal who, we were told, still frighten their children with tales of the *bargis*.

That the Marathas should take the lead and lasso the others was the 'best solution in the circumstances,' Savarkar asserts:

---

[44] Ibid, pp. 229–32.

. . . But had the Hindus been capable of being welded into such a political unity at a stroke, the Muhammadans would not have been able to cross the Indus at all. We must take the facts as they are and judge a people in the light of their environments. *No nation, any more than an individual, can rise entirely above her environments, or can help breathing the general atmosphere of their times . . .*[45]

Another strange roll. After all, from *Essentials of Hindutva*, the assertion has been that from times immemorial we have had a unique and deeply embedded *sanskriti*—this has been the 'environment', the 'general atmosphere' that has defined us. It has kept us one, separate from others. And suddenly we are told that even Marathas could not weld the Hindus together, or the Marathas themselves could not overcome their mutual frictions because no one can rise above his 'environment', or 'help breathing the general atmosphere of the times.'

Savarkar is not done with pasting the blame on others:

Secondly, to persuade others to a better mood depends as much on the skill of the person who persuades, as on the honesty of the purpose or moral sensitiveness of the person to be persuaded. Even had the Marathas taken only to persuasion, would the others have allowed themselves to be persuaded to lose voluntarily their individual existences as principalities and kingdoms in the name of Hindu *pad-padshahi,* in which all equally shared the rights and responsibilities? Where was this patriotic impulse to come from? Amongst those Hindus whose petty thrones were often soaked in the blood of civil feuds before they could ascend them, who freely invited the Moslems and the English to decide their civil wars and would rather bow down to the Mogul who trampled upon their Vedas and broke their images than to their brother? It is foolish to expect a people at this stage of political level and

---

[45] Ibid, pp. 232–33.

national integrity to rise at a bound to the height of political thought
and feeling and practice, which is implied in such absolute supposition
as that; and to blame only one amongst them for not doing that which
none else of his generation could even conceive the probability of doing
and especially the performance of which devolved at least as much on
others as on himself, is not only unjust but even absurd . . .[46]

Every clause in every sentence in that announces that no section had
pan-Hindu consciousness.

Again, that sudden qualm: 'Have I gone too far?'

And still, as it is, efforts to persuade other Hindu brethren to join
hands in the great task of building up a Hindu power were not
altogether wanting; nor were noble responses wanting from some of
the noblest of our Rajputs, Bundelas, Jats, and other northern and
southern Hindu comrades to such appeals.[47]

Savarkar comes close to giving up the claims that he has been advancing,

Taking into consideration, then, only the relative merits of the case,
one realises that the *Hindus as such were yet far from developing a
Pan-Hindu sense so intensely as to render them willing to sacrifice their
individual, parochial or provincial existence altogether and entirely to
the Hindu cause.*

But then what about the claim repeated at every turn since *Essentials of
Hindutva,* of all being steeped in an 'undying and unifying' pan-Hindu
consciousness?

Bearing also in mind the fact that the Marathas themselves, in spite
of the relatively more consolidated public life and more intense

---

[46] Ibid, pp. 233–34.

[47] Ibid, p. 234.

national spirit that they developed as a people and in spite of their being passionately devoted and dedicated to the great and holy cause of delivering the Hindu Race and the Hindu Faith from the political bondage of alien fanaticism, were naturally far from nationalistic or Pan-Hindavi perfection though steadily and even rapidly progressing towards it . . .

A slip there. For that is as close as one can get to the expression—'a nation in the making'—for using which Savarkar traduced others no end.

'Far from *perfection*?' Is that how the misdeeds are to be characterized?

And how far can one get away from what is manifest on, as they would say in courts, the face of the record? Can one say that the types of deeds that we glimpsed the rulers and courtiers were doing, and which are recorded in history books, suggest that they were done out of a passionate devotion and dedication to 'the great and holy cause of delivering the Hindu race and the Hindu faith from the political bondage of alien fanaticism'?

It does seem that what Savarkar is saying is again just to fortify what seems to be the over-riding concern—to proclaim that the Marathas alone were capable of leading the struggle for establishing an independent Hindu kingdom:

> . . . and finding, after a careful analysis of the relative strength of the different Hindu states or peoples in all Hindustan, that of all the scattered centres of Hindu life the only nucleus round which the forces of Hindu revival could rally and offer resistance to the mighty foreign foes with some chance of success was to be discovered in Maharashtra alone, we cannot, even from the Pan-Hindu point of view, help justifying the tenets and efforts of Ramdas and Shivaji's generation to rally all Maharashtra under the banner of Hindu Faith to create first a Maratha kingdom strong and independent to serve as a basis, as a powerful lever

for the uplift of the Hindu race, and then to extend the War of Hindu Liberation beyond the frontiers of Maharashtra . . .[48]

And that explains why the Marathas had to beat into line other Hindu kingdoms. Many a Hindu ruler was content to have and were so attached to 'their slavish ease and canine comforts of bondage,' Savarkar points out, that they would ally with, and subordinate themselves to Mughal and other Muslim rulers like the Nizam rather than accept the primacy of the Marathas, even of Shivaji personally, in the drive to establish a Hindu Empire. And so, the Marathas and even Shivaji had on occasion to 'unsheathe his sword' against other Hindu rulers, against other Maratha chieftains. And what acquits Shivaji acquits his successors too:

> What acquits Shivaji of any special responsibility or guilt for facing the inevitable, though regrettable, necessity of at times unsheathing his sword against some of his Maratha brethren themselves or Ranjit Singh for reducing the several Sikh *misals* and coercing them into submission towards him, acquits the Maratha Confederacy, too, for forcing many a recalcitrant Hindu chief to submission to their Empire.

Again, that qualm: 'Have I gone too far?'

> It must again be clearly pointed out that a few of those Hindu chiefs, though not all, cannot also be blamed for their opposition to the Maratha claim of sovereignty. For they too were, taking into consideration the general level of political and Pan-Hindu thought as well as their own ambitions to carve out independent Hindu kingdoms for themselves, naturally and rightly tenacious of their individual independence.

---

[48] Ibid, pp. 237–38.

But now, 'Have I said too much for the other side?'

> But as the very existence of the Hindus as a race, as a civilisation, as a faith, and as a nation, depended on the establishment of a powerful, consolidated and Pan-Hindu Empire, whether it be monarchical or confederate, autocratic or plutocratic, Bengali or Rajputi, Tamilian, or Telugu, but a Pan-Hindu and centralized and mighty empire, the Marathas who alone of all Hindu people could vanquish the foes of Hindudom and found and maintain that Empire, must be absolved from any special guilt or responsibility for using at times force against the Hindus themselves. The responsibilities, as we said, must be shared either by all Hindus alike or by none: at any rate not by the Marathas alone.

As they alone could lead the fight, Savarkar says, the Marathas had a right to force their way:

> Their fitness to lead the War of Hindu Liberation and establish a mighty Hindu Empire *gave them the right to expect all other Hindus to forego their individual ambitions and interests and submit and if recalcitrant to be forced to submit to its suzerainty.*[49]

No one had stopped the others from taking the lead, Savarkar says. But some of them would neither do something themselves to establish the Hindu Empire nor follow the lead of the Marathas. There was no alternative to coercing them to submit and follow the Marathas:

> Of these some were grown so callous and insensible to the fetters they wore—fetters riveted by Moslem power—that they actually prided themselves on them. They would not mind calling themselves

---

[49] Ibid, pp. 244–45.

dependents and tributaries, subjects or even slaves of the Moslem, of this Nabob or that, of the Nizam, or the big *padasha* at Delhi, but would not tolerate any proposal on the part of the Marathas to pay fealty to the Hindu Empire that stood before their eyes warring for the rights and honour of the Hindu race. *They had to thank but themselves for the chastisement they received at the hands of the Maratha horsemen who naturally looked upon them as allied to the Moslems, and did not cease teasing them, till they were coerced into acknowledging the sovereignty of the Hindu Empire of Maharashtra, or till their Moslem ruler became a tributary to it.*[50]

The Marathas had proven their ability to take the lead by the way they had dealt with the Portuguese, the Mughals and others. To expand the Hindu Empire, they had to consolidate the scattered pockets of Hindu power. And

as consolidation necessarily meant the reduction, submission and sacrifice, willing or forced, of all constituents to the dictates and interests of the supreme and sovereign constitution, the highest interests of Hindudom demanded the subordination of all Hindus to the Maratha Empire which, of all other Hindu sections, was the only organised state that could, as in fact it wellnigh did, establish and maintain a Hindu-*pad-padshahi*.[51]

As others too felt that they were equally entitled to be the leaders in this venture, a struggle between the Marathas and them was inevitable—as 'a regrettable necessity'. That is what had lain at the foundation of the ancient institution of 'Chakravarti', Savarkar says. Various kings would fight to determine who among them was best suited to take on the foreign foe. And the Hindus have always recognized this necessity, he argues:

---

[50] Ibid. p. 239.

[51] Ibid. p. 241.

Whenever national exigency demanded formation of a strong empire, the moral forces of the Hindu people instinctively rallied round the banner of a Hindu world-conqueror and not only condoned his fighting with and vanquishing all other Hindu rivals to that honour, but actually hailed it as the only test practicable under the circumstances to hit upon the best candidate to whom they could safely entrust the preservation and defence of their land and people.[52]

Did the Hindus instinctively rally round the victor? Is the rallying round not being imposed by Savarkar? Did they see in the suicidal fights between their rulers a contest to determine who is best suited to repulse the foreign foe?

In any case, that qualm again: 'Have I gone too far?'

Nor did they look down on those also who challenged him in the field before they acknowledged his right to suzerainty over them. Harsha could not consolidate his empire in the north, nor Pulkeshin in the south, without forcing into submission their mutual rivals, even if they too were Hindus like them, sometimes their castemen or actually their blood relations. We condemn not these latter, for it was but human, nay, in the absence of any other higher motive, even manly, that they did not surrender their individuality for the mere asking of it.[53]

You mean the 'higher motive' was so pervasively missing? And what happens when Harsha and Pulkeshin go to war against each other? On Savarkar's telling, the Hindus are most understanding, and so is he:

Nay, later on when Harsha and Pulkeshin both came to measure their swords against each other, we from the Pan-Hindu point of view

---

[52] Ibid, p. 247.

[53] Ibid, p. 247.

watch the struggle with parental impartiality and tolerate the sight of this internal fight even as a gymnast or a general tolerates, as a necessary evil, the combat between his own disciples or tournament parties with a view to train them and find out the best of them who could safely be trusted to face the hostile camp when and if the time comes.[54]

Savarkar does not, of course, mention that often the Hindu kings fought and crushed their neighbouring Hindu kings even when there was no foreigner to be pushed back. Perhaps just to keep in practice? Perhaps because they knew from their knowledge of the past that it would not be long before another foreigner came riding down the Khyber? Perhaps because they could see far, far into the future? And what if the contest to select who would be the best to fight the foreigner so weakens all the contestants that the foreigner has a walk-over? Isn't that what happened and cleared the way for the British? And what about the corruption and licentiousness in the courts of the fledgling Hindu State? These weakened the nascent Hindu State from within. Were they necessary weapons in doing in the neighbouring Hindu regimes?

Not Loot, Just Taxation?

But what about the wanton loot that contemporary chroniclers reported? Savarkar is clearly anxious about these reports. He knits several answers.

First, the great project of establishing a Hindu State required resources. All Hindus ought to have been contributing to the success of the project. If they were not doing so voluntarily, it was but right of the Maratha armies and generals to exact the amounts by force.

Second, in those days all armies relied on extraction, on living off the land. And so, the Marathas cannot be blamed.

---

[54] Ibid, pp. 247–48.

Third, engaged as they were in enlarging the Hindu Empire, Maratha armies were spread from Punjab to Arcot, from Kolaba to Bengal and Orissa. They had to fight foes simultaneously on several fronts. Their operations just could not have been sustained from the State treasury.

Fourth, 'everything is fair in a war,' Savarkar says, 'or without citing the juster rule that everything is fair in a righteous war—we need waste no words beyond quoting the reply which the great Shivaji himself gave to his opponents once for all: "Your Emperor had forced me to keep an army for the defence of my people and my country, that army must be paid by his subjects".'

Fifth, yes, on occasion the Hindu subjects of the lands that were being invaded suffered, and amounts were extracted from them also. To begin with, such are 'the cruel necessities of war.' Next, it is not possible to discriminate between different shades of people in the fury of war. In any case, 'as the Moslems or other hostile people had to pay contribution as indemnity, so also the Hindus, too, who ought to have actively sided with the Marathas and yet remained supine, nay, even hostile to them and would not pay for the national struggle and were therefore often made to pay it. It was a war-tax informally levied and collected from all Hindus for the maintenance of those armies of the Hindu Empire to whose valour alone they owed the existence of temples, race and civilization, and but for whose might they would have probably been converted perforce to Muhammadanism and ceased to be Hindus at all.'

Sixth, of course, excesses are not to be condoned, Savarkar says. But we must remember that excesses said to have been committed by Maratha forces were nothing as compared to those committed by the Muslims, by the Portuguese, and others. They did not convert people forcibly, they did not pull down mosques and churches, 'not even their worst enemies could attribute to them any wholesale butchery, or crimes against the honour of womanhood, or reckless and fanatical persecution, burning of the sacred books of hostile faiths and the like.'

Seventh, as for burning crops and stocks of grain, etc. this they did only to deprive Muslim foes of the wherewithal to fight. They did the same thing to their own lands and crops back in Maharashtra when the British attacked. And this singular measure did much to deprive the British of victory. Indeed, excesses must be condemned, Savarkar says, but it must be remembered that they have marked all wars—Mazzini's and Garibaldi's conquest of Italy, the struggle of the Irish, the American war of Independence . . .[55]

One Question and One Observation

How well do these arguments stand in the light of contemporary accounts of what people experienced at the hands of Maratha forces? Recall the eyewitness accounts of Gangaram and Vaneshwar Vidyalankar that we find in history books. Do those suggest that all that was being done was that a 'tax' was being extracted informally? Would people have developed as much antipathy towards these forces as we are told they did, had these arguments of Savarkar reflected what actually transpired? In any case, if the soldiery had to go to such extreme lengths to exact the 'tax', that shows how little the people were stirred by pan-Hindu consciousness, the consciousness that is the bedrock of Savarkar's claims.

Such assertions are often couched in terms of what Shivaji, and the forces under his direction did. Just as the example of Shivaji should never be forgotten, it should not always be used as if it represents what happened later.

In Any Case . . .

In any case, the main point that Savarkar strains to emphasize is that, in spite of what their forces might have or might not have done, the Marathas

---

[55] For the foregoing, *Hindu Pad-padshahi*, op. cit, pp. 258–63.

are entitled to the same respect that all Hindus accord to Harsha and Pulkeshin. 'Nay, more,' says Savarkar:

> For, as the national urgency that propelled the Maratha movement was far more pressing, the moral justification from a Pan-Hindu standard for these efforts and wars and conquests must also be far nobler than a Harsha or a Pulkeshin could claim. It was not a mere zeal or a lust of conquest that made them draw their sword. It was not only the glory of being a Chakravartin that made them subjugate others to their rule. It was the question of the very existence of the Hindus as a nation—as a Faith.[56]

And doubly more than those who faced Alexander:

> Foreign histories talk glibly of Alexander's Indian conquest. But in fact it means only the conquest of the Punjab. The centre of Hindu strength at Pataliputra remained unhit though supine.

In fact, Savarkar proceeds to insist, the Marathas deserve more respect than even Chanakya and Chandragupta, his heroes in another book:

> The genius of Chanakya and the strength of Chandragupta forced Nanda to abdicate for his failure to drive Mlenchhas out, took upon themselves the imperial burdens and with the resources of this empire at their command ably drove away the Greeks from the Indian soil. But compared to this, how difficult was the task the Marathas had to undertake, how gigantic the contrast of the dreadful magnitude of the danger and the poverty of the means they had to face! All India lay trampled under the feet of the Moslem, the Portuguese and several other alien and powerful foes for centuries: all virility and even hope

---

[56] Ibid, pp. 249–50.

squeezed out of it : demoralisation born of constant defeats fed itself on the vitals of the nation till it grew into a superstition that the Mogul Emperor was born to rule and possessed a divine right to do so: the sword literally broken, the shield literally torn: and yet they rose, yet they fought and yet they won in a contest the like of which the Hindus as a nation were never called upon to confront . . .[57]

It is precisely this kind of attitude that would have been one of the factors that kept others from signing up. Who would want to sign up for a 'joint struggle' as the subordinate of someone who is so convinced that he is far above the others?

---

[57] Ibid, 250–51.

A Revolutionary Fashions a State

Sutras for the State

'... Nothing makes [the] Self conscious of itself so much as a conflict with [the] non-Self,' Savarkar wrote in his tract, *Essentials of Hindutva*. 'Nothing can weld peoples into a nation and nations into a State as the pressure of a common foe. Hatred separates as well as unites. Never had Sindhusthan a better chance and a more powerful stimulus to be herself forged into an indivisible whole as on that dire day, when the great iconoclast crossed the Indus...'[1]

Hatred separates us from whom? Those who we should hate. Hatred unites us with whom? With those who should hate. The most effective prerequisite? 'A common foe.'

Just a few pages earlier, giving his version of the reasons on account of which Buddhism was erased from India, Savarkar had set forth the other half of his maxim 'Hatred separates as well as unites': '... everything that is common in us with our enemies weakens our power of opposing them.' Hence, 'the necessity of creating a bitter sense of wrong and invoking a power of undying resistance...,' he wrote. Therefore, 'What was the use of a universal faith that instead of soothening the ferociousness and brutal egoism of other nations only excited their lust by leaving India defenceless

---

[1] V.D. Savarkar, *Essentials of Hindutva*, in *Hindu Rashtra Darshan*, Abhishek Publications, Chandigarh, 2022, p. 487. As is well-known, Savarkar completed this tract in 1920/21 [another edition puts the date as 1921/22]. It was published under a pseudonym, 'A Maratha'. The lines quoted above occur in the context of the invasion of India by Mahmud of Ghazni.

and unsuspecting?'² So much not only for Buddhism but for the much-vaunted tolerance in Hinduism: we are tolerant because the text proclaims, *Vasudhaiv kutumbakam* . . .

The 'Sturdy Habits' We Must Develop

The maxims are in the tract written in 1920-21 when he was still serving his sentence for complicity in murder. He continued to preach hatred, revenge, cruelty till, as we shall see, his closing years. An instance will give us a glimpse of what is to come. M.R. Jayakar had been a member of legislatures. He had been a Judge of the Federal Court, a Vice-Chancellor and much else. He was also a member of the Hindu Mahasabha. Among his many public works, Jayakar had helped set up the Vedanta Ashram in Khar, Bombay, and persuaded Swami Yati Ishwarananda, one of the principal disciples of Swami Vivekananda, to take up residence at the Ashram. As part of celebrations to mark the 19th anniversary of the Ashram a public meeting was held in Bombay. In his memoir, Jayakar recalled the meeting:

---

² Ibid, p. 475. The full passage—a part of Savarkar's rationale for erasing Buddhism—is as follows:

> Moreover, everything that is common in us with our enemies, weakens our power of opposing them. The foe that has nothing in common with us is the foe likely to be most bitterly resisted by us just as a friend that has almost everything in him that we admire and prize in ourselves is likely to be the friend we love most. The necessity of creating a bitter sense of wrong and invoking a power of undying resistance especially in India that had under the opiates of Universalism and non-violence lost the faculty even of resisting sin and crime and aggression, could best be accomplished by cutting off even the semblance of a common worship—a common Church which required her to clasp the hand of those of her co-religionists whose had been the very hand that had strangled her as a nation.
>
> What was the use of a universal faith that instead of soothening the ferociousness and brutal egoism of other nations only excited their lust by leaving India defenceless and unsuspecting? No; the only safe-guards in future were valour and strength that could only be born of a national self-consciousness. She had poured her life's blood for sophistry that tried to prove otherwise. [Ibid, p. 475.]

The function was very successful. Some eminent speakers participated. Among them, Savarkar the Hindu Sabha leader made an extraordinary speech, the main theme of which was that, until we are a free nation, we must not think of practising soft virtues like humility, self-surrender or forgiveness. On the contrary, we must, during our subjection, develop sturdy habits of hatred, retaliation, vindictiveness and such other features. In other words, we must postpone, until we are free, the virtues inculcated by our religion. Though this speech was delivered in attractive language, there was commotion in the audience. Savarkar strengthened his argument by misconceiving Tilak's observation that Indians must postpone the delights, the ease and dignity of scholarship and research until India was free. A few speakers supported Savarkar's view, though a large majority differed and the danger appeared to be that a meeting called chiefly to popularise the lofty teachings of Shri Ramakrishna was likely to be misused for the propagation, in the name of patriotism, of views bordering on spiteful retaliation, vengeful hatred, vindictive punishment and the like. Consequently, in my concluding remarks from the Chair, I had to combat Savarkar's views, and establish a balance between the claims of patriotism and spiritual life. I said:

Whatever the value of Tilak's views may be in the region of literature or philosophy, they cannot be used to sustain a claim for a systematic reversal of the claims of religious or spiritual life.[3]

Perverted, Imbecile, Suicidal . . .

Savarkar went to great lengths to distinguish his 'Hindutva' from Hinduism. Indeed, the very values that we have been taught since childhood are the essential attributes of Hinduism, he decried as the values that must

---

[3] M.R. Jayakar, *The Story of My Life, Volume 2, 1922–25*, Asia Publishing House, Bombay, 1959, p. 541.

be jettisoned. He called them 'perverse', 'perverted', 'imbecile', 'suicidal', 'foolish', 'ridiculous', 'silly', 'anti-national' . . . the hallmarks of a people who are 'morbidly virtuous', 'this incurable disease of the Hindu mind', 'this suicidal disease of the perverted conception of virtues', and much else.

Among these were the 'seven *bandies*' that we have encountered earlier. These truly deserved the adjectives that Savarkar used—'perverse' and the rest. But these were not the only ones for which he used the adjectives.

Religious Tolerance

Yes, it can be a virtue—but, Savarkar said again and again, only if the other religion, group, person is also tolerant. If the other side is not, then you must be super-intolerant. Here is one set—from literally scores that can be reproduced—of representative passages from *Six Glorious Epochs of Indian History*:[4]

> 429-430. Every Hindu seems to have been made to suck, along with his mother's milk, this Nectar-like advice that religious tolerance is a virtue. But nobody ever explains to him the essence of that precept. If that alien religion is also tolerant of our own religion, our tolerance towards it can be a virtue. But the Muslim and the Christian religions, which boldly proclaim it to be their religious duty to destroy most cruelly the Hindu religion and to eradicate from the face of this earth the *kafirs* and the heathens, can never be described as tolerant of other religions. In respect of these intolerant foreign religions the very extremely enraged intolerance, which seeks to retaliate their atrocities with super-atrocious reprisals, itself becomes a virtue!
>
> 431. Even if we were to restrict our discussion to the period under discussion, it will be seen that every Muslim aggressor went

---

[4] This was the last book that Savarkar wrote. It was completed a short while before he passed away in 1966. The page numbers refer to the 2022 reprint, *Six Glorious Epochs of Indian History*, Abhishek Publications, Chandigarh, 2022.

on demolishing Hindu temples at Mathura and Kashi (Benaras). The most sacred idols in the various magnificent shrines from all over India right up to Rameshwaram were not only purposely taken to the Muslim capitals like Delhi and plastered into the portal steps of their royal palaces, but, for the sole purpose of hurting the feelings of the Hindus and insulting them, they were also used as slabs and tiles for lavatories, water-closets, and urinals. To be tolerant towards those Muslims who called these and many other atrocities their religious duty is the very negation of virtue, its sacrilegious perversion! Nay, for the Hindus to show such tolerance was the greatest sin to be punished in Hell! But the Hindus committed this very sin under the name of virtue! Even after overthrowing the various Muslim powers, i.e. even when the Hindus had acquired political ascendancy, they did not destroy the various masjids at Kashi (Benares), Mathura or Rameshwaram nor used their ruins as tiles for the various building constructions along roads. At the most, the Hindus reconstructed and renovated their old temples which were razed to the ground by the Muslims. They did nothing more! On the contrary, there are astonishing instances of grant of new lands for their maintenance and assurance of protection of the masjids which had been built by the Muslim aggressors, by the Hindu powers![5]

In a word, 'to meet cruelty with super-cruel blows, craft with super-craft, violence with extreme violence and to consider this war policy to be a highly religious duty of a brave warrior'—and this policy is to be followed not just in 'war' as we usually understand the term but also on the 'religious front'.[6] In fact, Savarkar laid greater emphasis on following a policy of this kind on the 'religious front' because, on his telling, the Hindus had often worsted enemies on the secular front. It is just that they could not capitalize

---

[5] Ibid, pp. 149–50.

[6] Ibid, pp. 226–27.

on these victories and roll back the enemy on the religious front because of that 'perverted sense of virtues'. Savarkar summarized the teachings of an Acharya he admired, Medhatithi.[7] Do not wait till your neighbouring State or your enemy has done something to provoke you; pounce on him. The fact that the enemy exists at all is enough:

491-492. Medhatithi clearly declares that to invade another kingdom— especially, an enemy state—can never be an injustice in political science. It is, on the other hand, the duty of a king, he said, to pounce upon the non-Hindu enemy and crush him before he grows powerful enough to invade the former. In statesmanship, the protection of the Aryavarta is the supreme duty of a king. That is why he condemns as suicidal, dilatory and so adverse to the kingly duty, everything that the other impudent, foolhardy critics recommend as proper code of conduct: viz. that while attacking a foreign kingdom, and especially the Muslim kingdom, the Aryan kings should not strike till the other gives offence of some sort or the other. On the contrary, he says that the neighbouring king is an enemy is in itself his fault; at an opportune moment he should be pounced upon and crushed. What more, if the neighbouring non-Aryan kingdom is seen to be getting stronger and

---

[7] 425. According to Savarkar, Medhatithi lived sometime between 850 and 950. Savarkar said, 'He tried to erect before the perplexed Hindus of the 9th and 10th centuries a huge light-house tower of the former Aryan imperialism and expansionism of Chanakya and to regenerate into them new courage to push ahead determinedly and strike hard at the aggressor. His intention was clearly to animate his society with the vibrant inspiration to repulse instantly the armed religious aggression of the Muslims of those times in the same magnificent tradition of the Aryan empires of old and with their military strategy in fighting down the aggressive Rakshasas (enemies). He wanted the Hindus to establish not only the old empire of Aryavarta, but to conquer and annex the Muslim states even beyond the limits of Aryavarta and establish Hinduism there, if necessary even with force. The Aryan slogan "*Krunvanto Vishvam Aryam*" (We are going to make the whole world Aryan) of the Vedic times resounds incessantly throughout his critique on Manusmriti . . .' Ibid, pp. 170–71.

mightier than our Aryan state, whether it is guilty of any tangible offence or not, we should ourselves form alliance with other friendly or unfriendly powers and go to war against this non-Aryan state, the moment we are assured of success.[8]

Moreover, one must not be squeamish about reasons for assaulting the other. Any pretext will do, and is fully justified, Savarkar believed, and taught:

493-95 . . . Once you are engaged in war with the enemy, you should throw kindness and generosity to the winds and crush the enemy outright. The crafty enemy should be struck down with super-cunning and skilful deception under any pretext whatsoever. In war the so-called virtues like honesty, simplicity, consistency in speech and action and politeness, gentility and generosity themselves prove fatal to the nation. Hence, a king should not fall a prey to them—should keep himself aloof from them.[9]

In his reconstruction of our past, Savarkar listed the damage that resulted from 'this confessed religious thought, the distorted sense of virtues and the blind religious tolerance which culminated in the religious suicide of the Hindus.'[10] The net result of not hitting back with that 'very extremely enraged intolerance,' of letting the Muslims continue to live on was, on Savarkar's telling, disaster:

. . . And in thousands of cases during the long period of Hindu-Muslim war, these very minority Muslims who had been living as refugees in the Hindu states never failed to rebel or sabotage the Hindu war-

---

[8] Ibid, p. 172.

[9] Ibid, pp. 172–73.

[10] Ibid, pp. 149–52, at p. 151.

efforts as soon as there was any foreign Muslim invasion. Even while they were seeing all these treacherous activities of the Muslims, the Hindu kings went on practising, and committing to their memory, the precepts of religious tolerance and large-heartedness in utter disregard of the proper place, time or person and, of course, they fell as miserable victims. This is verily the distortion of virtue itself![11]

The moral?

469. Religious tolerance! A virtue! Yes, It can be a virtue only where the other religion is tolerant of our own. But to tolerate the Muslim religion, the followers of which right from the Sultans like Mahmud of Ghazni and Ghori and others to the various Shahs and Badshahs thought it their religious obligation to massacre the *kafir* Hindus to celebrate their accession to the throne and had been carrying on horrible religious persecution of the Hindus for nearly a thousand years, was tantamount to cut the throat of one's own religion! It was not tolerance towards other religions, it was tolerance of irreligion! It was not even tolerance, it was impotence! But this truth never dawned upon the Hindu society of those days even after the horrible experience of a thousand years or so. They on their own part went on tolerating even such a hideous religion as the Islam and considered it a glorious virtue of their own—a special ornament in the crown of the Hindu community!

470. O thou Hindu society! Of all the sins and weaknesses, which have brought about thy fall, the greatest and most potent are thy virtues themselves.

471-472. Ahimsa (non-violence), kindness, chivalry even towards the enemy women, protection of an abjectly capitulating enemy, *Kshama veerasya bhushanam* (forgiveness, a glorious

---

[11] Ibid, p. 153.

emblem for the brave!) and religious tolerance were all virtues no doubt—very noble virtues! But it is blind and slovenly—even impotent—adoption of all these very virtues, irrespective of any consideration given to the propriety of time, place or persons that so horribly vanquished them in the millennial Hindu-Muslim war on the religious front.[12]

Savarkar returns to this theme repeatedly. The only way is 'to reciprocate atrocities with counter-atrocities, and reprisals with super-reprisals!' He held up what Jaswant Singh of Jodhpur did. Towards the end of his reign Aurangzeb mobilized his army for 'the most determined offensive against the Hindus', Savarkar wrote.

517 . . . But no sooner did he [Aurangzeb] go away to the South, the Rajputs retaliated with the same vehemence and vigour and made up for the humiliation and numerical losses of the Hindus. The glaring instance of Jodhpur may be cited here. Under the leadership of the powerful Maharana Jaswant Singh and the brave Durgadas Rathod, not only the Masjids erected by Aurangzeb on the ruins of Hindu temples, but all other Masjids also were razed to the ground and on their site Hindu temples were built. The Jodhpurian Rajputs reconverted not only the Muslimized Hindus but as many of the Muslims as they could on an extensive scale. If the Muslim armies went on throwing beef into the Hindu temples and wells, the Rathod armies cast pork in Masjid after Masjid and paid them in the same coin. Hundreds of Muslim women were converted to Hinduism and married to the Rajputs or were simply kept as concubines like the Hindu women by the Muslims before them. The whole of the Muslim society in Rajputana was horror-stricken to see this ferocious outburst of Hindu rage. Not merely for the sin of eating and drinking

---

[12] Ibid, pp. 164–65.

with the Muslims, but for having cohabited with and married Muslim women, and even keeping them in their houses, Hindus were no longer socially ostracized. For at least thirty to forty years this Hindu retaliatory aggression on the Muslims spread and glowed and resounded through town after town and village after village in the Hindu states in Rajasthan . . .[13]

Unfortunately, such instances were 'only exceptions', Savarkar said. It is because the Vijaynagar rulers followed maxims such as those of Medhatithi that Muslim armies did not dare pursue the fleeing Hindus in the environs of that empire.[14] Where this rule was not followed, the enemies worked their havoc again and again. The Marathas defeated the Pathan and Rohilla armies of Abdali. But they did no more. The example they should have followed, Savarkar proclaims, was that of Spain, Portugal, Bulgaria, Greece—which did not just defeat Muslims in battles, they finished each one of them:

> 1074-A . . . the Hindu Society (of the time) was haunted by a false and perverted sense of virtues and as such . . . the Hindus did not even slightly avenge the unbearable and unlimited persecution and the diabolic atrocities perpetrated by the Muslims on the Hindu religion. Unlike Spain, Portugal, Bulgaria, Greece and other (European) nations which saved Christianity from extinction (from their lands) by ridding completely their homeland of Muslims, the Hindus did not extirpate the Muslims from India. They refrained from inflicting similar, not to speak of greater, atrocities even on the enemy like the Muslims who considered religious persecution and diabolic and heinous atrocities themselves to be their religious duties! Every drop of blood in the Hindu veins and arteries was surcharged,

---

[13] Ibid, pp. 179–80.

[14] Ibid, p. 325.

as it were, with the false and suicidal and perverted conception of religious tolerance towards the aliens. The notion that whatever the nature of atrocities of the aliens on our religion, we should not, even for resisting them, retaliate against these very aggressive alien religionists, was the essence of their religious tolerance. And it was considered by the Hindus to be their religion! It is because of this suicidal notion of religious tolerance that Hindus, even when they had gained unparalleled victories over the Muslims on the battlefields and in the political arena, did not oppose them in the least on the religious front. Naturally on this religious front the Muslims in India were not extirpated, nor were they subdued. Root them out completely the Hindus never did! as they had done with the Greeks, the Sakas, the Huns and other ancient aggressors![15]

Savarkar describes in burning text the atrocities that Abdali had committed, and deeply laments the fact that after defeating him, the Maratha general, Raghunathrao, did not order his troops to 'retaliate with the same atrocities on the Muslims as were indulged in by the latter, that the Muslims as a whole were to be slaughtered, that just like (the ruined) heaps of the Hindu temples the Muslim Masjids should be pulled down without any exception, that the Muslim women should be put to the same indescribable humiliation and shame as the Hindu women folk were done by the Muslims; that it was their duty to take such a revenge for the wrongs done to Hindu religion and Hindu society!'[16]

'Purity' to the Enemy's Rescue

On Savarkar's reckoning, Hindus put up unbroken resistance against Muslim rulers for centuries, but there was one thing that Muslims had no

---

[15] Ibid, pp. 393–94.

[16] Ibid, pp. 395–96.

reason to fear: even if they won, the Hindus would not reconvert those who had been converted to Islam—and that because of the very same 'perverted sense of virtues', of maintaining purity, etc.

597. . . . in order to protect their states and religion the Hindus had fought grim and determined battles right from the times of Mahmud of Ghazni's and Ghori's demonical raids. They lost their states, they won their states! Defeat and victory, victory and defeat! The fortunes of the fields changed in quick succession! But for more than seven centuries the Hindus kept on fighting the Muslims throughout the whole of India, fought every inch of it and finally brought the mighty Muslim enemy to his knees in abject surrender! To say that these Hindus would have ever cared a two-pence for the fiercer rage of the Muslim revenge is in itself a fine illustration of self-contradiction!

598. Of course, the Muslims had never to worry in the least about the security of their religious domination in India! The Hindus were firm as regards one thing: never to convert any Muslim, not to counter-attack the sphere of the Muslim religious influence; nor again to harm them in any way in matters religious; for, all these actions were completely contrary to the Hindu religious faith! The Muslims had only one anxiety as to how to spread the Islamic faith incessantly throughout the length and breadth of India, even if the Hindus had reconquered political power.[17]

As a result, Muslims conquered more Hindu land via conversion than by military conquest[18] . . . The Hindus, and more particularly the Marathas, wrested back practically all political power throughout the whole of India from the Muslims towards the end of this 'epic Hindu-Muslim war.' Yet the

---

[17] Ibid, pp. 211–12.

[18] Ibid, p. 212. All caps in the original.

Muslims retained their hold individually or collectively on the masses and on property too![19] . . .

> 603. And the fun of it was that this religious domination of the Muslims and their individual right to that land had been constitutionally and legally protected by the Hindu kings themselves, giving them equal civil status as subjects along with the Hindus![20] . . . 605. These big or small Islamistans were really the time bombs laid by the covert Muslim religious authority in the foundation of the Hindu political superstructure.[21]

Savarkar urges the reader to 'read again and again and very carefully' the part of the book in which he has 'explained the inestimable wrong done to the Hindu society by this suicidal disease of the perverted conception of virtues . . .'[22]

Forgiveness of, Generosity Towards the 'Vanquished and Abjectly Surrendering Enemy'?

Savarkar is livid with Hindus who forgave their enemies, who showed generosity towards adversaries. Not just an 'eye for an eye', for an eye not just two eyes, the very life, and torn away in the manner that would inflict maximum pain. He builds his norm by citing instances where Hindu rulers are said to have defeated their adversaries and then let them go. In each case, his question is: what would the adversary have done if he had vanquished the Hindu ruler? And in each case, the account leads to the lament: if only the Hindu ruler had done what the Muslim enemy would have done.

---

[19] Ibid, pp. 212–13.

[20] Ibid, p. 213.

[21] Ibid, pp. 213–14. Bold caps in the original.

[22] Ibid, p. 396.

. . . so enemies like the ungrateful Mohammed Ghori and the Rohilla Najib Khan, were set free. And what did they do in return for this noble act of the Hindus? The first brutally murdered his former benefactor, Prithviraj Chauhan, while the second conspired against the very Marathas who let him go alive, and brought about their unprecedented destruction at Panipat. Having only learnt by rote the maxim, to give food to the hungry and water to the thirsty is a virtue, the Hindus went on giving milk to the vile poisonous cobras and vipers! Even while the Muslim demons were demolishing Hindu temples and breaking to pieces their holiest of idols like Somnath, they never wreaked their vengeance upon those wicked Muslims, even when they had golden opportunities to do so, nor did they ever take out a single brick from the walls of Masjids, because their religious teachers and priests preached the virtue of not inflicting pain on the offender . . .[23]

If Prithviraj had been captured, Ghori would have killed him, Ghori would have butchered his troops, captured the women, and distributed them among his soldiers. The offspring would have been brought up as Muslims . . . Ghori would have thus established his sway over Prithviraj's lands.

To such a damned, demoniacal enemy of our religion, like Mohammed Ghori, was mercy shown by Prithviraj and the other confederated Rajput rulers following sheepishly the textual maxim *Kshama veerasya bhushanam* . . . Nay, they showed mercy not only to Mohammed Ghori but even to the whole Muslim army, only to respect the noble Rajput tradition of assuring full protection from fear to those who surrendered meekly. Only an oral promise was obtained from Mohammed Ghori that he would not again invade India and he was allowed to go alive. His domain of Ghazni, too, was returned to him. And proud, more of their

---

[23] Ibid, p. 148.

suicidal and credulous generosity than of their having defeated the Muslim army of Mohammed Ghori, those Rajput warriors marched triumphantly to Delhi and celebrated their victory![24]

And again, a little later, Savarkar turns to Qutb ud-Din Aibak. He invaded the Rajput kingdoms. He was defeated repeatedly:

691. But it must be remembered here that even while the Muslims launched repeated attacks on the Hindu states, the Hindus as a rule never invaded them nor ever pursued the fleeing Muslim army, nor again besieged the Muslim localities left behind and destroyed them or their Masjids. It is because the Hindus never thus retaliated the Muslim aggression owing to their perverse sense of virtues, the latter again and again perpetrated these crimes against the former.[25]

The same perverse notion led to the same fatal blunder by Rana Kumbha, Savarkar pointed out:

841. . . . Sultan Mohammad Khilji of Malwa was at last caught alive by Rana Kumbha. But grossly affected as he was by the age-old malady of the perverted sense of virtues, as the other Hindu heroes before him were, he allowed the Sultan to go free, considering it a noble act on his own part. Had but Rana Kumbha been taken captive by the Muslim Sultan Mohammad Khilji, he would very likely have been deprived of his eye sight, as Prithviraj was, and brutally murdered according to the diabolic war-ethics of the Muslims. In fact, this diabolic war-ethics is the only one which is beneficial to a nation in such fiendish wars! and hence is highly pious and thoroughly sound![26]

---

[24] Ibid, p. 238.

[25] Ibid, p. 246.

[26] Ibid, pp. 297–98.

The Example of Gods

And yet, this was not always so, Savarkar laments. Rakshasas were disrupting rituals, killing rishis, drinking their blood, so much so that the bones of the rishis had piled up. Ram was taken to the Dandakaranya forest by Vishwamitra and shown the ravages that the Rakshasas had rained down on the rishis. Savarkar says that 'at that time those gods and god-like emperors, too, considered it the holiest religious duty to show super-savage cruelty to beat down the cruelty of the Rakshasas, to be arch-devils against the devils!'[27]

'. . . a nation has, as a rule, to adopt a war-strategy far stricter, crueller and more unrelenting than that of the unscrupulous enemy it wants to conquer,' Savarkar wrote.[28] The story of Kacha, he said, also shows that in the war our gods followed the policy to 'fight the crafty enemy with super-craft, to destroy barbarism with hyper-barbarity, as the only effective means of annihilating the foe'. This, he said, 'was the praiseworthy principle of religious warfare of our ancestors till at least the close of the Puranic era.'[29]

640. During the Vedic and the Puranik (mythological) period, the ancestors of the Hindu Nation had to fight the Daityas, Danavs and the Rakshasas, the cruellest, most atrocious and cunning cannibals of the time. It is because (as the Vedic and Puranik stories show) those of our ancestors, our gods, our emperors, the Vedic Rishis who chanted war canticles, the epic poets of the Puranas and all those who actively participated in the war could become more atrocious, more deceptive and cunning, and far crueller than those enemies—like the Rakshasas and others—it is because they could formulate an adequate war policy to meet the ever changing guiles of the enemy and practise

---

[27] Ibid, pp. 225–26.

[28] Ibid, pp. 225.

[29] Ibid, p. 226.

it effectively—that they could always succeed in those various wars, and our nation too became stronger and more expansive than before.

642: To fight the crafty enemy with super-craft, to destroy barbarism with hyper-barbarity, as the only effective means of annihilating the foe, was the praiseworthy principle of religious warfare of our ancestors till at least the close of the Puranic era . . . to face religious aggression with counter religious offensives—to meet cruelty with supra-cruel blows, craft with super-craft, violence with extreme violence and to consider this war policy to be a highly religious duty of a brave warrior . . .[30]

Truth, Ethics and the Rest

What is true of violence, cruelty, barbarity is equally true of truth itself:

645. Generally speaking, truthful conduct is a virtue. To satisfy a promised gift or word is also a virtue! But when in the heat of extolling virtues to the skies the Puranas (mythological stories) told the story of Harishchandra who made good his promise given to Vishwamitra in his dream by presenting him with his kingdom and such other childish stories, they definitely changed the national war-policy into an imbecile, weak and suicidal one. No words can adequately condemn this influence of the Puranas. More respectable than this truthful conduct was considered the practice of non-violence as the highest form of virtue not only by the Jains and the Buddhists but in some of the Vaishnav texts also, which later on hastened our terrible downfall as determinedly and as enormously as even our enemies, the Muslims, could not perhaps accomplish. Manliness and valour came to be condemned as the vilest of vices. The unmanly, the imbecile, the valour-lacking coward, not only lacking the ability but even the

---

[30] Ibid, pp. 225–27.

desire to avenge the national insult and injustice, came to be highly respected in religious circles as the greatest and most magnanimous saint, ripe for an honourable place in heaven.[31]

647. Naturally, when the Islam invaded Hinduism with far more ferocity and bitterness and with more dangerous weapons than the Rakshasas of the Puranik age, our Hindu ancestors of the seventh century had no other war-strategy to face it with than the imbecile, impotent and suicidal one which offered milk to a venomous serpent. To encounter the wolf, the sheep had proferred its own neck![32]

673. Were a serpent (an inveterate national enemy) to come with a view to bite the motherland, he should be smashed to pieces with a surprise attack, deceit or cunning or in any other way possible. Although this war-strategy of Shree Krishna and Chanakya was taught to the Hindus long ago, at that time it appeared to them like one of the five deadliest sins . . . the whole of the Hindu nation was at that time utterly infatuated with the perverted sense of virtues . . . But the Muslims, however, followed this very war-strategy most scrupulously.[33]

A lie is to be countered with a bigger lie, a canard by a more vicious canard, a rumour by an even more extravagant rumour, he wrote recounting the success with which rumours spread by Pathan guards were set at rest in the Andamans.[34]

And truth is but one element of ethical conduct. Ethical conduct in general is appropriate only when the other side is conducting itself by equally exalted ethical standards. And that holds in day-to-day life as much as in war. If the other side is not restrained by ethical considerations,

---

[31] Ibid, p. 228.

[32] Ibid, pp. 228–29.

[33] Ibid, p. 238.

[34] *My Transportation for Life,* Abhishek Publications, Chandigarh, 2022, p. 193.

then we should also deploy deceit, deception, lying . . . Rama killed Vali in this way, Savarkar reminds readers. The Pandavas used the truthful Yudhishthira to mislead Dronacharya with the half-truth, 'Ashwatthama is dead', and Krishna himself was their counsellor. A snake obeys none of the rules that you have set up for yourself, Savarkar warns: so kill it by all means, with every stratagem, with every ruse that you can devise. As Hindus did not live by this, they were trodden upon. To get out of the hands of Prithviraj, Mohammed Ghori had promised never to invade India again. He broke the promise again and again.

> 680. But the breach of promise which could Muslimize the whole of the Kafir state was a highly religious duty for the Muslims, and because Mohammed Ghori broke his promises again and again he became a Ghazi among the Muslims! This fact also must be engraved on the hearts of the Hindus that the Muslims who acted irreligiously according to Chand Bhat were blessed with success by God whereas the Hindus who never broke any promise but showed the quixotic greatness of setting the enemy free alive were crushed outright owing to their steadfast adherence to their so-called religious conduct![35]

Slaughter Wholesale

All this had been forgotten by the Hindus, Savarkar complained. They should have retaliated by massacring the Muslims, he declared:

> 466. An effective way of liquidating the Muslim religious authority could easily have been availed of by the Hindus of those times, if they had but done what the Muslims had been doing in their hundreds of offensives against Hindu states. The Muslims went on slaughtering wholesale the Hindu population. Similarly, whenever the Hindus

---

[35] *Six Glorious Epochs of Indian History,* op. cit., p. 241.

gained an upper hand, they could have retaliated by massacring Muslim population and making the region Muslim-less! devoid of Muslims! Even their ban on repurification (*shuddhi*) would not have prevented them from doing this. For in doing this there was no question involved of eating or drinking or of having any dealings with the Muslims! But—! But if not the ban on repurification, the suicidal Hindu creed of religious tolerance was certainly a major obstacle!

And so, instead:

467. Instead of massacring *en masse* the hundreds of thousands of Muslims, who from time to time fell in their hands completely vanquished and utterly helpless, in order to avenge the untold wrongs and humiliation heaped by them on Hindus, the Hindus in their turn refrained themselves from doing the Muslims even the slightest harm because they were in minority, and belonged to another religion. On the contrary, the Muslims were allowed to enhance the glory and scope of their own religion without the least possible hindrance. Not only like the Hindu citizens, but even more leniently and with more facilities were the Muslims allowed, by Hindu states of those days, to enjoy the legal rights!—a fact which is borne out by pages after pages of Indian history.[36]

The consequences were inevitable, Savarkar writes:

In the chaos that followed Taimurlang's depradations and then his having to rush back to Samarkand, Delhi's hold was greatly weakened. Several holy places were reconquered by the Hindus. For that matter, the holy places of the Hindus like Kashi, Prayag and others had, even before this time, been reconquered from the Muslims. But!—Although

---

[36] Ibid, pp. 163–64.

the Muslim political power there was defeated and uprooted, their colonies and there religious centres like their Masjids and mosques were not destroyed—as did the Muslims, whenever they conquered the Hindu territories, slaughtering the Hindus irrespective of their age or sex and pulling down the Hindu holy places of worship, so as to make mere existence impossible for them. But because the Hindus did not emulate the Muslims in this respect, these local Muslims who were left, alive and unmolested, turned traitors, like serpents fed and fostered as pets, and invited again and again the Muslim aggressors for help and made life miserable for the Hindus in those holy places and cities. But the Rajput malady of the suicidal generosity even now persisted without any moderation.[37]

What Should Have Been Done

Savarkar sets out several instances in gory detail. To take one instance, he writes of 'the warriors from Tipu's select company of the direst young Muslim scoundrels whom he fondled as his "sons",' and of 'the fairest young and innocent Hindu women, who were given away as rewards to those Muslim young rogues from this brigade for their brutal atrocities towards the Hindu . . .' What would have been the proper course once Tipu's army had been defeated? Here is Savarkar's answer:

616. Then in order to reward the meritorious services of the choicest Maratha warriors in this Hindu-Muslim war at least as many young and beautiful Muslim girls should be captured, converted to Hinduism and presented to them as were the Hindu girls distributed by Tipu amongst the daredevil warriors of his select brigade.

617. Thereafter the thousands of Muslim rascals and scoundrels, who have, in this Hindu-Muslim war, inflicted harrowing atrocities on the

---

[37] Ibid, pp. 296–97.

Hindus, raped Hindu women and girls, have broken holy images of Hindu gods and goddesses and have demolished their temples and who will have been locked as per the above-mentioned order in various prisons, shall be conducted under strong military guard to the four or five chief cities . . . They should especially be taken to Nargund and Kittur—the places where Tipu himself had inflicted inhuman atrocities on the Hindu men and women with the aid of his diabolic army, so that Tipu's devilish acts might be avenged with equal ferocity and with the harshest punishments meted out to the dare-devil soldiers of his Islamic brigade in the very presence of the afflicted people there. On the appointed day, during the reconversion week, these hundreds of Muslim devils should be brought under strong armed guard of soldiers and cannons to the vast parade-grounds and after the charge-sheets against them, indicating their fiendish acts against the Hindus, have been read out to them, they should be blown off from cannon-mouth, before the joyful eyes of the thousands of Hindu spectators.[38]

Women and Children

What goes for soldiers, mosques, lands, goes for the women and children of the adversary, says Savarkar. Allauddin's son is captured in the battle to retake Chitod. But, much to Savarkar's chagrin, he is not converted to Hinduism. 'He should have been at least to pay the enemy in its own coin!' Savarkar exclaims. 'This is the very same suicidal generosity of the Hindus.'[39] The same perversity prevailed in regard to Tipu's two sons who fell into the hands of the invading Maratha armies and were taken as hostages by the Marathas and the British to ensure that Tipu adhered to the treaty that he had signed, Savarkar reminds readers. They were treated

---

[38] Ibid, pp. 216–17.

[39] Ibid, p. 259.

with solicitous consideration. He recalls the letter that Haripant Phadke wrote to Nana Phadnis:

> Lord Cornwallis sent the two sons of Tipu to me. When I saw them they pleaded they were hungry. I sent them to a neighbouring tent and ordered that they should be well fed. Then after some time they were returned to the English camp of Lord Cornwallis![40]

And what did the Muslims do to the two sons of Guru Gobind Singh, aged 12 or less, who fell into their hands? Savarkar asks. They were buried alive against a wall, brick by brick.

The same question:

> 591. Supposing that by an adverse turn of events two children of our Peshwas were to fall in the hands of Tipu or any other Muslim ruler—what then? He would not have fed, as the Hindu-hearted Haripant Phadke did, the two tender-aged children and returned them to the Peshwa! Such a behaviour would have been considered sacrilegious and cowardly according to the Muslim religious belief; they would most probably have been built up alive in brick walls or else would have been crushed under an elephant's foot. The Hindus, on the other hand, would not have avenged such brutality with any hyper-brutal retaliation, even if they had had the strength and opportunity to do so. For, the virus of the perverted sense of virtues had been flowing through their arteries and veins for centuries, together.[41]

The women too: Hindus should treat Muslim women the way Muslims treated Hindu women, Savarkar declared. Muslims kidnapped Hindu girls and women. They forced them to become Muslims and took them as wives or

---

[40] Ibid, pp. 207–08.

[41] Ibid, p. 209.

kept them as concubines and housemaids in the most humiliating conditions, Savarkar wrote in passage after passage. The Muslim women in the household egged their menfolk to commit such atrocities, he said. By contrast,

> 449. The Muslim women never feared retribution or punishment at the hands of any Hindu for their heinous crime. They [the Hindus] had a perverted idea of woman-chivalry. If in a battle the Muslims won, they were rewarded for such crafty and deceitful conversions of Hindu women; but even if the Hindus carried the field and a Hindu power was established in that particular place (and such incidents in those times were not very rare) the Muslim men alone, if at all, suffered the consequential indignities but the Muslim women—never![42]

He listed instances where Muslim women were left untouched. In the process he scolded Shivaji also for returning the daughter-in-law of the Muslim Governor of Kalyan; and Chimaji Appa for returning the wife of the Portuguese Governor of Bassein.[43]

And so, the same question:

> 455. Suppose, if from the earliest Muslim invasion of India, the Hindus also, whenever they were victors on the battlefields, had decided to pay the Muslim fair sex in the same coin or punished them in some other way, i.e. by conversion even with force, and then absorbed them in their fold, then? Then with this horrible apprehension at their heart they would have desisted from their evil designs against any Hindu lady. If they had taken such a fright in the first two or three centuries, millions and millions of luckless Hindu ladies would have been saved all their indignities, loss of their own religion, rapes, ravages and other unimaginable persecutions. Our woman-world would not have

---

[42] Ibid, p. 157.

[43] Ibid, pp. 157–58.

suffered such a tremendous numerical loss, which means their future progeny would not have been lost permanently to Hinduism and the Muslim population could not have thrived so audaciously. Without any increase in their womenfolk the Muslim population would have dwindled into a negligible minority.[44]

Forefathers' Concept of Chivalry

The Hindus of the pre-Islamic era never interpreted chivalry to women in this 'anti-national and suicidal' way, Savarkar maintained:

460. A serpent, whether male or female, if it comes to bite must be killed. The enemy women who enforced conversion and heaped all sorts of humiliation on our mothers and sisters, had by that very devilish act, lost their womanhood, and their right to chivalrous treatment, and deserved nothing but only the most stringent punishment for their atrocious crimes. Hence, when Tratika, the she-demon marched on Ramchandra with other demons, he killed her immediately, without a moment's thought. When Shoorpanakha, another she-demon, rushed to eat away Seeta like cucumber, Laxman deprived her of nose and ears and sent her back—not honourably with generous gifts of ornaments to show off his chivalry to women! When Narakasur carried away thousands of Aryan women to his Asur kingdom (Assyria of to-day), Shree Krishna marched upon the demon and killed him in the war. But he did not stop with military and political defeat he inflicted on Narakasur! He rescued all the thousands of imprisoned Aryan females, undergoing all sorts of humiliation there, and brought them back to his own kingdom; and thus took a social revenge! Shree Krishna's army did not forsake their kinswomen, simply because they were forcibly polluted and violated—a dastardly thought which he never entertained

---

[44] Ibid, p. 159.

for a minute. On the contrary Shree Krishna as the Bhoopati, the Lord of the whole Earth, brought all those sixteen thousand or more women to his kingdom, rehabilitated them honourably and took upon himself the responsibility of feeding and protecting them. This very act of Krishna, as the Bhoopati, has been fantastically construed by the writers of the Puranas as to describe him the husband of those thousands of women. He was later thought to have married all of them . . .[45]

Two Facts

What the Hindutva State should be like, and what Hindus should do is evident from Savarkar's angry criticism of what Hindus did and failed to do. His advocacy—of 'super-savage cruelty', 'hyper-barbarity', 'retaliation', 'revenge', the bigger lie, 'super-cunning', 'super-reprisals', 'extreme violence', any pretext will do—establishes two facts beyond doubt:

- He was right in emphasizing that his 'Hindutva' is very different from 'Hinduism'—at least from what we have been taught Hinduism is
- In fighting the Islamic State through 'Hindutva', it is not a 'Hindu State' which will be established but the very thing Savarkar goaded it to fight—an Islamic State in saffron

The State

To be able to act in these ways, and to ensure that Hindu society lives by these values, the State, Savarkar maintained, would necessarily have to be a centralized State, a strong State not a loose, weak 'democracy':

Today everybody is praising democracy. That type of government is suitable where the voters are well educated and know how the

---

[45] Ibid, pp. 160–61.

democratic government machinery works. But in India where the voters are ignorant and do not know whom to vote and the elected representatives are also selfish it would bring about the ruin of Hindus. Therefore I would not recommend democracy. I would support any other form of government that would suit the interests of the Hindu nation.[46]

Godbole also reproduces what Savarkar said in Poona in 1961 at a celebration marking his birthday:

It is not good saying, this democracy or that democracy. What is more important is the public good. Instead of today's weak democracy (of Nehru) I would prefer thousand times one-man rule of Shivaji or Chandragupta. We have won independence. You do not know how easily you could lose it, if you keep on voting the men of straw time after time. Rajaji once said, the first duty of a government is to govern. I would not mind if we have a one-man government, so long as he makes India strong and powerful. That is thousand times preferable than the present government, which capitulates to every aggressor (i.e. China and Pakistan). It does not matter how we achieve it but we need a strong government. Once this is achieved, history will tell you that the processes and organisations that would give us national strength would lead to the change in the form of government at a later date. We do not need worry about that.[47]

Armed Might

Material strength, armed might, power in the large—that is what is required, Savarkar said. Not religiosity, not even literature. Leave Vedanta

---

[46] V.S. Godbole, *Rationalism of Veer Savarkar,* op. cit., epub, 451–52.

[47] Ibid, pp. 452–53.

to the Europeans and Americans.[48] We need to build factories, we need to acquire and manufacture arms, we need to join the army and learn the new ways of warfare. When the temples were being destroyed none of the gods enshrined in them came out to help. When the great library at Nalanda was burnt, it must have had thousands of great books and shastras in it, and so many scholars, pandits and Bhikkus. The pandits and Bhikkus, so learned though they were, could do nothing to stop or prevent the fire. As for the books so full of learning, they only helped the fire rage even more fiercely.

---

[48] Writing from the Andamans, Savarkar observed:

I wish that such popular series as the *Bharat Gaurav Mala* realize their responsibility of guiding and not only tickling the popular fancy and so publish every now and then political history, science and economy, e.g. Mill's Representative Government, etc. About the books on Vedanta philosophy, well, I fear it is not opportune that such men should be busy with such things. The Americans need Vedanta philosophy, and so does England; for they have developed their life to that fullness, richness and manliness—to Kshatriyahood and so stand on the threshold of that Brahminhood, wherein alone the capacity to read and realize such philosophy can co-exist. But India has not. We are at present all *Shus* [shudras] and cannot claim access to the Veda and Vedanta. That is the underlying idea why shudras were not allowed to study Vedas; not, certainly not, for cruelty, nor for narrow or vested interest—otherwise Puranas would not have been written by the very Brahmins expounding the same philosophy more lucidly. We, as a Nation, are unfit for these sublime thoughts, for it is well known that Bajirao II was a great Vedantist and that is why, perhaps, he could not see the difference between a kingdom and a pension. Let us study history, political science, science, economy, live worthily in this world, fulfil the *grihashram*—the householder's duties—and then the *vaanuh thaum* and its philosophic dawn might come. And whatever these works are meant to do, they might be left to be written by widows, old men and pensioners out of offices. They should live in the past—old works and old puzzles of God and soul and man. The young, the youth—why not live in the future? Talk of Vedanta!— Benares has not produced a single martyr and they cannot give up a farthing for their fatherland!!! [V.D. Savarkar, *Letters from Andamans*, Letter 3, 15 February, 1914, www.savarkar.org, p. 9.]

The people of each religion have claimed that the one true God is on their side, Savarkar wrote. So long as they were winning—think of the period when Islamic armies swept over the Middle East, North Africa, southern Europe, India—they pointed to those victories as proof of the facts that their God was the one true God and *that* God was with them. But soon, they were vanquished by the very people—say, the Christians of Europe—they had crushed. Now the Christians pointed to *their* victories as proof of the same facts: *their* God was the one true God, and He was on *their* side. The fact is that Islamic armies had swept over the others because Islamic kingdoms were united at the time and their military strength and tactics were superior to those of the Christians. When this balance was turned, the Christians prevailed. That is why it is not our Gods whom we have to please, we have to build a stronger army, we have to out-do our enemies in arms and ammunition, and we have to be more united as a people. Asked for a message on his 59th birthday, Savarkar replied that he had only one message: *'Hinduise politics, militarise the Hindu race.'*[49] The form of government—democracy or its opposite—is but a means to this end, he said. If it does not help achieve that end, it has to be replaced.

---

[49] The birthday fell in May 1941. At that time, Savarkar was at pains to justify aligning with the British, and his campaign to enrol Hindus into the British Army. The passage in *Savarkar Samagra* is as follows:

I have just one message: Hinduise politics, militarise the Hindu race. Whatever politics is beneficial to the Hindu rashtra internationally and nationally, adopt only that. That which is harmful to the Hindu interest is to be shed, it is sin. It really should be uprooted. On the principle of equality, one should not assault the lawful rights of anyone. But not to let anyone assault the lawful rights of Hindus, this being the *sootra* of Hindu politics, it is impossible for the Hindu race to go against not just what is required for the good of the nation but it is also impossible for it to go against the interests of humanity. As a notice of this Hindu statecraft, do not cast a single vote for any Congress candidate or any candidate who is not devoted to the philosophy of Hindutva. [*Savarkar Samagra*, Volume VIII, p. 554.]

Singular Aim

And the State has to have one exclusive, singular aim: it must work for its interests alone. Actually, that is too wide a formulation. In Savarkar's view, it has to work in the interests of the Hindu rashtra alone. In striving for these, as we have seen, it is not to be constrained by any fetish of morality or ethics. The means he advocates turn out to be the very means he accuses Muslims of deploying, the very Muslims he calls rakshasas, barbarians, and much else.

The One Trait of Muslims He Admired

The first prerequisite is to suffuse the people with a pan-Hindu consciousness. Savarkar maintained, as we have seen, that this permeated, and had always permeated every section of Hindu society—in 1857, for instance, from Mangal Pandey to Rani of Jhansi; that it underlay every battle, that it pervaded the relentless resistance that Hindus put up against conquerors. On the other hand, he also bewailed the fact that this consciousness had been lost and had to be rekindled.

It was the one thing that he admired in Muslims—their religious zeal, their pride in their religion, their commitment to restoring Muslim rule over India, their identification with Islamic empires elsewhere. Even a few passages from his account of his experiences in the Andamans will give a glimpse of what struck Savarkar. Turkey enters the war on the side of Germany. This sends a thrill down the spines of the Pathan guards, Savarkar writes. And when they hear that the Amir of Afghanistan has joined the Turks, their excitement knows no bounds. They begin believing all sorts of extravagant rumours—Muslim rule is going to be re-established over India; Enver Pasha has 'decimated thousands of British regiments'; he has taken Basra. The Amir has taken Lahore one day, Sirhind another. The Kaiser has taken London . . .

But behind the ridiculous behaviour of the Pathans there was one quality which I never failed to impress upon those who simply laughed at them. I always asked my Hindu brethren not to forget how enthused they [the Muslim guards] were, to a man, over the prospect of Muslim Raj in India, or over the invasion of India by a Muslim power. This pride of race and religion was a virtue worthy of emulation, and it was this pride that would instantly translate itself into action at the right moment and with the right opportunity. The Hindus lacked this pride, this fervour, this unity of action, and, therefore, they had suffered.

This was a matter of compliment for the Pathans but was full of menace to the Hindus, and the Hindus must be ever vigilant about it. Eternal vigilance was the price of liberty. Also they had to bear it well in mind that the Mussulman imbibed this religious fervour and this spirit of Pan-Islamism with his mother's milk. In every Muslim household he was taught from his childhood to love his religion and to stand by the Muslim Raj. What had the Hindus to show in comparison with this fervour, with this ardent, burning passion? Not one in ten thousand Hindus knew or cared to know what was Hindusthan, what was Hindu power, Hindu Raj, or the meaning of the term Hindu. What then of a common bond of sympathy among them? The Pathans had, at the moment, only one place to call their own and that was Kabul. But they swear by it at all times, while they eat, drink and sleep. The Hindus have a place which is their own, but very few know of it, and know that the place goes by the name of . . .[50]

I omit the name of the place for now as an exercise for the reader: today, all the more so, but even then, the place and its supposed power would have

---

[50] *My Transportation for Life*, op. cit., pp. 338–40.

appeared as a fantasy of Savarkar. But it was a recurring fantasy, and we will return to it later.

In the book that he had written earlier, *Hindu Pad-padshahi*,[51] Savarkar had commended for emulation more than mere pan-Islamic consciousness and pride. Muslim invaders prevailed because they had, and the Hindus did not, 'fierce unity of faith, that social cohesion and valorous fervour ... the irresistible strength in the principle of theocratic unity, indissolubly wedded to a sense of duty to reduce all the world to a sense of obedience to a theocracy, and Empire under the direct supervision of God ... fanatical fury and greed.' In the ensuing centuries, he wrote, the Hindus too 'became more conscious of those ties that united them as a people and marked them out as a nation than the factors that divided them.'[52] But there was much more to be imbibed: 'the fierce unity of faith, social cohesion, valorous fervour ... theocratic unity ... fanatical fury ...' By implication, these and similar traits are what the Hindutva State and society has to have.

Once again, we reach the same point: the Hindutva State becomes an Islamic State *sans* Islam.

National Language, Calendar, Flag

Of course, Savarkar urged several other things. Sanskrit-*nishtha* Hindi in Devanagri script to be the national language. Foreign words, in particular Urdu words and those based on Persian or Arabic, must be purged.[53]

---

[51] V.D. Savarkar, *Hindu Pad-padshahi, Or a review of the Hindu Empire of Maharashtra,* B.G. Paul & Co, Madras, 1925.

[52] Ibid, pp. 226–29.

[53] Savarkar reiterated this time and again—for instance, in his Presidential Speech to the 21st session of the Hindu Mahasabha at Calcutta in 1939. Several speeches and essays on Sanskrit-*nishtha* Hindi as the national language written in Devanagri script are collected in Veer Savarkar, *Hamari Samasyaein,* Rajpal & Sons, Delhi, no date. He began proposing Hindi as the national language while he was confined in the Cellular Jail: Cf., *My Transportation for Life,* op. cit., pp. 458–72. And *Savarkar Samagra,* for instance Volume VII, pp. 448–61; on reforming the script Volume IX, pp. 625–722.

Cities must be renamed—Ahmedabad to be Karnavati, Allahabad to be Prayagraj, Punjab to be Panchnad, etc. And what are today countries also—Burma to be Brahmadesh. The country is to run by the Hindu calendar. And while local languages and scripts, flags of organizations shall be respected, like the local *panchaang,* all must subscribe to what has been accepted as the national language, the national flag, the national calendar. His prescription was:

Ek Deva, ek desh, ek bhaashaa
Ek jaati, ek jeev, ek aashaa[54]

As for the national flag, when the Constituent Assembly adopted the Tricolour as our national flag, Savarkar said that the one good feature he saw in the Tricolour that had been adopted as the national flag by the Constituent Assembly was that the spinning wheel of the Congress flag had been replaced by the chakra. He claimed that this had been done because he had urged the Flag Committee to make the change. In any case, it is not 'Ashoka Chakra' but the 'Dharma Chakra'—Ashoka had it inscribed on the Sarnath pillar to commemorate the 'Dharma Chakra Parivartan' discourse the Buddha had delivered after his enlightenment; and so it is the 'Dharma Chakra'. But the insignia had to be pulled away not just from that villain, Ashoka, but also from the Buddha! And so, 'The second merit of adopting the Chakra,' he said, 'is that it reminded us of one of the Glorious

---

[54] That prescription was preceded by two other vows. He would recall that in 1908-10 when they lived in India House, before going to bed the youngsters "would stand and in all seriousness repeat the national vow. Among it were these two resolves:

> *Hindi ko rashtra bhasha karoongaa*
> *Nagri ko rashtra lipi karoonga*
> *Ek Dev, ek desh, ek bhasha*
> *Ek jaati, ek jeev, ek aashaa*"
> [Cf., for instance, *'Rashtra bhasha aur rashtra lipi,'* in *Hamari Samasyaein,* op. cit., pp. 49–50.]

Epochs of Hindu history: of the time when Chanakya and Chandragupta Maurya drove back the armies of Alexander and Seleucos.' That said, 'I must emphatically state it [the Tricolour] can never be recognised as the National Flag of Hindusthan,' he declared. He gave two reasons—he repeated these on subsequent occasions also:

> Firstly, because the State of Indian Union and the so-called Constituent Assembly are the creation of the British will and not of the free choice of our people ascertained by a national plebiscite and their ultimate sanction even to-day is the British bayonet and not the national consent or national strength. Secondly, the very mention of the Indian Union reminds us of the break-up of the Unity of India as a nation and a State, the vivisection of our Motherland, and the treacherous Congressite abetment of that crime. How can a genuine nationalist salute such a Flag adopted by such a party with no mandate from the nation as a National Flag!

What then is to be the National Flag?

> The authoritative Flag of Hindusthan, our Motherland and Holyland, undivided and indivisible from the Indus to the Seas, can be no other than the Bhagava with the Kundalini and the Kripan inscribed on it to deliver expressly the message of the very Being of our Race! It is not made to order but it is self-evolved with the evolution of our National Being. It mirrors the whole panorama of our Hindu History, is actually worshipped by millions on millions of Hindus and is already flying from the summits of the Himalayas to the Southern Seas. Other Party Flags will be tolerated, some may even be respected in corresponding courtesy but Hindudom at any rate can loyally salute no other Flag but this Pan-Hindu Dhwaja, this Bhagava Flag, as its National Standard.[55]

---

[55] V.D. Savarkar, *Historic Statements,* S.S Savarkar, Bombay 1967, pp. 126–27; statement issued on 29 July 1947—a week after the Constituent Assembly adopted the National Flag.

At a function to venerate the *bhagvaa dhwaj* in Poona, on 3 August 1947, he repeated these objections, added a slight concession, and an emphatic exhortation:

> This Constituent Assembly is not ours. It stands on the strength of British arms, and on which we do not have faith, such is the Constituent Assembly.[56] This is not an Assembly that has been chosen by the nation—bear this in mind. Even though this is the case, in the flag approved by it there is the *Dharmachakra*. That is God's *Chakra*. The emblem of Emperor Harsha.
>
> This was the emblem of the army of Emperor Chandragupta and Chanakya when it had succeeded in extending their boundary up to Hindukush, Gandhar. In other words, this *Chakra* is not that of Ashoka—history testifies to this.
>
> We are told that the colours do not denote communities. Then, why such love for just these three colours? If one is talking of attractiveness, I do not have anything to say.

A little concession:

> We should not disrespect this flag. I will not feel upset if it is respected.

And immediately:

> But do not forget that this is the flag of the Indian Union. But when we do not accept the Indian Union after Pakistan has been hacked off from it—where then is the question of the flag of that Indian Union?

Also, *Savarkar Samagra*, Volume VIII, pp 639–40. He explained, that 'Kundalini [was] to signify the spiritual pursuits and achievements of our people, and the Kripan [was] to signify power and fighting spirit.'

[56] Recall that in speech after speech at election-time—for instance, in the run-up to the 1945 elections—Savarkar used to exhort people to vote for Hindu Mahasabha candidates on the ground, among others, that the result would determine who mans the Constituent Assembly!

We know only of *Akhand Hindusthan* [applause]. And the flag of that should only be *bhagva*. [Slogans venerating the *bhagva dhwaj*, and clapping.] This is like sacrificing the head and accepting the torso of one's mother. It is very distressing. It is like giving up the Khyber Valley and trying to protect the remainder. How shameful is this situation.

That *bhagva dhwaj* used to remind us of the valour of our ancestors, it does so today and will continue to do so in the future. The very same as our *bhagva dhwaj* with the *Kundalini* and the *Kripan*. And that is the *dhwaj* that should be our *rashtra dhwaj*. Whoever wants to make Hindusthan *akhand*, whoever wants to take back Pakistan, he will have to accept the *bhagva dhwaj* with the Kundalini and the *Kripan* as the *rashtra dhwaj*. [applause] If Hindu Dharma has a *dhwaj*, then this is the *dhwaj* . . . It is under this flag that the forces of the Peshwas shattered the throne of Delhi . . . It is the symbol of consciousness within the body . . . It is the *dhwaj* that was unfurled over Attock . . . To those who ask where is the tradition of this *dhwaj* of yours, I ask where is the tradition of your *dhwaj*? It is the hoary tradition of just 27 years, isn't it? [laughter and applause]. If you will respect our *dhwaj*, then we shall definitely respect your *dhwaj*. If the green flag of the enemy will be opposed then it will be by this *bhagva dhwaj* alone. [applause] The *bhagva dhwaj* is the one that has torn the green flag to shreds, not your flag of the Indian Union.

Die for the *bhagva dhwaj*, go to the gallows for it, let the entire generation die. It is possible that the situation may arise tomorrow when the one who considers the flag of the Indian Union approved by the Constituent Assembly to be the *rashtra dhwaj* shall be looked upon as a traitor. But bear in mind—should such a situation arise, then for ensuring respect for the *bhagva dhwaj*, for ensuring, for protecting the respect for it, go to prison, kill, be killed, go to the gallows. Even if the generation sitting in the front perishes, it will succeed in the time to come. Keep the *bhagva dhwaj* as the *dhwaj* of the Hindu rashtra.[57]

A Must

As we would expect from Savarkar's denunciation of those seven *swadeshi bandies,* he emphasized repeatedly the imperative of *shuddhi*—that we must resist conversion by all means, we must convert persons from other religions and reconvert back into Hinduism those who have been converted to other religions.

Numbers themselves are important, he wrote. After all, when one Hindu becomes a Mussalmaan or a Christian, it is not just that person who has been lost. The generations that will follow too will grow up in those other religions. Moreover, the injury is greater, far greater than mere numbers. A person who is converted to another religion loses his nationality, he wrote. The person disowns his ancestors. He disowns and will soon learn to denounce everything that his ancestors venerated. He will strain to prove his loyalty to the new community he has joined or has been forced to join, and that means that he will exert to bring harm to Hindus, Hinduism, Hindu rashtra. Aurangzeb and Tipu, Savarkar pointed out, were sons of converted Hindu mothers.

In a word, resist conversion to other religions. *Shuddhi* for those who were converted or whose ancestors were converted. The simplest ceremony. Embrace those who come back . . .

The procedure for taking the person back into the fold of Hinduism must be as simple as can be: he or she may be asked to eat a *tulsi* leaf, to repeat a mantra, to take a dip in a nearby river. The ceremony is not important. The heart must be transformed.

---

[57] *Savarkar Samagra,* Volume VII, pp. 368–70.

Each of us, he repeated in lecture after lecture, essay after essay, can play a part—especially in transforming the heart. We can welcome the person back, we can resume social relations with him or her and their family, we can invite the person to our houses to share meals with us. This is where we are letting our society and ourselves down, he would tell audiences. He would cite cases of persons and groups who had come back and were distressed that, even though they had done so, their fellow-Hindus kept them at a distance, even spurned them. We should reverse this. As he did in programmes for abolishing untouchability, he would make his audiences chant, 'Sparsh karoongaa, Svikaar karoongaa.' He often spoke about the work of Swami Shraddhanand, of Masurkar Maharaj, and urged people to donate funds to persons and organizations that are engaged in conversion and *shuddhi* work.

Savarkar cited authorities from the past—Medhatithi, Deval—who had urged *shuddhi*. He cited precedents—Shivaji himself welcomed back persons into the Hindu fold, Savarkar would point out. Because of greed and some bodily tormenting, Bajaji Nimbalkar became a Mussalmaan, he recalled. Shivaji did not just bring him back into the Hindu fold through *shuddhi*, he honoured the family of Nimbalkar by marrying a daughter from his own family into the family of the latter. In the same way, the Maratha commander, Netaji Palkar had fallen into the hands of the Mughals. He had been forcibly converted to Islam and sent off to the Frontier by Aurangzeb. He had somehow returned to Maharashtra and sought to be converted to Hinduism. The matter went to Shivaji. He saw to it that he was accepted back as a Hindu again through *shuddhi* . . . [58]

So, *shuddhi*.

---

[58] *Savarkar Samagra*, Volume V, pp. 463–64. Also *Hindu Pad-padshahi*, op. cit., pp 269–70.

Three Other Programmes and Practices He Praised

We have already encountered Savarkar's admiration for what in his reckoning Mussolini and Hitler had accomplished for their people and countries, and his repeated admonition that what they did at home was no concern of ours. We should admire them for what they have accomplished, he said. We should be grateful for the help they have given us in the past, he said. It would be wrong to attribute those speeches lauding Hitler's Germany as having been triggered merely by unexpected successes of Hitler in 1938/39. To do so would be to lose sight of the admiration that Savarkar had for several of the actual tenets and practices of the Nazi State.

Improving The Breed

Consider a single example—Nazi eugenics, the project of the Nazi regime to breed 'perfect' Aryan children. Under this project men and women were selected and paired by officers of the State so as to produce children who would raise even higher the 'superiority' of the Aryan race. Children who turned out to be 'defectives', so to say, were culled. One segment of the programme was run by the SS, and was a special priority of Himmler himself. Leap decades. Savarkar is writing his book, *Six Glorious Epochs*. He is eighty years old, confined to bed, as he reminds us several times during the book. He holds up two ancient Republics of the Hindus—Saubhootis and Katha—as having had a democratic constitution:

> The constitution of both these republics was democratic. Writes a Greek writer Diodoros, 'they were governed by laws in the highest degree salutary and their political system was admirable.'

That is all about their democracy. He reserves the bulk of his account about them for a particular programme of the two republics and for the thoroughness with which they enforced it. Here is what Savarkar writes:

35. One special feature of these republics was that with a view to promoting healthy, strong and handsome progeny, the procreation of human species was not left to individual whims and fancies, but was controlled by the State. They were very fond of physical beauty. Hence marriages were arranged not with an eye on the handsome dowry, but with proper consideration of mutual physical fitness, beauty and health, and the ability of the bride and the bridegroom to bring forth healthy and sturdy children . . . Their laws regarding the proper production of human species were so strict that within three months of their birth children were medically examined by the State authorities, and if a child were found with some native defect or to be suffering from some incurable disease or deformed, it was immediately put to death under State orders without any mercy.

35A. Readers of history know well that Republic of Sparta had similar laws about heredity.

36. Though not so very strict and ruthless as the Saubhootis and the Kathas, there were other Ganas or republics in India who paid special attention to heredity, and the bringing forth of strong and handsome children . . .[59]

Such ideas were not very original. In the late nineteenth and early twentieth century, variants of these ideas were in wide circulation in Europe and America—through books, pamphlets, the press, in academia and political circles. That certain races—Asians, Blacks, Yellows—and certain groups—Jews, Gypsies—are inferior. That the Nordic race is superior—in Germany, 'Nordic' came to be particularized as 'Aryan', and that as German. That for humanity to continue to progress, the superior race must multiply, it must prevail; the inferior races must function as the slaves and servants of the superior race. That being the case, all means required to ensure that the superior race prevails are justified, indeed they are mandated. Every

---

[59] *Six Glorious Epochs in Indian History,* op. cit., pp 25–26.

supposition, every argument, every scruple, every teaching that weakens the resolve of the superior race to vanquish and replace the inferior race is immoral—it is coming in the way of human progress. Therefore, only that which enables the superior race to prevail is moral; what comes in the way of its progress is immoral.[60] Indeed, at many a turn, the very sentences seem to have been plucked from publications that were common in late nineteenth and early twentieth century Europe.

It would be a great mistake to take such praise, such fascination to be the fleeting emotion of some adolescent. Remember that it occurs in *Six Glorious Episodes*—the book was written when Savarkar was in his late seventies, early eighties, it was the last book he wrote. He was distilling models from history so that generations to come emulate them.

There is another reason to pay the closest attention to Savarkar's commending such examples. The premises underlying such a practice underlie Savarkar's programme, they are the very foundation of his 'ethics':

- The Hindu nation, like all individuals, groups, nations, States is engaged in a struggle for survival
- In this struggle, the fittest, the strongest alone will survive
- Indeed, only the fittest and strongest *should* survive—else the progress of that group, of the Hindu nation and State will be impeded, and it will fall prey to the stronger ones
- Therefore, everything that is required for strengthening the Hindu nation and its progress is moral; anything, any teaching, any activity which weakens it is immoral
- Therefore, as one lemma, only those who are fit and strong enough to contribute to that struggle can be allowed to survive

---

[60] Numerous studies speak to this. See, for instance, Andre Pichot, *The Pure Society, From Darwin to Hitler*, David Fernbach [tr.], Verso, London, 2009; and Richard Weikart, *From Darwin to Hitler, Evolutionary Ethics, Eugenics, and Racism in Germany*, Palgrave, Macmillan, New York, 2004.

With the singular difference that they were advocated in favour of the 'Nordic'/ 'Aryan'/ 'German' race, these were the premises that constituted the foundation for Nazi eugenics. The 'theses' advocating that programme, the course that the programme took show the other devilish feature of such pursuits and fascinations: programmes that set out to 'improve' human stock swiftly mutate into programmes to weed out the 'inferior'.

Like the republics that so fascinated Savarkar, the Nazis set out to populate their nation with the 'superior' lot. For this, they selected handsome men and women to cohabit and produce children. To this was added the natural corollary: to sterilize the deficient, the unfit. And then the next natural step: to eliminate the unfit. The list—in the literature, much of that consisting of scholarly volumes, as well as official policy—of those who were unfit kept ballooning. It started with malformed children. To this were added the 'mentally deficient', the 'abnormal', the 'defective', the 'degenerate', those suffering from neurological problems, those with genetic illnesses. The Physicians' Ordinance of 1935 made it the duty of doctors to report such patients to the authorities. To categories such as the foregoing were added 'weaklings', those suffering from 'incurable diseases'. And soon enough, the 'old'. All these categories were dubbed as being a 'burden on society', to be 'useless', to be of 'negative value'. Soon, the programme corralled entire groups—Gypsies, for instance. '. . . in 1944,' we read, 'the Nazis considered extending extermination to common-law criminals who were ugly (whatever their crime), this ugliness being considered proof of their insufficient humanity . . .'

Children were taken from cradles in hospitals. Patients were taken from lunatic asylums. The elderly were taken from hospices. From 275,000 to thrice that number are estimated to have been killed in this pursuit. Some were killed by injections, some were gassed, some were starved to death . . .

The killings were not just benefiting the Nazi State and nation, it was said. They were 'mercy killings', it was said. Through them, the State was sparing the individuals—the 'defectives' as well as their relatives—the suffering which would otherwise have been their unavoidable fate.[61]

Remember three things. This programme to improve the racial stock by both 'positive' and 'negative' measures predated the War. Second, remember, that this was independent of the 'final solution' to the 'Jewish problem'. Third, the change it wrought was not limited to these hundreds of thousands. The pursuit upturned discourse, it upturned ethics. Kindness, compassion, charity became perversities that weaken a nation by keeping the weak and defective alive. Hunting the weaklings and defectives out, injecting poisons into them, gassing them, starving them became 'manly'. They equipped one better for serving the Fatherland. Performing them became a duty towards the Nazi State and the Aryan nation.

'The Splendid . . . Magnificent . . . Tradition'

The second practice writing about which sent Savarkar into raptures was *jauhar*. He called it a 'splendid tradition', 'this magnificent and awe-inspiring tradition', 'this martyrdom, this noblest type of self-sacrifice', 'the age-long glorious tradition'. Sounds strange? Well, here are a few examples from just one book:

> 66. We generally believe that this magnificent and awe-inspiring tradition of 'johar' or self-immolation of large groups of men and women in times of national crisis was originally practised by the Rajputs only. But instances, like the one just mentioned, cited by

---

[61] For all this, as a beginning see the volumes that I have cited earlier: Andre Pichot, *The Pure Society, From Darwin to Hitler*, David Fernbach [tr.], Verso, London, 2009, in particular Chapter 11; and Richard Weikart, *From Darwin to Hitler, Evolutionary Ethics, Eugenics, and Racism in Germany*, Palgrave, Macmillan, New York, 2004, especially Chapter 1, 'The origin of ethics and the rise of moral relativism'; Chapter 5, 'The spectre of inferiority: Devaluing the disabled and "Unproductive" '; Chapter 6, 'The science of racial inequality'; Chapter 8, 'Killing the "unfit" '; Chapter 10, 'Racial struggle and extermination'; and Chapter 11, 'Hitler's ethics'.

the Greek writers who were astounded to witness them, go to prove that, even before the name of the Rajputs was ever heard of, this splendid tradition was followed by our Indian warriors right from the ancient days. The word 'johar' is comparatively modern. It was perhaps derived from the war-cry *'Jai Har'*. The Indian God of war and destruction is *'Har! Har! Mahadev!!'* That is why the Indians fought desperately inspired by this deafening war-cry! The Marathas too used the same war-cry *'Har, Har, Mahadev!'* After fighting to the last, when every hope of success was over, or every chance of escape from the enemy was lost, this Johar, this martyrdom, this noblest type of self-sacrifice was resorted to by the Hindus as the last unfailing weapon to save their religion, their nation, their own self-respect and to avoid captivity, abject slavery and hateful conversion! As soon as all men of fighting age were slain on the battlefield after taking the greatest toll of the enemy blood, their wives, mothers, daughters, hundreds of them, with babies at their breasts, used to leap into the burning pyres, specially kept ready for the purpose, and were reduced to ashes. This was what was known as 'Johar'! It was not an easy job. It was the limit of valour and endurance for the sake of keeping up the prestige of one's self and one's own religion!

67. Whoever had donned this exceptional armour of 'Johar' and its leaping flames were beyond all attempts of an Alexander, an Allaudin or a Salim—why, even of Satan himself—to pollute them and convert them to his religion! Confronted with this horrible sacrificial fire the enemy stood aghast, discomfited and crest-fallen.[62]

A few pages later, writing about 'the martial spirit and prowess of Vedic Hindus in Kamboj, Gandhar, Panchnad [his name for Punjab] straight to Sind,' he remarks,

---

[62] Ibid, pp. 25–26.

Not only the Kshatriyas there, but in some of the states all the citizens, men and women, young or old, took the field to face the aggressive foreign enemy. Where unfortunately a certain republic got beaten, the brave Indian ladies there leapt into the fire with the dauntless children . . . at their breasts![63]

Yet again. Jalalludin, the uncle of Allaudin, is defeated at Ranthambor. And, Rana Bheemsingh of Chitod has refused to turn over his wife, Padmini, to Allaudin:

732. In order to avenge the defeat inflicted by the Rajputs in this battle and for the sake of Padmini, Allauddin once again invaded Chitod in A.D. 1303, when once again the brave Rajputs donned the 'Kesaria' (saffron garments) and fought till the end, slaying hundreds of Muslims, and died to a man. Seeing the victory smile upon the Muslims and fortune darken upon the Rajputs, about ten thousand Rajput women, including Rani Padmini, leapt into the blazing fire with their children at their breasts. Allauddin conquered Chitod, only to collect the ashes of Padmini! When the Hindu warriors and Hindu women fought, they fought thus![64]

Glorification of the practice occurs at several other places also. The Rajputs of Chitod have turned down Akbar's overtures. Akbar lays siege to the fort of Chitod:

946. The Rana of Chitod at that time was Uday Singh, who had not even a small percentage of the dauntless valour of his celebrated father, Rana Sang, who had earlier fought with Babar. But the one courtesan who was at that time wielding real power in Chitod inspired the

---

[63] Ibid, pp. 62–63.
[64] Ibid, pp. 258–59.

Rajputs to extraordinary valour. Even when Uday Singh fled away to the forest, the great feudatory lords of Chitod like Jaymalla, Patta and others continued to fight with the Moghals. Later when Jaymalla and Patta were killed on the battle-field and defeat was absolutely certain, the Rajput Hindus of Chitod instead of becoming dispirited and dis-heartened were touched to the quick and infuriated to the extreme. All the soldiers desperately entered the battle-field and with the war-cry 'Har, Har Mahadev' heaped up mounds of the massacred Muslim warriors. But ultimately when the Rajputs themselves were almost killed in the battle, all the Rajput ladies of Chitod set ablaze the big fire which was kept ready for the purpose and leapt therein from the ramparts of the fort according to their age-long glorious tradition, with small children at their breasts and the acclamations in praise of their religion on their lips. These brave ladies reduced themselves to ashes but did not allow the hateful Muslim-touch to defile their pure bodies! This was the third great self-immolation by the ladies of Chitod.[65]

Even more than *Jauhar*, Savarkar admires assassination that, in his view, has to be executed at times as a national duty. The setting for them covers eighty pages of his book, *Six Glorious Epochs of Indian History*. And I do hope you will read them as they illustrate how Savarkar wants our history to be written. For the moment, we will just have to rush through them.

'Simply a National Duty'

Alexander has invaded India. 'In India he had to face the bitterest opposition at every step,' Savarkar writes. 'Although he never lost a battle as such, his Greek army was completely exhausted and exasperated in the very process of winning them. These victories were far too costlier [sic.]

---

[65] Ibid, pp. 338–39.

than the ones in Persia, and all their vauntful declarations of conquering India as easily as Persia proved to be empty words . . .'[66] Alexander appoints governors—two Greek, two Indian—and leaves. He hears that 'local democratic institutions [have] refused to accept his over-lordship,' and that revolts are brewing in Gandhar and Panchnad to overthrow him completely. 'But Alexander could at that time do nothing to thwart any such attempts at revolt. During his campaign against India not only his army but he himself was completely exhausted . . .' He dies on the way. '. . . some of the Indian politicians began hatching out a secret plan against the Greeks in the Punjab to win back their lost freedom. But it was not merely aimed at the recovery of the lost territory. It was essentially to overhaul and revolutionize the whole gamut of the political life of India and to bring about a sweeping change in the internal life of the country. Even if Alexander had not died so soon, the deep-laid Indian plot was destined to achieve this daring political revolution.' The two Greek Governors are beheaded . . . Within six months all signs of Greek rule are erased. Who were the 'Indian politicians' who conspired to get rid of the Greeks? 'History as yet is ignorant of their names! Still two of them at least have become immortal! . . . The first was a brilliant and smart youth, who had just completed his studies at the University of Taxila, Chandragupta! And the other was Acharya Chanakya, who had been a teacher at that University and who later on gave practical lessons in political craft and political revolutions to the young Chandragupta!'

Mahapadmanand, whom we have encountered earlier, is the emperor—and this is only because he is the brother of the previous emperor. His only obsession seems to be to amass wealth—people call him 'Dhanananda'. People are disgusted with his extravagances and his unwillingness to face the Greeks. Fearing that Chandragupta—his son from his concubine, Mura, or the son of someone else from Mura—will become the rallying point for a revolt, Mahapadmanand banishes him. Chandragupta reaches

---

[66] Ibid, pp. 28–29.

Taxila, where Chanakya is teaching. Together they gather an army and invade Magadha. In the melee, Mahapadmanand escapes. He is caught and beheaded.[67]

Chandragupta is succeeded by Bindusar. He too is brave. Extends his empire to the south. Succeeded by his son, Ashoka. Embraces Buddhism. Enforces Buddhism. Incalculable harm to India. Dies after ruling for 25 years. As the empire has been weakened to the extreme, within 30 years of his death, the Bactrian Greeks invade.

Brihadrath, a descendant of Ashoka, is the emperor. Incapable of doing anything about the Greeks. 'Perhaps that Buddhist King was trying to win over the Greeks by his unrestrained observance of the Buddhistic principle of "non-resistance" and the one which preached, "Anger should be conquered by the negation of anger" and was trying to succeed in the application of the Buddhistic doctrine by keeping indoors!' Wave of anger among Vedic Hindus, especially in Kalinga and Andhra—'The kings of both these provinces were staunch followers of the Vedic religion and so equally staunch Indian patriots.' Kharvela, the king of Kalinga, takes on the task and routs the Greeks.

Buddhists turn traitors, sympathize with and help the Greeks.

Vedic Hindus decide to overthrow Brihadrath Maurya.

184. The Vedic community and their leaders in North India had already experienced a surge of heroic spirit because of the victory of the brave Kharvela of Kalinga. To add to it the news arrived of Menander's menacing invasion! Besides, the Indian Buddhist populace showed clear signs of defection and betrayal of their co-nationalists to Menander. The nationalist Indian leaders, therefore, formed a revolutionary body with a view to dethrone the vacillating and weak Brihadrath Maurya from the royal seat of Magadha and

---

[67] Ibid, paras 71 to 119, pp. 32–51.

replace him with one of the Vedic sect, who was of proven metal like Chandragupta Maurya. But everybody was confronted with the difficult question as to who was there so bold and powerful as to take the lead in this national revolution and to destroy the Yavanas (the Greeks) completely.

They turn to Pushyamitra, who has been Commander-in-Chief of Brihadrath's army. During the hustle-bustle of a military parade, Pushyamitra executes Brihadrath by severing his head.

Savarkar's conclusion:

189. This unexpected and horrible turn of events caused a great furore in the large crowd assembled there. But did any of the armed warriors or anyone from those of the royal household who were sitting near King Brihadrath attack General Pushyamitra? No, not at all. On the contrary, the whole army hailed him as their leader.

190. For, General Pushyamitra had done exactly what the soldiers themselves and many others wanted to do but could not, as nobody in the whole of India dared shoulder the responsibility for such an hazardous deed. Pushyamitra had simply done the unavoidable national duty of killing Asoka's descendant, Brihadrath Maurya, who had proved himself thoroughly incompetent to defend the independence of the Indian empire.

191. Chandragupta and Chanakya had to assassinate, as an unavoidable national duty, Samrat Mahapadmanand who had proved himself thoroughly incapable of repulsing the Greeks for the protection of the Indian empire and its independence at the time of the first Greek invasion of Alexander. Just for the same reason Pushyamitra had to cut off the head of Brihadrath Maurya, the nominal Buddhist emperor, simply as a national duty.[68]

---

[68] Ibid, p. 78.

Consequences

We have already noted two.

The values that Savarkar declared the Hindutva State must have made the State exactly what he declared he was fighting against, an Islamic State.

Second, the means he championed were the very means that the ones he was denouncing, Muslims, deployed—untruth, cruelty and the rest. His devotees become indistinguishable from the ones he hates.

The consequences of his advocacy do not stop with those two. Indeed, they just set the stage for many more.

The 'Negative Example' to Bear in Mind

After all, an 'Islamic State' is not some disembodied figment of imagination. We see it in scores of countries. Pakistan, as we have seen earlier, provides a ready 'negative example'. We have seen earlier how they started by persecuting Ahmediyas. Then graduated to the Sunnis falling upon Shias. And then variants of Sunnis—Barelvis, Deobandis, Ahl-e-Hadis . . . falling on each other. Soon, the sects began organizing private armies and hit squads. Soon, the State machinery was patronizing one gang against another. Soon, the State machinery lost the capacity to control the gangs for it was itself riven by the same 'ideological' rifts. We can see where this sequence has got Pakistan. The same splintering and animosity are bound to occur among Hindus once they embrace the violent certainties and precepts of Savarkar, all the more so once they are liberated from ethical restraints as Savarkar most emphatically tries to liberate them.

Remember: just as the perfidy and violence of the 'other' rationalize our perfidy and violence, our perfidy and violence rationalize the other's perfidy and violence.

Hence: a dictatorship, a dictatorship that is all-powerful against individuals and simultaneously is weak, a dictatorship unable to confront feuding, violent, armed packs. That State held up by a society saturated with hate and vengeance. A society in which there is no place to escape that perverse State nor those murderous gangs. For one of the consequences of the hatred that Savarkar espouses is that his 'ideology' provides a rationalization to the neighbourhood bully as much as it does to the bureaucrat and judge. Pull out a truck driver and kill him; overturn the little basket of a helpless, poor bangle-seller and beat him up; frighten schoolgirls; beat up couples to deter 'love-jihad'; insist that people boycott shops owned by or employing Muslims; demand that Muslim tenants move out; bulldoze houses . . . Values erased. Norms gone. The fist is all. Soon the terror spreads to Hindus—those who speak up against such bulldozer treatment of citizens, those who raise any question about the one decreed version of faith . . . Society and State get bogged down in such issues. The essential tasks are neglected. Again, look at what Pakistani institutions and people have been preoccupied with since it declared itself to be an 'Islamic State', and the ditch into which it has descended as a result.

Nor is public life alone that is affected. The hatred, cruelty, barbarity, revenge and reprisals, 'extreme violence', untruth, cunning, deception that Savarkar mandates poison ordinary, day-to-day life as well. The place becomes unliveable. Those who have any skill, any asset that can help them vault away, leave. The State and society are left in the grip of worse and worse scoundrels.

No one is safe. Not even, in fact, certainly not a Gandhi. Who has weakened India by preaching *ahimsa*, who has been unable to stand up to the enemies of the Hindus, who has 'proved himself thoroughly incompetent to defend the independence of the Indian empire'—who it is who is guilty of all this is drilled into those unscrupulous, violent devotees by the Chanakya who has been giving 'practical lessons in political craft and political revolutions' . . . Among the devotees, a Godse who takes on the task that no one else dares to execute . . . And the historian writes,

This unexpected and horrible turn of events caused a great furore in the large crowd assembled there. But did any of the armed warriors or anyone from those of the royal household who were sitting near

King Brihadrath attack General Pushyamitra? No, not at all. On the contrary, the whole army hailed him as their leader.

For, General Pushyamitra had done exactly what the soldiers themselves and many others wanted to do but could not, as nobody in the whole of India dared shoulder the responsibility for such an hazardous deed. Pushyamitra had simply done the unavoidable national duty of killing Asoka's descendant, Brihadrath Maurya, who had proved himself thoroughly incompetent to defend the independence of the Indian empire.

Once you have indoctrinated devotees—do go through extracts from *Agrani,* the magazine Godse edited and Savarkar patronized, that we will come across soon—into believing who is selling the Hindus down the line, once you have indoctrinated them into believing who is responsible for cutting the Motherland in two, once you have indoctrinated them into believing who is weakening the Hindus by his incessant talk of *ahimsa* and truth and loving the enemy, once you have drilled the 'hard virtues' into them—revenge, retaliation, 'super-cruelty', 'hyper-barbarity', 'super-reprisals', 'extreme violence', 'super-cunning'—and once you have liberated them from all ethical shackles, you can sit back and relax, and write your next book. You don't have to procure pistols as of old. You don't have to give them any instructions. You don't have to bless them—'Succeed and return.' Someone among them will go and shoot the villain dead.

So Many Villains,
and a Saviour in Waiting

Savarkar's world is full of villains, of course. Akbar: *Din-I Ilahi* turns out
to have been a ploy of Akbar to get himself acclaimed as the *'paigambar'*,
as 'the spiritual lord of the human race'; a schemer and deceiver, 'heartless',
'this devilish destroyer', the one with 'fiendish fanaticism', he turns out to
have been as intolerant of Hindus as Allauddin and Aurangzeb.[1] Tipu in
Savarkar's eyes was 'Tipu Sultan, the savage': not a word that he is one
of the very few who defeated the British—a public holiday was declared
in England to mark his death; not a word that he ran an efficient state
apparatus—even the British who hated him referred to his domains as a
'garden'; the funds and facilities that he gives to temples turn out to have

---

[1] While concluding his account of Akbar Savarkar does allow a concession—but with a
caveat:

> 990-A. However, of the many great emperors that lived at the time in Europe or
> Africa or Asia, Akbar was the greatest in respect of his strategy, his wielding of
> the widest power, bravery, founding of a vast empire, his patronage of learning
> and arts and crafts. Although according to some writers he was illiterate, he
> patronized great authors and encouraged the writing of famous books! This
> comparative greatness history can concede to him, and we do not hesitate to call
> him as great as he really was. But with all that greatness he was, from our Hindu
> point of view, foreign, belonging to another religion and mean-minded and as
> such he should be decried by us, Hindus! [*Six Glorious Epochs of Indian History*,
> Abhishek Publications, Chandigarh, 2022, p. 357]

been given out of fear of the advancing Maratha armies . . . One feature in this long list of villains stands out: there is not one Englishman among them.

The three chief villains are the Buddha, Ashoka and, as you would guess, Gandhiji. And on Savarkar's telling they have one thing in common: each of them weakened India and thus left it an easy prey for predators.

The two communities that are villains are Buddhists and, as you would guess, Muslims. Again: not the British.

The 'Good Sportsman'

Quite the contrary. While talking of the British, he was, to use his expression, the 'good sportsman'. Savarkar's *Hindu Pad-padshahi* is devoted to arguing that the Marathas were the ones who broke the back of the Mughal Empire, that, among Indians, they were the ones best suited to do so, and establish a Hindu Empire. At the penultimate moment, the prize was stolen 'slyly' by the British. There is little in Savarkar's many books about the collaboration that helped the British triumph, the occasional traitor, yes, but little more than a passing allusion to wholesale collaboration by communities at large. The British were better equipped to take over from the Mughals, Savarkar wrote:

> For England was then relatively far better equipped in all those essentials that contributed to great conquests. Their nation had long since passed the period of incubation, civil feuds and Wars of the Roses and religious persecutions and star-chamber tyrannies. Unlike the Marathas, they had long been trained into all those public virtues of how to obey and order and of how to rule and submit, of patriotic loyalty to their country and their king—the national emblem of sovereignty—and, above all, racial cohesion and solidarity of aim and aspiration and loving subjection which a strongly consolidated nation-state engenders in a people. Even the Marathas—who of all

Indian people were the best fitted in all these qualities—were woefully lacking in them relatively to the English.

Still single-handed they [the Marathas] stood, they fought even frantically, knowing later on full well that it was a struggle for existence . . .[2]

And again on the next page:

We acknowledge that it is not without a keen agony that we write this epitaph on the grave of this our great national [Maratha] Empire. But we grudge not England her victory. Like a good sportsman we admire her skill and might that, stretching her hand over oceans and seas, over continents and countries, snatched an Indian Empire from our struggling hand, and on that Foundation has raised a magnificent World-Empire, the like of which history has scarcely recorded.[3]

The Buddha and His Devotee

Savarkar starts his account of 'some of the anti-national Buddhist preachings and practices' with a formal genuflection to the Buddha. 'I consider it my duty to state in the beginning—so that there may not be any misunderstanding or perversion of my views—,' he says, 'that on the whole, I have a very high regard for Lord Buddha and his religion. In Indian history there are several lofty Himalayan peaks of world famous personalities, and the name of one of those sublime heights is Bhagwan

---

[2] V.D. Savarkar, *Hindu Pad-padshahi, Or a review of the Hindu Empire of Maharashtra,* B.G. Paul & Co, Madras, 1925, p. 286.

[3] Ibid, p. 287.

Buddha! . . . The Hindu nation too, which gave birth to such a divine considers him the ninth incarnation of Lord Vishnu.'[4]

That this is just a formal bow becomes evident almost immediately. He asserts at great length that Buddhism did not decline for the reasons that are generally adduced. It was consciously erased by an enraged Hindu population because Buddhists turned traitors—they actively assisted invaders; and because its teachings weakened the country thereby leaving it incapable of fending off the foreign marauders. This weakening was not the work only of the Buddha's followers. It is not long before we find Savarkar pointing to 'the Greek states beyond the Indian border and farther off than these the more ferocious wild tribes of the Saka-Kushan-Hun type, who recognized "violence" as the only means of achieving their objectives were anxiously waiting for an opportunity to pounce, like a lion, on India,' but had been deterred thus far by the army built by Chandragupta and Chanakya. 'Would they all not have taken this golden opportunity to throttle the "*bhikku*-ridden" India and Asoka's "religious triumph without the use of arms" and drawn its blood?' he asks. And answers, 'But it is hardly necessary to indulge in these "ifs" and "whens". At that very time, India had unfortunately to suffer the grievous consequences of the preaching, not only of Asoka but of the Buddha himself, as has been shown in my play, '*Sanyasta Khadga*'[5] . . .And again when he is talking of centuries later and urging Hindus to have Narsimha as their inspiration, he writes, 'in those days of bitter warfare between the most cruel and diabolic Muslim invaders on the one hand and on the other the tolerant Hindu Society emasculated to suffer persecution and indignities to the last limits of endurance by the thoughtless preaching of the Buddhist cult from the days of Gautam Buddha himself . . .' Only Narsimha could have inspired 'in spineless Hindus of the day instinctive and effective reaction

---

[4] V.D. Savarkar, *Six Glorious Epochs of Indian History,* Abhishek Publications, Chandigarh, 2022, pp. 53–54.

[5] Ibid, p. 57.

to retaliate every wrong done them, and also violent valour which could strike terror in the hearts of the enemy.'[6] But they couldn't do so as the spine had been pulled out of Hindus—of course, by the teachings of the Buddha himself.

Ashoka

Ashoka is very high on Savarkar's list of villains. According to Savarkar, in several ways Ashoka weakened India and enabled foreigners to invade it. He abandoned war. He preached, and indeed, he enforced ahimsa. Deploying 'tyrannical' force and punishments, he banned Vedic practices, and thus drained the national spirit. His patronage of Buddhism emptied the treasury.

It does seem that given his own fixation on a 'blood and iron' State, Savarkar is manufacturing a villain, and finding in Ashoka's abandonment of violence and war the root cause, if not the one cause of the disintegration of the Mauryan empire. After examining the matter thoroughly, scholars who put together the Bharatiya Vidya Bhavan volumes concluded that, given the natural difficulties of running such a vast empire two thousand years ago, the wonder is that it was governed centrally for a hundred years and not that it collapsed in the following fifty. Their summary of the point is really worth reading for it awakens us to how much Savarkar shuts out— that should read, 'how much Savarkar typically shuts out'—when pushing his pet thesis. Here are a few paragraphs. Do read them:

Theoretically this view [that the Mauryan empire collapsed because Ashoka foreswore violence and thereby weakened it] appears plausible enough, but it is difficult to ascertain the extent to which the weakness of the empire is to be attributed to this cause alone. We cannot forget the fact that, considering the circumstances of

---

[6] Ibid, p. 311.

those days, it is a far greater wonder that so vast an empire should have been governed continuously by a central authority for nearly a century, than that it should have fallen to pieces within the next fifty years. Many other empires, far less in extent, rose and fell in India both before and after Asoka, and there must have been some natural causes at work in all these cases. Among them we may reckon the spirit of local autonomy, the difficulty of communication with distant provinces, the oppressive rule and rebellious disposition of their governors, palace intrigues and official treachery. Foreign invasion is another such factor, which invariably accelerates other causes. In the case of the Mauryas we have positive evidence that some, if not all, of these causes were at work. The repeated revolt of the distant province of Taxila, due mainly to the oppression of local officials, is perhaps typical of what was happening in other parts of the empire.

The Kalinga Edicts show that Asoka himself knew of the oppression of his officials and vainly tried to stop them. That the officials at the capital were not all loyal and devoted servants is proved by the treacherous conduct of Pushyamitra.

There are also good grounds to believe that the Maurya court was divided into two factions, one headed by Pushyamitra, the Commander-in-Chief, and the other by the Ministers who managed to make their sons respectively governors of Vidisa and Vidarbha. The immediate causes that brought about the end of the Maurya dynasty were no doubt, the invasion of the Bactrian Greeks . . . and the assassination of king Brihadratha by Pushyamitra. [The very same assassination that Savarkar lauds as having been carried out 'simply as a national duty.'] It is not unlikely that this coup d'etat was helped, if not prompted, by the foreign invasion. It is also equally likely that the weakness caused by internal dissensions invited foreign aggression. On the whole these natural causes might have been sufficient to bring about the decline and downfall of the Maurya Empire. It is not necessary, therefore, to postulate that the pacific policy of Asoka was responsible for this catastrophe, though this cannot be altogether ignored as a possible factor.

But even if Asoka's policy brought about the downfall of the Mauryan Empire, India has no cause to regret the fact. That empire would have fallen to pieces, sooner or later, even if Asoka had followed the policy of blood and iron of his grandfather. But the moral ascendancy of Indian culture over a large part of the civilized world, which Asoka was mainly instrumental in bringing about, remained for centuries as a monument to her glory and has not altogether vanished even now after the lapse of more than two thousand years.[7]

Two thousand years later, 'the natural difficulties of governing a large empire' would have been much less. The Maratha rulers were certainly not wedded to ahimsa. And yet the Maratha empire which Savarkar regards as the epitome of Hindu achievement, an empire that was scarcely larger than Ashoka's empire, an empire that had mastered new methods of warfare and weapons, an empire every pore of which on Savarkar's telling was imbued with pan-Hindu consciousness, collapsed within a hundred and forty years of Shivaji's death. After a few decades of conquest and dominance, the rulers had been less and less able to govern. And that, as we have glimpsed, because of all the familiar reasons: tussles between and within families, rivalries among chieftains, loot, sullen hostility of peoples they had walked over and 'taxed'—from Rajputs to Bengalis, rival factions cutting deals with foreigners. The end was swift as can be: the empire disintegrated in just twenty-three years—from 1795 to 1818. Yet, on Savarkar's telling, Ashoka with his conversion to Buddhism robbed the people of their identity, and with his abandonment of violence weakened the country and opened it to

---

[7] *The History and Culture of the Indian People,* Volume II, *The Age of Imperial Unity,* R.C. Majumdar, General Editor, Bharatiya Vidya Bhavan, Bombay, 1951/1990, pp. 90–92.

foreign invasions while the Marathas imbued the people with a sense of identity and wrested the country from foreign rule.

Only to hand it to another set of foreign rulers.

Buddhism and Buddhists

But all this weakening was not the work of just the Buddha or even of Ashoka by himself. The Buddhists en masse had turned traitors, and, in their fury, Hindus en masse annihilated them and their religion, asserts Savarkar.

The erasure or disappearance of Buddhism from India presents genuine problems. One cannot maintain that it disappeared because Mandana Misra and Shankaracharya defeated Buddhist scholars in debates. The fact is that the doctrine of Adi Shankarachrya was in many ways so akin to what the Buddha had taught that the former was said by some to be a 'crypto-Buddhist'. In any case, the points at issue were so esoteric that they could not have been of much concern to common folk— Hindu or Buddhist. Nor, on the other hand, can one put the erasure to, and I am plucking something Gandhiji said, '. . . if the legends are true, the great Shankaracharya did not hesitate to use unspeakable cruelty in banishing Buddhism out of India. And he succeeded!' For that would call into question the claim that we have been Maoists all along ensuring 'let a hundred flowers bloom, let a hundred schools of thought contend.' And that would also undermine the claim—advanced till today—that Buddhists, Sikhs, Jains are all Hindus. Nor can one say, as Savarkar does time and again, that the Buddhists had to be eliminated because they taught ahimsa, and this weakened India. Why would the Vedantists not have had to be eliminated for the same reasoning? After all, their teaching of *maya*, their teaching as much of others that the real goal to strive for is inner realization and liberation from this cycle of births and deaths than this-worldly attainments, this teaching would have turned people away from this world and its concerns and thus sapped their urge to combat worldly foes. Nor can one claim that it was necessary to erase Buddhism because its doctrine of universalism and love weakened India for, going by what Savarkar says, having an enemy, and cultivating hatred for the enemy are what unite people. For that would call into question the claim that Hindus are tolerant. The erasure also undermines the claim that ancient Indian society, but for foreign invaders, in any case till the time the Muslims came, was all peace-and-harmony.

Just 'the Most Appropriate Punishment for Treason'

Savarkar is inventive. He makes villainous traitors of the Buddhists and makes out that out of burning patriotism the Hindus finished them— much like Pushyamitra executed Mahapadmanand, 'simply as a national duty'! 'No religious persecution,' proclaims the section heading in his *Six Glorious Epochs*, 'but the most appropriate punishment for treason.'[8]

For three hundred years, Savarkar says, the Buddhists were allowed to 'observe their own rituals according to their own beliefs and likings. Besides, they could openly preach by sweet persuasion and discussion'. During and till the time of Chandragupta and Chanakya 'they had not . . . formed any anti-national and political alliances detrimental to the interests of the nation either with Alexander or Seleucos'. The reason they did not? 'It was not then possible for them!' 'That is why alone' they, 'along with many other religionists,' were allowed to practise their rituals and preach their doctrines.

But when the Greeks came a second time under Demetreos and Menander, and were about to 'dethrone the reigning king of Magadha and endanger the independence of the Indian empire,'

205 . . . the Indian Buddhists played a brazen-faced treacherous role, as is seen from the fact that these Buddhists swore their loyalty to

---

[8] *Six Glorious Epochs of Indian History,* op. cit., p. 72.

the Greek Emperor, Menander, whom they called Milind. When the latter adopted the Buddhist cult, they accepted him as the King of the region conquered by him. The Buddhist scholars and '*bhikkus*' proudly strutted in the Indian courts of those Greeks, as if they were moving in some national court. In order to put down as sternly as possible these highly objectionable treacherous acts of these Indian Buddhists, the plots hatched to undermine the national independence, and the open instigation to do anti-national acts which went on incessantly through various Buddhist monasteries and *viharas*, Pushyamitra and his generals were forced, by the exigency of the time, when the war was actually going on, to hang the Indian Buddhists who were guilty of seditious acts and to pull down the monasteries which had become the centres of sedition. It was a just punishment for high treason and for joining hands with the enemy, in order that Indian independence and empire might be protected. It was no religious persecution. As the supreme authority in the imperial administrative structure of India, it was Pushyamitra's duty—a religious and kingly duty according to the national legal code—to chastise perfidy, whether it was on the part of the Buddhists or on that of the Vedic Hindus![9]

The Buddhists did not learn, it seems, and the punishment had to be repeated time and again. Kanishka presents a problem. His achievements and conquests are too huge not to be appropriated. But he is a foreigner. And among his conquests are large swathes of India—from the Hindukush mountains to Saurashtra and right down to the tip of Konkan. Moreover, if not formally a Buddhist, he is a patron of the religion. A Buddhist king defeating Hindu kings? Does that not show that the Hindu nation had already become weak by then—that is, around the first and second century AD? Savarkar can't let that pass. Yes, Kanishka patronized Mahayana Buddhism. But 'it must be borne in mind that Buddhism that was embraced

---

[9] Ibid, pp. 72–74.

by Kanishka was not the unadulterated original one of Lord Buddha nor that of Asoka. It was the Kanishkan edition of Buddhism. For example, although the Emperor had surrendered his loyalty to Buddhism, he still worshipped the Vedic deities like Rudra. Kanishka's Buddhistic faith had nothing to do whatever with the non-violence of Asoka . . .' As for his defeating the Hindu rulers, we were defeated in good company:

> 237. The propriety of recounting this whole incident here is to show clearly that this sudden eruption of the Saka-Kushans throughout Asia did not convulse India alone; it discomfited even the then strongly built and well-organised empire like China too for a time on the battlefield. But just as it is tom-foolery, born out of jealousy, to say that the Chinese nation had been weak throughout all these years and was never better fitted for anything else than to be rotting in slavery simply because they suffered temporary defeats against the Saka-Kushans or at some such other times, it is equally foolish and jealously blind to say, as some of our enemies do, that the Indian national life was a series of defeats.

Incidentally, that phrase—'a series of defeats'—is that of, and the 'enemy' in question is Ambedkar.
It only shows that they cannot read history properly.

> 238. It is not the number of foreign aggressions over a nation that is the last criterion of deciding its vitality or virility or the absence of both, but the query, whether that nation was destroyed as a result of those aggressions or whether in the final phase of that national struggle that nation was able to overcome those foreign aggressions, that determines a nation's prowess, its vitality and its right to live.[10]

---

[10] Ibid, pp. 86–89.

That is what shows that the Hindu nation has had more vitality and virility than either the Muslim or the English nation, to say nothing of the Greeks, Sakas, Kushans, Buddhists. QED.

The problem was not Kanishka and his victories. The problem was the Indian Buddhists, in particular the 'hereditary disloyalty of the Buddhists'. Kanishka was a foreigner, after all. 'His empire was in fact an aggression on India. His was not an indigenous Indian empire.'

> 245. So the patriotic Vedic population of India fought furiously with Kanishka as it did with the Sakas, in order to overthrow his empire and to liberate all those Indian provinces which had the misfortune to grovel under his political domination. But what were the Indian Buddhists doing at that time? They tendered their submission to the Mlenchcha enemy, the Kushan emperor, as soon as he courted the Buddhistic cult and began to perpetrate acts of treachery against the Indian nation and the brave patriotic Vedic people, who were fighting for her liberty!

They had 'sold their loyalty to the Greeks' at the time of Menander's invasion, Savarkar says. They remained indifferent when the 'Vedic patriotic republics and states . . . were engaged in a life and death struggle with the Saka-Kushans for a hundred and twenty-five years'.

> But as soon as the strongest of these national enemies, Kanishka proclaimed his conversion, albeit half-heartedly, to Buddhism, the whole of the Buddhist population submitted their most affectionate loyalty at the feet of that national foe. They extolled him like a God to the skies! They prayed fervently in their *viharas* for the everlasting existence of that Saka-Kushan Mlenchcha State. What wonder if the inevitable consequence followed! As a result of the extreme hatred which the Vedic Hindus felt towards the Buddhists for their high treason, Buddhism continued to decline, as it had begun to do right

from the time of Pushyamitra, in spite of the royal support of Emperor Kanishka.[11]

Fortune turns. Kanishka is killed fighting in China. His son and successor is 'comparatively cold in his sympathy towards the Buddhists'. His grandson gives up Buddhism all together and embraces Hinduism.[12] Indian Buddhists 'lost both ways'. Soon, Samudragupta takes charge. His campaigns lead historians to call him 'The Indian Napoleon,' Savarkar records with pride. The Kushans ultimately surrender to him and sue for peace. In the ensuing decades, the Sakas are also defeated and driven out. Waves of assaults by the Huns follow. The patriotic Vedic Hindus and their kings repulse them, Savarkar writes. The head of the Huns, Mihirgula becomes an ardent worshipper of the Vedic God Rudra. Savarkar falls back on Vincent Smith, and writes, 'Of these people, Vincent Smith says, "The savage invader who worshipped his patron deity Shiva, the God of Destruction, exhibited ferocious hostility against the peaceful Buddhistic cult and remorselessly overthrew the Stupas and Monasteries which he plundered of their treasures".'[13] Even so, in the eyes of Vedic Hindus, Mihirgula remains 'a foreign aggressor and as such a national enemy,' and 'everybody was seething with indignation at seeing a foreign tyrant like Mihirgula occupy the throne of the Great Vikramaditya at Ujjain . . .'[14] The 'Vedic kings' get together. Mihirgula is defeated, caught, ordered to be hanged. But a member of the alliance, the King of Magadha, secures his release, and he is set free to return to the Hun-held lands of the northwest.[15] He sweeps Kashmir, usurps the kingdom, and 'persecuted the people of the land and especially liquidated the pockets of Buddhist influence after

---

[11] Ibid, pp. 90–91.

[12] Ibid, p. 91.

[13] Ibid, p. 103

[14] Ibid, pp. 104–05.

[15] Ibid, p. 106.

slaughtering wholesale thousands of Buddhist monks and nuns'.[16] The rationalist Savarkar remarks, 'It is very difficult to say if fate had brought to life this Mihirgula only to give a practical lesson to the Indian Buddhists who were intoxicated by the delirious idea, viz. "Religious victory was greater than armed victory," and to show that without one's own armed support even religion, cannot survive the onslaughts of the barbarous enemy's fire and sword.' The moral? 'Milk offered to snakes brings venom only.' These 'milksops of Buddhists' have done nothing to thwart the depredations of Mihirgula. All they now do, all they *can* do now, Savarkar remarks, is to consign him to hell in their fables. The Huns are extirpated in the decades that follow, and India remains free of foreign invasions for 500 years.[17] In fact, Vedic Hindu kings, Savarkar tells us, extend their rule to Ghazni and other regions of Afghanistan.

'Hereditary Traitors'

Buddhists remain the 'hereditary' traitors they are. In 711 AD, Mohammed bin-Qasim launches his invasion of India. The Vedic Hindus under their Vedic king, Dahir put up a gallant resistance. After the persecutions of Mihirgula, Buddhists had been left 'free to follow their own religion so far as it concerned only with their own selves'.[18] But a hereditary traitor will not change his spots. Hence, in spite of the freedom they have been given by the Vedic king and population, '. . . these Indian Buddhists were elated, to see the Muslim foreigners march against the Hindu kingdom. These Buddhists, who bore malice towards the Hindus, perhaps thought that these new Muslim aggressors might embrace their Buddhist cult, as did their forerunners, the Greeks under Menander or the Kushans under Kanishka, and establish a Buddhist empire over India. So they went and

---

[16] Ibid, pp. 106–07.

[17] Ibid, pp. 106–08.

[18] Ibid, p. 117.

greeted the Arabian-Muslim leader, when he captured Port Deval from the hands of King Dahir . . '. They surrender to Qasim, pledge loyalty to him and 'helped the Muslims in every possible way, while the latter marched onwards, by showing them difficult passes, providing them with foodstuff and fodder and supplying them secret military intelligence'. Savarkar adds for good measure, 'Some few Vedic Hindus also were guilty of this treachery; but their attempts were individual and exceptional.'[19]

The Arabs in Dahir's army refuse to fight Qasim 'since the latter was a Muslim as they themselves were, and that it was a religious crusade against the kafirs'. The Hindus fight 'fiercely'. Dahir dies in battle. The deed that Savarkar admires so much follows:

330. However, the moment she received the horrible news of King Dahir's death on the battle-field, the Queen and hundreds of other brave Hindu ladies leapt into a great fire and burnt themselves to death. It was the limit of warlike spirit, the *Kshatriyadharma*! The enemy's attempts to capture and molest the Queen and other ladies of high-rank were mostly foiled.[20]

'Mostly' because Dahir's two daughters and 'hundreds of other women' are captured and taken as concubines.

The traitors celebrate:

332. At the news of the fall of King Dahir and the victory of the Muslims, these Buddhists began to ring bells in their *vihars* to greet the Muslim conquerors, and prayed in congregations for the prosperity of the Muslim rulers!

333. But what they thus asked for as a boon proved to be an inexorable curse for them. After winning the final battle, when the Muslims

---

[19] Ibid, pp. 107–08.

[20] Ibid, pp. 118–19.

rushed violently, like a stormy wind, throughout Sindh, they went on beheading these Buddhists even more ruthlessly than they did the Vedic Hindus. For, the Vedic Hindus were fighting in groups or individually at every place and so they struck at least a little awe and terror in the minds of the Muslims. But as there was no armed opposition in Buddhist vihars and Buddhist localities, the Muslims cut them down as easily as they would cut vegetable. Only those of the Buddhists who took to the Muslim faith were spared, while all their *vihars* throughout Sindh and the innumerable shrines in them were knocked down, and hammered to pieces; for the Muslims hated these 'Buddh parastis'—these shrine-worshippers.[21]

'Collective High Treason'

Having set out this record of perfidy, Savarkar summarizes the causes for 'the total extinction of the Buddhists in India.' 'The successful theoretical refutation of the Buddhist philosophy and religious tenets by the stalwart Vedic theologians and pandits' is well known, Savarkar says. Accordingly he will focus on other factors, he declares. The first cause, he writes, is the 'collective high treason' of Buddhists: 'Being convinced beyond doubt by actual experience that these Buddhist congregations were inherently anti-national and unpatriotic, and treacherous institutions, the patriotic politicians and the kingly courts gave them hardly any support anywhere in India.' And this finished them as they had become accustomed to largesse from Ashoka's time. The second cause was their fanatical insistence on *ahimsa*. Ashoka and Harsha had enforced this on the Hindus 'misusing their political authority'. Even the killing of a louse invited severe punishment. This insistence on non-killing deprived 'millions of Indian hunters, fishermen, seamen, gamekeepers, foresters and others'

---

[21] Ibid, pp. 121–22.

of their livelihood. Third, contrary to what you might believe, Buddhism aggravated untouchability, Savarkar says. Therefore,

> 345. Those, who ignorantly or maliciously blame the Peshwas for the evil treatment given to the untouchables when they entered the town, should also criticize, equally vehemently and for the same offence Asoka, Shree Harsha and Buddhist kings, and all the Kshatriya kings right from Vikramaditya to the Rajput rulers, when they see this evidence. For this evil tradition of untouchability was not begun by the Peshwas for the first time but it had been prevalent even since the Vedic, the Buddhist and the Jain regimes; and in the Buddhist period especially instead of being weakened it was most scrupulously and mercilessly observed.

Hence, to no one's surprise,

> the untouchables like the Chandals and others preferred the Vedic regimes, as more congenial, to the unrelenting and uncompromising Buddhist ones, and those thousands of them who in the past had voluntarily (or helplessly and under pressure) embraced Buddhism, now renounced it and declared their allegiance to the Vedic religion.[22]

Finally, there were the Muslims. They had 'an innate hatred for that sect', namely the Buddhists. Therefore, they killed every Buddhist they could lay their hands on, and burnt libraries, vihars, stupas, idols of the Buddha to the ground. And what did the Buddhists do in return?

> As most of the Buddhists showed, through fear of death, willingness to embrace Islam, they were all converted . . . On seeing Bakhtyar Khiljee march on Bihar several Buddhists took their religious books and fled to Tibet and China. The rest were polluted and taken over

---

[22] Ibid, pp. 123–25.

into the Muslim fold. Some might have preferred to die rather [than] to be Muslims but no one fought for life and religion![23]

And this is what explains a paradox. How is it that there are so many Muslims in East Bengal? Simple: 'Quite obviously! This province had numerically more Buddhists than the Hindus and those numerous Buddhists became Muslims! It is natural, therefore, that this province alone should become, since then, a Muslim-majority province.'[24]

Homework

That is a lot to heap upon the Buddhists. While writing his book, Savarkar wrote that he was very unwell. He must have skipped listing the sources for that reason. S.T. Godbole who prepared the volume for the press noted in his introduction, 'A book of this type had to be substantiated with proofs, especially when it is replete with thought-provoking—sometimes even shocking—statements and conclusions. Basic references were, therefore, an unavoidable necessity; but the author, who had already crossed the bar of eighty years, and whose physical ailments had already created insurmountable difficulties in the very writing of this book, could not be expected to stand the rigour of pinpointing his references, voluminous as they were. I, therefore, had to shoulder that responsibility . . .' Godbole was satisfied that the 'basic references' that he had listed 'will clearly show to the reader that the facts mentioned in this volume are fully backed by evidence.'[25]

I leave it as an exercise for the reader to look up the references to ascertain whether they hold up Godbole's confidence. A few small things will indicate that the exercise will be worthwhile.

---

[23] Ibid, pp. 125–26.

[24] Ibid, pp. 126–27.

[25] Ibid, p. ii.

A Contemporary Account?

Recall the vivid details in Savarkar's account of Mohammed bin-Qasim's invasion, right up to the *Jauhar* by the Queen, the treachery of Buddhists, how they helped the invader, and how they celebrated his victory. Where does Savarkar get all these details from? Delving into Savarkar's sources, Godbole traces them to *Chachnama*.[26] This book is said to have been the translation into Persian of an earlier account in Arabic. The Arabic volume was never found, but was presumed to have been a contemporary account of the Muslim conquest of Sindh. The first translation of the full text of *Chachnama* into English was published in 1900.[27] Even at that time, the translator—Mirza Kalichbeg—and his associate noted that the volume contained some fabulous accounts. It spoke, for instance, of 'a sorceress, who could "put a girdle round about the earth" in somewhat more than forty minutes, could bring fresh nutmegs from Ceylon in the twinkling of an eye, and, by means of her weird second sight, discover whether a person was alive on the face of the earth . . . '[28] They also noted the difficulty of establishing the accuracy of various events described in the volume 'or to choose between the conflicting versions of one and the same event occasionally given by the author, or, rather by the authors . . .' 'Authors' not 'author', they wrote, for the volume was manifestly the product not of one author but of the labours over time of a family. The family had been very industrious in collecting information about the campaign of their kinsman, Mohamed bin-Qasim, they said, though one had to make allowances for the 'natural bias of the Sakifi family'. Moreover, the sources on which they had relied were varied.

---

[26] See end notes 15 to 27 and 32 to Chapter VI of V.D. Savarkar, *Six Glorious Epochs of Indian History,* translated and edited by S.T. Godbole, Bal Savarkar Sadan, Bombay, 1971, pp. 497–498.

[27] *The Chachnamah, An ancient history of Sind giving the Hindu period down to the Arab conquest,* Mirza Kalichbeg Fredunbeg, Commissioner's Press, Karachi, 1900. Kalichbeg was the Deputy Collector of Naushahro, Hyderabad district, at the time.

[28] Ibid, p. ix

Apart from the correspondence that passed between Qasim and Hajjaj, who had sent him on the expeditions, the translator and his associate wrote, the authors had relied on the following sorts of sources:

1. Arab historical plays, and ballads.
2. Family traditions of the Sakifis [the family in question], recorded and unrecorded.
3. Stories told by individuals whose names were forthcoming.
4. Stories told by individuals of a certain class, e.g. Brahmans.
5. What may be called the Flotsam and Jetsam hearsay.[29]

Not the sort of evidence on which one would base charges as severe as the ones that Savarkar hurls.

But modern scholarship points to much more. In his persuasive and erudite book,[30] Manan Ahmed Asif advances a pile of reasons to maintain that the *Chachnama* is an original work and not the translation of some earlier Arabic book—it was common for authors to trace their book to some Arabic text to make it sound authoritative just as it was common for them to trace the lineage of their patron or ruler back to the family of the Prophet, and that of their own family to some well-known family of scholars and writers. Nor is the book a record of conquest. It is a prescriptive work that sets out how a multi-cultural, multi-religious and politically diversified kingdom of early 13th century should be ruled. For advancing its prescriptions, the *Chachnama* invokes events, some of which transpired five hundred years earlier, and lore. It blends lessons that inhere in Persian, Arabic and Sanskrit texts that were poured over by the learned in early 13th century. What it says in regard to the conquest of Sindh—which

---

[29] For the preceding observations, see Ibid, pp. ix–x.

[30] For the following, Manan Ahmed Asif, *A Book of Conquest, The Chachnama and Muslim Origins in South Asia,* Harvard University Press, Cambridge, Mass. 2016. See, in particular, the Introduction and Chapters 2 and 3.

had happened five hundred years earlier—is based primarily on the brief section on that subject towards the end of Baladhuri's history[31], which itself was 'produced for the Abbasid court, [and itself] is removed from the earliest historical events it narrates by more than two hundred years and is thus itself an act of imagining the past.'[32] In a word, the book is not a history of what had happened in the 8th century, it is a book of counsel that addresses the concerns and circumstances of a court and society in a principality[33] in the 13th century. And yet, Savarkar—and others—snatch passages and descriptions in it to prove their assertions about not just events that happened five hundred years earlier than the composition of the book, but also the motives of individuals and entire communities that were involved in them.

Consider next an event that Savarkar sets out to prove his thesis.

'The Martyr Louse'

Consider first 'the martyr louse' as Savarkar calls it. Savarkar devotes an entire page to the incident. But it leaves one in doubt. On Savarkar's telling the king who decreed punishment for killing that little creature was not a Buddhist but a Jain! Savarkar writes,

> 338 . . . Kumar Pal, a *Jain* King of Gujrath, imposed savage penalties upon violators of his (similar) rules. An unlucky merchant who had committed the atrocious crime of cracking a louse was brought before a special court at Anilhawada and punished with the confiscation of his whole property. Another wretch who had outraged the sanctity of the capital by bringing a dish of raw meat was put to death. The special court constituted by Kumar Pal (for this purpose) had

---

[31] *Kitab Futuh al-Buldan, 'Book of the Conquests of Lands'.*

[32] M.A. Asif, op. cit., p. 35.

[33] With its capital at Uch, about 70 km north of modern Karachi. For the foregoing, M.A. Asif, op. cit., Introduction and Chapters 1 and 2.

functions similar to those of Asoka's censors. And the working of the later institutions sheds light on the unrecorded proceedings of the earlier one.

339. Out of the proceeds obtained by selling the confiscated property of the offender who committed the 'atrocious crime' of cracking the said louse was built a big temple worth lacs of rupees and it was named 'Yukvihar'—the temple of the Louse!

340. Were this incident described by any other writer it would have been as a parody of the *Jain* faith. But it is the *Jain* writers themselves who cite it with evident pride. Hence it has to be taken as true.

341 . . . It is because of this 'Ahimsa', more ruthless and more violent than violence—'Himsa'—itself that millions of Indian hunters, fishermen seamen, gamekeepers, foresters and others who lived by hunting and fishing, lost their professions.

342. When these millions of flesh-eaters jointly protested and demonstrated how they and their wives and children would starve to death and how this would spell violence of an enormously grave nature King Kumar Pal of Gujrath most graciously issued another order that these millions of people, who have been carrying on violent professions ought to leave those professions themselves. However as per their demand, the state was to subsidize them for three years.[34]

So, we are given the name of the king thrice—'Kumar Pal of Gujrath'—and we learn thrice over that, according to *Jain* sources, he was a *Jain* king who ordered this punishment in accordance with the *Jain* faith. But the incident is said to confirm what the Buddhists were doing, and why they enraged common folk enough to erase all trace of them.[35]

---

[34] Ibid, pp. 121–22.

[35] The printed edition of 2022 has no footnotes or endnotes, and therefore no indication of sources. Fortunately, the electronic version has endnotes. It is through that edition that the reader will have to find out both how well the sources confirm the story, and how

A Different Explanation

Second, Savarkar had himself given a different explanation for Hindus turning against Buddhists. In *Essentials of Hindutva*, he maintained not that Buddhists had assisted and joined up with invaders but rather that they had failed to stop the invaders. His allusion to their having teamed up with invaders had been put in a tentative way.

Corruption and laziness in the *sangha* could not have been the cause for disappearance of Buddhism, he wrote. There is no reason to believe that Jain monasteries or Hindu *mutts* had been more diligent and pure. Yet, Jainism and Hinduism survived. Nor could disagreements over arcane points have ignited Hindu anger. Hindus were accustomed to and revelled in different points of view. The real reason must have been something else. As successive waves of invaders—Greeks, Sakas, Kushans, Huns— descended on India, as they began trampling on our temples and all else, it became evident to the patriotic Hindus that no arcane argument of the Buddhists, no formula in Buddhist logic was going to stem the invasions, Savarkar said. The only answer was to be militarily strong. But, with their fanatical insistence on ahimsa, the Buddhists would not equip armies to do battle. 'So the leaders of thought and action of our race had to rekindle their Sacrificial Fire to oppose the sacrilegious one and to re-open the mines of Vedic fields for steel, to get it sharpened on the altar of Kali, "the Terrible", so that Mahakal, the "Spirit of Time" be appeased . . .'

Rulers abroad who had become Buddhists had invaded India to conquer it, and some Buddhists here would have helped them, 'even as Catholic Spain could always find some important section in England to sympathise with their efforts to restore a Catholic dynasty in England.' Very different from what Savarkar would say later. 'Sympathising with' as against actively working for . . . 'Eventually, invasions by foreign Buddhist rulers

---

relevant the incident involving this Jain king is for getting to know what the Buddhists were doing.

were defeated', Savarkar had written. Naturally, the fact that Buddhism had no answer in its doctrine or logic-chopping to foreign invasions and the fact that their doctrine of ahimsa kept them from taking steps which were required to forestall the invaders had led to strong antipathy towards Buddhists and Buddhism within India, he said, and concluded that for this reason a strong reaction set in which ignited the Vedic Hindus to erase Buddhism and Buddhists. Institutions like the four varnas were revived. Ban was placed on visiting countries abroad where a Hindu could not practice his rituals and varna code . . .

The emphasis is on foreign invaders who had become Buddhists. Not on local Buddhists. Moreover, the latter are charged with having possibly 'sympathis[ed] with' not with having actively worked for . . .

And yet there may be a hint of a more potent reason on account of which those controlling the Hindu order had been enraged with the Buddha, his teachings, and the Buddhists in general. Institutions like the four varnas were revived, Savarkar noted. Precisely. A major factor which would have invited the wrath of the Brahmanical order was the Buddha's opposition to castes, in particular to castes based on birth, and the order based on them. The dominance and power of the upper castes had rested entirely on this division of society, and on the myths and rationalizations that had been conjured up for it. Could this have been the reason for pushing away Buddhism and Buddhists rather than patriotic rage at their not having been able to defeat the invaders?

Did the Doctrine of Ahimsa Hold Back Anyone?

Third, several scholarly studies refute Savarkar's conjectures. Consider Savarkar's repeated assertion that it is the Buddha's doctrine of ahimsa that weakened India and thus opened the gates for the invaders. In his book, *Bhagwan Buddh,* the distinguished polymath, D.D. Kosambi, gives a brief and telling reply to the assertion:

The *parinirvana* of the Buddha occurred in 543 BC Two centuries after that, Chandragupta established his empire. It is said that Chandragupta himself was a Jain. His dharma's *ahimsa* did not prevent him from throwing the Greeks out of the country. His grandson, Ashoka was wholly a Buddhist. And yet he reigned over a large empire.

Mohammed bin Qasim invaded Sindh in 712 CE. By that time, Buddhism had disappeared from the western parts of Bharat and the Brahmanical faith had gained predominance. In spite of this being the situation, in a short time this subordinate of the Khalifa brought Sindh under his heel, killed the Hindu king, captured his daughters and sent them off to the Khalifa as *nazaraanaa*.

A hundred years after the Muslims had established their sway over Sindh and Punjab, the Shankaracharya rose. The whole objective of his Vedanta was that Shudras should not study the Vedas. If a Shudra hears a Vedic verse, molten glass or shellac should be poured into his ears. If he recites a *Vedvaakya,* his tongue should be cut off, and if he adopts/*dharand karey* a *Vedmantra,* he should be killed—this was his Vedanta. Our *sanatani* brothers did not learn anything from even the Muslims. Buddha was in any case their enemy. Where was the question of learning anything from him?

The Rajputs were strict *sanatanis*. They did not subscribe to *ahimsa* even in the slightest. When the occasion arose, they would die fighting each other. Then how did Mahmud Ghazni trample upon these true-believers in violence as dust under the hooves of his horses? Is it because they believed in the *ahimsa* of the Buddha?

The Peshwai of us Marathas was in any case in the hands of exalted Brahmins. The last Bajirao was famous for his industry and assiduousness. Yet violence crossed the limits under the Peshwas. They were fighting others, of course, but fighting against each other was also not infrequent. Once Daulatrai Shinde looted Pune city and the next time Yashwantrao Holkar looted it. The empire of these true-devotees of violence should have spread over all of India. Why did they have to seek shelter with the British, who were a hundred times more non-violent than them? Why did one Maratha chieftain after another become the vasal of the British? Is it because they were the devotees of the Buddha?

Japan has been Buddhist for the last 1000-1200 years. How did they at once become unified when Commodore Perry made them the target of his canons? Why did Buddhism not make them impotent?

Eminent critics should definitely answer these questions. '*Mirvisi sushatva vrithaa anyaalaa svakrit taap laavuni*' (Why are you *sugyatva baghaartey ho* by pasting your own deeds on others?) Has this poetic line been written by the Marathi poet Moropant with such persons in mind? They are showing off their learning by blaming the Buddha for the sins committed by their forefathers.[36]

Naturally, the examples in Kosambi's brief response are just a sample of instances that refute Savarkar's assertion. In another essay, Kosambi himself adds to the list:

... As for the waning practical effect of Buddhism, we might note that Asoka had turned to the non-killing religion after a single gruesome campaign in Kalinga. In contrast, the devout Buddhist emperor, Harsha Siladitya (A.D. 605-655) of Kanauj, fought incessantly for at least thirty years to bring most of India under his sway. For that matter, Jenghiz Khan (Temujin) and the Mongol princes who succeeded him conducted military operations over most of the Eurasian continent, notorious in history for their scale of carnage and destruction compared to which Alexander's campaign looks like a border raid; but

---

[36] D.D. Kosambi, *Bhagwan Buddh,* Rajkamal Publications on behalf of the Sahitya Academy, Delhi, 1956, pp. 12–14.

these Mongol emperors, too, pass for good Buddhists. No Buddhist king, however, killed or crusaded for the glory or propagation of religion.[37]

There is no shortage of other examples that refute Savarkar's charge that the doctrine of ahimsa preached by Buddhism led people to shed violence, and warfare in particular. A substantial volume can be filled describing the internecine violence among Vedic Hindu rulers of South India, for example.

Had We Forsaken Violence?

There is an even more elementary point. The question of whether the doctrine of ahimsa weakened us would arise if we had embraced it. Had we embraced it? Here is none other than the keenest devotee of the doctrine in recent times, Gandhiji himself. His friend, C.F. Andrews has written to Gandhiji about how a step that Gandhiji is propagating goes contrary to Indians having shed their lust for blood. Gandhiji responds:

You say: 'Indians as a race did repudiate it, bloodlust, with full consciousness in days gone by and deliberately took their choice to stand on the side of humanity.' Is this historically true? I see no sign of it either in the *Mahabharata* or the *Ramayana*, not even in my favourite Tulsidas which is much superior in spirituality to Valmiki. I am not now thinking of these works in their spiritual meanings. The incarnations are described as certainly bloodthirsty, revengeful and merciless to the enemy. They have been credited with having resorted to tricks also for the sake of overcoming the enemy. The battles are described with no less zest than now, and the warriors are equipped with weapons of destruction such as

---

[37] D.D. Kosambi, *The Culture and Civilization of Ancient India in Historical Outline*, Vikas, NOIDA, 2001, Chapter 7.2, 'The evolution of Buddhism,' pp. 147–56.

could be possibly conceived by the human imagination. The finest hymn composed by Tulsidas in praise of Rama gives the first place to his ability to strike down the enemy. Then take the Mahomedan period. The Hindus were not less eager than the Mahomedans to fight. They were simply disorganized, physically weakened and torn by internal dissensions. The code of Manu prescribes no such renunciation that you impute to the race. Buddhism, conceived as a doctrine of universal forbearance, signally failed, and, if the legends are true, the great Shankaracharya did not hesitate to use unspeakable cruelty in banishing Buddhism out of India. And he succeeded! Then the English period. There has been compulsory renunciation of arms but not the desire to kill. Even among the Jains the doctrine has signally failed. They have a superstitious horror of blood(shed), but they have as little regard for the life of the enemy as an European. What I mean to say is that they would rejoice equally with anybody on earth over the destruction of the enemy. All then that can be said of India is that individuals have made serious attempts, with greater success than elsewhere, to popularize the doctrine. But there is no warrant for the belief that it has taken deep root among the people.[38]

Muslims in East Bengal

Consider next the explanation that Savarkar produces for the large number of Muslims in East Bengal: that this area had a disproportionately large number of Buddhists and they gave themselves up to Islam. This is directly contrary to what careful study of contemporary records establishes. Conversions in this area were of the same kind and by the same sort of

---

[38] *Collected Works of Mahatma Gandhi,* Volume XVII, p. 121.

methods as elsewhere: they were done by force as well as by Sufi preachers, and they were of Hindus.[39]

A Contradiction in the Thesis

Another reason for examining Savarkar's charge that Buddhism with its 'anti-national' teaching of ahimsa weakened India is to find out how it squares with his account that throughout the centuries that followed the Buddha, including the seven hundred years of Muslim rule, Hindus gave ceaseless, violent resistance to every foreign onslaught? How does it square with his account of Hindus setting up empires in distant lands? How does it square with the violent struggles between Hindu empires and between as well as within Hindu dynasties? How does it square with the violence against untouchables, tribals? Either the Buddhists were a fringe element of little consequence, and their teaching of ahimsa got nowhere, or, while Buddhists were numerous and influential, the Vedic Hindus were alert enough not to let Buddhist teachings of ahimsa percolate into themselves, and, therefore, all these things followed despite Buddhism and Buddhists.

Internal Decay

Finally, the array of reasons advanced by authorities equally concerned about Hinduism and Hindus, as well as by scholars, themselves constitute a ground to examine how far Savarkar's sources bear out his charge. Consider a sample of these, and inquire whether, taken together they are not sufficient to explain the disappearance of Buddhism.

---

[39] As an example, consider the thorough study of an authority who the current lot would find difficult to disown, Dr K.S. Lal. His book, every paragraph of which is based on contemporary and authoritative sources, deals in detail with the agencies who converted, the means they used, and who were converted. Buddhists of Bengal hardly figure in the account. K.S. Lal, *Indian Muslims, Who are they,* Voice of India, Delhi, 1990. Conversions in Bengal are dealt with at pages 56–70 of the book.

Unlike Hinduism, Buddhism had come to depend on monks and monasteries. And these degenerated. Hsiuan-tsang's description of degeneration in many monasteries is often cited. Patronage from rulers and the rich had led to simple huts being replaced by buildings several storeys high, they had led to the mendicant's robe being replaced by robes of fine silk . . . Monks would be rewarded with higher positions, better facilities, attendant monks, an attending escort, depending on their performance in verbal duels . . . Eighteen schools had come into being. 'The tenets, of the Schools keep these isolated,' Hsiuan-tsang wrote, 'and controversy runs high; heresies on special doctrines lead many ways to the same end. Each of the Eighteen Schools claims to have intellectual superiority, and the tenets (or practises) of the Great and the Small Vehicles differ widely . . . many are the noisy discussions.' The result was not just ever-finer parsing of each hair, but hierarchy upon hierarchy: 'Wherever there is a community of Brethren, it makes [its own] rules of gradation. Those who bring forward fine points in philosophy, and give subtle principles their proper place, who are ornate in diction and acute in refined distinctions, ride richly caparisoned elephants preceded and followed by a host of attendants. But as for those to whom religious teaching has been offered in vain, who have been defeated in discussion, who are deficient in doctrine and redundant in speech, perverting the sense while keeping the language, the faces of such are promptly daubed with red and white clay, their bodies are covered with dirt, and they are driven out to the wilds or thrown into the ditches.' Commenting on such changes, Kosambi observed, 'Clearly, this was nowhere near the Buddhism preached by the Founder in sixth-century B.C. Magadha.'[40] The Buddha was a mendicant. He lived an

---

[40] C. f., Thomas Watters, *On Yuan Chwang's Travels in India, 629–645 A.D.*, T.W. Rhys Davids and W. Bushell [eds.], Royal Asiatic Society, London, 1904, p. 162. See also, D.D. Kosambi, *The Culture and Civilization of Ancient India in Historical Outline*, op. cit., 7.2 'The evolution of Buddhism.' As well as his 1956 essay, 'The decline of Buddhism in India,' in D.D. Kosambi, *Exasperating Essays*, People's Publishing House, New Delhi, 1957.

austere and simple life. A corpse's sheet was his robe . . . As centuries pass, recollections of him become more and more elaborate. To compress an entire history in a sentence, the original teachings and order of the Buddha were superseded by the in-some-ways-austere form Hinayana, which in turn was superseded by the more elaborate Mahayana, and then the latter was infected by Tantric practices.

Swami Vivekananda, for instance, speaks of the utter degradation of Buddhism from within, how invaders completed the job, and how the arena is being reclaimed. That Indian Buddhists betrayed the country, and, therefore the patriotic Vedic Hindus turned on them do not figure in the account. As an illustration take just one of his lectures, 'The sages of India.' '. . . the Temple of Jagannatha is an old Buddhistic Temple,' he says. 'We took this and others over and re-Hinduised them. We shall have to do many things like that yet . . .'

> . . . The Tartars and the Baluchis and all the hideous races of mankind came to India and became Buddhists, and assimilated with us, and brought their national customs, and the whole of our national life became a hotch-podge of the most horrible and the most bestial customs. That was the inheritance which that boy [Adi Shankaracharya] got from the Buddhists, and from that time to this, the whole work in India is a reconquest of this Buddhistic degradation by the Vedanta. It is still going on, it is not yet finished. Shankara came, a great philosopher, and showed that the real essence of Buddhism and that of the Vedanta are not very different, but that the disciples did not understand the Master [the Buddha] and have degraded themselves, denied the existence of the soul and of God, and have become atheists. That was what Shankara showed, and all the Buddhists began to come back to the old religion.[41]

---

[41] 'The sages of India,' *Selections from the Works of Swami Vivekananda*, Advaita Ashram, Calcutta, 1998, pp. 316–17.

Monks and Monasteries

Or take a person of the opposite persuasion, Ambedkar. According to him, Muslim invasions crippled and extinguished Buddhism. Muslim invaders were equally violent towards the Hindus. But Buddhism died and Hinduism did not—because of three facts particular to Buddhism of the time. First, at that time Brahminism had official patronage and Buddhism did not: as a result, when Hindu temples were destroyed, they could be restored at least in areas which remained under the control of Hindu rulers; but when the Buddhist monasteries, universities and libraries were reduced to ashes, they could not be revived. Second, Ambedkar said, Buddhism had become monk- and monastery-centric. When the monasteries were destroyed and the monks slaughtered, Buddhism died. Brahmins were also killed, but in Hinduism every Brahmin is a potential priest, Ambedkar said, and so the functions of priests would be performed by any Brahmin who happened to have survived and was around. Performing these rituals did not require much preparation. A Buddhist monk, by contrast, had to go through rigorous training for years, and had to conform to a strict code of conduct. Not so in Hinduism. Third, Ambedkar did speak of mass conversions to Islam, but for a reason that Savarkar would not countenance: '. . . the Buddhist laity was persecuted by the Brahmanic rulers of India and to escape this tyranny the mass of the Buddhist population of India embraced Islam and renounced Buddhism.'[42]

---

[42] Ambedkar cites an address by Surendranath Sen to the effect that Buddhists in Sindh 'lent their wholehearted support' to the Islamic invaders:

> 'According to the *Chachnama*, the Buddhists of Sind suffered all sorts of indignities and humiliations under their Brahman rulers, and when the Arabs invaded their country, the Buddhists lent their whole hearted support to them. Later on, when Dahir was slain and a Muslim Government was firmly established in his country, the Buddhists found to their dismay that, so far as their rights and privileges were concerned, the Arabs were prepared to restore status quo ante bellum and even under the new order the Hindus

received a preferential treatment. The only way out of this difficulty was to accept Islam because the converts were entitled to all the privileges reserved for the ruling classes. So the Buddhists of Sind joined the Muslim fold in large numbers.'

Prof. Sen then adds this significant passage:

'It cannot be an accident that the Punjab, Kashmir, the districts around Behar Sharif, North-East Bengal where Muslims now predominate, were all strong Buddhist Centres in the pre-Muslim days. It will not be fair to suggest that the Buddhists succumbed more easily to political temptations than the Hindus and the change of religion was due to the prospects of the improvement of their political status.'

Ambedkar proceeds to say:

Unfortunately the causes that have forced the Buddhist population of India to abandon Buddhism in favour of Islam have not been investigated and it is therefore impossible to say how far the persecution of the Brahmanic Kings was responsible for the result. But there are not wanting indications which suggest that this was the principal cause. We have positive evidence of two Kings engaged in the campaign of persecuting the Buddhist population . . .

Coming nearer to the time of the Muslim invasions, we have the instance of Sindh where persecution was undoubtedly the cause. That these persecutions continued up to the time of the Muslim invasions may be presumed by the fact that in Northern India the Kings were either Brahmins or Rajputs both of whom were anti-Buddhists. That the Jains were persecuted even in the 12th century is amply supported by history. Smith refers to Ajayadeva, a Saiva King of Gujarat who came to the throne in A.D. 1174–6 and began his reign by a merciless persecution of the Jains, torturing their leader to death. Smith adds, 'Several other well-established instances of severe persecution might be cited.'

There is therefore nothing to vitiate the conclusion that the fall of Buddhism was due to the Buddhists becoming converts to Islam as a way of escaping the tyranny of Brahmanism. The evidence, if it does not support the conclusion, at least makes it probable. If it has been a disaster, it is a disaster for which Brahmanism must thank itself. ['The decline and fall of Buddhism,' in *Dr. Babasaheb Ambedkar, Writings and Speeches,* Volume 3, Vasant Moon, Hari Narake (eds.), First Edition by Education Department, Government of Maharashtra, 14 April,

There is a telling essay by R.C. Majumdar, 'Hindu reaction to Muslim invasions.'[43] As we have seen, Majumdar thought very highly of Savarkar. He even wrote the introduction to *Hindu Pad-padshahi,* and it was a very appreciative one, a note that echoed Savarkar's thesis. The essay is interesting for another reason also: it presages the lines that Savarkar would pursue in *Six Glorious Epochs.* This is what Majumdar says about treachery in Sindh:

> Treachery of the Hindus seems to have played an important part in the success of Muhammad from beginning to end. The Buddhist priests of Sindh, we are told, had been carrying on secret correspondence with Hajjaj and openly helped Muhammad in capturing several strongholds. But it appears on a close scrutiny of the Muslim accounts that some Buddhists, at any rate, were patriotic enough to fight against the Muslim, and many of those—chiefs and common people alike— who betrayed their king and country were not Buddhist. Some of the leading chiefs, including the chief minister, and even 4000 warlike Jats of Sindh, helped Muhammad in subduing their own country.

A much more complex picture than the one Savarkar would have us see.

Two and a half centuries pass. The invaders are again at India's door. By now Buddhism has been more or less pushed out of the region all together. What do the Hindu rulers do? Majumdar's account accords with our record much better than mere treachery:

1987. Re-printed by Dr. Ambedkar Foundation, Ministry of Social Justice & Empowerment, Government of India, January, 2014, pp. 229–47, at pp. 236–38.]

In this account also we have Buddhists becoming Muslims but for a reason that is quite the opposite of what Savarkar had advanced—not the reason which would have sent the patriotic Vedic Hindus into a fury and thereby led to the extermination of masses of Buddhists by masses of outraged, patriotic Hindus.

[43] In *Mahamahopadhyaya Prof. D.V. Potdar Commemoration Volume,* Surendranath Sen, (ed.), S.R. Sardesai, Poona, 1950, pp. 341–51.

Nor were the northern rulers fully alive to the danger that threatened them. During the long period of two centuries and a half that elapsed since the Muslim conquest of Sindh, great upheavals took place in the Islamic world, which must have rendered the position of Muslims in India very precarious; and there were many powerful rulers in India like Lalitaditya, Bhoja, and Dharmapala who even singly could have driven them out of India. But they were either deterred by the superstitious faith, as in the case of Multan, or did not sufficiently realise the gravity and importance of the task. In either case we are bound to hold that they were devoid of national feelings and far-seeing statesmanship as we understand them today. If, instead of fighting with other Indian states, they had turned their arms against the Muslims of Sindh, India would have been rid of a grave danger.

Scholars who put together the Bharatiya Vidya Bhavan volumes on the history and culture of the Indian peoples lead us to attribute the decline and assimilation of Buddhism not to extermination launched by outraged Vedic Hindus, but first, to the destruction of monasteries in Bihar and Bengal by Muslim invaders, and then to internal developments within Buddhism itself. To reach out to the people at large, they point out, Buddhism came down to the 'popular' level. It reintroduced rituals, idols, mantras, superstitions, etc. It thus became less distinguishable from, and therefore, all the easier to assimilate into Brahmanism.[44] One of the main

---

[44] The scholars write,

> The developed doctrines and rituals of Mahayana and Brahmanical religion made such a near approach to each other, specially through the stress upon faith and devotion, worship of images of numerous gods and goddesses, and the use of Sanskrit in liturgical texts, on the part of the Buddhists, and the acceptance of the principle of ahimsa, specially in regard to diet, on the part of the Brahmanas, that a merger of the two was not only rendered quite easy but became almost inevitable. The identification of the Buddha with Vishnu by means of the theory of incarnation completed the process, and Buddhism silently merged itself into

reasons Jainism survived is the very one that also limited the numbers who followed it: it retained its conservative, orthodox character. The other development made the two religions—Hinduism and Buddhism— equally degenerate, the analysis of the scholars suggests. Tantra developed in both religions. This led to debasement of ethics and morality in both. The adulteration was all the greater among monks and priests. And as Buddhism had become more monk- and monastery-centred, the effect of this degradation in ethics was greater on Buddhism. This degradation, it would seem from their reconstruction of our past, was part and parcel of the degradation in society in general and had been induced by peace and prosperity of the preceding centuries. Islamic invasions provided the final rites: they cremated the degenerate remains.[45]

Again, we do not encounter enraged Vedic Hindu patriots killing off or driving away the traitorous Buddhists.

Other Reasons

Could it then be that Savarkar alighted on his assertions for other reasons? First, there is Savarkar's repeated prescription—which we have encountered—that history must be written for a purpose. It was important

---

Brahmanical religion. Even today images of Buddha are worshipped as Siva or Vishnu in many places in Bengal. It is also interesting to note that Siva and Buddha were identified in Java, and in modern Balinese theology Buddha is regarded as a younger brother of Siva. Further, Siva, Vishnu and Buddha were all regarded as identical and so were their Saktis. These no doubt truly reflected the religious conception of the motherland. [Cf., The section on 'Buddhism' and, in particular 'General Review' written by R.C. Majumdar in Chapter XVI, 'Religion and philosophy,' in *The History and Culture of the Indian People*, Volume V, *The Struggle for Empire*, R.C. Majumdar, General Editor, Bharatiya Vidya Bhavan, Bombay, 1957/1979, pp. 398–426. The passage quoted above is at p. 402. For the baneful effects of Tantra on both Hinduism and Buddhism, pp. 400–01.]

[45] Ibid, pp. 400–01.

to emphasize the deep animosity between Hindus and Muslims at the time of Shivaji, he wrote, but the opposite is required in the first decade of the twentieth century—when he wrote his account of the 1857 uprising against the British. Could a change in circumstances between the 1920s when he wrote *Essentials of Hindutva* and the 1960s when he wrote *Six Glorious Epochs* have accounted for his new insistence—that the Buddhists had betrayed India to foreigners, that they were 'hereditary' traitors? One thing which had upset Savarkar no end had certainly happened, and that too in spite of his admonitions: under the banner of Ambedkar, a large number of Mahars and others had embraced Buddhism. Could forestalling the possibility that such conversions may continue have been the new purpose?

The other reason is also embedded in *Essentials of Hindutva*. As we have seen, Savarkar was of the view that hatred unites, that aspects which we share with others weaken our resolve to fight them. Was he setting up two opposites—the patriots, the Vedic Hindus, and the 'hereditary' traitors, the Buddhists? Was he conjuring an internal enemy for accomplishing the task that he felt was the most important one—to unite the fractious Hindus?

In any case, the Buddha having been proclaimed an avatar of Vishnu, the practices of the two religions having become so similar that many came to proclaim Buddhism to be just a sect of Hinduism, the Buddhists having been erased or having disappeared thousands of years ago, pasting hereditary treason on them could serve Savarkar's end only to a very limited extent. Islam and Muslims, by contrast, were a major and conspicuous presence. Targeting them would certainly sow fear, hatred, alarm in Hindus, and thus prod them to unify behind him and his organizations.

The third possible reason is the most obvious. All of Savarkar's historical writing had one theme: a pan-Hindu consciousness suffused our people from the very beginning. Inspired by this consciousness, we conquered, we created, we achieved heights that others can scarcely dream of. The Muslims came and spoilt everything. But then how to account for the defeats, the deterioration, the sapping of creativity in the pre-Islamic era?

An internal enemy had to be invented, and the defeats attributed to its perfidy, the decay attributed to its corrupt influence.

Islam and Muslims

Trashing Buddhism was to box the air. Thrashing Buddhists was to cane ghosts. Buddhism had disappeared. Buddhists had already been erased. A palpable, living enemy was needed.

Exceptions apart, Islamic rule had been violent, oppressive in the extreme. Savarkar had counseled that we should put those bitter memories behind us. In his *The Indian War of Independence of 1857,* he had celebrated the fact that Hindus and Muslims had fought together. In passages that are often quoted, he had written, '. . . The nation ought to be the master and not the slave of its own history. For, it is absolutely unwise to try to do certain things, simply because they had once been acted in the past. The feeling of hatred against the Mahomedans was just and necessary in the times of Shivaji—but, such a feeling would be unjust and foolish if nursed now, simply because it was the dominant feeling of the Hindus then.'[46] Around the same time, on 10 May 1908, Savarkar organized a function in London to mark the fiftieth anniversary of the 1857 Uprising. In the homage to the martyrs that he wrote, he said,

> The war began on the 10th of May 1857 is not over on the 10th of May 1908, nor shall it ever cease till a 10th of May to come sees the destiny accomplished, sees the beautiful Ind crowned, either with the lustre of victory or with the halo of martyrdom.
>
> But, O glorious Martyrs, in this pious struggle of your sons help. O help us by your inspiring presence! Torn in innumerable petty selves, we cannot realise the grand unity of the Mother. Whisper, then, unto

---

[46] An Indian Nationalist, *The Indian War of Independence of 1857,* The Publishers, London, 10 May 1909, Author's Introduction, pp. vii–viii.

us by what magic you caught the secret of Union. How the *feringhee* rule was shattered to pieces and the Swadeshi thrones were set up by the common consent of Hindus and Mahomedans. How the higher love of the Mother, united the difference of castes and creeds, how the venerated and venerable Bahadur Shah prohibited the killing of cows throughout India, how Shreemant Nanasahib after the first salute of the thundering cannon to the emperor of Delhi, reserved for himself the second one! How you staggered the whole world by uniting under the banner of Mother and forced your enemies to say 'Among the many lessons the Indian Mutiny conveys to the historian and administrator, none is of greater importance than the warning that it is possible to have a revolution in which Brahmins and Shudras, Mahomedans and Hindus were united against us and that it is not safe to suppose that the peace and stability of our dominion in any great measure depends on the continent being inhabited by different races with different religious systems, for they mutually understand each other and respect and take part in each other's modes and ways and doings. The mutiny reminds us that our dominions rest on a thin crust ever likely to be rent by titanic fires of social changes and revolutions.' Whisper unto us the nobility of such an alliance of Religion and Patriotism, the true religion whichever is on the side of patriotism, the true patriotism which secures the freedom of religion.[47]

After Andamans

Two years later, he is arrested, transported back to India, convicted, and sent to the Andamans. His writings after he comes out are full of fire and pejoratives against Muslims. He writes of them as 'evil', 'devilish', 'diabolic', 'devils', 'highly fanatical', 'ruthlessly destructive', 'wicked', 'the inveterate and crafty Muslim enemies', 'Muslim wolves', 'those Muslim demons', '. . .

---

[47] http://savarkar.org/en/encyc/2017/5/22/Oh-Martyrs.html

seething in their brains another fierce religious ambition, not heretofore dreamt of by any of the old enemies of India. Intoxicated by this religious ambition, which was many times more diabolic than their political one . . .', 'malevolent and atrocious Muslim invaders', 'treacherous and dangerous', '. . . such a hideous religion as the Islam [sic.]', 'the Muslim pestilence', 'the traditional Muslim malignity towards Hindus', '. . . According to the shameless but proud vaunt of the Muslims in general that to kidnap the non-Muslim beautiful women openly was a Muslim's religious duty . . .', 'the Muslim diabolism towards the hapless Hindus', 'the combative marauding, aggressive and fanatic Muslim and Christian nations'. And so on.[48]

This transformation in his assessment of Muslims is often attributed to the cruelty and partisanship of Muslim guards in the Cellular Jail. All accounts of the jail portray them as cruel, greedy, ones who targeted Hindu prisoners especially. They would certainly have contributed to the drastic change in Savarkar's new aversion. But several factors suggest that there must have been other considerations also.

First, Savarkar himself makes a distinction among the Muslim guards— the Pathan, Baloch and Sindhis on the one hand and the Muslims from Punjab and Bengal on the other. The former are the ones who were cruel and partisan, he says, the latter not as much.[49] But that does not make him differentiate between Muslims. He paints them all as vile and worse.

Second, the chief architect of the regime in the prison, the one on whose command and to please whom all the guards acted was the dreaded Barrie. In *My Transportation for Life*, Savarkar always refers to him as 'Mr. Barrie', sometimes as 'Barrie Baba'. He was an Irishman. That did not lead Savarkar to hate the Irish.

---

[48] The adjectives and expressions in the text are from just one of his books, *Six Glorious Epochs of Indian History*, op. cit.

[49] 'The Pathans, the Sindhis and the Baluchi Muslims, with a few exceptions, were, one and all, cruel and unscrupulous persons, and were full of fanatical hatred for the Hindus. Not so the Mussalmans from the Punjab, and less even than they, those of Bengal, Tamil province and Maharashtra.' *My Transportation for Life*, op. cit., p. 93.

Third, the British are the ones who had sent him to that jail in the first place, and who kept him there, who turned down his successive mercy petitions. That did not ignite any hatred for the British in Savarkar. On the contrary, as we have seen, he strove hard to be of service to them.

And then there is his own account, or that of his alter-ego, *Life of Barrister Savarkar*, the book we have encountered earlier. From that we learn how Savarkar had developed a visceral hatred for Muslims even when he was in school. Hindu-Muslim riots broke out. They enraged him and his fellow students, he wrote. They decided to 'attack' an abandoned mosque as revenge. They inflicted a little damage with sticks and stones. Later there was a fight with Muslim students. He began instructing fellow students on how to fight and defeat the Muslims. In these mock battles, the Hindus were to always win.[50]

Even in *Hindu Pad-padshahi* which was published in 1925, Savarkar said that the purpose is not to perpetuate enmities of the past but to see what factors led to them and learn to avoid them, and that we should not be emphasizing enmity between Hindus and Muslims at present:

It would be as suicidal and as ridiculous to borrow the hostilities and combats of the past only to fight them out into the present, as it would be for a Hindu and a Muhammadan to lock each other suddenly in a death-grip while embracing, only because Shivaji and Afzal Khan had done so hundreds of years ago. We ought to read history, not with a view to find out the best excuse to perpetuate the old strife and stress, bickerings and bloodsheds whether in the name of our blessed motherland, or of our Lord God, that divided man from man and race from race, but precisely for the contrary reason of finding out the root causes that contributed to, and the best means to the removal of that stress and strife, of those bickerings and bloodsheds, so that man

---

[50] Chitragupta, *Life of Barrister Savarkar*, Acharya Balarao Savarkar, Veer Savarkar Prakashan, Bombay, 1987, pp. 4–6.

may be drawn towards man because he is man, the child of that our common father God—and nursed at the breast of this our common mother—Earth—and weld humanity in a World-Commonwealth.[51]

It would seem, therefore, that while the cruelties of Muslim guards would have incensed Savarkar, as they would have infuriated everyone, there were prior and later triggers that convinced him that Muslims had to be put down. The first factor is the intense desire of a prisoner to be of use to his captors. Recall what Savarkar had written in his 'mercy petitions'—that he would do his utmost to help work the scheme that the British put in place. And this was not just in regard to the constitutional arrangements to govern India. The moment Turkey joined the War on the side of Germany, Savarkar started pleading with the British that he be given the opportunity to enlist and fight Germany, Turkey, etc. There is real danger that Turkey along with other Islamic powers from the Hejaz to Afghanistan will team up and attack India, he wrote. They will be assisted by traitorous Muslims within India, he wrote. This became an *idee fixe* with him. He would invoke this prospect time and time again in the following decades. Indeed, as we will see, he even charged Gandhiji for having joined this conspiracy to help Muslims fulfil their singular aim—the re-establishment of Islamic rule over all of India.

His tract, *Essentials of Hindutva,* fits the same objective. As has been pointed out repeatedly, by Ambedkar to begin with, the central concept in it was very carefully formulated to exclude Muslims. Only those could be full-fledged members of our nation, he wrote, for whom this land was the land of birth, the land in which they performed their karma, the land of their ancestors, and also their sacred land—their *punyabhoomi.* Hindus, Sikhs, Jains were automatically included. Parsis, Jews, Zoroastrians, Christians, Muslims could never be included at par. Their parents may have been Hindus—the mothers of most Mughal emperors, including

---

[51] *Hindu Pad-padshahi,* op. cit., pp. xi–xii.

Aurangzeb, had been Hindus before their conversion, Savarkar pointed out. They may do good work in India, they may fight valiantly for India. But because their sacred places were elsewhere, their loyalty would always lie elsewhere.

As readers of his books and articles would have noticed, so that there is no ambiguity that this is the place of the Hindus, Savarkar always spelt 'Hindustan' with an 'h'—'Hindu*sthan*'. 'Howsoever many rats, lizards, spiders, etc. may be staying in a house,' he wrote in one of his characteristic similes, 'the house does not become theirs. It remains the house of the master. In the same way, however many other types of people may be staying in the country, the country is of the Hindus.'[52]

This was the two-nation theory—a theory that was so convenient to the British. The British could, and did explain away their decision to not delegate power to Indians at a faster pace on the grounds that there were irreconcilable differences between Hindus and Muslims. Savarkar began advancing this unbridgeable separateness much before Jinnah alighted on the same thesis.

This rigid, uncompromising line had another advantage. Savarkar hated Gandhiji more than he hated anyone else. His harshest criticism and abuse were directed at ahimsa and other norms around which Gandhiji was mobilizing the masses. But was the basic reason sheer jealousy? As we noticed, Savarkar had probably seen himself as the heir to Tilak—from the community, Marathas, that had smashed the Mughal empire; from the caste—Chitpavan Brahmins—that had produced one leader after another right up to Tilak—the revolutionary strategist. And here was Gandhi from distant South Africa, stealing the prize. The worst of it was that while Savarkar was the one who had staked his all on Hindutva, the one who was pressing the case for Hindutva, the Hindus were flocking to Gandhiji—they as well as others looked to Gandhiji as the representative of Hindus, as the epitome of Hindu culture and civilization.

---

[52] *Savarkar Samagra,* Volume VII, p. 363.

Gandhiji's politics was built on the premise that there were three earth-faults in Indian society and polity which the British would widen so as to paralyze the national movement—Princes versus British India; Harijans versus caste Hindus; and Hindus versus Muslims. So, he did everything he could to hold them together. The thesis on which Savarkar had alighted differentiated him from Gandhiji and the Gandhian approach completely.

Savarkar maintained that Muslims will just not join Hindus in a struggle to secure joint-rule over India. To do so would be to repudiate their religion and a sin, he argued. They may under compulsion stay as drenched cats [*bheegi billies*] in such a land—but they will do so out of fear not with conviction, not with faith, he maintained. Not just that. They believed what they had been taught—that they would have to atone for committing the sin. For them to re-establish Islamic rule over India was a religious duty. They felt that they had a special position as they had been rulers over this land for centuries. In whatever they decide, the British must keep this fact in mind, they told the British. And now because they were in a minority, they must be given special treatment—for instance, higher representation in higher posts, in the army and police—so that their interests are safeguarded.

This is where the Congress, and Gandhiji in particular had made two fatal mistakes, Savarkar argued. First, they had fallen for 'Territorial Nationalism'—that anyone who lived in India would be an Indian citizen, with the underlying premise that all would devote themselves equally to the interests of the country. Second, the Congress and Gandhiji in particular had worked on the premise that if only their latest demand were to be conceded, the Muslims would join the national struggle. The record showed that the moment one demand was conceded, they started pressing yet another demand.[53] Because of such erroneous premises, the Congress had pushed itself into a trough of always feeling that *it* had to prove its *bona*

---

[53] In his book, *Pakistan or the Partition of India,* Ambedkar gave a comprehensive list of these concessions and their fate, an account that is truly worth reading: Cf. B.R. Ambedkar,

fides. This is what the Muslims exploited. Instead of saying that Congress is a national organization, Savarkar wrote, that there are no Hindus and no Muslims in it, the Congress leaders started saying, 'How can an organisation in which there are no Muslims be a national organisation?' As a result, they decided that, whatever the cost, we must have some Muslims in it. Seeing this, the Muslims began saying, 'If you give this then we will join, if you give that we will join.' A loot started.

As evidence, Savarkar often cited the autobiography of Surendranath Banerjee.[54] In recounting the third session of the Congress, Banerjee had remarked, '. . . The Mohammedan community under the leadership of Sir Syed Ahmed had held aloof from the Congress. They were working under the auspices of the "Patriotic Association" in direct opposition to the national movement. Our critics regarded the National Congress as a Hindu Congress and the opposition papers described it as such. We were straining every nerve to secure the cooperation of our Mohammedan fellow countrymen in this great national work. We sometimes paid the fares of Mohammedan delegates and offered them other facilities.'

It becomes obvious from this that the Congress kept these 'rented Mussalmaans' near itself only because they were Musalmaans, Savarkar said. Within two years of its formation, to keep up this *tamasha* of Hindu-Mussalmaan unity the Congress had become mad and besieged. This mentality of Congress leaders of giving fares and wages swelled into giving Gandhi's 'blank cheques' . . . Unwittingly the leaders of the Congress thus introduced this time-bomb of touching the feet of Mussalmaans in the very foundations of Bharatiya *rajniti*. No one had even imagined that when

---

Pakistan or the Partition of India, now Volume VIII of *Dr. Babasaheb Ambedkar, Writings and Speeches,* Government of India, New Delhi, 1979/2014.

[54] One of the founders of the Congress. Worked for Hindu-Muslim unity. Broke with the Congress over support for the Montagu-Chelmsford reforms.

this time-bomb explodes it will blow up the very ribs/*dhajiyaan* of united Hindusthan and the oneness of Bharat, Savarkar wrote.[55]

The Congress and Gandhiji had fallen into these twin mistakes because they had not looked the religion of Muslims in the eye. The Congress policy of '*Haanji, haanji*'/'Yes Sir, Yes Sir' is only going to lead Muslims to demand more and more. The answer to obstinacy is obstinacy, Savarkar argued.

The Remedy

In retrospect, the dispute is not about the attitude of the Muslim leadership, especially after Jinnah took over. The long list of concessions that Ambedkar documented settles the matter. The problem is that with all his bluster, Savarkar did not build, the RSS did not build, no one else built or was able to build a countervailing force. In his public speeches as well as in private exchanges, Savarkar kept assuring people that three sinews of strength would keep the Muslims from achieving their nefarious aims—of establishing Islamic rule over all of India or breaking India.

The first, he maintained, was the strength that the Hindu Mahasabha had accumulated to counter the Muslims. The second was the leverage that his policy of having Hindus enter the military had given. This would ensure that they could seize Independence by arms when required, and thwart Muslim designs. His published speeches are full of such claims. An intelligence report about the discussions he had with Hindu Mahasabha workers in Poona gives a glimpse of the airy talk:

> In Savarkar's view there can never be Pakistan in India: if Jinnah were to start riots on this issue, the Sabha's volunteers were already strong enough to oppose the Muslims, or even to start riots on their own in order to teach the Muslims a lesson.

---

[55] The writings and speeches in which Savarkar pressed these points fill volumes. As an example, see his 'Autobiography' in *Savarkar Samagra*, Volume I, pp. 96–103.

As regards, independence, Savarkar hopes to achieve this goal along the path of militarization, and not by direct action. He thinks that the Sabha's policy of militarization, though slow, is sure, and he is confident that when the Mahasabha has its own men and officers in the Army in sufficient numbers, its pressure on Government will be irresistible and that it will be able to free India by a Revolution, if necessary, as was done in Russia.

To a private enquiry whether he would be prepared to ask Indians to turn their guns against Government, Savarkar said that he had never openly ventured any such advice in any of his public speeches, though the burden of his utterances might be interpreted as having this effect. Should he be prosecuted on this issue, his defence would be forthcoming.[56]

During a meeting to felicitate him on his 61st birthday, we have him holding forth with the same confidence, though on different grounds:

In spite of the various invasions by foreigners India had been able to preserve its culture. Referring to the Muslim demand for Pakistan, he said that Government in their own interest were against it. He blamed the Congress leaders for giving undue importance to the Muslim demand and declared that the Hindu Mahasabha would always oppose all such insidious moves.[57]

'Oppose' by issuing press statements or by actual action on the ground? When the time came, neither Savarkar nor any other organization could unleash violence on a scale that would make either the Muslim League desist from pressing its demand for Pakistan or keep the British from accepting it.

---

[56] Home Department (Spl), File No. 1009/303, Part III, 1942, Directorate of Archives, Maharashtra State, Mumbai.

[57] Home Department (Spl), File No. 1009/309, Part III, 1942, Directorate of Archives, Maharashtra State, Mumbai.

The third force Savarkar held up was of saviours in the wings, in particular one saviour—who would swoop down to thwart the Muslims.

The Saviour

Muslims must remember that the possibility of a Hindu-Buddhist alliance has come into being, he declared. The reason for this, to say nothing of evidence for it, he provided was curious: 'If the Mussalmaans can see daydreams of a pan-Mussalmaan alliance, can we not dream of a Hindu-Buddhist alliance stretching from Jammu to Japan?'[58]

The even more formidable superpower that was going to swoop down to save the Hindus and their Motherland was the one and only Hindu kingdom in the world—Nepal.

In his Presidential Addresses to sessions of the Hindu Mahasabha, Savarkar repeatedly returned to Nepal—that Hindusthan and Nepal were one, Nepal was as integral a part of India as Maharashtra, Punjab, Madras; that Nepal faced the same dangers from Mussalmaans as we do in India; that the King and Prime Minister of Nepal were alive to these facts; that Nepal had legions of Gurkhas—well-armed and battle-hardened; that they would sweep down into Bihar and Bengal in the east and down the Indus in the west to save our common Motherland; that, in fact, the British Government should restore to Nepal the lands which at one time belonged to it and were subsequently annexed by the British. All this from one who considered himself to be a major strategic thinker.

Sounds Incredible?

Do these fanciful notions sound incredible?

Well, here is Savarkar delivering his Presidential Address at the 19th Session of the Hindu Mahasabha at Ahmedabad/Amravati in 1937. At

---

[58] *Savarkar Samagra,* Volume VIII, pp. 548–49.

the very outset, he delivers 'Homage to the Independent Hindu Kingdom of Nepal'.

'I feel it my bounden duty to send forth on behalf of all Hindus our loyal and loving greeting to His Majesty the King of Nepal, His Highness Shree Yuddhsamasher Ranajee—the prime minister of Nepal and all of our coreligionists and countrymen there,' he tells the delegates, 'who have even in the darkest hour of our History, been successful in holding out as Hindu Power and in keeping a flag of Hindu Independence flying unsullied on the summit of the Himalayas.' Nepal is the only kingdom that is recognized as an independent Hindu kingdom. The King is the only one among twenty-five crores Hindus 'who can enter in the assemblage of Kings, Emperors and Presidents of all the independent nations in the world, with head erect and unbent, as an equal amongst equals.' We are bound together not just by the exigencies of the current situation, he says, but also by 'the dearest ties of a common race and religion and language and culture, inheriting with us this our common Motherland and our common Holyland.' 'Our life is one,' Savarkar says. 'Whatever contributes to the strength of the Hindudom as a whole, must strengthen Nepal and whatever progress the latter records is bound to elevate the first.' Hence every Hindusangathanite looks forward to Nepal being 'rapidly brought to an up-to-date efficiency, political, social, and above all military and aerial so as to enable Her to hold out Her own in the National struggle for existence that is going on all around us and march on to fulfil the great and glorious destiny that awaits Her ahead.'[59]

As the War speeds up, Savarkar returns to Nepal at the Bhagalpur Session. He conveys his 'Loyal Homage to His Majesty the King of Nepal'. 'I tender on behalf of Hindudom as a whole our most loyal homage

---

[59] V.D. Savarkar, *Historic Statements,* 1967, Bombay, and *Hindu Rashtra Darshan,* e-book composed by Chandrashekhar Sane. The latter book contains Savarkar's Presidential Addresses at six annual sessions of the Hindu Mahasabha during the time he was its President from the 19th session at Ahmedabad in 1937 to the 24th Session in Cawnpore, in 1942.

to his Majesty the King of Nepal as a defender of the Hindu Faith, the Sovereign of the only Independent Hindi[60] Kingdom today, the foremost representative of the glorious Hindu past and the Hope of still more glorious Hindi future,' he told the delegates. By good fortune, he said, 'the present Prime Minister of Nepal realizes more than anyone else that the future of the Hindu Kingdom of Nepal is indissolubly bound up with the future of Hindudom as a whole. Hindus in fact are a National unit and it is given to Nepal today to shape its destiny.' Given what is happening around us, it has been wise of the kingdom of Nepal to have allied itself with the British Government 'and sent our brave Gurkha armies to protect Indian Frontiers and to some other theatres of war to check new alien invasions.'

And then comes crucial advice to the British: 'The British Government too would do well to recompense for this effective assistance they receive at Nepal at least those districts in Bihar and on the Borders of the Punjab which were a part of the Kingdom of Nepal only a century ago and were then annexed by the British.'[61]

'It is encouraging to note that the land-forces of Nepal are already so efficient and up-to-date as to match the resistance,' he says. 'But we are anxiously waiting for the day when even the aerial forces of Nepal will be as efficient, up-to-date and powerful enough to protect not only herself but even Hindudom as a whole.'

---

[60] Savarkar often used the word 'Hindi' rather than 'Hindu' to conform better to 'Hindutva' which he maintained is wider than mere 'Hinduism'. The latter is one part of it—it is a religion. The former is a 'history', encompassing everything that the race has experienced and achieved.

[61] Going by Bhide's volume, the exhortation at the 21st session of the Hindu Mahasabha, Calcutta, in 1939, was more explicit. In his Presidential Address, Savarkar said,

> In this connection it must be emphasized that the British Government should also restore some of those territories on the borders of Nepal which the British had wrested from her in the past, back to the King of Nepal. Such a step will cement the friendship between the two Nations as nothing else can do.

Moreover, now the same villain threatens us: 'From sources which are more or less reliable,' Savarkar says, 'it seems that the Moslems are trying to make their influences felt and stealthy and treacherous advances [sic.]. Mosques are multiplying rapidly in Nepal and the numbers of unwary Hindu girls and lads are being kidnapped or duped in surrounding tribal districts and ultimately converted to Mohammedanism. There are more ways than one by which a well-planned scheme of increasing the numerical strength of the Moslems in and about the Hindu Kingdom is long being worked out.' The Nepal Government should be as alert as possible to this danger, Savarkar says. Mosques are built. At first, they act as places for prayer. But 'they soon develop, as we have found in so many cases all over India, into hot-beds of anti-Hindu fanaticism.' Similarly, 'The campaign of kidnapping and abduction does on the face of it seem a stray outburst of individual crime,' at first. 'But then if history has anything to teach us Hindus, it teaches us that it was by these means, howsoever despicable they may seem, that the Moslems continued and are even now continuing to increase their numerical strength and strengthen their hold in India.' Nepal should not fall prey to the 'suicidal madness' which enabled non-Hindus to take over all of India. 'The erstwhile guests are threatening to oust the master of the house himself, out of it. Consequently, the Government of Nepal should make it clear to all concerned that no anti-Hindu activity or designs would be tolerated in Nepal and should watch ceaselessly so as not allow any non-Hindu section and especially the Moslems to grow in numerical strength in Nepal beyond what it recorded a century ago,' he urges.

Denouncing Gandhiji for saying that were the British to leave and were, say, the Nizam to become the ruler of India, that still would be *swadeshi* rule, Savarkar declares that, in that case, the ruler of India would be His Highness the King of Nepal and not the Nizam.

The collective might of Hindu Rajas-Maharajas, of the awakened Hindus is enough to deal with any Nizam or ruler of Bhopal . . .

When all the Hindu Maharajas from Udaipur to Kolhapur and in the south all the Hindu Naresh from Mysore to Cochin pounce on the Mussalmaan rule, then from the Dakshin sea to the Yamuna, not a scrap of Muslim rule will remain . . .

It would be foolish to imagine that what Nadir Shah and Ahmedshah Abdali could not accomplish at the height of their power will be accomplished by some tolies from the Frontier now. Apart from this it will be very costly for them to forget the might of the independent, Hindu kingdom of Nepal with its disciplined guns. And in Gandhiji's terms, his rule will be Swarajya in any case . . .

The strategist's plan:

Should any Mussalmaan raise his head to re-establish Muslim hegemony over Hindusthan with the help of Muslims from the Northern and Southern provinces, the King of Nepal, the protector of Hindus will surely sweep down as the Commander-in-Chief of the Hindu army. At the least, he will not let go of a golden opportunity to establish its power. Given the current situation, the Gurkha battalions can invade Bihar, Bengal up to Assam with ease. The gundas of Mian Haq in Noakhali and the Khaksars roaming around with just phawadaas [62] on their shoulders will be inadequate to meet the might sweeping down of the Akhil Hindu Sangathan soldiers of independent Nepal. Can mere sand dunes stop the mighty ocean . . .?

Muslims and those backing them should beware:

. . . it never occurs to us that while the Moslems are building castles in air for their independent Nizam to lodge, there is already in fact an independent Hindu Kingdom of Nepal with a hundred thousand

---

[62] Shovels.

seasoned Hindu soldiers shouldering up-to-date rifles in defence of the Hindu cause!

But we have been also saying repeatedly, all this is academic. If Hindus from a 'pan Hindu' viewpoint assess how much strength can be gathered in our hands in comparison with Bharatiya Mussalmaans, and from time to time gather all those centres together, then what is today an academic discussion can become actual. This dream of a united, strong and independent Hindu saamrajya can be realised in so short a period that one cannot have the courage to even imagine it.[63]

The Saviour Ends Up Swallowed

As far as rescuing India is concerned, all this may sound Quixotic. But the embrace left the Nepalese apprehensive.

Under Savarkar's guidance, a movement was launched for Nepal. The essays he wrote and statements he delivered in connection with this movement had one theme.[64] Nepal and Hindusthan are not two separate rashtra at all. Because of British rule over India, Nepal, being independent, is out of 'British Hindusthan' but not out of 'Hindusthan'. Just because Nepal did not fall into the hands of the British, should we look upon it as a foreign land?[65] 'The Gurkhas,' he says, 'are the direct descendants of Rajputs and went to Nepal only some three centuries ago!'[66]

How is it that, when the Congress' national council has drawn up a list of provinces on the basis of language, it has not included Nepal, Savarkar demands. Nepal should be counted as one of the provinces of Hindusthan, like Portuguese Goa and French Pondicherry. Does anyone

---

[63] *Savarkar Samagra,* Volume IV, pp. 688–95.

[64] See, *Savarkar Samagra,* Volume IX, pp. 501–624.

[65] *Savarkar Samagra,* Volume IX, pp. 562–65.

[66] *Hindu Rashtra Darshan,* op. cit., p. 88.

have the courage to say that the independent Hindu kingdom of Nepal does not have as much right to see to the future of Hindusthan that the lifeless provinces groaning under foreign rule have? The *dhwaja* of an independent Hindu rashtra is flying over Nepal. Even today sixty thousand Hindu soldiers trained in the latest European arts of warfare, having bravely battled German tanks and bombers, answering the orders of a Hindu Commander-in-Chief, are poised under the Hindu *dhwaja*. So, Savarkar declares, in the enumeration and demarcation of provinces along linguistic lines, the independent Hindu Kingdom of Nepal should be enumerated along with other provinces of India.[67]

By the time he comes to write *Six Glorious Epochs*, the proud and independent kingdom of Nepal has become firmly a part of India:

> . . . in fact, Nepal is as much an indivisible part of India as are Maharashtra, the Punjab or Madras. These regions might have been governed by different rulers at different times but the term Hindu Nation is equally applicable to all of them . . .[68]

The great, independent Kingdom of Nepal that was going to rush to our rescue had become just another province of India.

Good strategic thinking!

---

[67] *Savarkar Samagra*, Volume IX, pp. 540–42.

[68] *Six Glorious Epochs of Indian History*, op. cit., para 984, pp. 353–54.

Learning to Read a Revolutionary

' . . . Gandhiji and Myself Lived Together as Friends . . .'

Savarkar is being tried, along with Godse, Apte and others for the assassination of Gandhiji. He files a detailed written statement in his defence. During the course of this, among many other things he says:

I have been accused of so wicked a crime as to abet the murder of Gandhiji and of an incitement against the life of Pandit Nehru too. It is absolutely relevant if I try to bring to the notice of Your Honour the personal feelings I cherished regarding Gandhiji and Panditji too. I shall not refer to my relations personal and public with Gandhiji in the rather remote past by reciting how in 1908 Gandhiji resided in 'India House' in London owned by the well-known personality, Pandit Shyamji Krishnavarma, and placed under my management and led by me; how Gandhiji and myself lived together as friends and worked together as compatriots; how later on he paid a personal visit with his wife to me and my family and spent hours in happy talks about our old comradeship and current politics. I would not waste the time of the Court in telling how Gandhiji wrote now and then kind notes about me in 'Young India' too. Because those memories would naturally be held as too distant in so far as this case is concerned. Enough to say that in spite of fundamental differences in our ideologies on some points and in virtue of close affinity on others, there ever continued a mutual respect for and a personal goodwill to each other.[1]

Even so brief an extract gives us several insights into Savarkar, and alerts us to the care with which we must read what he says. In these few sentences, apart from the allusion to what Gandhiji may have written about him in *Young India*, Savarkar says:

- 'in 1908 Gandhiji resided in "India House" in London'
- 'Gandhiji and myself stayed together as friends'
- We 'worked together as compatriots'
- Gandhiji and his wife came to visit me and my family in our house in Ratnagiri 'and spent hours in happy talks about our old comradeship and current politics'
- 'there ever continued a mutual respect for and a personal goodwill to each other'

1908

Let us just start with 'in 1908 Gandhiji resided in "India House" in London.' It so happens that

- Gandhiji was not in London in 1908 at all
- He never 'resided in 'India House'—he did spend one night, though not in 1908, and that is all
- Neither in 'India House' nor anywhere else, neither in 1908 nor at any other time did Gandhiji and Savarkar 'live together as friends and work together as compatriots' at all

---

[1] For the full statement that Savarkar made in court, *Savarkar Samagra,* Volume II, pp. 590–633.

'India House' was inaugurated in July 1905. It had accommodation for around 25 students. Gandhiji had left England for India in 1891. From 1896, he was in South Africa. As is well-known, he became involved in several public activities there, especially directed at opposing discrimination against and the condition of persons of Indian origin. In 1906, he and another Indian, Haji Ojer Ally, were deputed by the Indian community to go to London to canvas their case. They reached Southampton on 20 October 1906. Conscientious about his assignment and punctilious about expenses, Gandhiji used to send information regularly to the community back in South Africa through letters and as despatches to *Indian Opinion* about what he was doing. We therefore have a record of, among other things, when and where he stayed. From the despatch he sends on 3 November 1906, we learn:

> . . . On the first day of our arrival, both Mr. Ally and I went to stay at India House, and we were very well looked after. But as our work requires our getting in touch with important people and as India House is rather remote, we have been obliged to come and live at this Hotel at great expense.[2]

In the coming days and months, he puts himself through what for us would be gruelling and far-from-heartening toil—letters, memoranda, waiting on British worthies, rushing from one to another, meetings, lectures.[3]

Gandhiji leaves for South Africa on 1 December 1906.

He does not come to England either in 1907 or 1908.

---

[2] Despatch in *Indian Opinion*, 1 December, 1906, *Collected Works,* Volume V, pp. 490–91.

[3] 'Often working through the night, and writing an incredible 5,000 or so letters during the six weeks . . .,'Rajmohan Gandhi writes about Gandhiji's work during this brief visit. Rajmohan Gandhi, *Mohandas, A true story of a man, his people and an Empire,* Penguin, 2006, p. 127.

1909

In 1909, Gandhiji is deputed a second time by the Indian community to represent their case to the authorities in London. Sir Curzon Wyllie, the Political Secretary to the Secretary of State for India, is assassinated by a young Indian, Madanlal Dhingra, on 2 July 1909—we will return to this in a moment. Gandhiji reaches London just days later, on 10 July 1909. This time, as we learn from the *Deputation Notes* that he sends back with unfailing regularity, he goes straight to Hotel Cecil,[4] and then to Westminster Palace Hotel. He stays there till 13 November 1909. 'Hectic' would hardly be an adequate word to describe his engagements and activities. They are a whirlpool. They tell on him physically. He has sent his colleague in South Africa, H.S.L. Polak to India to sensitize leaders there to the problems of the Indian community in South Africa. In a letter to Polak written just four days into this visit, he describes the endless rounds of meetings and remarks in passing:

> . . . I am already working under double pressure: have not yet been able to go to bed before one o'clock in the morning, and you know what that means to me. The legacy of a swollen leg, which I inherited from the Pretoria gaol, has not yet left me; this, however, by the way.[5] . . .

And, as we learn from his *Deputation Notes*, in many ways the endless activities are enough to try even his patience:

> The more experience I have of meeting so-called big men or even men who are really great, the more disgusted I feel after every such meeting. All such efforts are no better than pounding chaff. Everyone appears preoccupied with his own affairs. Those who occupy positions

---

[4] *Collected Works,* Volume IX, p. 402.

[5] *Collected Works,* Volume IX, p. 406.

of power show little inclination to do justice. Their only concern is to hold on to their positions. We have to spend a whole day in arranging for an interview with one or two persons. Write a letter to the person concerned, wait for his reply, acknowledge it and then go to his place. One may be living in the north and another in the south. Even after all this fuss, one cannot be very hopeful about the outcome. If considerations of justice had any appeal, we would have got [what we want] long before now. The only possibility is that some concessions may be granted through fear. It can give no pleasure to a satyagrahi to have to work in such conditions.

I think it will be far better to submit to still further suffering than exhaust ourselves in such efforts and waste so much money on them . . .[6]

Pressed in this manner, would Gandhiji have had the kind of time to spare for Savarkar that the latter implied in his statement to the Court?

Gandhiji leaves England for South Africa on 13 November 1909.

After 1909

Gandhiji does not return to England till August 1914.

Now let us look at Savarkar's whereabouts after 1909 when Gandhiji left England for South Africa.

He is captured in London on his return from Paris on 13 March 1910.

He is put on a ship going to India in July 1910.

He is convicted and sent to the Andamans. He enters the Cellular Jail on 4 July 1911.

In a word, Gandhiji left England in November 1909 not to return till August 1914. Savarkar was shipped out of England in July 1910. There is no way that Savarkar and Gandhiji could have 'stayed together as friends'.

---

[6] *Indian Opinion*, 21-8-1909, *Collected Works*, Volume IX, pp. 440–41.

There is an even more conclusive reason why Gandhiji would not have stayed at 'India House' any time during his 1909 visit.

The Conclusive Reason

For a moment, we should step back a little to the previous visit—in 1906. Here is a letter that Gandhiji wrote on 6 November 1906:

> Hotel Cecil, London,
> November 6, 1906
>
> Dear Mr. Brown,
>
> I thank you for your letter of the 5th instant. I send you the last two copies of *Indian Opinion*, which will give you some more information about the Ordinance, and also on the general movements of the Indian community in South Africa. You will also see that the last number contains photographs of the Delegates.
>
> It was very kind of you to introduce Mr. Ritch and me to Sir Curzon Wyllie, though at the time you introduced us I did not know that Sir Curzon was the Political A.D.C. to Mr. Morley . . .[7]

When Gandhiji lands in 1909, all England is agog with the assassination of one of the persons named in in that letter: Sir Curzon Wyllie. He had served in various capacities in India, and was at the time ADC to Lord Morley, the Secretary of State for India. Just ten days before Gandhiji was to land, a young Indian, Madanlal Dhingra, an understudy of Savarkar, and a part of the group that congregated at India House, had killed Curzon Wyllie.

A meeting over tea had been organized by Indians. Britishers too were invited. As Curzon Wyllie was coming in, Dhingra shot him at point-blank range. A Parsi doctor, Cawas Lalcaca, who was visiting from Shanghai, tried to shield the victim. Dhingra killed him too. Dhingra was overpowered.

---

[7] *Collected Works,* Volume VI, pp. 7–8.

During the trial, he acknowledged that, yes, he had indeed done what he was accused of doing.

Savarkar was exultant at the assassination. Gandhiji was appalled.

Apart from everything else, the assassination of Curzon Wyllie, as Gandhiji was to record later, had 'complicated' his mission: he had come to plead the cause of Indians with Britain's leaders, and the thought uppermost in everyone's mind was that an Indian had murdered an Englishman. The deed was all the more galling because, as we just saw, Gandhiji had been introduced to Curzon Wyllie during his previous visit, and because Curzon Wyllie had been killed at a function to which he had been invited by Indians, and was, as Gandhiji noted in his letters, their guest. Murdering, and murdering one you have invited as a guest. It doesn't take much to imagine Gandhiji's revulsion.

He did not, and just would not have gone to 'India House' to 'live together as friends' with anyone, much less with one who had been the guide of Dhingra and who was exulting in the deed.

The 'Biography'

We have already come across, *Life of Barrister Savarkar* by 'Chitragupta', a 'biography' that was probably written by Savarkar himself. As we saw, it is quite as effusive in recalling the killing of Curzon Wyllie as it is about the reported admiration of Lloyd George and other British leaders for Dhingra's statement. Chitragupta also recounts the 'rumour' that Savarkar had written the statement, that he had smuggled it out of the prison after meeting Dhingra.

The point that is significant for our present concern is whether Gandhiji would have stayed at India House with the assassination having been carried out just days before his arrival. All the more so in light of what Chitragupta states: that he, Dhingra, *'till then was a prominent member of the India House brotherhood'.*[8] Later, the book reproduces

---

[8] Chitragupta, *Life of Barrister Savarkar,* op. cit., p.58.

the view of the authorities about 'Dhingra, *a resident of the India House* who assassinated Sir Curzon Wyllie with a Browning pistol at a party in London in June 1909'.[9] Another point which this book spells out is just as relevant. After the assassination, and in particular after Dhingra is hanged, Chitragupta tells us,

> Now a whole troop of detectives and police was let loose on the Indians in London. Almost every second man was marked out and watched. The India House was the special victim. The whole street was dotted by detectives. They would dog the very steps of every Indian who passed by and scare him away. But Savarkar and his band continued their work unperturbed . . . The India House was ultimately stopped as it enabled the Police to watch the center of Revolutionists all the more easily in a group. But, as Mr. Savarkar said, the India House was closed not before it had done its work of propaganda: for every room where an Indian youth stayed was turned into an Indian House.[10]

---

[9] Ibid, p. 164. This is from the judgement of the Special Tribunal that convicted Savarkar later. The context is a pamphlet many copies of which were found along with the twenty Browning pistols that the Court held Savarkar had forced on Chaturbhuj, the cook at India House, to smuggle into India. The Court observed,

It is a pamphlet in praise of Dhingra, a resident of the India House, who assassinated Sir Curzon Wyllie with a Browning pistol in London in June 1909. The pamphlet strongly advocates political assassination in India and whether or not it is from the pen of Vinayak Savarkar, it at all events represents doctrines which he was anxious to disseminate in India. The following passage may be quoted as indicating its aim: 'Terrorise the officials, and the collapse of the whole machinery of oppression is not very far. The persistent execution of the policy that has been so gloriously inaugurated by Khudiram Bose, Kanailal Dutt and other martyrs will soon cripple the British Government in India. This campaign of separate assassinations is the best conceivable method of paralysing the bureaucracy and of arousing the people. The initial stage of the revolution is marked by the policy of separate assassination.' Ibid, pp. 164–65.

[10] Ibid, pp. 69–70.

Now,

- Gandhiji is totally opposed to the violence, in particular the assassinations which these India House youngsters think are the only way India can secure freedom
- The victim of this particular assassination is someone to whom Gandhiji has been introduced on his previous visit to London
- The person who has killed him is a 'resident of' India House, 'a prominent member of the India House fraternity'
- The suspicions of the authorities are focused on India House
- The assassination, having been executed just a few days before his arrival, has, as he wrote, 'complicated' his mission of getting British leaders to take a sympathetic view of the condition of Indians in South Africa.

Given all this, would Gandhiji have stayed in the same India House so soon after the assassination when the killing, the killer, his trial, his hanging were the one subject that was being discussed in the town?

Savarkar's claim in his statement to the trial Court turns out to be completely fabricated.

And now let us see whether Gandhiji and Savarkar could have, as Savarkar claimed in his statement to the Court, 'worked together as compatriots'.

'Worked Together as Compatriots'

In late nineteenth and early twentieth century, revolutions, violence, assassinations and secret societies were much in the air throughout Europe and Russia. Not just Marx and Engels, but Mazzini and Garibaldi, the Nihilists, the Anarchists, and a host of other theoreticians and practitioners of violence, the groups and movements they had spawned, were the staple of heated debates. Russian young men, and those of other nationalities roamed European cities imparting instruction on how to organize work in secret, on how to make bombs. In India, the 1857 uprising had been suppressed—only to give rise to new 'schools' of violence. Nothing will be gained by petitioning the British, they maintained. But the British have the capacity to overwhelm violence of the 1857 kind, especially as the people have been completely and meticulously disarmed; so that is out—in any case, the people are not ready for it. So, we must frighten the rulers out of India through assassinations—of selected officials as well as others picked at random—and through raids at official establishments. Inspiration and guidance for such a course could be inferred from the writings of even such a great figure as the Lokmanya. This sentiment had taken root in Bengal, Maharashtra, Punjab. The killing of Rand, the Plague Commissioner in Poona, and Ayerst, his military escort, by the Chapekar brothers, their trial, the hanging of the three that followed, had become household legends throughout Maharashtra. In Bengal, the partition of the province had enraged the people. Agitations and murders had become frequent. Khudi Ram Bose, a young lad of 18, had flung a bomb at Kingsford, the District Magistrate of Muzaffarpur; the bomb had missed Kingsford. A Mrs Kennedy and her daughter were killed. The Sub-Inspector, an Indian, Nandlal, who arrested Khudi Ram Bose, was also killed. And so was Narendra Gosain, approver in the Alipore Conspiracy Case. In 1909, Ashutosh Biswas, a Public Prosecutor, was shot dead, while leaving the court in Calcutta. And so on.[11]

In distant South Africa, Gandhiji was observing all this and growing more and more convinced that objectives achieved through violence would turn out to be poison. He was hewing a different path. On it, work would be in the open—in contrast to the secretiveness that characterized the path of violence. It would involve people at large—in contrast to assassinations which of necessity were the work of the fewest possible. Most of all, it would be non-violent. Instead of inflicting suffering on others, people would

---

[11] Cf., Note in *Collected Works*, Volume X, p. 253.

invite suffering for themselves and, through that, move the authorities to do right. He had been able to mobilize the Indian community. Indians there and he himself had been hauled into prison. They had not flinched. Their sticking to peaceful methods on the one hand and, on the other, the heavy hand that the authorities had brought down on them, had begun to attract considerable attention—especially in England. The authorities were struck by its novelty. They also saw its potential power. Young Indians in London, especially those weaned, so to say, by Shyamji Krishnavarma, thought of Gandhi's method and teaching as worse than useless. They parodied it, they denounced it.

This was the backdrop against which Gandhiji's 1909 trip to England was planned. But it wasn't just his current mission that Gandhiji was worried about, and not just about the killing of Curzon Wyllie. He had been worried to the bone about what this 'cult of the bomb' would do to the people at home—how among Britishers ruling India it would become the reason for ever greater suppression of Indians, of ever greater expenditure on armed forces out of funds extracted from Indians; how Indians, having begun to kill others, would all-too-soon fall on each other, how it would harden hearts and coarsen minds of the people at large.

An Assassination

We have earlier encountered the assassination of Curzon Wyllie, and how enthused Savarkar was by it—recall the dispatches in the 'newsletter' that he used to send home for publication. On the other hand, Gandhiji was revolted by it. In his *Deputation Notes*, Gandhiji called the assassination 'a terrible thing'.[12] A while later, he referred to it as 'an illustration in its worst and [most] detestable form of the method'—the method of violence,

---

[12] 'Deputation Notes' written on or just after 16 July 1909, *Indian Opinion,* 14 August 1909, *Collected Works,* Volume IX, pp. 427-29.

'one of the accepted and "time-honoured" methods to attain the ends . . .'[13] Reminding his readers that Curzon Wyllie had been invited to a tea-meeting by Indians, Gandhiji said, 'Sir Curzon Wyllie was [thus] a guest of the assassin. From this point of view, Mr. Madanlal Dhingra murdered his guest in his own house . . .' And said that as such the murder was an act of cowardice: 'If I kill someone in my own house without a warning—someone who has done me no harm—I cannot but be called a coward. There is an ancient custom among the Arabs that they would not kill anyone in their own house, even if the person be their enemy. They would kill him after he had left the house and after he had been given time to arm himself. Those who believe in violence would be brave men if they observe these rules when killing anyone. Otherwise, they must be looked upon as cowards.'

But the principal blame did not lie on Dhingra, Gandhiji pointed out:

> Mr. Dhingra's defence is inadmissible. In my view, he has acted like a coward. All the same, one can only pity the man. He was egged on to do this act by ill-digested reading of worthless writings. His defence of himself, too, appears to have been learnt by rote. It is those who incited him to this that deserve to be punished. In my view, Mr. Dhingra himself is innocent. The murder was committed in a state of intoxication. It is not merely wine or *bhang* that makes one drunk; a mad idea also can do so. That was the case with Mr. Dhingra.

On the day Dhingra's case comes up in Court, Gandhiji presses the same point:

> Mr. Dhingra's statement, according to me, argues mere childishness or mental derangement. Those who incited him to this act will be called to account in God's court, and are also guilty in the eyes of the world.

---

[13] *Indian Opinion*, 25 December 1909; *Collected Works*, Volume X, p. 243. He repeated the characterization in the Preface he wrote while publishing Tolstoy's 'Letter to a Hindoo': 19 November 1909, *Collected Works*, Volume X, p. 243.

There are immediate consequences of such acts, Gandhiji writes—for the victim, for oneself, for others. Shyamji Krishnavarma's *The Indian Sociologist* had 'published a categorical statement that homicide for the good of one's country was no murder', Gandhiji noted. The Government had taken action against it. The action was not limited to the publication. The authors, being in Paris, could not be acted against but the poor printer, 'an innocent Englishman', who knew nothing of what the issue contained had been sentenced. 'Such acts will not advance the progress of the nation. So long as the people do not throw up men who will be prepared to invite the utmost suffering on themselves, India will never prosper.'[14] Moreover, they ignite a cycle of revenge. With the exchanges in London much in his mind, Gandhiji wrote about 'The futility of brute force' in *Indian Opinion.* He took as the news peg an instance which was being talked about across Europe. It concerned 'a famous man in Spain, [Francisco] Ferrer by name, who worked to spread education among the people.' He was, besides, an atheist, a strong opponent of the Roman Catholics. He believed in violence, and, in turn, was shot dead. And now '. . . his comrades want to avenge his death . . . Because he lost his life, revolutionaries in Europe have given way to a frenzy of excitement, abandoning all reason. There is no concern for justice in all this. "Kill, kill", that is all they want. If this is the way things go on, no one's life will be safe in Europe . . . Some Indians have been thinking of introducing these methods in India. I think Ferrer's case should serve as a warning to them.'[15]

And there is the larger point about the ultimate consequences of such acts, the consequences for the country. If freedom is attained for the country through murder, who will rule the country? The murderers:

---

[14] *Indian Opinion*, 21 August 1909, *Collected Works,* Volume IX, pp. 436–37.

[15] *Indian Opinion*, 20 November 1909, *Collected Works,* Volume X, p. 188.

I must say that those who believe and argue that such murders may do good to India are ignorant men indeed. No act of treachery can ever profit a nation. Even should the British leave in consequence of such murderous acts, who will rule in their place? The only answer is: the murderers.

India can gain nothing from the rule of murderers—no matter whether they are black or white. Under such a rule, India will be utterly ruined and laid waste.

Any meeting ground for Gandhiji and Savarkar to have worked together as comrades and compatriots?

A Gathering

Because of his intense worry on this score, and in spite of his incredibly heavy duties, Gandhiji made time to exchange views with the young men. Where others had refused, he agreed to participate in an event with them. It was a function in a hotel to celebrate *Vijaya Dashmi.* About 70 persons attended. It had been agreed that no one would speak on political issues. Gandhiji was asked to preside and speak. He spoke of the greatness and goodness of Sri Rama. 'If India again produced a Ramachandra, a Sita, a Lakshmana and a Bharata, she would attain prosperity in no time,' he said. 'It should be remembered, of course, that before Ramachandra qualified for public service, he suffered exile in the forest for 12 years. Sita went through extreme suffering and Lakshmana lived without sleep all those years and observed celibacy. When Indians learn to live in that manner, they can from that instant count themselves as free men. India has no other way of achieving happiness for herself.'

The young Savarkar also spoke. He said that because of the decision that had been taken, he would not speak on any political question.

He would speak only on the Ramayana and what had happened then. From the Ramayana we learn that Rama defeated Ravana not through passive resistance or nonviolence but by the force of arms, he said. It was violence which had conquered evil. Gandhiji described it as 'a spirited speech': 'Savarkar delivered a spirited speech on the great excellence of the *Ramayana* and said that every Indian should realize the significance of the fact that *Vijaya Dashami* is preceded by *Navratri (Roza).*'

The account of the occasion in Chitragupta's *Life of Barrister Savarkar* is more fulsome. Gandhiji had been invited to the meeting, the author of the book reported, in spite of the India House group thinking of him to be, like Gokhale, 'a man of moderate views who was too good-natured or perhaps weak to think of any vigorous line of action.' Gandhiji spoke 'a few non-committal words,' we are told, 'and resumed his seat after saying "But Mr. Savarkar, the speaker of the evening, is to follow me, and I should not like to stand between you and him!" 'Although that veteran orator Mr. B.C. Pal was one of the speakers of the evening,' Chitragupta's account continues, 'Savarkar rose in all confidence of one who was admitted to be easily the first and who himself felt as much, and delivered one of the finest speeches I have ever heard.'[16]

This is the one exchange between the two of which there is a record. But Gandhiji did exchange views with young Indians, and it is possible that he did so with Savarkar also. Neither was able to move the other by an inch. On the contrary, various accounts written later by Savarkar's admirers suggest that from these initial encounters themselves, Savarkar

---

[16] Gandhiji's account was written around 24 October 1909, and is available in the *Collected Works,* Volume X, pp. 189–90. For Chitragupta's account, *Life of Barrister Savarkar, op. cit.*, pp. 151–52.

developed an aversion to Gandhiji and everything he espoused. And not just the accounts written by others. In his autobiography, Savarkar reports that he was convinced from his childhood itself that the only way to secure freedom for the country would be through violence. By the time he got into his teens, on his own account this belief had hardened so much that he had begun forming secret societies and setting out the steps by which violent uprisings are to be brought about. In London, again on his own account, he was converting others to the path of violence, and on the account of the authorities he was preparing manuals on how to make bombs, etc. In this background, we can well imagine how strongly he must have revolted against Gandhiji's approach. A passage from his autobiography—the autobiography was written much later, in the early 1950s—conveys the indignation:

Most thought that Home Rule could be attained without violence. Some thought violence was not opportune. But no one till then had preached the hypocrisy and deception that even if violence is unavoidable in some circumstances or is possible or opportune, to indulge in it is a great sin. And that therefore, we will neither indulge in violence nor accept independence attained through violence . . . No one had preached a doctrine so full of hypocrisy, so laughable and delusory a sermon . . . From Naoroji . . . to Wacha they had spoken against the British decision to disarm Indians and even passed resolutions for these laws to be repealed. Till then the utter hypocrisy of ahimsa had not appeared in the Congress . . . The extremist side thought that armed revolution should not be attempted because in the circumstances prevailing at that time, it was impossible. Not because it is a sin, and only absolute ahimsa is dharma. This madness of absolute ahimsa was rubbed into the Congress fifteen-twenty years later—by the advent of Gandhi.[17]

In a word, Savarkar continued to view with disdain Gandhiji's insistence on non-violence. And, on the other side, Gandhiji never wavered from his view that non-violence was the route to India's independence. His entire life is testimony. As is everything he wrote whenever the subject came up.[18] Where then was the common ground for them to have 'worked together as compatriots'?

---

[17] *Savarkar Samagra,* Volume I, pp. 414–15. That the autobiography was written around 1952 is suggested at p. 417.

[18] As an instance, see his reaction to a bomb being planted and going off under the Viceregal train: 'The cult of the bomb,' *Young India,* 2 January 1930, *Collected Works,* Volume 48, pp. 184–86. A person joined issue with him: you did not use your influence to protect the accused, you did not condemn the policies of the Government which led them to the deed. Gandhiji was forthright:

> They forfeited their lives when they dedicated themselves to their creed. That they keep themselves in hiding does not mean that they fear death, but it means that they want to hang on to life as long as possible so as to carry out their project. They stand in no need of my protection, active or passive. They know that I hold their lives as dear as my own, but they know too that I am a determined enemy of their creed. But my enmity resolves itself into an attempt to convert them to my own. Condemnation of the outrage was a method of conversion. That it may fail in its purpose does not affect it. I must act according to my lights and leave the result to the Higher Power.

As for not having condemned the policies which lead persons to throw bombs, Gandhiji pointed out that every issue of *Young India* contains censure of some policy of the Government. Making the same point in this article would have been irrelevant: 'The point to be made in the article was that violence was ineffective, no matter how wicked was the policy of the Government.' *Young India,* 6 February, 1930. *Collected Works,* Volume 48, pp. 298–99.

The Young Men's Views Continue to Disturb Gandhiji

Exchanges with the young men settled nothing. They remained in Gandhiji's mind as he boarded the ship, *Kildonan Castle*, back to South Africa. It is during this journey that Gandhiji wrote *Hind Swaraj*. So disturbed had he been by what the India House type had been arguing, and even more so by the consequences that would befall India were such ideas to spread further in the country that he devoted an entire section of *Hind Swaraj* to answering their ideas.[19] Means determine ends as much as a seed determines the tree, he emphasized again . . . Courage consists not in killing others but in killing one's self . . . Yes, soul-force has been used since time immemorial, it is used every day—for instance, when a mother wins over the angry child by her love. You do not see this because for you history is only the doings of kings . . .

In every particular, Savarkar's convictions were the direct opposite, and he spent his life denouncing Gandhiji's views. The end alone matters . . . The means that will attain the goal at the least cost to us and inflict the maximum harm to our enemy are the ones that we must use . . . The British can never be made to leave by non-violence . . . They *will* yield to terror spread through assassinations . . . These ideas had congealed in him even before he had gone to London. They were certainly rooted deep in him when he encountered Gandhiji. They continued in him throughout his life.

So, yes, Gandhiji reached out to the youngsters, but not because he found anything right in their approach, rather, as he told Lord Ampthill, 'in order if possible to convince them of the error of their ways' and thereby to wean them away from what they had set out to do.[20] And while he dedicated his life to preaching and to demonstrating that non-violent

---

[19] *Hind Swaraj*, in *Collected Works*, Volume X, pp. 245–315, in particular pp. 283–98.

[20] Letter to Ampthill, 30 October, 1909. *Collected Works*, Volume 10, pp. 200–01. Lord Ampthill was both a sounding-board for Gandhiji during his visit in 1909, and also one who shared his views about what would and what would not shift opinion of the British rulers.

means could indeed attain great objectives, his contact with this lot of 'revolutionaries' ended with these exchanges.

Where is the basis for Savarkar's assertion 'and we worked together as compatriots'? Could it be that they agreed to a sort of division of labour? 'All right. The "revolutionaries" will take care of the violent part, and Gandhi will take care of the nonviolent part'?

Let us now look at the next assertion in Savarkar's statement to the Court during the assassination trial.

The Visit

Was Savarkar making up things when he told the Court, 'later on he paid a personal visit with his wife to me and my family [in Ratnagiri] and spent hours in happy talks about our old comradeship and current politics'?

Fortunately, we have the contemporaneous account of the visit—how Gandhiji happened to visit Savarkar, whether they 'spent hours in happy talks about our old comradeship and current politics,' and all. Mahadev Desai was Gandhiji's secretary, indeed his amanuensis. A very substantial part of what we know about what Gandhiji was doing and saying, we owe to Mahadev Desai. We have his account of the visit in his 'Weekly Letter' in the *Young India* of 17 March 1927.

Gandhiji was touring the Konkan region. As part of this tour, he naturally came to Ratnagiri—the birthplace of the Lokmanya. He addressed a public meeting. 'Lokmanya's birth-place is a place of pilgrimage not only for me but for the whole of India,' Gandhiji said in his speech. Gandhiji went on to recall, Mahadev's account informs us, 'that his old friend Sri Savarkar whom he had known well in England and whose sacrifice and patriotism were well known was also residing in Ratnagiri. "We had our differences then," he added, "we have them now, but they have not affected in the least our friendship. Differences of opinion should never mean hostility. If they did, my wife and I should be sworn enemies of one another. I do not know two persons in the world who had no difference of opinion, and as I am a follower of the Gita, I have always attempted to regard those who differ from me with the same affection as I have for my nearest and dearest."' Notice: the differences persist, and the fact that these 'have not affected in the least our friendship', as differences never should.

'After addressing the meeting,' Mahadev continues, 'he had a note from Sri Savarkar to say that he had been ailing for some time,' 'and Gandhiji called at his place on his way to the women's meeting . . .' Notice the occasion for the visit: 'After addressing the meeting he had a note from Sri Savarkar to say that he had been ailing for some time'. Notice too, 'on his way to the women's meeting.'

And now the meeting, and the exchanges during it: 'The meeting with Sri Savarkar was a pleasant one. He emphasised that Gandhiji was there not as a political leader, but as a friend, and that he would not therefore engage him in a discussion as some friends had desired.' 'But incidentally he asked Gandhiji to clear his attitude about untouchability and *Shuddhi*. Gandhiji cleared some of the misrepresentations and said: "We cannot have long talk today, but you know my regard for you as a lover of truth and as one who would lay down his life for the sake of truth. Besides, our goal is ultimately one and I would like you to correspond with me as regards all points of difference between us. And more. I know that you cannot go out of Ratnagiri and I would not mind finding out two or three days to come and stay with you if necessary to discuss these things to our satisfaction." The conversation was all in Hindi. "I thank you" said Sri Savarkar, "but you are free and I am bound, and I don't want to put you in the same case as I. But I will correspond with you."'[21] He didn't—just kept caricaturing and thereby vilifying Gandhiji and his ideas.

---

[21] Mahadev Desai, *Day to Day with Gandhi*, Volume 9, pp. 233–35, Sarva Sewa Sangh Prakashan, Varanasi, 1974, and *Collected Works of Gandhi: Volume 38*, Page 176–180. Gandhiji had already addressed the question of *Shuddhi* in his speech: 'I am asked to take part in the *Shuddhi* movement. How can I, when I wish that its Muslim and Christian counterparts should also cease? It is unthinkable that a man will become good or attain salvation only if he embraces a particular religion—Hinduism, Christianity or

Contrast this with what Savarkar told the Court twenty years later: that they 'spent hours in happy talks about our old comradeship and current politics'.

'Friends'

'But Gandhi *did* speak of Veer Savarkar as his friend. He *did* talk of their friendship. Did he not address him as "*bhai*"? Therefore, how was Veer Savarkar wrong in alluding to their friendship during his statement in Court?'

The question should be the other way round: did Savarkar talk of Gandhiji as one talks of a friend—other than asserting in the statement when he was being tried in the assassination case that they were friends? Did he speak of or behave towards Gandhiji as anyone would towards a friend? As far as Gandhiji is concerned, he spent his life teaching—as he manifestly is doing even in that Ratnagiri speech—that even if we think that a person is doing evil things, we must not think of him as an evil person. We are out to get rid of British rule, he taught, but we must not hate the British. As for addressing someone as 'friend', Gandhiji addressed even Hitler as 'Dear friend', and closed the letter with, 'I remain, Your sincere friend'![22] He wrote a second letter in which also he addressed Hitler as 'Dear friend'. And explained why he was doing so—it turns out to be the same reason as we just came across in the Ratnagiri speech. 'That I address you as a friend is no formality', Gandhiji wrote to Hitler after addressing

---

Islam. Purity of character and salvation depend on the purity of heart. I therefore say to the Hindus, "Do whatever you like, but don't ask a man like me, who has come to his conclusions after the maturest thinking, to take up what he cannot." Man's capacity is after all limited. I can do what is within my power, not what is beyond it. I cannot do a hundred or even half a dozen things at a time. If you agree with me that the Charkha is the best *sangathan* (organization) that is possible, give me as much help as you can render.' [Mahadev Desai, *op. cit.*, p. 241.]

[22] Gandhiji to Adolf Hitler, 23 July 1939, *Collected Works*, Volume 76, pp. 156–57. The Government withheld this letter.

him as 'Dear friend'. 'I own no foes. My business in life has been for the past 33 years to enlist the friendship of the whole of humanity by befriending mankind, irrespective of race, colour or creed . . .'[23] That did not keep him from speaking the truth to Hitler, for the very next paragraph reads:

I hope you will have the time and desire to know how a good portion of humanity who have been living under the influence of that doctrine of universal friendship view your action. We have no doubt about your bravery or devotion to your fatherland, nor do we believe that you are the monster described by your opponents. But your own writings and pronouncements and those of your friends and admirers leave no room for doubt that many of your acts are monstrous and unbecoming of human dignity, especially in the estimation of men like me who believe in universal friendliness. Such are your humiliation of Czechoslovakia, the rape of Poland and the swallowing of Denmark. I am aware that your view of life regards such spoliations as virtuous acts. But we have been taught from childhood to regard

---

[23] Gandhiji to Adolf Hitler, 24 December 1940. *Collected Works,* Volume 79, pp. 453–57. As is well known, Hitler's prescription for dealing with Gandhiji was somewhat different. Lord Halifax who had been Viceroy and had dealt long and patiently and fruitfully with Gandhiji was meeting Hitler. The two were as unlike each other as can be. At one point, Hitler took off on how to deal with India:

. . . After this dismal lunch, Hitler told Halifax how his favourite film, 'Lives of a Bengal Lancer', was compulsory viewing for the SS as 'this was how a superior race must behave', and he lost no time in expounding his answer to the problems of India. 'Shoot Gandhi,' he told the ex-Viceroy, 'and if that does not suffice to reduce them to submission, shoot a dozen leading members of Congress; and if that does not suffice, shoot 200 and so on until order is established.' During this tirade Halifax 'gazed at Hitler with a mixture of astonishment, repugnance and compassion. He indicated dissent, but it would have been a waste of time to argue.' [Andrew Roberts, *'The Holy Fox', The life of Lord Halifax,* Phoenix Giant, London, 1991, p. 72.]

them as acts degrading humanity. Hence we cannot possibly wish success to your arms.

Nor did it keep him from warning Hitler:

> If not the British, some other power will certainly improve upon your method and beat you with your own weapon. You are leaving no legacy to your people of which they would feel proud. They cannot take pride in a recital of cruel deeds, however skilfully planned. I, therefore, appeal to you in the name of humanity to stop the war. You will lose nothing by referring all the matters of dispute between you and Great Britain to an international tribunal of your joint choice. If you attain success in the war, it will not prove that you were in the right. It will only prove that your power of destruction was greater. Whereas an award by an impartial tribunal will show as far as it is humanly possible which party was in the right.

Recall what Savarkar was saying about Hitler being the best to judge what was good for Germans, about the great and mighty progress that Germany had made under Hitler, about his and the Germans having a right to Sudetenland and Czechoslovakia, and Poland, and about why we should not be concerned about what he was doing within Germany to the Jews, etc. . . .

Indeed, Gandhiji insisted that we keep an open heart not just for persons with whom we differ but even for persons who, having promised to be with us, leave us. It would seem that he looked upon this as an index—one of several—of a person's control over his mind! An incident will illustrate the point and bring home the meaning of what he said about Savarkar at the public meeting in Ratnagiri. As is well known, in spite of much opposition, Gandhiji had been projecting Muhammad Ali and Shaukat Ali during the Khilafat agitation. He would invite them to meeting after meeting.

He would take them to all public meetings and make much of them. The Khilafat agitation petered out—Ataturk abolished the Caliphate itself. Even before this end had come, the two brothers had started drifting away. Citing one reason or another, they would absent themselves from meetings. We find Gandhiji saying again and again during public meetings, 'I miss brother Shaukat . . .' But he continued to patronize them. Muhammad Ali was even made the Congress President in 1923. He soon left the Party, and became the President of the Muslim League, a party of which he had been one of the founders. Gandhiji's followers expressed anger at the about-turn of the Ali brothers. His counsel was that instead of being angry at the brothers for having left us now, we should be thankful that they travelled with us thus far.

As for his having spoken of Savarkar as '*Bhai* Savarkar',[24] Gandhiji referred even to Abdul Rashid, the assassin who murdered Swami Shraddhanand, as '*Bhai* Abdul Rashid'—something for which few denounced him as vociferously as Savarkar.

The question, as we just noticed, should be the other way round: did Savarkar speak of Gandhiji as a friend, did he behave as one would towards a friend?

Many differed with Gandhiji—recall Subhas Bose—but few hurled the kind of invective and vicious scorn on him that Savarkar did. No one drilled as much poison about Gandhiji into his followers as he did, poison that propelled them.

'A Walking Plague'

The ridicule and scorn continued over decades. The writings in which it occurs would make a tidy volume. Here are just a few examples from just one section—*Gandhi Aapaadhaapi*—of one volume of *Savarkar Samagra*:

---

[24] Much is read into this: as an example, Arun Anand, 'Gandhi admired Hindutva icon Savarkar as "lover of truth", addressed him as bhai,' *The Print,* 28 May 2020, https://theprint.in/india/gandhi-admired-hindutva-icon-savarkar-as-lover-of-truth-addressed-him-as-bhai/430707/

- *Paagal*
- These epileptic fits that he has, *in mirgi ke dauraan . . .*
- *Is-se pehley hi ki is vishailey 'tatva-gyan' kaa sarp apnaa phan uthaaye, usey kuchal denaa chaahiye . . .* Before this poison-filled snake of 'true-knowledge' unfurls its hood it should be crushed . . .
- This *dalaal,* broker of the British . . .
- His intelligence is as narrow [*sankuchit*] and unripe [*aparipakva*] as his heart is wide
- Because he does not have the intelligence to know the meaning of the words he uses, and does not have the strength to acknowledge that he does not know, to evade the subject he spews one kind of nonsense one day and another kind of nonsense another day—*voh kabhi kuchh aur kabhi kuchh bak detey hain . . .*
- In the last five-six years he has fomented so much *ghaplaa* [scam, bungling] with words such as swarajya, khadi, pure swadeshi, non-cooperation, satyagraha, ahimsa, etc. that at least Maharashtra has got tired. He has given so many and such contradictory definitions of each of these words that if they were strung together even a madman would roll about laughing. But they have pulverized national work to such an extent that, and scattered national resolve so much that, and made the rashtra so unable to act that along with hatred/*ghrinda*, instead of laughter, a deep sorrow and furious contempt arises
- His *sanaki*/crazy, eccentric ideas
- The odiousness of his *jhakkipan*/craziness, whimsicality
- But in this regard, remaining silent and joining his Mussalmaan colleagues he is uttering such *bakwaas*/nonsense as 'What is there in numbers?'
- *Sankipan* Mahatma ki atma: the soul of the crazy/eccentric Mahatma
- His *anoothi jhakkipan*: his singular/queer craziness

- He should change the name of his paper from 'Young India' to 'Old India', adding that he—Gandhi—is a 60-year-old 'Back Number' of that paper
- When Gandhiji puts forth his ideas as they are, even while laughing at them one does not feel sad, but several of his political entanglements proceed beneath the cover of 'truth'. His falsehood is pushed fearlessly/ *bedhadak asatya* . . . 'My mind is sound'—it becomes difficult to prove this to oneself; and there isn't the courage to say, 'My thoughts were thoughtless'. *Tab prasang nibhaaney ke liye,* then to talk away the subject, *jo muhn mein aayaa, baktey hain*/he jabbers out whatever comes to his mouth—this conduct of his is laughable . . .
- *Moorkhataa   poorand   aatmvanchanaa*/foolishness   filled self-deception
- *Aviveksheel*/discrimination-less Rahu
- Guilty of spreading '*ahimsa kaa paakhand*'/the hypocrisy of ahimsa
- Commenting on Gandhiji writing of Abdul Rashid, the assassin of Swami Shraddhanand, in *Young India* as 'Bhai Abdul Rashid', Savarkar writes that there is no doubt that the writer of the paper at least till this expression *asatya kaa prachaarak, chaltaa-phirtaa plague hai*/is the spreader of falsehood, a walking plague. Gandhi is saying all this [sanctimonious stuff] to establish his greatness. This is cowardice. Not calling it cowardice, we call it foolishness/ *moorkhataa* . . . Instead of calling this habit of always casting as much blame on Hindus as on Mussalmaans—*moorakhataa*/ foolishness, we have to call it cowardice and *paakhandsoochak*/ hypocritical. This is the partisanship of a *duraatma*/wicked being, not the impartiality of a Mahatma
- *Do kaudi kaa 'chakravarti'* . . . this two-peenies' worth world-conqueror . . . [25]

---

[25] For these examples of vituperation, *Savarkar Samagra,* Volume IV, pp. 639–42, 643, 645–47, 653, 662, 663, 667, 668, 678, 681, 682, 712. His epithets for Pandit Nehru:

This is what Savarkar must have meant when he told the Court that between Gandhiji and him 'there ever continued a mutual respect for and a personal goodwill to each other.' And presumably, the ban on taking part in politics did not cover spewing venom on Gandhiji.

A Counter-Example

The point certainly is not that X or Y should not have differed with Gandhiji, with his beliefs, his campaigns like Khilafat, his decisions regarding them. Many did, and they expressed their reservations in the strongest terms. In fact, *Young India* is full of the critics' views as, before answering his critics, Gandhiji freely reproduced what they had written to him. The difference lies in the malice, the hatred, the jealousy that come through in Savarkar's writing, and of which there is not a tinge in the criticisms of others. Perhaps a counter-example will bring the point home. As is well-known, Subhas Chandra Bose had the strongest reservations about many of Gandhiji's views and decisions. And there also can be no doubt that without Gandhiji's consent the manoeuvre by which Bose was forced to resign from the Presidentship of the Congress could not have been initiated. Bose's *The Indian Struggle* lists without let one decision of Gandhiji after another which he characterizes as 'blunders'. He bemoans the passing of Lala Lajpat Rai, Motilal Nehru and C.R. Das as, after them, he says, there is no one in the Congress who will stand up to the Mahatma and tell him where he is wrong. 'The leader of the Congress is Mahatma Gandhi,' Bose explains for the foreign reader, and adds, '—who is the virtual dictator. The Working Committee since 1929 has been elected according to his dictation and no one can find a place on that committee who is not thoroughly submissive to him and his policy.' He is sharp in his

---

nipunsak—impotent; *hijda*—eunuch; *buddhuram*—*Mr Fool*: see, for instance, his last public address, delivered at Pune, 15 January 1961. The occasion was a function to felicitate him. *Savarkar Samagra,* Volume VIII, pp. 320–34; at pp. 321, 328, 329, 332.

criticism of individual decisions of the Mahatma and traces them to traits in his very nature. When Gandhiji suddenly shifts the focus from civil disobedience to fighting untouchability, Bose says that 'this side-tracking of the civil-disobedience movement was the result of that subjectivism which seizes him at times and makes him utterly blind to and oblivious of objective realities . . .' 'The effect,' Bose says, 'was the same as it would be if in the middle of a battle a general gave the order to his troops to start excavating a canal in order to supply water to the thirsty people of the countryside.' The Mahatma 'alternates between obstinacy and leniency and moreover,' Bose writes, 'he is too susceptible to personal appeals—and with such habits of mind, it is difficult to get the better of one's opponent in political bargaining.' The result is that campaigns are begun, but then they get lost in calls from the inner voice. Bose quotes with approval C.R. Das' comment: 'The Mahatma opens his campaign in a brilliant fashion; he works it up with unerring skill; he moves from success to success till he reaches the zenith of his campaign—but after that he loses his nerve and begins to falter.' Indeed, Bose says that Gandhiji's asceticism, his religious persona and idiom have fanned among the people some of the very traits that have kept us backward—the reliance on faith, on faith in individuals, on faith in religious-looking individuals. And this has led to, it should foment a rationalist revolt against the Mahatma's ways . . .[26]

But it is the same Bose whom Gandhiji continued to consider as his son, whose sacrifice, drive, integrity, dedication to the cause of the country and whose ability to weld Indians into one people, Gandhiji said, were 'unsurpassed'. Gandhiji continued to have the greatest regard and affection for Bose even as he would not bless the path the latter had chosen. Similarly, even as he had to part ways with the Mahatma and the Congress, Bose stated that 'it will always be my aim and object to try and win his

---

[26] The expressions quoted are from Subhas Chandra Bose, *The Indian Struggle, 1920–42*, Netaji Research Bureau, Asia Publishing House, Bombay, 1964. pp. 28, 69–70, 114–15, 210, 230, 249–50.

confidence for the simple reason that it will be tragic for me if I succeed in winning the confidence of other people but fail to win the confidence of India's greatest man.' And in an oft-quoted speech that Bose delivered from Bangkok on Gandhiji's birthday in 1943, he said, 'The service which Mahatma Gandhi has rendered to India and the cause of India's freedom is so unique and unparalleled that his name shall be written in letters of gold in our national history for all time.' Further that,

> For twenty years and more Mahatma Gandhi has worked for India's salvation, and with him the Indian people too have worked. It is no exaggeration to say that if in 1920 he had not come forward with his weapon of struggle, India would today perhaps have been still prostrate. His services to the cause of India's freedom are unique and unparalleled. No single man could have achieved more in one lifetime under similar circumstances . . .[27]

And who anointed Gandhiji as the 'Father of our Nation'? None other than Subhas Chandra Bose. These days when Bose also is being yoked to the project of erasing Gandhiji, how necessary it is to remind ourselves of this. These days when, following Savarkar and his type, when every disagreement becomes the occasion for pasting motives on the other, for abuse, how necessary it is to remind ourselves of the way leaders who held fundamentally and profoundly differing views looked upon each other.

'Father of Our Nation'

The occasion has been described by S.A. Ayer, a close associate of Netaji. Ayer notes that Netaji firmly held to the view that the British would have to be thrown out by violence, and that for this help from foreign sources was unavoidable. Ayer says that on both these counts, he differed from

---

[27] *Selected Speeches of Subhas Chandra Bose,* Publications Division, Government of India, 1962, pp. 201, 203.

Gandhiji, and that he—Bose—never wavered from these two propositions. And then Ayer recalls the broadcast that Bose made from Rangoon Radio on 6 July 1944. In it he addressed the people of India, of course, he addressed Gandhiji directly and personally. 'For obvious reasons, I attach the greatest importance to this broadcast,' Ayer wrote, 'which I hope and trust will be read by Indians who wish to know in what high esteem Netaji held Gandhiji when the former was in the midst of a life and death struggle for India's liberation.' The address was a 'soul speaking to soul', Ayer wrote. 'Every line of his personal references to Gandhiji is the handsomest and most sincere tribute that one leader has ever paid to another.'

'I accompanied Netaji to the broadcasting station night after night, and it was my official privilege to sit at the same mike, facing Netaji, and to introduce him to his listener,' Ayer recorded. 'I had read beforehand what he was going to tell Mahatmaji over the Radio that particular night. I was dying to see the expression on Netaji's face when he would come to the concluding words of his broadcast to Gandhiji . . .'

As I remained seated across the mike desk, my eyes were glued to Netaji's glowing face. He was coming to the last poignant words, I was all agog in my seat. I looked at his face.

There was a pause.

Then he began: 'Father of our Nation!' His voice had become somewhat hoarse; then it quivered a bit; a solemn look came over his face; then his throat cleared, the words now came out clear and strong: 'In this holy war for India's liberation,' then again a slight pause, a slight lowering of the pitch, a tone of supplication, 'we ask for your blessings and good wishes.'

If Gandhiji had been there on the spot, I am sure the great man would have granted a prayer like this which was profoundly genuine.[28]

Yet today, knaves and fools write articles and deliver speeches using Bose to erase Gandhiji. The poisonous design of those whose idols and icons were doing nothing—either violently or non-violently—to secure independence for our country.

The second feature of the scorn and abuse that Savarkar hurled at Gandhiji is just as important: they resulted from a method.

The Method

Savarkar cites a passage from Gandhiji's *Autobiography*: I will first give the passage as it appears in Savarkar's *Samagra*:

> You are the one who thinks himself glorious by singing the anthem of the British Empire, God Save the King. In connection with the Zulu war you yourself write in your Autobiography—The Zulu people had not caused even the slightest harm to Indians. It was with great difficulty that the charge of rebellion had been thrust on them. They were being killed in a very brutal way. But the moment I heard that the British had launched war against them, and that there had been a call for volunteers for that project, it seemed necessary to me to take part in this war of the English, because it was my belief that the British Empire is for the betterment of the world. It was my earnest desire that this Empire should not end.[29]

---

[28] S.A. Ayer, *Unto Him a Witness, The Story of Netaji Subhas Chandra Bose in East Asia*, Thacker & Co, Bombay, 1951, pp. 255–56

[29] *Savarkar Samagra*, Volume IV, p. 674.

and keeps hammering away: See, here is the real Gandhi. This is what he really believes. This is what he believes even today. The very first sentence that Savarkar writes after citing this passage is:

> *Aur aaj bhi aapki yahi ichha hai*—And today also this is your wish. It is possible that you have not realised this. But the British have.[30]

That is why they give you special privileges—for instance, when you travel by train. And that is why you have drugged the country into following what is most convenient to the British—nonviolence, non-cooperation . . .

First, that is not quite what Gandhiji had written. The actual passage in his *Autobiography* is as follows:

> The papers brought the news of the outbreak of the Zulu 'rebellion' in Natal. I bore no grudge against the Zulus, they had harmed no Indian. I had doubts about the 'rebellion' itself. But I then believed that the British Empire existed for the welfare of the world. A genuine sense of loyalty prevented me from even wishing ill to the Empire. The rightness or otherwise of the 'rebellion' was therefore not likely to affect my decision. Natal had a Volunteer Defence Force, and it was open to it to recruit more men. I read that this force had already been mobilized to quell the 'rebellion'.
>
> I considered myself a citizen of Natal, being intimately connected with it. So I wrote to the Governor, expressing my readiness, if necessary, to form an Indian Ambulance Corps. He replied immediately accepting the offer.[31]

---

[30] Ibid.

[31] M.K. Gandhi, *My Autobiography, or The Story of My Experiments with Truth*, Translated from the original in Gujarati by Mahadev Desai, Navjivan Publishing House, Ahmedabad, 1927/1959, pp. 231–32.

Savarkar omits the lines that indicate what Gandhiji was volunteering for—
for recruiting an ambulance corps. Nor does he mention that Gandhiji got
together all twenty-four volunteers, and that they attended to Zulus who
had been injured—and injured not so much in battle but by having been
flogged by the British. But let that be incidental. Savarkar's main point is
that Gandhiji was, on his own telling, loyal to the British, that he thought
the British Empire existed for the good of the world. And that he had
continued to be, and was at the time of writing—Savarkar was writing in
1927—loyal to the British just as he had been in 1897. He completely omits
that by this time Gandhiji was involved in full-scale struggle against the
Raj. Even as declarations go, Savarkar shuts the readers' eyes from, to cite
just one example, the statement that Gandhiji made in 1922 when he was
charged with sedition. He had told the judge, *'I plead guilty on each count
of the charge'*—sedition. This was in the wake of the non-cooperation
movement that he had launched and had called off after the Chauri Chaura
incident. He had explained how 'I came reluctantly to the conclusion that
*the British connection had made India more helpless than she ever was
before, politically and economically* . . . No sophistry, no jugglery in figures
can explain away the evidence that the skeletons in many villages present
to the naked eye . . .'

> I wanted to avoid violence. I want to avoid violence. Non-violence is
> the first article of my faith. It is also the last article of my creed. But
> I had to make my choice. *I had either to submit to a system which
> I considered had done an irreparable harm to my country, or incur the
> risk of the mad fury of my people bursting forth when they understood
> the truth from my lips.* I know that my people have sometimes gone
> mad; I am deeply sorry for it. *I am, therefore, here to submit not to
> a light penalty but to the highest penalty. I do not ask for mercy. I do
> not ask for any extenuating act of clemency. I am here to invite and
> cheerfully submit to the highest penalty that can be inflicted upon me*

for what in law is a deliberate crime and what appears to me to be the
highest duty of a citizen.

Gandhiji pointed to how unjustly 'justice' was being administered in India,
how the sedition section itself was being used:

> . . . the section under which Mr. Banker and I are charged is one
> under which mere promotion of disaffection is a crime. I have studied
> some of the cases tried under it, and I know that some of the most
> loved of India's patriots have been convicted under it. I consider it
> a privilege, therefore, to be charged under it. I have endeavoured to
> give in their briefest outline the reasons for my disaffection. I have
> no personal ill will against any single administrator, much less can
> I have any disaffection towards the King's person. *But I hold it to be a*
> *virtue to be disaffected towards a Government which in its totality has*
> *done more harm to India than any previous system. India is less manly*
> *under the British rule than she ever was before. Holding such a belief,*
> *I consider it to be a sin to have affection for the system. And it has been*
> *a precious privilege for me to be able to write what I have in the various*
> *articles tendered in evidence against me.*

And therefore,

> . . . Non-violence implies voluntary submission to the penalty for non-
> cooperation with evil. *I am here, therefore, to invite and submit cheerfully*
> *to the highest penalty that can be inflicted upon me for what in law is a*
> *deliberate crime and what appears to me to be the highest duty of a citizen . . .*

Contrast all this to Savarkar's mercy petitions. The judge imposed the
maximum sentence under the law—six years' imprisonment. While doing
so, he observed:

Mr. Gandhi, you have made my task easy in one way by pleading guilty to the charge. Nevertheless what remains, namely, the determination of a just sentence, is perhaps as difficult a proposition as a judge in this country could have to face. The law is no respecter of persons. Nevertheless, it will be impossible to ignore the fact that you are in a different category from any person I have ever tried or am likely to have to try. It would be impossible to ignore the fact that, in the eyes of millions of your countrymen, you are a great patriot and a great leader. Even those who differ from you in politics look upon you as a man of high ideals and of noble and of even saintly life. I have to deal with you in one character only. It is not my duty and I do not presume to judge or criticize you in any other character. It is my duty to judge you as a man subject to the law, who has by his own admission broken the law and committed what to an ordinary man must appear to be grave offences against the State . . .

There are probably few people in India who do not sincerely regret that you should have made it impossible for any Government to leave you at liberty. But it is so. I am trying to balance what is due to you against what appears to me to be necessary in the interests of the public, and I propose, in passing sentence, to follow the precedent of a case, in many respects similar to this case, that was decided some 12 years ago, I mean the case against Mr. Bal Gangadhar Tilak under this same section. The sentence that was passed upon him as it finally stood was a sentence of simple imprisonment for six years. You will not consider it unreasonable, I think, that you should be classed with Mr. Tilak, and that is the sentence, two years' simple imprisonment on each count of the charge, i.e. six years in all, which I feel it my duty to pass upon you and I should like to say in doing so that, if the course of events in India should make it possible for the Government to reduce the period and release you, no one will be better pleased than I.

Gandhiji said in turn:

I would say one word. Since you have done me the honour of recalling the trial of the late Lokmanya Bal Gangadhar Tilak, I just want to say that I consider it to be the proudest privilege and honour to be associated with his name. So far as the sentence itself is concerned, I certainly consider that it is as light as any judge would inflict on me, and so far as the whole proceedings are concerned, I must say that I could not have expected greater courtesy.[32]

Surely, even if we shut out all the campaigns against the British that Gandhiji was leading and confine ourselves just to statements, Savarkar could not have been unaware of this statement—it had resonated across the country and beyond, and was regarded, it is still regarded as one of the greatest statements made in the defence of liberty and justice. Savarkar could not have been unaware of the trial and the sentence—these had shaken the country. But all of that is shut out. What Gandhiji said in 1897 is all. And that in an autobiography which from beginning to end establishes one thing—not that Gandhiji remained wedded to the positions he had taken at some time but how his convictions had changed, how *he* had changed. Most of all, Savarkar who often projected himself as one carrying on the work of the Lokmanya, could not have been unaware of the fact that in the judgement Gandhiji had been classed with the Lokmanya—perhaps this is what had jarred all along.

Let us move to another speech, another conference, another declaration of loyalty to the British.

Speech at the Round Table Conference

Consider the following passage from a speech at the Round Table Conference:

---

[32] *Young India*, 23 March 1922. *Collected Works*, Volume 26, pp. 377–86. How I wish that the illiterates who are rewriting our textbooks were to include the proceedings of this trial in those textbooks instead of hagiographic passages about the real collaborators.

I should like to begin my speech by expressing my heart-felt gratefulness to Lord Peel for the noble and courageous lead that he gave yesterday by saying that we should speak frankly and sincerely. He may be legitimately proud of having brought a contribution of sincerity to the business before this Conference, and for having paid this Conference the compliment of frankness. I can assure him that in my speech he will not be disappointed; he will have the most frank, sincere and honest views of *a man who has proved his loyalty to the British Empire, even running the risk of losing his life in doing so, when he was a young man and comparatively unknown, and when he showed his loyalty in the actual fire of the Boer War.* It is such a man who now speaks frankly and sincerely and may even appear to be a rebel at the present time.

Could there be a more explicit declaration of loyalty to the British Empire? And these were the speaker's sentiments in 1931, not 1897. What would Savarkar not have made of the declaration had the speaker been Gandhiji? It so happens that the speaker was B.S. Moonje. And he was speaking at the Plenary Session of the First Round Table Conference.[33] Moonje was President of the Hindu Mahasabha—it was when he demitted the Presidentship that Savarkar became President of the Mahasabha. He was the one who suggested to Hedgewar how RSS should be organized. He had been invited to the Conference as a representative of the Hindus, and, as Savarkar was to state later, he spoke on behalf of, and as the true representative of the Hindus.

Outright Fabrication

The third instrument of the method behind the abuse that Savarkar hurled at Gandhiji was outright fabrication. A single example will do.

---

[33] *Indian Round Table Conference, 12 November 1930–19 January 1931, Proceedings,* Government of India, Central Publications Branch, 1931, p. 74. The Congress did not attend. Participants were chosen by the British Government. Among 'British-Indian Representatives,' 'Hindus' were represented by B.S. Moonje, M.R. Jayakar, and Raja Narendra Nath.

From the time he was in the Andamans to the Second World War, whenever Savarkar wanted to convince the British of how useful he could be to them, he would paint one bogey: the Mussalmaans of Afghanistan, backed by and allied to the Islamic powers in the Middle East and Central Asia are going to invade India, and the Mussalmaans of India will ally with them to overthrow the British and re-establish Islamic rule over the country. And that he and his Hindu Sangathan are the ones who could and would help the British ward off this menace.

This thesis of his reached an apogee during the Khilafat agitation. For decades after that, he kept saying that the Muslim leaders, and Gandhiji had entered into a conspiracy, that they had been in secret communication with Amanullah, the Amir of Afghanistan, and had invited him to invade India.[34] He kept repeating this gross falsehood even in 1947:

> . . . Had not Gandhiji himself conspired with the Ali Brothers to invite
> an invasion by the Pathans and to enthrone the Amir of Afghanistan
> as the Emperor of India? . . .[35]

Impossible to believe that anyone could allege or even imagine that Gandhiji would conspire with anyone to get him to invade India? Just proves that you haven't read Savarkar. Incredible or not, such allegations are consequential, that Savarkar peddled them is hugely important. They speak to his nature. And they illustrate how poison was spread—poison that ultimately led to assassination.

In fact, at the height of the Khilafat and non-cooperation movements, Gandhiji had said that 'It is, I hold, the duty of every Hindu to resist any inroad on India even for the purpose specified as it is his duty to help

---

[34] See, for instance, 'Swatantra Bharat kaa samraat kaun hai?', Savarkar Samagra, Volume IV, pp. 688–95, at pp. 688–89. Savarkar repeated the canard in his Presidential Address to the 21st session of the Hindu Mahasabha, Calcutta, 1939 as well as his Presidential Address to the 23rd session of the Hindu Mahasabha, Bhagalpur, 1941.

[35] Statement issued on 22 October 1947: Veer Savarkar's Historic Statements, S.S. Savarkar, Girgaon, Bombay, 1967, p. 132. http://savarkar.org/en/encyc/2017/5/23/2_12_15_55_historic_statements_by_savarkar.v001.pdf_1.pdf

his Mussulman brethren to satisfy their just demands by means of non-
cooperation or other form of suffering, no matter how great, so long
as it does not involve loss of India's liberty or inflicting of violence on
any person.'[36] None of this mattered. Savarkar just kept repeating the

---

[36] What had propelled him to say this was an exchange between Hindu and Muslim
participants at a Conference at Allahabad in June 1920. As the editors of the *Collected
Works* note, 'the Hindu representatives had expressed their fear that complications might
arise from the Indian Muslims welcoming an Afghan invasion of India. The Muslim
speakers gave an assurance that they would resist any foreign invasion undertaken purely
for conquest, but added that any invasion undertaken to uphold the prestige of Islam and
to vindicate justice would have their full sympathy, if not their actual support.' While
stressing that he was not for armed conflict, that he was at the time devoting himself to
non-cooperation as the instrument for bringing the Government to respect the legitimate
sentiment of Muslims, Gandhiji wrote:

> Whilst I am considering the Hindu connection with the Khilafat movement,
> even at the risk of repetition I would like to clear up my own position. As
> I consider the Muslim claim to be intrinsically (as distinguished from religiously)
> just, I propose to go with them to the extent of fullest non-cooperation. And
> I consider it to be perfectly consistent with my loyalty to the British connection.
> But I would not go with the Mussulmans in any campaign of violence. I could not
> help them in promoting, for instance, an invasion of India through Afghanistan
> or otherwise for the purpose of forcing better peace terms. It is, I hold, the duty
> of every Hindu to resist any inroad on India even for the purpose specified as
> it is his duty to help his Mussulman brethren to satisfy their just demands by
> means of non-cooperation or other form of suffering, no matter how great, so
> long as it does not involve loss of India's liberty or inflicting of violence on any
> person. And I have thrown myself Wholeheartedly into the non-cooperation
> movement, if only because I want to prevent any such armed conflict. [*Young
> India*, 23 June 1920. *Collected Works*, Volume 20, pp. 416–19, at p. 419.]

The tussle with the Government intensified with every passing month: Jallianwala Bagh, the
Rowlatt Act, Khilafat, non-cooperation . . . The following year, Gandhiji had to again warn
the people not to fall for the 'Afghan bogey'. Such an invasion was not going to happen, nor
the other invasion that was said to be imminent—from Russia. Were the Amir to invade
India, 'I would, in a sense, certainly assist the Amir of Afghanistan if he waged war against
the British Government.' And that in a particular sense—that is, by continuing to non-
cooperate with the Government. He would not ask Indians to take up arms on behalf of the
British Government—in part because that would mean violence and he was against violence;
and in part because 'it would be a crime to help a Government which had lost the confidence

lie—from the early 1920s to, as we saw, 1947. Goebbels anticipated by decades: the bigger the lie, the more often it is repeated, the greater the chances it will stick.

And he kept twisting and turning what Gandhiji was saying—putting constructions on what Gandhiji was saying which would inflame. June 1947: There have been riots and killings in Bihar. Savarkar congratulates the Hindus of the province for standing up to the attacks that were launched against them. See what he says, and what he says Gandhiji is saying. And ask whether pasting such constructions would not eventually create the atmosphere in which some zealous follower will take it upon himself to put an end to the source of all the trouble.

> I have fullest knowledge of the shameful propaganda that has been let loose against you by the Mussalmaans staying in Bharat and the Hindu *pancham stambhiyon*. According to them your great crime is that your blood boiled at the atrocities that have been committed on Hindus in Bengal. These *akal ke putley* will prohibit you from hitting with a lathi even a snake biting your leg. These fools do not even know that the Hindu *jagat ek rashtriya mahapurush* . . .
>
> I have heard that Gandhi is preaching to you that before the rains commence you give shelter in your own house to homeless Mussalmaans. It seems that even after breaking the Motherland into pieces this Mahatma does not think that his life's work is done. As a result, even before Jinnah, he is demanding that a Pakistan be set up inside each house and behind it a Noakhali. Seeing that this is the preaching of a deluder, do not pay heed to his sermon. If a corner or

---

of the nation to remain in power . . . [a Government] that has deliberately emasculated us . . . [a Government that is] unwilling to give up O'Dwyerism . . .' ['The Afghan bogey', *Young India*, 4 May 1921, *Collected Works*, Volume 23, pp. 110–11.]

a little grain is left in anyone's house, then give it to Hindu refugees coming from Bengal and Punjab . . .[37]

The Ventriloquist

But Savarkar did not just speak himself. As his own writing about himself states again and again, as his biographers tell us *ad infinitum*, he had tremendous, magnetic, hypnotic influence over others. He inspired them to revolutionary acts, he says, his biographers say. He inspired a poor cook to smuggle 20 pistols into India for assassinations. He propelled Dhingra, he was charged with propelling Godse and Apte. Given that he could propel them to wield weapons, inspiring them to speak would be, as they say, *baayein haath kaa khel.*

He would set up, he would encourage and help others to set up publications. They would naturally carry content that he wanted disseminated to the public.

Agrani was one such publication. It was started by two devotees of Savarkar—Godse and Apte, with the former as editor and the latter as proprietor. Savarkar gave Rs. 15,000 to them for the publication—he was to insist during the trial that he had given this amount as a loan. The first issue came out on 16 January 1944. Because of the incendiary stuff the paper was publishing, it was warned. The warning had little effect. Security was demanded in 1946 under the Press Emergency Powers Act. It was forfeited. Security was also demanded from *Maratha,* a publication of the same hue. That too was forfeited. On 3 July, 1947 a security was demanded again from *Agrani,* this time of Rs. 5000. The paper did not deposit the security, and instead stopped publication. But, in spite of objections from the police, it was allowed to recommence publication on 15 July 1947

---

[37] *Savarkar Samagra,* Volume 8, pp. 636–37.

under a new name, *Hindu Rashtra*—'which' Justice Kapur was to remark later, 'cannot be a credit to the efficacy of the Press Act.'[38]/[39]

On reviewing the publications, Justice Kapur found that *Agrani* was 'writing in a rabid strain',[40] that the *Hindu Rashtra* followed 'the same rabid policy', that *Hindu Rashtra* was 'if anything more violent and fire-eating in its writing than *Agrani* against the Congress and Congress leaders though the language was carefully shrouded', that they 'were writing violent articles', that they were inciting violence, that they were preaching 'Savarkar ideology'.[41]

---

[38] In this and the next section, there are frequent references to the report of the Jiwanlal Kapur Commission, *Report of Commission of Inquiry into Conspiracy to Murder Mahatma Gandhi,* Parts I and II, Ministry of Home Affairs, Government of India, 1970. Henceforth, *Kapur Commission.* Justice Kapur was a retired Judge of the Supreme Court. The Commission was constituted in 1965 to examine aspects of the assassination of Mahatma Gandhi, and the investigations that followed. It did not examine what happened during the trial. The Commission was set up because several persons claimed that they had received advance information about the plot to assassinate Gandhiji, and that some of them had even shared the information with ministers and others in both the Bombay and Central governments, and alerted them to the danger. The final report was submitted on 30 September 1969. It was published by the Ministry of Home Affairs in 1970. The full report is in six volumes. Parts I and II have been digitized by the South Asia Citizens Web (www.sacw.net), and are available on *Internet Archive.* Cf:

https://archive.org/details/JeevanlalKapoorCommissionReport/JeevanLalKapur CommissionReport_PART1-A/page/n3/mode/2up

[39] As we shall see in a moment, Savarkar was to make much of the securities that were demanded from *Agrani* and *Hindu Rashtra.* In fact, securities were demanded from other papers also—with a not-difficult-to-guess ending: As the Kapur Commission recorded, security was demanded from *Kesari;* from the *Maratha* security demanded was Rs. 20,000; it was reduced to Rs. 10,000. From the *Kal* security of Rs. 3.000 was demanded in 1946 and was deposited. That paper was given a warning in 1947. 'On the 4th August, 1947, the Provincial Press Advisory Committee advised that these securities be returned as a gesture of goodwill. This recommendation was accepted . . . Mr. Morarji Desai said that securities were returned to the newspapers as gesture of goodwill in order to celebrate ushering in of Independence.' *Kapur Commission,* para 15.25, also para 26.74.

[40] *Kapur Commission,* para 15.59.

[41] *Kapur Commission,* paras 15.59, 15.272

Justice Kapur's report contains several extracts from these publications which exhibit their virulence and the poison that they were seeding in the minds of readers. Just two or three will have to suffice. Once such poison has been spread, one need not pull the trigger oneself. Someone or the other will do so 'on his own'.

A Few Samples

Here are representative extracts from *Agrani* and *Hindu Rashtra*, publications patronized by and lauded by Savarkar:[42]

> *Agrani*, dated the 12th April, 1947.
> *The thirst for blood of the advocate of non-violence*
> *has not been quenched.*

Mr. Gandhi who cherishes (lit. taken to heart) as his life time ideal to annihilate the mentality of residence [sic.: resistance?] of the Hindus by advocating unilateral non-violence, has now clearly stated in his post-prayer speech that he is anxious to see (Barrister) Jinnah adorn the Presidential chair (lit. Presidentship) of independent India. Mr. Gandhi had already revealed his pro-Islam slavish mentality, at the beginning of his political career (lit. life) by inviting the Amir of Afghanistan to invade India under the gorgeous pretext (lit. name) of achieving independence. After that by raising the issue that some impostor's rule might be established in India as a result of anarchy due to war this false (lit. nominal) devotee of freedom and this hypocritical worshipper of truth and non-violence was eager to place the crown of India's sovereignty on the head of the Nizam and to pay respects to (lit. to wave five-lamped platter round the face of) such a Nizam. Mr Gandhi had already tried to entrust power again to Jinnah

---

[42] The text, including the words within parentheses, is from the reports of the Kapur Commission.

through the mouth of Rajaji by offering (Barrister) Jinnah the prime ministership of the Interim Government, and now feeling definitely that independence is knocking at the door, this quisling of the Hindu nation is openly wooing (Jinnah) saying (Ba)rrister Jinnahbhai why do you demand only Pakistan, that is India's one third or one fourth? Why do you not accept when this humble servant is prepared to offer at your feet the whole of India? From this, we are constrained to say that the thirst for Hindu blood which this 'Mahatma' (i.e. 'great soul') is feeling has not yet been satisfied.

* * *

Mr. Gandhi, Commit Suicide.

It is the height of (lit. to reach the height of) shamelessness that the coward who cannot go out without taking the aid of the police and soldiers so that no harm is done to his person, the touch of whose feet converts many an Ahilya occupying ministers' posts into Shurpanakhas, who cannot step forward in carrying on the administration without bombs, cannons and British soldiers, should advise (the Hindus) to sacrifice themselves without offering resistance. Does the Sultan blinded with power consider the blood of the Hindu people as not worth a pie, so that this Bania who is a traitor to his community (meaning Mahatma Gandhi) should despite the flowing of several rivers of it, devise fresh means of satisfying the blood thirst of these monstrous aggressors? Does he not think the blood-shed at Noakhali, Punjab and Bihar as adequate? We clearly tell Mr. Gandhi that if the rivers of Hindu blood that he has made to flow or the encouragement that he has indirectly given to such outrages, by the advocacy of which [sic.] cowardly philosophy, is at least to be partially undone then Gandhi should accept the defeat of his cowardly and worthless non-violence and should, for the defence of his self-respect (if any is left of it) commit suicide; if not, he should bid goodbye for ever to Indian Politics. Does this Sokaji who has been so generous about the lives of others consider lakhs of his countrymen? Is it not the duty of the people to determine from this the real worth of this hypocritical patriot?

In the issue of 3 January 1941, the paper taunted the youth to do more than hurl abuse at Gandhi, Nehru, Patel, etc. After all, every day they read in the newspapers that 'Jawaharlal killed Hindus only; Vallabhbhai tolerated the molestation of a Hindu woman and Gandhi (lit. and what of Gandhi) he is always eager to start for a tour in order to annex every day, a new province to Pakistan . . .' *Hindu Rashtra's* issue of 9 July 1947 held up the example of Apte—he will later be hanged because of his part in Gandhiji's assassination—and exhorts the youth to do the most they can: it says that punishment such as transportation for life would be trifling compared to what they would have avenged:

Brothers, You have been knowing Mr. Nanarao Apte as the Manager of the *Agrani*, a close friend of Mr. Nathuram Godse, a founder of Hindu Rashtra Dal, and one of the best orators and workers of Hindusabha. But now, it is necessary to have more information (lit. acquaintance) of this youth.

Mr. Apte became extremely uneasy at the incident of arrogance which has reached its climax. He began to think that 'if I had no power to punish these arrogants, I should not call myself a 'Savarkarite'. Readers! There is not a single word of exaggeration in this.
Brothers! Mr. Apte himself and I, who am his very intimate friend, do not feel the pain caused by (lit. of blows dealt by) intoxicated power.

The motherland was vivisected, the vultures tore pieces of flesh (from her), the chastity of Hindu (lit. Arya) women was violated on the open streets, everything was lost and the big guns of the Congress eunuchs watching the rape committed on their own wives have begun to growl at you. How long can one bear this? And if this suffering is going to be a matter of habit, what greater agony can there be in transportation for life?

The *Hindu Rashtra* of 7 September 1947, declared that all that the *swaraj* which the Congress people had secured amounted to was that they go on tours with Liaquat Ali, and for that 'deity of *swaraj*' Gandhi could drink *musambi* juice from the cup of Suhrawardy. It demanded,

Where has the bravery gone?

Has the Hindu community really become so devoid of valour that it should live as refugees in large numbers running into lakhs not at all taking to heart even the dishonouring of its own women, for living somehow . . .

and counselled, if readers and followers had decided to sacrifice their lives for Hindutva, they should remember not to strike at the wrong target:

And if anyone has really the urge for Akhand Hindustan (lit. undivided India) and if a feeling of sacrificing one's own life for its sake has been created, then do not strike at a wrong place! Remove these obstacles (lit. bolts). The flood of Indian bravery will in no time integrate the whole of India into one.

and then, to use Justice Kapur's expression, it shrouded its message:

Of course, all this (will be done) by peaceful ways of elections, meetings, propaganda, etc.! What more than that can we tell?

'It shrouded its message in words whose import every zealot would have seen,' I should have typed.

In the issue of 16 December 1947, *Hindu Rashtra* proclaimed Gandhiji to be 'the father of all these wicked conspiracies'—from ensuring that Hindi would not be the national language to all others. In its issue of 24 January 1948—that is, in the issue just three-four days before Godse, the editor and Apte, the proprietor, leave for Delhi to assassinate Gandhiji, *Hindu Rashtra* had advice for the Government:

> We request that the Government of India should provide more armed soldiers for Gandhiji's protection so long as he (Gandhiji) makes anti-national and terrible statements as above. As Gandhiji has made gift (lit. provided) of [Rs.] 55 crores to Pakistan and also expressed the above statement, the Government of Pakistan should invite this Friend to visit Pakistan.

It charged him with seeking to harm the state of Gwalior, and indirectly urging the Ministry of States to take that state to task. It attributed what Gandhiji was saying to his habit, the habit of this 'well-wisher and friend of Muslims' of blaming the Hindus without looking into a situation . . .[43]

The same venom was hurled through mere 'reporting'. Issues of late December 1947, carried reports of a speech by Ketkar in which he said that Gandhism was 'Enemy Number 1', and a speech by Parchure, the boss of Hindu Mahasabha in Gwalior, in which he said that 'Gandhi and Nehru will soon reap the fruits of their sins'—this was in late December 1947; a bomb was thrown at Gandhiji just three weeks later, and he was assassinated within a month.[44]

---

[43] For these and other examples of writings from *Agrani* and *Hindu Rashtra*, see *Kapur Commission*, para 19.93.

[44] *Kapur Commission*, para 15.57.

How did Savarkar view what was being written by *Agrani,* the publication that he had helped start? We don't have to look far.

The Ventriloquist's Voice

As we saw, because of its incendiary writings, *Agrani* was asked to deposit security in 1946 also. Savarkar took up its cause. He issued an appeal that was carried by the paper in October that year. The appeal was fulsome approval and more for everything that was being done through the publication:

> The priceless work that was being done by 'Shraddhanand' for the protection of Hindu rashtra and for sowing the seed of reawakening, after it the same work is being done today with the same conviction and confidence by the 'Daily *Agrani*'. The work that is being done in support of Hindu rashtra according to their capacity by different publications is praiseworthy, of course. But the way this *Agrani* is fighting for those devoted to the Hindu cause is truly *agrani* [leading, foremeost]. *Agrani* has acquired this standing by the effective [*prabhaavshaali*] propaganda it is doing throughout greater Maharashtra.
>
> The six thousand rupees that have been demanded as a deposit can be collected from just a handful of five–ten persons. Their devotion to Hindutvata is commendable. But my wish is that this time there should be a collective cooperation of those committed to Hindutva. Keep this 'Agrani Nidhi' open throughout October, and let Hindus throughout Maharashtra shower funds on *Agrani.* For this, let every *Hindunishtha* family contribute at least Rupee one. Let that family not see even one film for one week. By doing only this much and without having to take on any economic burden every family will be able to save as much. Poona city will be able to collect the amount just by itself.

But we need the collective leadership of *Hindunishtha*. For this, from village to village, from house to house, through one's friends, women and men, every Hindu with pride rooted in Hindutva should collect at least Rupee one and send it at the earliest possible to the office of *Agrani*. I hope that thousands of Hindus in Maharashtra will heed my prayer.[45]

During the trial, Savarkar was at pains to distance himself from *Agrani*, and, of course, from Godse and Apte. However, the editors prefaced the text of the appeal with a note that tells the tale:

> The publications *Agrani, Kaalkesari, Sadrish, Savarkarnishth* were working to encourage all workers committed to Hindu interests, who were working under the open or secret guidance of Savarkar and answering at place after place a knife with a knife and fire with fire. *Ateh,* the Government demanded a deposit of Rs. 6,000 from *Agrani*. Even a year had not passed when this blow fell on this daily. To get over this difficulty, the editor of *Agrani*, Nathuram Godse and the publisher, Nana Apte appealed for funds. Writing in the paper in October 1946, Savarkar said . . .[46]

Non-Editorial Activities

Godse and Apte, the ardent devotees of Savarkar, continued to be involved in other activities also. Two examples will suffice to illustrate both what they were doing, and also the tone and tenor of the publications.

Gandhiji was at Panchgani, recovering from the malaria that he had got after his release in May 1944. An incident occurred which should have awakened everyone, and we will return to it in a moment. Here we may just note the milder version of it that Justice Kapur set out:

---

[45] *Savarkar Samagra*, Volume VIII, pp. 625–26.

[46] Ibid

Ex. 52 is an extract from the *Agrani* of July 23, 1944 of which the editor was Nathuram Godse. There also the incident given is that of demonstration organised by the Hindus against Rajaji's 'unpious formula of Pakistan in this land of Shivaji' . . . Apte is stated to have made a speech which is published in this issue of *Agrani* in which he said:

'Gandhiji! you have committed an offence of stabbing the nation by giving your consent to Pakistan formula. You have already confessed that you have no right to speak on behalf of Hindus. Today we are demonstrating peacefully on behalf of Hindu youths. You bear in mind that if you do not change your behaviour more difficult situations and ill fame are awaiting you. We will treat them as traitors who will try to vivisect our motherland. We, by this statement call on national minded people to treat Gandhi-Rajaji formula in this manner.'[47]

For the second incident, we have to glance through just one small part of the evidence of Morarji Desai—at the time Home Minister in the Bombay Government—before the Commission:

Evidence of Morarji Desai: . . . (8) A bomb was thrown in Poona in which the proprietor of the *Agrani*, N.D. Apte, was stated to have been involved, but due to lack of evidence that case could not proceed. Thereupon Mr. [B.G.] Kher [the then Chief Minister] wrote a strong note to the effect that the local police should be more vigorous in the investigation of such cases. Mr. Kher did not like confiscated securities to be returned to papers like the *Agrani* but the return of confiscated securities evidently was done as a measure of general goodwill towards all newspapers on the advent of independence.[48]

---

[47] *Kapur Commission*, para 9.29.

[48] *Kapur Commission*, para 18.50.8.

Unfortunately, Justice Kapur recorded, 'neither the confiscation nor the refund had any effect on the hymn of hate' which the *Agrani* broadcast. The columns of *Agrani* continued to be 'particularly venomous.'[49]

The Government was functioning at cross-purposes:

On the 9th July, Mr. [B.G.] Kher wrote a note on the file, when the matter of the Poona bomb went to him after passing through the various Secretariat echelons, wherein he said 'Was not the Editor of the *Agrani* arrested? I would like to know the progress' ...[50]

When the papers came to Mr. Desai for sanction for prosecution under the Explosive Substances Act (exhibit 158) he recorded a note on 5th August that his information was that the confession had been retracted and if that was so what was the evidence to prove the guilt of the accused persons. On this Mr. Kher wrote: 'This matter must be treated more seriously. We must impress it upon the D.S.P. that he is to investigate the case thoroughly. The *Agrani* has stated it is a matter of high honour that the Hindu Sabha should be accused of throwing a bomb—H.D. [Home Department] is returning his security. Is terrorism to be allowed to be openly encouraged? I would like to see Secretary H.D.' This is demonstrative of Mr. Kher's anxiety in relation to the incidents of bomb throwing.[51]

While ministers squabbled in files, what did bomb-throwing mean for *Agrani*? 'The activities of and writings in the newspaper the *Agrani* regarding

---

[49] *Kapur Commission*, para 26.74.

[50] B.G. Kher was a distinguished and gentlemanly statesman. He was the Prime Minister of Bombay Province in 1937–1939 and 1946–1947, and the first Chief Minister of the state between 1947 and 1952. It was during this latter tenure that the Bombay Government lifted the ban on Savarkar's translation of Mazzini's autobiography. Savarkar and his publishers/editors were to claim later that Kher had taken the vow of Abhinav Bharat in his youth: Cf., *Savarkar Samagra*, Volume I, pp, 466–68.

[51] *Kapur Commission*, paras 18.16 and 18.17.

the arrest of Athawale and Apte in connection with the bomb explosion on June 26, 1947, are both important and reflective,' Justice Kapur recorded. 'On July 6, 1947, Ex. 152, the editorial, was rather aggressive in tone saying that it was gratifying to note that Government had started suspecting the Hindu Mahasabha of a bomb conspiracy; the connection of the Sabha with the actual war weapon was worthy of the high honour and that it was possible that Godse also might not escape the attention of the police; that the Congress Government was seeking to obstruct the Hindu Mahasabha organization by these arrests and even the *Agrani* might be stopped; and that the Black-Day observance was the beginning for the fight of "Hinduistic" movement.'[52] And later, referring to two reproductions from the paper, Justice Kapur remarked, 'These passages from. Ex. 152 to 154 show that the *Agrani* was lauding the prosecution of Hindu Mahasabha workers for bomb throwing and it was directing all its energies against the Government and the Congress High Command so much so that it called upon the Hindu volunteers to be up and doing something and it wanted to know how long the Hindus will bear what was happening.'[53]

An Organization for Secret Work, and Its 'Fuhrer'

1942: Savarkar is the President of the Hindu Mahasabha. On 15 May he addresses a training camp in Poona.[54] The evidence placed before Justice Kapur showed that Savarkar 'emphasised the necessity of forming a volunteer organisation for secret activities, as that [sic.] could not be undertaken by the Sabha'. As a result, the Hindu Rashtra Dal was formed. Among its founding members were two who would be convicted of murdering Gandhiji—Apte and Godse. Ostensibly the organization was meant to assist the Hindu Mahasabha. 'But,' Justice Kapur noted, 'they

---

[52] *Kapur Commission*, para 15.21.

[53] *Kapur Commission,* para 19.97.

[54] The following is based on *Kapur Commission*, paras 16.57, 19.82, 19.89, 19.98, 26.15.

made no effort in popularising the movement of the Dal or to increase its membership.' The reason is implicit: its work was to be secret, and therefore it was to be limited to a few.

A year later, on 29 May 1943, 'V.D. Savarkar held private discussions with the Hindu Rashtra Dal in Anandashram, Poona,' the Commission learnt. 'He required the volunteers to owe an implicit allegiance to him irrespective of who the President of the Hindu Mahasabha was.' The organization's task was not to be limited to assisting the Hindu Mahasabha. 'It was to remain a distinct body, its primary duty being to protect Hindudom,' and it was to 'help every Hindu institution in their attempt to oppose encroachment on their rights and religion.' It was to work to realize 'Savarkar ideology': this was said to be 'attainment of Hindudom, opposition to Pakistan and indivisibility of India.'

'From its very inception the Rashtra Dal was a movement of extremists which had adopted the ideology of Savarkar to whom the members and the volunteers were required to show unreserved and implicit allegiance and faith,' the Commission found.[55] As its 'dictator', Savarkar nominated the

---

[55] During the assassination trial, of course, Savarkar insisted that his acquaintance with Godse and Apte was of a distant and formal kind—that he knew them as and to the extent that he knew other workers of the Hindu Mahasabha. Godse too was careful. In describing his relationship to Savarkar he limited himself to saying: 'I emphatically deny that we saw Savarkar on the 17 January, 1948 or that Savarkar blessed us with the words "Yashasvi Houn Ya," "Be successful and come" . . . I have worked for several years in RSS and subsequently joined the Hindu Mahasabha and volunteered myself to fight as a soldier under its pan-Hindu flag. About this time Veer Savarkar was elected to the Presidentship of the Hindu Mahasabha. The Hindu movement got verily electrified and vivified as never before, under his magnetic lead and whirlwind propaganda. Millions of Hindu Sanghatanists looked up to him as the chosen hero, as the ablest and most faithful advocate of the Hindu cause. I too was one of them. I worked devotedly to carry on the Mahasabha activities and hence came to be personally acquainted with Savarkarji.' Cf. Nathuram Godse, May it Please Your Honour, paragraphs 22, 29. Others, on the basis of interviews, etc. have imputed a much closer relationship: see, for instance, Larry Collins and Dominique Lapierre, Freedom at Midnight, HarperCollins, London, 1997, e-book 2017, locs 575–76, 582–84, for an attribution that we may not even reproduce today.

next 'dictator' and General Secretary of the Dal. He asked the volunteers 'to assist the villagers in securing arms' licences within the provisions of the law', to establish 'mass contact' and spread 'Savarkar-vad' among the villagers, 'and to inculcate in the villagers a spirit of aggression.' In four speeches to the volunteers that were reported to the Commission, Savarkar, 'talked about Muslim atrocities in the Punjab, Bengal and N.W.F.P. and said that they would not stop until the Hindus retaliated in the same spirit including raping of women and destroying of mosques, etc. if Hindu women and Hindu places of worship were treated in that manner.' He 'emphasised the necessity of the Hindu Rashtra Dal and referred to Muslim atrocities in the Punjab and in Bengal, and preached retaliation.' In another part, the Commission noted what Savarkar had urged the volunteers: 'You should not stop until you retaliate in the same spirit and manner. If Hindu women were raped and Hindu temples damaged, equal number of mosques should be destroyed.' This emphasis on retaliation and revenge struck the Commission. It observed: 'Though ostensibly it was a protective movement yet it was a movement which in action was expected to be retaliatory in the sense that it was to behave towards the Muslims in the same manner that Muslims behaved towards the Hindus in Pakistan, even to the extent of destroying places of religious worship and treating men and women in the same manner that Hindus were treated in Pakistan.' In addition, Savarkar 'advised the Dal volunteers to oppose the Constitution to be framed by the Constituent Assembly if it was against the interests of Hindus and Hindudom.'

'From its very inception the Rashtra Dal was a movement of extremists which had adopted the ideology of Savarkar to whom the members and the volunteers were required to show unreserved and implicit allegiance and faith,' Justice Kapur observed, and remarked, 'It is not surprising that the brains behind the conspiracy to murder Mahatma Gandhi were the leaders of the Rashtra Dal.' And again, after reviewing further evidence, he observed that '. . . As things turned out, the persons who were responsible for the conspiracy to murder and the murderers of Mahatma Gandhi were

Savarkarites belonging to the Hindu Rashtra Dal who were blind followers of Savarkar whom they treated as the Fuhrer . . .' And yet again, '. . . All this shows that the brains behind the conspiracy were the Poona people belonging to the Hindu Rashtra Dal group of Savarkarites.'

The Inevitable Consequence

The venom that had been poured into the tight little group had its inevitable consequence, a consequence and inevitability that deserve repeating so that they are driven into our minds.

Indoctrinate a fellow, poison his mind against your target. And he will kill him 'on his own', 'autonomously', by his own 'free will'. Recall all the things that Savarkar had been drilling into his audiences that, he said, Gandhiji was doing to harm the Hindus, to pander to the Muslims, to help the British. Recall the pages of *Agrani* and what they show of the poison that had already been drilled into the minds of Godse and Apte. Savarkar had manufactured robots. He did not need to tell them 'Succeed and come back', or that 'Gandhi's hundred years are over'—the sentences that the approver in the assassination trial said he heard from Godse and Apte as they left the house of Savarkar.

The Aftermath

This is the point that would have struck anyone. It certainly struck Sardar Patel. Being briefed every day on the arrests and interrogations, he did not have much doubt. Pandit Nehru wanted that the net be spread wider. Sardar Patel explained that almost everyone who seemed to have been involved in the conspiracy to assassinate Mahatma Gandhi had already been arrested, as had the principal functionaries of organizations that might foment trouble. He wrote:

> . . . It also clearly emerges from these statements that the RSS was not involved in it at all. It was a fanatical wing of the Hindu Mahasabha

directly under Savarkar that [hatched] the conspiracy and saw it through. It also appears that the conspiracy was limited to some ten men, of whom all except two have been got hold of . . .

And later in the letter,

After having dealt with these matters at first hand and discussed these matters in detail with Sanjeevi and other officers who are in charge of this investigation, including the Public Prosecutor of Bombay, Mr. Pettigarah, who has been advising the investigators on legal points, I have come to the conclusion that the conspiracy of Bapu's assassination was not so wide as is generally assumed, but was restricted to a handful of men who have been his enemies for a very considerable time—the antipathy can be traced right to the time when Bapu went for his talks with Jinnah, when Godse went on a fast and some others of the conspirators went to Wardha to prevent him [Bapu] from going.

Sardar Patel went on to remark later in the letter,

. . . Of course, his assassination was welcomed by those of the RSS and the Mahasabha who were strongly opposed to his way of thinking and to his policy. But beyond this, I do not think it is possible, on the evidence which has come before us, to implicate any other members of the RSS or the Hindu Mahasabha. The RSS have undoubtedly other sins and crimes to answer for, but not for this one . . .[56]

Panditji remained unconvinced, and continued to press for stricter and wider action against the RSS. A few months later, Syama Prasad Mukherjee—he had been President of the Hindu Mahasabha and was now Minister for Industry

---

[56] Cf., Letter from Pandit Nehru to Sardar Patel of 26 February 1948, and Sardar Patel's reply of 27 February 1948 in *Sardar Patel's Correspondence, 1945–50,* Volume 6, Durga Das [ed.], Navjivan Publishing House, Ahmedabad, 1973, pp. 55–56 and 56–58 respectively.

and Supply in the central Government—wrote to Sardar Patel urging that the assassination was the work of a very small group based in Poona, that others should be released, that strictest vigilance should be exercised over what the communists were doing, and Muslims in general, and that Hindu opinion must not be pushed into a corner as we would need it were Pakistan to move against India. In his reply, Sardar Patel said, inter alia,

> As regards the RSS and the Hindu Mahasabha, the case relating to Gandhiji's murder is sub judice and I should not like to say anything about the participation of the two organisations, but our reports do confirm that, as a result of the activities of these two bodies, particularly the former, an atmosphere was created in the country in which such a ghastly tragedy became possible. There is no doubt in my mind that the extreme section of the Hindu Mahasabha was involved in this conspiracy. The activities of the RSS constituted a clear threat to the existence of Government and the State. Our reports show that those activities, despite the ban, have not died down. Indeed, as time has marched on, the RSS circles are becoming more defiant and are indulging in their subversive activities in an increasing measure . . .[57]

Fomenting the atmosphere is quite the point. Once an atmosphere of hatred is fomented, the leader does not have to actually tell anyone

---

[57] Cf., letter from S.P. Mukherjee of 17 July 1948, and Sardar Patel's reply of 18 July 1948, Ibid, pp 320–23 and 323–24 respectively. Nathuram Godse's brother, Gopal Godse, said later that they had grown up in the RSS, that it was family to them, that their connection with the organization had never ceased. Godse had been striving to bring the RSS and the Hindu Mahasabha closer together. Much has been written about Gandhiji's assassination— the botched investigation, the ground on which the approver's evidence about Savarkar's role was set aside, the apprehension that if the Government proceeded further regarding Savarkar, Hindu opinion could be inflamed, the precise nature of the relationship between Savarkar and Godse, etc. As these aspects are not covered in this book, the reader would want to look up some of the numerous books that directly deal with this subject.

to pull the trigger. He can retain his mask of goodwill and friendship. The *bhakt* will 'do the needful' 'simply as a national duty'.

What survives?

And now recall what Savarkar told the Court: 'how Gandhiji and myself lived together as friends and worked together as compatriots, how later on he paid a personal visit with his wife to me and my family and spent hours in happy talks about our old comradeship and current politics . . . how Gandhiji wrote now and then kind notes about me in "Young India" too . . .' and how 'in spite of fundamental differences in our ideologies on some points and in virtue of close affinity on others, there ever continued a mutual respect for and a personal goodwill to each other.'

Not a syllable survives scrutiny.

Read Savarkar, not his hagiographers, and remember that when you read Savarkar.

And So

And So, My Plea

The essence of Hinduism is the inner-directed search.

Hindutva, by contrast, is a project to capture, dominate, retain, twist and turn the State.

For the inner-directed search, adherence to truth, humility, service, ethical conduct in general are the *sine qua non*.

Hindutva, by contrast, shouts that we capture and dominate the State, that we subjugate society by all means—falsehood and force, intimidation and cruelty, deceit and bribery—in a word whatever is 'necessary', which, in practice, means whatever the Leader, indeed the Leader of the moment fancies.

In Hinduism, all practices—rituals, observances, worship, meditation—are aids to the inner-directed search. Hindutva perverts these, making of them devices for dominating and controlling the State, for demarcating and segmenting society. Contrast what a pilgrimage is meant to be with the new fad, 'Religious Tourism'. Contrast quiet contemplation with shrill, bombastic propaganda. Contrast the Path of many paths, which is what Hinduism has been, with 'Follow the Leader'.

No surprise, therefore, that the moment a religion is dragooned and made an instrument in the pursuit of the State and its purposes, it gets devoured—look at what has happened to the Christianity of Jesus, look at what has happened to Islam of the Sufis.

And so, my plea:

SAVE HINDUISM FROM HINDUTVA

Index

Scan QR code to access the
Penguin Random House India website